Mr. Bob Boase

With Compliments

Huijiong Wang

2003.8.14

Integrated Study of China's Development and Reform

— Preliminary Exploration of Social System

Huijiong Wang

Foreign Languages Press

First Edition 2003

Written by Huijiong Wang

English text editor Li Zhenguo
Editor Cui Lili and Yu Ying
Cover design by Zhang Tao

ISBN 7-119-03335-2
©Foreign Languages Press, Beijing, China, 2003

Published by Foreign Languages Press
24 Baiwanzhuang Road, Beijing 100037, China
Home Page: http://www.flp.com.cn
E-mail: info@flp.com.cn
sales@flp.com.cn

Printed in the People's Republic of China

PREFACE

This book is a collection of papers by the author, who has worked for over twenty years in policy research for and gaving advice (strategic planning at macro and micro level) to the Chinese government. And he had been invited abroad to give speeches and read papers on various aspects of China's reform and opening-up. Eighteen papers are selected from his works in the area of development planning, science and technology, economy, social and environmental development; most of these papers had been published in books and journals abroad. The purpose to publish these selected papers in this book, titled *Integrated Study of China's Development and Reform*, represents an attempt to give the readers an overall picture on China's reform and opening-up from various perspectives, so as enable them to better understand the achievements and issues on China's development and reform as well as some possible challenges the country faces ahead.

The success of China's reform and opening-up since the late 70's has attracted worldwide attention. Many excellent papers have been written on China abroad, but most of them focused mainly on one or several specific areas. For example, China's economic development, or economic reform and its challenges, or sustainable industrial development had been studied extensively by many international organizations, such as the World Bank, IMF, OECD, ADB, UNIDO, etc. The feature of this book tries to provide a new perspective of study — an integrated approach. Of course, the author has also absorbed widely from the above-mentioned studies in preparing this book.

Although this book has presented five essential components in the consideration of China's development and reform, the author does not intend to pay too much attention on theoretical or quantitative explorations. To make an integrated study of China's development and reform is by no means a simple task, which is impossible to be completed by the effort of an individual. It calls for organized research and study of both Chinese and foreign experts. It took the author more than twenty years to complete a book *An Introduction to Systems Engineering* (published in 1979), when the author served as a chief engineer of electric power industry. The author also has rich experience, basic knowledge of general system theory, the capability of analysis and synthesis equipped with appropriate mathematical tools, a good senes of logic, as well as a sound understanding of the various disciplines of social sciences that he has aquired from learning and doing. But it should also be stressed that the author learned the lessons from his 33-year experience and continuous learning on engineering and 22-year work and study on economics and other branches of social sciences; economics, as a part of social science, is a very complicated field of study, because social science mainly focuses on the study of society and human relationship. The domain of it is still not fully clarified, and the study of human behavior is very difficult to be quantified. For example, psychology is often seen as a natural rather than social science, and economics is most likely to be regarded as a comparatively unproblematic social science. But the penetration of mathematics into economics and current economic modelling still suffer from certain difficulties due to the involvement of human behavior and political environment factors both domestically and internationally and development study. It is quite different from engineering in that there is not enough experimental data, and there is also the difficulty of measurement, in spite of the fact the functionalism of Talcott Parsons offers the fullest employment of systems theory in sociology. Therefore, this *Integrated Study of China's Development and Reform* will serve as a very preliminary study and experiment of system approach to social science and development study. From the "Contents" of this book, it can be seen that a few papers are collected in part IV, the social aspects, although the author had written a paper in Chinese titled "Some Studies on Cultural Industries," etc. I have no intention to have it translated and included in this book. Because this book is only an illustrative study to see how system approach can be applied to the objective world, the weakness of part IV is remedied somewhat in paper 12 and the "Conclusions" part. The mankind and the world it lives is developed and changed continuously. There is no end for the recognition of the objective world and themselves for the mankind through learning and practice. It is expected that more knowledge of the world can be learned and some relatively in-depth studies on this subject can be done by the author in the rest of his life through life-long learning process.

The author wish to thank sincerely his distinguished classmates and friends both at home and abroad, close colleagues, the sponsor and all the organizations that have assisted the preparation of these papers and the publication of this book.

All criticism and comments are sincerely welcome.

Huijiong Wang

May 15th, 2003

CONTENTS

INTRODUCTION

China's reform, opening-up and its development over last two decades since the late 1970s have achieved an extraordinary success; it has attracted wide attention from the global society. It can be seen from the fact that, the famous research project of the World Bank, "The East Asian Miracle," which was published in 1992, had not taken China's development into account. But the recent study "The Emerging Asia" of Asian Development Bank launched in 1997 and the study "Rethinking the East Asia Miracle" of the World Bank published in 2001 both have focused on China and treated it as a crucial component of the study of the experience of Asia's development. There are also several special studies focused on China recently, such as OECD's publication in 2002 "China in the Global Economy: Challenge of Domestic Policies", IMF's publication in 2003 "China: Competing in the Global Economy". In fact, there are enormous amount of publications and literature from various research institutions of different countries, developed or a few of developing countries, which focused on the experience and issues of development and reform of China in recent years.

Many studies on China have been done by large international organizations. They are generally carried out by assembling large numbers of experts from abroad. Sometimes, Chinese experts are also invited to participate in these studies. Generally speaking, most of these studies are of a relatively good quality, which had observed and summarized the experiences, lessons and issues of China's development and reform correctly in the relative sense; some useful suggestions have also been raised. They are deserved to be studied and learned seriously by the relevant institutions, organizations and professionals in China. They can also provide useful references for the developing countries as well as background information about China to developed countries. From the academic point of view, they represent a new accumulated pool of knowledge for the newly emergeing disciplines since World War II, the development economics, policy science and policy analysis,

7

and also the transitional economies emerged in recent years. Those new disciplines have been continuously improved and developed. New experiences have been provided by them. But it is regretted that there are relatively few publications, written directly in English by Chinese scholars to introduce systematically the experiences of and issues in China's reform and development.

The enormous amount of economic and social construction since the founding of the PRC, and particularly in past more than twenty years of reform and opening, have provided a rare good opportunity for the author who has done all sorts of practical work and plunged head and tail into the study of theory. Especially in the recent twenty years and more, the author worked in one branch of the Development Research Center of the State Council, formerly called "Technical Economic Research Center," my colleagues and I made use of the chance to engage in the study of macro and micro issues of development and reform of China, and made wide connections and exchanged views with various international organizations and academic professionals, and accumulated a fair amount of experience in doing joint research projects with them. In the recent ten years and more, I have been invited by various international organizations and academic institutions on more then 100 occasions to give speeches abroad, most of which had been published in publications of international organizations or academic institutions, some of them were translated into Japanese, French and Portuguese. Of them, I have selected fourteen papers, the other three papers are selected from international conferences held in China, and one is a report given at the National Conference of Academicians of Chinese Academy of Sciences and Chinese Academy of Engineering in 1998. The author has rewritten them into English with some supplements. These above eighteen papers are collected in this book titled *Integrated Study of China's Development and Reform*. The purpose is to provide a relatively overall picture of the development and reform of China as well as some other issues in a comprehensive perspective. On the other aspect, former PRC President Jiang Zemin had mentioned in his report to the Twelfth National Congress of Communist Party of China that the target of China's economic restructuring is to establish a system of socialist market economy, which is a very complicated social system engineering. Therefore, on the part of this author, this book is a very preliminary exploration in the study that ranges from engineering systems engineering to social systems.

This book is divided into five parts.

Part I is an overview. Four papers are collected in this part. The first paper is "System Concept of Sustainable Development—Sustainable Development of Mode of Production and Consumption and the Impact of Social Culture". This paper was originally a speech the author was invited to give at the National Conference of Academicians of Chinese Academy of Sciences and Chinese Academy of Engineering in 1998. The content in this paper reflects the author's overall academic perspective on China's development and reform. In fact, the basic concept is expressed nearly throughout all chapters of the book. The original speech is given in Chinese. It is rewritten into English based basically on the original speech, but is supplemented with some new materials.

The second paper is titled "The Experience of Development Planning in China". This was a speech delivered by the author on the invitation of the United Nations. It was presented in the National Planning Conference in Iran in October 1998. Planning and market had been a major subject of debate in the domestic economic field at the initial stage of China's reform and opening-up. It is also a focus of debate among scholars of international political economy. In reality, as the development of the contemporary world is related to the interaction of many factors, political, social, economic, technological, and environmental, it is fair to say that nearly all countries (include large corporations or large cities) of the world need to prepare a national (corporate or regional) development planning to certain extent, especially the strategic planning. It is well known that two famous economists, the Nobel Prize Winner Dr. Tinbergen of Netherlands, and Arthur Lewis of the United States had contributed to the study of development planning. It is necessary to have a "vision" or certain "target" to be achieved, and make preparations to take actions in implementation. This is true both for a nation or even an individual. But, it is also necessary to emphasize that the function, the process, the content and the techniques of planning are evolving and developing internationally as times goes on. In this national planning conference of Iran, there were large numbers of participants coming from governments, corporations and enterprises and academic institutions. Three experts from China, the Republic of Korea and USA were invited to give speeches on their countries' experience. This can show the general trend of the study of development planning in contemporary world takes. In the report presented by the author, a brief introduction of international experience on development planning was given in the very beginning, a relatively detailed explanation of the history, achievements and issues confronted at different stages of development planning of China since the founding of the PRC was presented, the methodology which was designed and applied in the important national project "China Towards the Year 2000" sponsored by the former Technical Economic Research Center of the State Council was also introduced in brief.

The third paper, "Redefining Regional Development Strategy, the Chinese Experience — Toward a Framework of Study of Regional Development Strategy," was written for the Global Forum on Regional Development Policy and the International Symposium towards Sustainable Urban and Regional Development jointly sponsored by UNCRD and UN/DESA on December 1-4, 1998, Nagoya, Japan. This paper explained that China was in transition from a former centrally planned economy to a socialist market economy. The gap between the regions in terms of economic, social and cultural development will diminish during this process. This paper gives the historical perspective on regional development of China, stating that new regional development strategies will be defined within the context of globalization and multipoliarization to tackle issues unique to different regions of China. Taking into consideration of the huge population and size of the country, the author holds the view that it is not sufficient to study the development strategy of China as a whole; it must be supplemented with the understanding and study of regional development strategies. This is one of the reasons that the center where I had worked had set up a Bureau on Development Strategy and Regional Development. The content in this paper represents a complement to the study of paper 2 in this part. This paper was abstracted in UNCRD Proceedings Series No. 37 in July 1999. It is incorporated in this book in its original English draft.

The fourth paper is "Two Decades of Experience of Policy Modeling of DRC". This paper is jointly written by I and two of my colleges, the two successive directors of the Bureau of Development Strategy and Regional Development of our center, based on the working experience our unit gained. This paper was written and presented at an International Conference sponsored by the China Association of Quantitative Economics. The major difference of contemporary economics and its traditional study is that a large number of mathematical tools are employed in statistics, projections, analysis and policy simulation of economic phenomena. The application of mathematics of the natural science to the study in social science, and particularly economics, represents an extension of the application of mathematics. This is also the natural result of the emergence of many new "interdisciplinary studies" to meet the necessary demand of complexity of the "object" to be studied. But it should be warned that people should have a clear understanding that there is difference in basic nature between the application of mathematics to natural science or engineering and to the study of social science. The basic definition of social science is "A general label applied to the study of society and human relationships."[1] Generally speaking, it is difficult to quantify human behavior, social behavior and the relationship between them. There is not enough experimental data to support this type of study. With the precondition of recognizing this, a right approach may be found to the policy modeling. We have not discussed the mathematical details of various models and their appropriate area of application. This paper is simply a retrospect and summary of lessons and experiences of policy modelling of the DRC (including the former Technical Economic Research Center of the State Council). It can be seen from this paper that the policy modelling of the center is developed in the past two decades relying not only on the cooperation of Chinese experts from other ministries and academic field, it also has been improved gradually through extensive international cooperative effort, thus illustrating greatly the necessity of opening-up and international cooperation. Although this paper summarized that the most important experience in the following: "The quantitative analysis should be applied in combination with qualitative analysis and sound judgement in policy modelling", we have been making continuous exploration for the improvement and application of quantitative method, in order to adapt to the requirement of policy studies to achieving the target to establish a better-off (*xiaokang*) society in China by 2020. This should be the basic concept in exploring the objective world of the mankind.

The second part of this book focuses on study related to science and technology. Strictly speaking, science and technology are two related terminologies with different meaning. Three papers collected in this part are based more on the

---

1. *The Concise Oxford Dictionary of Sociology,* edited by Gordon Marshall. Oxford University Press, 1994.

summary and exploration of China's technological development. There is no argument on the fact that science and technology are the engine of growth and development of the economy and society. On the other hand, science and technology are developed within the environment of specific socio-economic system; their development is promoted or constrained also by factors of their socio-economic environment. In the realm of micro-economics, technological innovation is inseparable with enterprise management. While under the market economy system, enterprise should be the major actor of technological innovation. Therefore, the issue of current technological innovation of China cannot be studied without the reform of the economic system. It is also necessary to keep in mind the following views: innovation is a process, the life cycle of a product is also a process. Technological innovation is not only occurred in the value chain of research, development, design, testing, engineering and production, it is also existed in the process of marketing planning and market development. Due to the influence of traditional centralized mandatory planning, China has relatively strong macro-capacity in technological management. But, the micro-management and the technological innovative capacity of the enterprises, which are the major actors in the market, are waiting to be further improved and strengthened. These are the major messages expressed in the three papers of this part.

One of these three papers "China's Experience of Technological Independence" was completed in 1986. This is a paper written for an international joint research project, "Self Reliance of Science and Technology in Development," sponsored by the United Nations University with the participation of six Asian countries (China, Japan, the Republic of Korea, the Philippines, Thailand and India). The twenty Chinese participants came from three units, with Madamn Li Poxi and I as the heads. The major English report was written by me. This research was not published at that time. The emergence of East Asia, especially the publication of a World Bank Policy Research Report titled "The East Asian Miracle" in 1993, had attracted the worldwide attention on the experience of development of East Asia. This research report was published by the United Nations University Press in 1994 titled "Technological Independence — the Asian Experience". The report, written by the author on behalf of the Chinese team, had presented a relatively detailed retrospect of the history of development of science and technology at different stages since the founding of the PRC; this study of development of S&T is linked closely with the development of the socio-economics as well as the social culture of China. Thus, the international society can understand better what is the potential of competitiveness of China in global manufacturing activities. The issues faced by China on S&T development are also pointed out in this paper.

The other two papers collected in this part, "Technology Innovation and Enterprise Management and a Case Study in China" and "Some Issues of Technology Management in China: A Challenge towards the 21st Century", were both written on the request from Professor Bela Gold, the guest editor of the *International Journal of Technology Management*, which changed its name into *International Jounal of Manufacturing Technology and Management* in 2001. The two papers were published in the journal at different times. Part of economic and technological data in the later paper are mainly those of the 80's and 90's, which can complement the first paper "China's Experience of Technological Independence". The contents of all three papers are mutually supplementary. All three papers expounded on role of the system concept to the development of science and technology in China at different depths. This is especially evident in the first paper of this part.

The third part of this book focuses on China's economic development and reform. Economics is a relatively matured discipline in international social science; it has developed continuously from qualitative study to quantitative study; and the areas studied are expanded continuously in depth and in breadth. For example, the growth rate of GDP, its demand (or expenditure) side includes investment, consumption and net export (export minus import); its supply side (or output) includes primary, secondary and tertiary sectors. All of them can be analyzed and predicted with simple arithmetic operation on the precondition that the available statistics are accurate. Along with the development of the financial market of the developed economies and the various ways to apply advanced mathematics in this field, there is now emerging the new discipline of "financial engineering" abroad, which is defined as the following: "The use of financial instruments, such as derivatives, to obtain a desired mix of risk and return characteristics. More broadly, the application of financial technology to solve financial problems and exploit financial opportunities."[2] Also emerging is the new occupation "financial engineer"

---

2. From "Dictionary of Financial Engineering" by: John F. Marshall, Ph. D. John Wiley and Sons. Inc. 2000

In the field of economics, a new branch, the "development economics," had also emerged during and after World War II; it deals with the problem of growth of developing countries. Even this new discipline has undergone considerable change in recent years. On the theoretical side, the relevance of neo-classical economics to developing countries has been questioned and there has been increasing emphasis upon institutions. With the termination of the cold war, many economists working in some large international organizations (such as the World Bank and IMF) are exploring a new field of study, the transitional economics. For example, *The World Economic Outlook* published by the IMF in May and October of 2000 respecgively focused on the study of transitional economies of Eastern European countries. Large amount of data was collected and statistical analysis was done, policy recommendation was given on the transition of the Eastern European Countries and on their membership in European Union. Again take the organization and management theory in the microeconomics for example. It has been subjected to a five-generation change within nearly one century since the term "scientific management" of the first generation was raised in 1910, coined after the view of Taylor who focussed primarily on increasing worker efficiency. The theory on management is now entering into the stage of "knowledge management." Furthermore, thanks to the separation of the right of ownership and operation, there have emerged large numbers of corporations and salaried professional managers or directors, who have acquired substantial powers in respect to the affairs of the corporations. They are paid to run the corporations or enterprises on behalf of their shareholders but not always had the best interests of shareholders in mind when performing their managerial functions. Thus, a series of issues occurred. The Cadbury Committee Report (1992) recommended a "Code of Best Practice" related to the appointment and responsibilities of executive directors, the independence of non-executive directors and tighter internal financial controls and reporting procedures. Then corporate governance became the new area studied by some economists. But in the real world, there are one after another news of scandals in USA in recent years. Enron is one of them. It is worthwhile for us to do further research of all facts of the real world and study the related theoretical study. One point can be further discussed, i.e., the issue of reform. China launched its economic reform in the late 70's. But we must be aware that 'reform' is not an issue unique only to the former central mandatory planning economies. It is also an issue existing in the entire process of economic development that all countries of the world must face. We must have a sense of its complexity. Paul E. Atkinson of OECD wrote a paper, "The Experience of Economic Reform in OECD-APEC Countries"; it was presented at a conference for preparation of the APEC meeting in New Zealand. In the paper, he pointed out, "Economic reform is usually a difficult and wrenching process. It involves substantially changing the way a society thinks about whatever it is that is being reformed and often dismantling of existing institutions and arrangements." The above quotation is to emphasize the point that the rapidly changing society would result in a trend of rapid change of economics theory and that the complexity of the reform should be fully recognized. It is expected that people working in the economic field of China strengthen their cooperation and exchange with people working in the economic field abroad, because it is necessary to absorb useful lessons abroad and combine them properly with the concrete domestic conditions. Discovering and solving problems are by no means a simple task.

Therefore, the six papers collected in this part cover only a limited scope of the study of economics. Their selection has the following considerations.

The first paper in this part is titled "Industrialization and Economic Reform in China". This paper was a report given in Brazil on Feb. 1993, when the author was invited by the Vargas Foundation. This report is divided into four parts: Overview; industrialization of China in the pre-reform era (1949-1978); development strategy of industrial economy in the 80's — the period of economic reform; China's economic strategy in 90's and recent policy of economic reform, issues and measures. The report discussed also the sectoral aspects, therefore it can complement the contents of part I of this book. The oral presentation was translated into Portuguese and published by the Vargas Foundation in 1994. The version collected here is the original draft in English.

The second paper is "Foreign Direct Investment Policies and Related Institutional Building in China". It was written at the request of ESCAP. Detailed descriptions of the development, policy and institutional building regarding the use of foreign direct investment are given in it. It is published in a symposium titled "Foreign Direct Investment in Selected Asian Countries: Policies, Related Institution-Building and Regional Cooperation" by ESCAP.

The third paper in this part is "Experience of Tax Reform in China". It was written at the request of ESCAP for a speech given to officials of the Ministry of Finance in Kyrgiz Republic on Nov. 1999. Both Kyrgiz and China were formerly centrally planned economies. From the author's perspective, the priority on the reform agenda should be given to fiscal reform in the transition from a former centrally planned economy to a market-oriented economy. In the reform of the banking sector in the financial system, due to its unique state owned enterprise nature in the former centrally planned economy, all difficulties faced in the reform of SOEs also exist in the reform of banking sector, which is even more difficult and complex, because monetary policy is essentially macro-economic policy of the government. While the reform of the fiscal aspect is related not too closely to the development of the market, it is, however, more closely related to the political issue. The author had discussed this point with one of the former vice presidents of the World Bank (an Israelite who has died). Both of us hold the same view. This paper has not explored the fiscal reform of China extensively. It simply lists the facts of evolution and reform of the fiscal system of China, evolution and reform of the tax system of China and major lessons of tax reform and future prospects. The issue of the central-local fiscal relationship and the extra-budgetary system are also discussed. The author had been asked by the ESCAP to publish this paper on their *Development Papers*.

In the above three papers, there are relatively detailed national statistics and analysis done by the author. All statistical data are currently easily available for economists abroad. Possibly, the author may understand better the history of China, its development and the cultural tradition. Therefore, his analysis based on the same statistical data may provide a new perspective for the international economic community to better understand the reform and development of China. So is the part related to the institutional reform for the utilization of foreign direct investment.

The fourth paper is "Corporate Governance — Challenge to East Asian Countries in the Process of Globalization." This paper was a speech given to visiting students (includes post graduate students) at the invitation of Beijing University which was responsible for that activity. The author deeply felt that although "Corporate Governance" is a hot issue within the domestic economic circle. Yet, it is a product of separation of the right of ownership from that of operation, and the emergence of stock companies. Based on the specific conditions of China, it seems to be a necessity to integrate the study of corporate governance with the development of the financial system (one of its component is stock market) of China. The international financial system is, in general, composed of three components: the banking system, the bond market and the equity market. The Asian Development Bank and ESCAP have summarized the lessons and experiences after the East Asian financial crisis. They both recognized that the share of the bond market is too low for most of the financial systems of East Asia—China has a similar situation regarding the share of bond market in the financial system. This is an issue that deserves to be studied.

The fifth paper is "Comments on *Rethinking the East Asian Miracle*." This is a speech given by the author in Tsinghua University at the launch of World Bank publication *Rethinking the East Asian Miracle*" in China on March 2002 when the author was invited by the World Bank to give comments on that activity. The publication of the World Bank *The East Asian Miracle* in 1993 had received worldwide response. Most of the response is confirmative and positive. But there were also different voices, particularly so after the East Asian financial crisis. Dr. Joseph E. Stiglitz (former vice president of the World Bank, a Nobel Prize Winner) and Dr. Shahid Yusuf (former chief economist of China) have organized many scholars to take a fresh look at the regional experience during the 1990s and to extend and revise as necessary the findings of the former publication. Three papers related to China and Vietnam are added. Although this is only a paper of comments, the author has expressed a number of views related to development and reform. I have endorsed highly the perception that "in the light of market and government failures, there are two alternative strategies; to focus on one and ignore the other or to try to address the weakness in both, view the public and private sector as complementary." This is an idea that China should learn seriously in its development and reform. Dr. Yusuf has also pointed out the universal weaknesses of corporate governance in East Asia, such as ineffective boards of directors, weak internal control, unreliable financial reporting, lacking of adequate disclosure, lax of enforcement to ensure compliance and poor audits, etc. All the above weakness also exist in corporate governance of China. I do expect the related authorities take care of all the above weaknesses in policy making on corporate governance.

In my comments to that book, I also stressed the role of social and cultural factors in development. This perception can remedy the insufficiencies of part four of this book.

The sixth paper is "E-Governance and Human Resource Development". This is a report presented to the ASEM Conference on Globalization and ICT on March 10-12, 2003 in Malmo and Helsingborg Sweden. This paper will be included in a collection of papers presented at the symposium by IKED Sweden. The author stresses in this paper that globalization is a process, a brief retrospect of the history of the process of industrialization is given, both positive and negative lessons of the process are summarized. It is emphasized in this paper that the developed countries, take the lead in marching toward establishing an information society (or knowledge-based society) should learn lessons from history. The second part of this paper explores e-governance, with a broad definition of governance. The author has prepared a comparative study of government organizational structure to the traditional hierarchical structure of enterprises, e-governance to the improvement of organizational structure is explored, a system concept of organizational structure in management theory is also described. A brief description of current status and prospect of e-governance is also presented. Difference between human resource development and traditional personnel management is clarified in Part Three of this paper; the strategy in application of ICT to human resource development and upgradation of skills in continuity is also emphasized. And finally, some recommendations on cooperation between Europe and Asia are raised. The author would like to mention here that there will be a world summit in 2004 and 2005 on "Information Society". People should keep abreast of changes at international level in the process of globalization. In domestic development, people must be sensitive and adaptable to global changes.

Part four of this book are related to some social aspects of China. It should be emphasized here that the study of contemporary society can cover very broad areas, far broader than that of economics. They may include: family, race, class, strata, poverty and welfare, institutional structure, work and economic life, government and politics, education, religion, mass media and culture. Contemporary study of development economics has also taken "cultural factor on development" to be a specific subject. In fact, one cannot isolate economic policies with the social and cultural aspects. Early in the mid 80's, some economists from the World bank had exchanged views with me on the progress of economic reform of China. They think that the process of China's reform seems to be too slow. I told them that the process of China's economic reform cannot be pushed too fast, because the established social welfare system cannot be changed overnight. Large and small countries differed in social rigidity. The failure of the shock therapy approach applied to the reform in the former Soviet Union is due to its neglect of the social aspects by Western economists. Social aspects are very complicated issues if they are studied in depth and breadth. An initial study has been done on social aspects in this book, only two papers are selected, i.e., the social issues that the Chinese government had, and it is continuous to be dealt with full effort. The first paper is "Social Security System and Alleviation of Poverty in China." This report is written by the author at the request of ESCAP. It was completed in April 1995, the contents of this paper cover poverty and current status, trend of social security policy framework and current system of social security; financial resource of social security system and future strategy. This paper also gave a brief description of "8-7 Poverty Alleviation Program of China". It was published in *Toward Social Security for the Poor in the Asia-Pacific Region* by UNESCAP in 1996.

The second paper in part IV is "Urban Poverty Alleviation and Development". Poverty and poverty alleviation is a dynamic process. Prior to the reform and opening-up, poverty was mainly a rural phenomenon in China. There are emergence of urban poverty and human settlement in urban area due to large amount of immigrants and industrial restructuring. This paper has discussed in general the process of change of urban poverty and human settlement in China before the 90's; the emerging issue of urban poverty and strategy to deal it; a new initiative for poverty alleviation in China, the "Brilliant Cause" (relevant institutions of UN show great interest in that initiative) is introduced briefly. And the final part of this paper concludes with a section titled "Poverty Alleviation and Improving Human Settlements, A Fuman Development Challenge". This paper is written at the request of UNCHS (United Nations Conference on Human Settlement) for the conference jointly sponsored with UNCRD (United Nations Center for Regional Development). It is published in *Regional Development Dialogue* by UNCRD in 1999.

Part V of this book focuses on some environmental aspects. The author has a relative detailed description of sustainable development in paper 1 of part I. Therefore, there is no need to give extra space to theoretical introduction in this part. Three papers are collected here. One paper is "Toward a Sustainable Development Society: A System Approach". This paper is a pilot study of paper 1 in Part I. It is written for the Club of Rome Conference in Fukouka, Japan in 1992 prior to the World Summit held in Rio de Janeiro, Brazil. *Declaration of Fukouka* was raised at that conference and sent to the World Summit. The speech given by the author was published, both in English and Japanese, at the symposium; it was titled "Global Environment and Local Action." The paper collected in this book is the original draft in English.

The second paper in part V is "Economic Development and the Environment in China". The co-author of this paper is Madam Shantong Li of our center. The contents of this paper includes, economic achievements of China, economic development and its impact to environment, economic development and energy demand, industrialization of China and its impact to environment, China's policy to environment, etc. This paper differs from most other papers included in this book in that relatively detailed technical aspects are discussed and analyzed. There are sectoral data on output and the amount of discharge of waste water, waste gas, and sulfur dioxide. This paper was written in 1995. It was published in a book titled *Economic Development & Cooperation in the Pacific Basin* by Cambridge University Press in 1998.

The third paper is "Sustainable Development in a New Millenium." It is written for an "expert groups meeting" sponsored by United Nations held in Malaysia in July 2001. This meeting was to make preparations for the World Summit in Johanesburg, South Africa 2002. The speeches delivered by all the experts were collected by the staff of UN to become internal references. The author has given a brief speech called "China: Agenda 21", which analyzed the issue and constraints of its implementation, new opportunities and challenges of East Asia and Pacific Region, ventured the prospects of the new millenium and put forward some recommendations.

Conclusions in the last part briefly discuss the challenges in and issues related to the "integrated approach," and some documents of international organizations on China's planning and development are introduced to provide a wider sharing of information with the readers.

This is a brief introduction of all parts of this book. It is expected that this brief introduction will give a bird's-eye view of the contents of the book. The academic perspective of the author is also expressed briefly in this introduction. It should be emphasized that China's reform and opening is a mega social systems engineering. This book is a very preliminary exploration of it. The author expects that, better explorations can be made of this gigantic project in my life-long learning and pooling of large amounts of domestic and international knowledge, through continuous summary of experience of the ever-changing real world.

Part I

Overall Perspective of
Development
Strategy of China

1. System Concept of Sustainable Development — Sustainable Development of the Mode of Production and Consumption and the Impact of Social Culture*

Introduction

Although it was raised early in 1972 in the Stockholm Declaration that "the protection and improvement of human environment is a major issue which affects the well being of people and economic development throughout the world," this issue and challenge were only recognized in consensus by all countries until the United Nations Conference on Environment and Development (UNCED) was held in Rio de Janeiro, Brazil in 1992. With the adoption of *Agenda 21, the Rio Declaration on Environment and Development*, world leaders had defined a clear agenda for sustainable development. China had also prepared *China: Agenda 21*, which was promulgated by the State Council in March, 1994. But implementation of sustainable development is a complicated system problem. This can be seen from a document of the UN, "Implementing Agenda 21," in Feb. 2002, that "There is undoubtedly a gap in implementation, which is particularly visible in four areas. First, a fragmented approach has been adopted towards sustainable development. The concept of sustainable development is meant to reflect the inextricable connection between environment and development. Sustainable development must simultaneously serve economic, social and environmental objectives. Policies and programmes, at both national and

---

* This paper was written in 1998. It is supplemented with a part from the reference, referred in the end of this paper.

international levels, have generally fallen far short of that level of integration in decision making."[1] Therefore, this paper will do a preliminary exploration of this subject in four parts:

1. System Concept of Sustainable Development;
2. Evolution of Development Strategy and Sustainable Development Strategy;
3. Current Global Situation of Implementing Sustainable Development and Issues under Exploration''; and
4. Exploration of Implementation of Sustainable Development Strategy of China.
   (1) Sustainable Development of Mode of Production;
   (2) Sustainable Development of Mode of Consumption;
   (3) Cultural Impact on Sustainable Development.
Finally, a brief conclusion.

1. System Concept of Sustainable Development

The global economy has undergone a period of high growth rate after World War II. The developed countries have experienced a long period of high rate of economic growth through reconstruction in the post-war period; the average annual growth rate of GDP reached around 4% from 1950 to 1975, and even reached around 5% in the ten-year period before the eruption of the oil crisis in 1973. Developing countries that got rid of the former rule of colonization, had also implemented strategy of industrialization. Most of them have experienced extraordinary rate of economic development which was described by some Western economists as the "Second Industrial Revolution". But the issues of environmental pollution and ecological destruction began to emerge acutely, i.e., atmospheric pollution, ozone depletion, climate change, marine pollution, destruction of freshwater resources and water quality, land degradation and desertification, deforestation and degradation of forests, loss of biological diversity, environmental hazards and discharge of toxic chemicals and hazardous wastes, etc.

These phenomena are direct results accumulated through more than two centuries of the process of industrialization, sharp increase of the world

---

1. "Implementing Agenda 21," Report of the Secretary-General 19, Dec. 2001, UN Economic and Social Council.

population since 1800, and increase of activities of the mankind with its natural environment. Then, economists, political leaders and sociologist began a reflective study of strategies of development. Various new concepts of "sustainable development" were raised. The definition of sustainable development broadly adopted, which has also been used in the World Summit of 1992 is "sustainable development... meets the needs of the present without compromising the ability of future generation to meet theirs...."

The above definition has philosophically expressed the basic concept of sustainable development. But in the implementation of this concept, there is the need to have an overall view of system concept.

(1) In the Domain of Time

The development of current mankind should be integrated with the consideration of the development of the coming generations, i.e., the process of development is a dynamic historical process. "Time" is an important parameter to be considered in development to deal properly the relationship of development of the current generation and the future generations, the current generation should not spend all the available resources to rob the chance of survival of the coming generations. The second aspect of time domain to be considered is that the "needs" and "ability" of the mankind are dynamic in essence. They change over time along with the various stages of development. It was described by our ancient great politician Guanzhong that "The people learned to be polite when the warehouse is full of grains; the people will have the feeling of glory and shame when they have enough food and cloth". Modern Maslow's theory in Western management had divided the "needs" of the people into five hierarchical levels: they are, respectively, the basic physiological needs; the needs of safety and security; the needs of love and be loved, a feeling of attachment; the needs of being respected and needs of self-realization. It can be found that the theory of Guanzhong raised 2,500 years ago is more or less in consistent with the theory of Maslow in 1970. It shows that a country, which represents the interests of its largest groups of people must evaluate in detail the historical period it is situated, to judge the overall needs and ability of its current generation, give appropriately possible estimation of the needs of its coming generations, and appropriate policies of sustainable development should be implemented. This is by no means a simple task, and requires coordinated efforts to study them by all of our scientists and engineers.

(2) In the Domain of Space and Role of Government

System concept of sustainable development should also take into consideration the differences of "needs" and "ability" of spatial region.

Although there are rich countries and rich regions in the world, there are also many poor countries and poor regions. It is necessary to have different priorities in the implementation of sustainable development. The fifth principle in the *Rio Declaration* emphasizes that all countries and all people should consider "alleviation of poverty" be one of the basic tasks of sustainable development, to cooperate together in this area, to reduce the disparity of living standard, to satisfy better the needs of most of the populations of the world. It is reconfirmed in the UN Document of 2002 (reference 1) that "Reducing poverty and improving opportunities for sustainable livelihoods requires economic and social development, sustainable resource management and environment." The later statement has clearly integrated the approach of poverty reduction with economic and social development as well as resource management. In academic terms, this is a system approach. And those are exactly the aspects pursued in current governmental policies of China. Therefore, poverty alleviation implemented in certain provinces and countries of China is also a concrete action in the implementation of sustainable development.

(3) The system approach of sustainable development strategy should consider the mutual interaction and impact among environmental, ecological, social, economic and technological sub-systems. In the part 4 of this paper, I shall analyze briefly the mutual interaction and impact among the modes of production and consumption and cultural aspects to illustrate this system concept.

2. Evolution of Development Strategy and Emergence of Sustainable Development Strategy

The emergence of sustainable development strategy is an outcome of evolution and innovation from the traditional mode of development, which is developed by practitioners and theorticians. In the post-War period, there are various theories of development strategy, several studies of OECD had summarized them as follows:

(1) Development Strategy of Monetarism

Development strategy of monetarism emphasizes the function of money. The theory emphasizes the importance of the need for a balanced relationship between the amount of money available to finance purchases of goods and services and, on the one hand, the ability of the economy to produce such goods and services. It emphasizes free enterprises and market force. It also put emphasis on the role of the government which should be restricted to provide a framework of necessary legal systems, institutions and financial system for the operation of economic system, while all the rest should be left to the operation of market system.

(2) Development Strategy through Industrialization

This is a terminology applied to the development of manufacturing sectors of the developing countries. There are three types. The first type focused on the development of consumer's goods to meet the domestic demand. At the meantime, it also put emphasis on protection of domestic market through the barrier of custom tariff. The second type relied upon the state mandatory planning system to focus on the development of producer's goods. This was exactly the development strategy that was pursued by China in the pre-reform era. The third type is to develop export-oriented industries through the guidance of planning and support of preferential policies of the government.

(3) Development Strategy of Open Economy

This strategy focuses on the opening of both domestic commodity and factor markets (labor market is an exception) to international market. It allows free flow of capital and trade liberalization. In fact, most of the developing countries put more emphasis on the export orientation and import of foreign capital in the implementation of this strategy.

(4) Development Strategy of Green Revolution

This strategy was raised on the background that some developing countries were biased too much on the development of the industrial sector and neglected the linkage of industry to agriculture, or they had neglected the comparative advantage of their domestic agricultural resources. This strategy puts priority on the development of the agricultural sector.

(5) Development Strategy of Redistribution

It focussed on income equality and are biased to the low level of income of all social strata. Its main contents are: (a) Primary redistribution of the assets; (b) mobilization of the local initiative to promote a broad scope of people to participate in the process of development; (c) investment on development of human resource; and (d) promoting growth of employment.

(6) Socialist Development Strategy

The feature of this strategy mainly focuses on a high rate of accumulation of capital with low consumption. It puts emphasis on public consumption (i. e., health care, education, public transportation) rather than private consumption. It emphasizes relatively equal distribution of benefits. This type of development is recognized to be a strategy with unique feature in international study of development economics.

(7) Sustainable Development Strategy

This strategy is raised on the basis of summarizing the various strategies adopted by different countries in the past centuries and the new challenges faced by the mankind. This strategy puts emphasis on equality among current and coming generations in considering development; it also puts emphasis on investment to natural capital and also the equality of development.

It can be seen from the above summary of development strategies, of which strategies (1)-(6) are summarized by several OECD publications, that China's experience of development in the pre-reform era and also the development strategy implemented in the current transitional economies (former socialist countries) had also been summarized. From my perspective, there is no single universal strategy that can be applied to all countries in different stages of development and with different historical backgrounds. China itself must summarize correctly from its own conditions, its historical experience in development as well as international experiences to establish its own appropriate development should be established. China is a huge country with regions of different characteristics, policy measures and goals of development should be carefully discriminated in short or even medium terms within the context of a long-term goal of national strategy of development.

3. Current State of Implementation of Sustainable Development Strategy of the World and Issues under Exploration

(1) Current State of Implementation of Sustainable Development Strategy of the World

Most countries of the world had developed their own national development strategies based upon *Agenda 21*, for example, China and Japan had taken the lead to prepare National Agenda 21 in Asia Pacific Region. It is disclosed in a very recent UN report (Reference 1) that about 85 countries have developed one or other kind of national strategies although the nature and effectiveness of those strategies vary considerably from country to country.

But the implementation of sustainable development is far from satisfactory due to four reasons: a fragmented approach; no major changes of unsustainable mode of production and consumption; a lack of coherent policies, and finally, the financial resources required for implementing *Agenda 21* have not been forthcoming and the mechanism for the transfer of technology have not improved. Therefore, it is concluded in a UN document (Reference 1) that "Some progress has been made in adopting measures to protect the environment. But the state of the world's environment is still fragile and conservation measures are far from satisfactory. In most parts of the developing world, there has been at best limited progress in reducing poverty. Some progree has been made in some area of health, but other problems have surfaced, such as HIV/AIDS." Therefore, a new round of World Summit on Sustainable Development was held in Johannesburg 2002 to review the progress of implementation of *Agenda 21* in ten-year period after the Rio summit.

(2) On-going Explorations

Implementation of sustainable development is a complex issue requiring co-ordinated efforts of global society as a whole. Two technical aspects of explorations will be briefed below.

(a) To include the natural resource and social impacts into national accounting system

In order to make the basic definition of sustainable development to be operational, it seems to be necessary to quantify the assets of all kinds to compromise the needs and capital (assets) available for current and coming generations. The World Bank had implemented a preliminary study of accumulated assets and its components of different countries and regions. It had classified the capital which is the basis of development into four categories, the man-made capital, the natural capital, the human capital and the social capital. Within the realm of social capital, it includes social institution, culture, information and knowledge. It can be seen the enormous difficulties faced in this classification, and there is not any means and method of calculation recognized by all. Therefore, this is an area under exploration. Based upon the preliminary results calculated by the World Bank, the composition of global total capital has a share of 64% of the human capital, 16% share of man-made capital and 20% share of the natural capital.

(b) Indicators of sustainable development

The international organizations and related countries have started to study and establish an indicator system of sustainable development. OECD had established a framework of sustainable development indicators based upon the concepts of "Pressure-State-Response" (PSR system).

The Commission of Sustainable Development (CSD) of the UN had initiated the Program of Work on Indicators of Sustainable Development in 1995, and a report titled "Indicators of Sustainable Development: Guidelines and Methodologies" (Reference 2) as the culmination of the CSD Work Program on Indicators of Sustainable Development (1995-2000). It provides a detailed description of key sustainable development themes and sub-themes and the CSD approach to the development of indicators of sustainable development for use in decision-making processes at the national level.

A framework and methodology sheets for 134 indicators were developed by the UN-lead agencies and others as a preliminary working list for testing at the national level, 22 countries (including China) from all regions of the world were engaged in the testing process to gain the experience with the selection and development of sustainable development indicators and to assess their application and suitability to assist the decision makers. Against the background of the national testing experience and overall orientation in decision-making needs, and through several rounds of iterative process, a final framework of 15 themes and 38 sub-themes has been developed to guide national development beyond the year 2001, which is shown in Table 1.

Table 1 CSD Theme Indicator Framework

SOCIAI		
Theme	**Sub-theme**	**Indicator**
Equity	Poverty (3)	Percent of Population Living below Poverty Line
		Gini Index of Income Inequality
		Unemployment Rate
	Gender Equality (24)	Ratio of Average Female Wage to Male Wage
Health (6)	Nutritional Status	Nutritional Status of Childern
	Mortality	Mortality Rate Under 5 Years Old
		Life Expectancy at Birth
	Sanitation	Percent of Population with Adequate Sewage Disposal Facilities
	Drinking Water	Population with Access to Safe Drinking Water
	Healthcare Delivery	Percent of Population with Access to Primary Health Care Facilities
		Immunization against Infectious Childhood Diseases
		Contraceptive Prevalence Rate
Education (36)	Education Level	Children Reaching Grade 5 of Primary Education
		Adult Secondary Education Achievement Level
	Literacy	Adult Literacy Rate
Housing (7)	Living Conditions	Floor Area per Person
Security	Crime (36,24)	Number of Recorded Crimes per 100,000 Population
Population (5)	Population Change	Population Growth Rate
		Population of Urban Formal and Informal Settlements

ENVIRONMENTAL		
Theme	**Sub-theme**	**Indicator**
Atmosphere (9)	Climate Change	Emissions of Greenhouse Gases
	Ozone Layer Depletion	Consumption of Ozone Depleting Substance
	Air Quality	Ambient Concentration of Air Pollutants in Urban Areas
Land (10)	Agriculture (14)	Arable and Permanent Crop Land Area
		Use of Fertilizers
		Use of Agricultural Pesticides
	Forests (11)	Forest Area as a Percent of Land Area
		Wood Harvesting Intensity
	Desertification (12)	Land Affected by Desertification
	Urbanization (7)	Area of Urban Formal and Informal Settlements
Oceans, Seas and Coasts (17)	Coastal Zone	Algae Concentration in Coastal Waters
		Percent of Total Population Living in Coastal Areas
	Fisheries	Annual Catch by Major Species
Fresh Water (18)	Water Quantity	Annual Withdrawal of Ground and Surface Water as a Percent of Total Available Water
	Water Quality	BOD in Water Bodies
		Concentration of Faecal Coliform in Fresh Water

Theme	Sub-theme	Indicator
Biodiversity (15)	Ecosystem	Area of Selected Key Ecosystems
		Protected Area as a Percent of Total Area
	Species	Abundance of Selected Key Species
Economic Structure (2)	Economic Performance	GDP per Capita
		Investment Share in GDP
	Trade	Balance of Trade in Goods and Services
	Financial Status (33)	Debt to GNP Ratio
		Total ODA Given or Received as a Percent of GNP
Consumption and Production Patterns (4)	Material Consumption	Intensity of Material Use
	Energy Use	Annual Energy Consumption per Capita
		Share of Consumption of Renewable Energy Resources
		Intensity of Energy Use
	Waste Generation and Management (19-22)	Generation of Industrial and Municipal Solid Waste
		Generation of Hazardous Waste
		Generation of Radioactive Waste
		Waste Recycling and Reuse
	Transportation	Distance Traveled Per Capita by Mode of Transport

INSTITUTIONAL

Theme	Sub-theme	Indicator
Institutional Framework (38,39)	Strategic Implementation of SD (8)	National Sustainable Development Strategy
	International Cooperation	Implementation of Ratified Global Agreements
Institutional Capacity (37)	Information Access (40)	Number of Internet Subscribers Per 1,000 Inhabitants
	Communication Infrastructure (40)	Main Telephone Lines Per 1,000 Inhabitants
	Science and Technology (35)	Expenditure on Research and Development as a Percent of GDP
	Disaster Preparedness and Response	Economic and Human Loss due to Natural Disasters

Source: *Indicators of Sustainable Development: Guidelines and Methodologies,* Sept. 2001,

4. Exploration of Implementation of Sustainable Development Strategy of China

It can be seen from the above that the implementation of sustainable development of China must be viewed from the coordinated perspective of sustainable social, economic and technological development, or from the perspective of the system concept I put forward. If exploration of the economic sub-systems is done, analysis should proceed both from the supply side and demand side. It is impossible to give a detail analysis of all aspects. The following brief analysis on the modes of production and consumption, and the impact of social culture is at the best only preliminary explanation.

(1) Sustainable Mode of Production in Development

(a) Economic Structure

There were structural changes of the Chinese economy from 1978-1997. The share of primary sector of GDP is decreased from 28.1% in 1978 to 19.1% in 1997; the share of the secondary sector is increased from 48.2% in 1978 to 50.0% in 1997; the share of the tertiary sector is increased from 23.7% in 1978 to 30.9% in 1997. This share of tertiary sector is very low in comparison with other developing countries. There is the need to have an in-depth study of this phenomenon. Generally speaking, the pollutant discharge per unit of GDP of the tertiary sector is relatively small. Therefore, it is necessary to develop the tertiary sector (service sector) from the development perspective, including distribution, retail sales, intermediary service, financial service, consultancy service, consumer's service and public service. It should be emphasized that the rapid growth of ICT has not only changed the pattern of manufacturing, such as CAD, CAM, etc., it has also changed the pattern of traditional commercial activity, such as the emergence of e-commerce. There is also a trend of increasing share of tertiary sector of global society, especially in developed countries and newly industrializing economies. It is pointed out in reference 1 that "There has also been a shift in industrial production, from the material and energy intensive traditional industries, such as iron and steel and petroleum refining, to electronic and electrical industries, telecommunications, data processing and advanced chemicals. That trend, coupled with energy efficiency improvements, has led to a reduction of energy intensity (per unit of GDP) of more than 25 percent in the last 20 years. However, the improvement in efficiency per unit of production has been offset by an increase in the volume of goods and services consumed and discarded". Therefore, sustainable production must be linked closely with a sustainable mood of consumption.

(b) Establishment of New Indicators

From the perspective of sustainable development, although CSD of the UN has established a system of indicators (as shown in Table 1), it seems to be feasible to develop an indicator system based on classification of different production sub-sectors, so as to help in the preparation of national industrial policies for sustainable development. This indicator system can include resource intensity (resource consumption per unit GDP), intensity of pollutant discharge (quantity of pollutant discharged per unit GDP), etc. Study and establishment of such an indicator system may be useful to study appropriate sustainable industrial structure. This study can compliment the traditional pattern to classify the industries, such as labor intensive, capital intensive or knowledge intensive, etc. From the perspective of sustainable development, industries can also be classified into resource intensive, pollutant intensive, etc., which should be reduced as much as possible in the consideration of industrial structure; suppression and monitoring of these sectors should also receive particular attention.

(c) Recycling the Production Process

In the complete life cycle of a product or service, i.e., production, circulation (transport, transmission and distribution) and consumption, pollutant(s) are inevitably produced to downgrade the "state" of the system may be the same as "entropy" in thermodynamic process. It is known from the information theory that feedback information will produce negative entropy to improve the performance of the system. It may also be possible that a "link" of "anti-pollutant" or recycling the pollutant into useful product can be added to improve overall system performance. More efforts and information are required through the efforts of scientists and engineers.

(2) Sustainable Mode of Consumption

(a) Type of Consumption and Some Comments

Consumption can be broadly devided into public consumption (or government consumption) and private consumption. With respect to public consumption, a lot can be discussed on the rational budget revenue expenditure. Therefore, it will not be dealt with in this paper. Consumption can also be classified into material consumption, and non-material consumption (services in general, or entertainment, or a fashionable terminology in Chinese popular magazine, "enjoyable consumption"). It should be emphasized again that the pattern of consumption is dynamic, according to Maslow's theory. There is consumption to satisfy the basic needs (clothing, food, housing) up to weathy type and luxuries. Basic needs of consumption can generally be quantified; for example, the basic energy from the food should not be less than certain amount of kilo-calories, etc. But the pattern of consumption in excess of basic needs depends upon very much the subjective "value system" and the value system of the community and society. I am in agreement with the view that "The rich or so-called elite on the high income ladder are also emulating western lifestyles and consumption patterns, characterized by high levels of dietary, energy, raw materials and manufactured goods consumption demand which may cause serious damage to the environment".[2] Under the concrete conditions of China, riding a "bicycle" in short distance is a pattern of sustainable consumption rather than a passenger car. China has limited resources of land and crude oil, public transportation is a better means of transport that China should advocate from the long-term view of sustainable development. This pattern of con-sumption is now advocated in Europe too. We must learn seriously from inter-national experience and combine it with China's practical conditions. Similarly, multi-story buildings may be more suitable in rural areas.

(b) The concept of sustainable development has been accepted generallly in Western developed countries; the market for "green and fair trade" products has grown rapidly since the 1980's, particularly in developed countries. Con-sumer organizations and other non-governmental organizations have played an important role in increasing consumer awareness of consumption choices. Other tools for promoting sustainable consumption patterns include greening the supply chain, shifting consumption from products to services, and life-cycle assessments of goods and services, and responsible marketing and ad-vertising should also be done. Recently, eco-system design of housing has been adopted in Western developed countries, such as the utilization of solar energy in housing heating system, energy saving lighting and household elec-tric appliances, water saving equipment in kitchen and bath room; collection of rain water for flashing the toilet; no passenger car is allowed to be parked in residence area, etc. It can be expected that all those modes of sustainable development will be emerged in China in the process of globalization.

(c) Sustainable mode of consumption is deeply effected by the culture. In recent years, there are many studies in Western countries on "economics and culture". China had also wanted to develop the cultural industries. Yet,

---

2. Introduction of "State of the Environment in Asia and the Pacific 2000 Executive Summary," UN, 2000, jointly sponsored by ADB and ESCAP.

it is a complicated issue and requires detailed studies. The following quotation can serve to illustrate the complexity. "Any self respecting university course or textbook on industry economics spends some time at the outset discussing the difficulties of defining an industry— i.e., whether the concept of industry can be delineated according to groupings of producers, product classifications, factors of production, types of consumers, location, etc. What is problematical for industries in general is especially so in cultural sphere because of uncertainties in the definition of cultural goods and services". But culture does have its impact on sustainable development which will be discussed in the following.

(3) The Impact of Culture on Sustainable Development

(a) Culture is the state of a specific society or community. Culture may be taken as constituting the way of life of an entire society or community, including the codes of manners, dress, language, rituals, norms of behavior and systems of belief. Sociologists stress that human behavior is primarily the result of nurture. They and anthropologists both describe and analyze the society. The mode of consumption is a social phenomenon. It is effected by the culture of a society. Because culture covers a broad area defined above, we shall only study the impact of culture on the modes of production and consumption. We shall first explore a little bit on the "high culture" described by historians, i.e., the expression of culture is recorded in printed material. But we shall not neglect the impact of so-called "low culture" in oral expression from ordinary people or even illiterate, or the mode of behavior which is not recorded in printed material.

(b) From the history of China, teachings of Confucius, which arose in the 6th century BC in China, had played a decisive role in the legitimation of Chinese society, and in providing a unified culture over many centuries Confucius advocated simple and thrifty and criticized luxury. Therefore, the Chinese has a traditional culture on thrifty, which is basically consistent with the principle of sustainable mode of consumption. There is also the other famous Chinese scholar, Xunzi, who advocated that anything that was not consistent with past institutions should be destroyed. This thought is counteractive with the innovation of production, and it is not compatible with the principle of sustainable mode of production. Therefore, we should inherit the sound tradition of culture and discard the unsound traditional culture. Possibly, this type of Eastern culture, pursuit of simple and thirfty, is one of the reason of the "East Asia

Miracle" that has raised many debates among Western economists.

(c) Culture is not rigid; it can be constructed and subject to change. It is studied in Reference 4 "that cultural goods and services involve creativity in their production, embody some degree of intellectual property and convey symbolic meaning". There is also the emergence of the study of cultural dynamics. It is pointed out by President Jiang Zemin in his report to the 16th National Congress of the CPC, "It is necessary to master the forward direction of advanced culture. Development of advanced culture in contemporary China means to create a national, scientific, popular socialist culture which gears towards the modernization, the world and the future, to enrich continuously the spiritual world and to strengthen the vital force of the people". He had also said in his report to 15th Party National Congress, "Establishment of a socialist culture with Chinese characteristics will promote the sustainable modes of production and consumption."

Brief Conclusion

In the realm of sustainable modes of production and consumption, and the impact of culture, there are many emerging new issues within the field of science and engineering waiting to be studied. Let us work together with all efforts to pursue the revitalization and sustainable development of the Chinese Nation!

REFERENCES

1. *Implementing Agenda 21—Report of the Secretariat General 19*, Dec. 2001.

2. *Indicators of Sustainable Development: Guideline and Methodology*, Sept. 2001, 2nd Edition, UN, 2001.

3. *State of Environment in Asia and the Pacific, 2000*, Executive summary UN 2000

4. Economics and culture by: David Thosby Cambridge university Press 2001

2. The Experience of Development Planning in China

Part I   Introduction — An Overview of the Development Planning

Conscious plans for the development of the economy as a whole were drawn up for the first time in the former Soviet Union in the 1920s. After 1945, the establishment of planning agencies in most of developing countries were working to provide medium- and long-term perspectives on development planning, which became a tool for economic management, supplementing the short-run control of the purse string by the Ministry of Finance, which has traditionally played a preeminent role in economic management in most of the countries. A part of the developed countries also practiced the planning system, such as France, Japan and others. All of them worked out a series of national economic plans since the mid-1950s, each of these plans focused on one or two themes within the framework of long-range economic analysis and prospects. For example, the first French plan during initial period of planning (1947-1950, later postponed to 1953) focused on providing adequate production means to produce more and produce more quickly. The purpose of the second French plan (1954-1957) no longer focused only on increasing production, but also on improving the quality and effectiveness of production (profitability). The third French plan (1958-1961)was to focus on full employment of the extra number of youths who would soon reach working age and the development of the common market. The Japanese first Five-Year Plan (1956-1960) was for economic self-support, which was the first one officially adopted by the government as an important means to coordinate government economic policies and activity. And along with the achievement of high economic growth in the 60's, Japan's new development plan focused more on promotion of social development and innovation of industrial structure. The United Nations Committee for Development Planning had prepared a report titled "Toward Accelerated Development" with the sub-title "Proposals for the Second United Nations Development Decade" and was published by the United Nations in 1970. It's basic objectives are abstracted into an "Hypothetical Intent Studies" through an academic research[1].

Practice throughout the world had encouraged the academic field to explore the theoretical aspects of "development planning", the two famous books on "development planning" written by Jan. Tinbergen and W. Arthur Lewis have summarized various essential components of a sound development planning with a survey of current conditions, objectives to be achieved, means and instruments in implementation (policies and measures), budget expenditure, and also mathematics in planning. Currently, there are a rich resources of reference on development planning.

In addition to the above mentioned, planning should be looked upon as an evolving process. Sound development planning depends very much on the capability and knowledge of the mankind in understanding the many aspects of the contents to be planned. For example, the United Nations Conference on Environment and Development held in Rio de Janeiro, Brazil, June 1992, has made the whole world focus on sustainable development as one essential objective in development, i.e., "... the exploitation of resources, the direction of investments, the orientation of technological development, and institutional change are made consistent with future as well as present needs". And the World Summit for Social Development held in Copenhagen, Denmark, March 1995, has placed priority concerns on social development. Therefore, a sound national development planning should be prepared within a broader global scope and context to combine closely with national concrete conditions. Different countries are in different stages of development with different natural endowment and socio-economic and socio-cultural conditions, a careful analysis of these conditions with long-term global and domestic development perspectives in mind is a prerequisite in the preparation of a sound development planning.

---

1. Reference 6, *Societal System* by Yohn N. Warfield, 1976.

Fig. 1. Hierarchy of Goals of Development
(from reference)

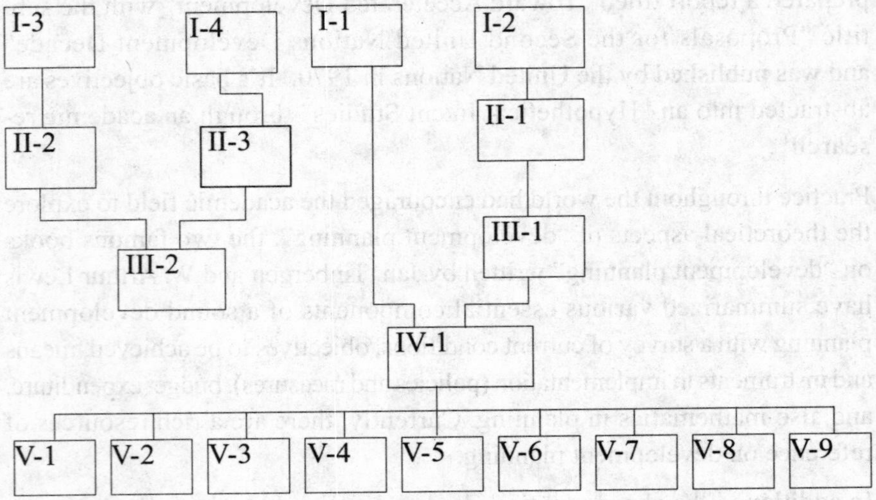

I-1   To dimension world tension
I-2   To provide opportunities for a better life to all sections of the population
I-3   To bring to fruition the hopes of mankind
I-4   To comprehend the inter relations among the elements in the development process
II-1   To eliminate glaring inequalities in distribution of income and wealth
II-2   To resoive the acute problems of poverty, disease and hunger
II-3   To use knowledge gained from experience
III-1   To attain a better distribution of income and wealth
III-2   To apply science and technology
IV-1   To increase the rate of development
V-1   To create internal environments conducive to rapid development
V-2   To expand employment opportunities
V-3   To eliminate mass poverty
V-4   To expand opportunity for all
V-5   To finance desired changes
V-6   To serve development needs through education
V-7   To identify obstacles and formulate measures to overcome them
V-8   To strengthen the United Nations system
V-9   To produce major changes in social and economic structures

China had learned from the Soviet model of planning since the First-Five Year Planning period (1953-1957). Despite the several cycles of centralization and decentralization from 1953-1978, the provincial and autonomous regional governments had also learnt from the planning techniques and procedure. The Soviet model of planning is characterized by its nature of short- and medium-term (annual and five-year plans), sector- and project-oriented (approval of projects are the key responsibility of the planning commission), centralization at the central level with inadequate co-ordination between sectoral and regional levels. This model of planning depends on administrative means rather than financial, fiscal and foreign trade policies. The planning process is a closed one; it is not open to the public to get consensus in the process of planning. It is more or less a top-down approach rather than a bottom-up approach. It focuses on too much details of every project and every product. Therefore, it is inappropriate when the society becomes so complex, the demand of the people is so much diversified, especially in a rapidly changing international environment and the environment of rapid progress of science and technology. Therefore, reform of the planning system is one crucial element of the reform program since the reform and open-up of China launched in late 1978. Formerly, the national development planning was under the sole care of the State Planning Commission (currently, the State Development Planning Commission), but our center (the Development Research Center of the State Council) and some international organizations also did research on development planning of China. Therefore, this paper will be presented as follows: part II and III will focus on the evolution of national development planning done by the State Planning Agency, part IV will summarize major research on development planning in China by our center (a government organization to provide policy consultation to the government) and other organizations (including international ones). One section of part V will deal with lessons and issues of development planning based on the Chinese experience and part VI will be brief concluding remarks.

Part II Evolution of National Development Planning of China (1949-1980)

2.01 Introduction

China's efforts for development over the past three decades have been consistently directed toward two main objectives in its development planning. First, industrialization, and in particular, development of a heavy industrial base. Second, elimination of the worst aspect of poverty. There are five planning periods, which are shown in table II-1. They will be described in relatively detail in 2.02.

Table II-1 The Chinese Planning Periods before 1980

National Economy Recovery Period	1950-1952
First Five-Year Plan Period	1953-1957
Second Five-Year Plan and Economic Adjustment Period	1958-1965
Third and Fourth Five-Year Plan Period	1966-1975
Fifth Five-Year Plan Period	1976-1980

2.02 Development Planning in the Pre-Reform Era

1. Industrialization and the First Five-Year Plan

Prior to 1949, the Chinese economy mainly relied on the production of its agricultural sector; the industrial sector was still at its stage of infancy, and moreover, it dominated by foreign investment. In 1950, the share of GDP of the primary, secondary and the tertiary sectors is 50.5%, 20.8% and 28.7% respectively. China was under the condition similar to other developing countries that severe deficiencies in their social and physical infrastructure made it diffucult for the building of its industrial capacity. The lack of experience in economic management exacerbated the problems. For most of developing countries, policies for industrialization include many aspects, such as the commercial policies, the fiscal and monetary policies, production and market control, labor policies, location policies, so on and so forth. But in the former central planned economies, centralization of administrative control was a common means of implementation; they rarely depended upon various policies and policy instruments as the means of control.

The speech to describe the major tasks of the "First Five-Year Plan" given by the former Primier Zhou En-Lai on Sept. 8, 1953 can serve to provide the background for understanding many aspects of the development objectives and policies of the Chinese economy in the First Five-Year Planning period. He stated, "First, to concentrate major forces to develop the heavy industry, to establish the foundation of national industrialization and modernization of national defense; create the technological human resource, develop transport, light industry, agriculture and expand commerce correspondingly; promote the cooperatives of agriculture and handicraft and also the reform of private industrial and commercial enterprises in appropriate steps; realize correctly the function of individuals of agriculture, handicraft and private industrial and commercial activities — All these are for the purpose to guarantee a stable increase of share of socialism in the national economy, to guarantee the gradual improvement of the level of physical and cultural lifes of the people on the basis of development of production." This statement can explain generally the guideline for various development policies in the First Five-Year Plan period.

2. Implementation of the First Five-Year Plan

(1) Implementation of industrialization as prescribed in the First Five-Year Plan was entirely through administrative means. Implementation based on heavy industry and modernization of the national defense as well as the creation of the technological human resource was successful. This can be shown from the change of the share of production of heavy and light industries, which is shown in Table II-2.

Table II-2 Share of Industrial Production (%)

Year	Heavy Industry	Light Industry
1953	37.3	62.7
1954	38.5	61.5
1955	41.7	58.3
1956	45.4	54.5
1957	48.4	51.6

Source: *China Statistics Year Book 1984.*

(2) According to the socialistic ideology, public ownership and socialist transformation were taken as the main goals. This process was accelerated at a higher rate than that stated in Zhou's speech. The state firms of commerce has increased their trade turnover from 14.9% in 1950 to 65.7% in 1957 while the trade turnover of private firms declined sharply from 85% in 1950 to 2.7% in 1957.

Because of the material allocation system (MPS) of the central planned economy, the commercial sector (which is considered to be non-productive in MPS) turned stagnated. This is also one of the negative experience of development of the Chinese economy and the other transitional economies too. Development experience shows that the commercial sector is inseparable with the growth of industrial sector, and the commercial sector can also provide more opportunities of employment through activities that serve the industry. Table II-3 shows this stagnation of the commercial sector in that period.

Table II-3   Figures for Commercial Services in China (1952-1957)
(Based on Every 10,000 People)

Item	1952	1957
Total Retail Sales (10,000 yuan)	48.15	73.34
Number of		
firms	95.16	41.8
retails	73.0	30.2
restaurants	14.8	7.3
other services	7.8	4.3
Work Force		
total	165.8	117.5
retail	123.5	87.7
restaurants	25.3	17.9
other services	17.0	11.9

Source: *Study of China's Sectoral Policy*, edited by Wang Huijiong, Li Boxi and Zhou Lin, China Financial and Economic Publisher, 1989.

(3) Fiscal, Monetary and Pricing Policies

Since the founding of the PRC, the central government tried all efforts in the unification and centralization of the fiscal and taxation system. But China had undergone several cycles of centralization and decentralization in regard to development planning and fiscal system, which can be shown in Table II-4.

Table II-4   Share of the Central Government and Local Administration of State Expenditure *(Various Periods) (%)*

Period	Central government	local government
"First Five Year"	74.1	25.9
"Second Five Year"	48.1	51.9
"Third Five Year"	61.1	38.9
"Fourth Five Year"	54.2	45.8
"Fifth Five Year"	49.4	50.6
"Sixth Five Year"	48.8	51.2
"Seventh Five Year"	39.6	60.4
1995	29.2	70.8

Source: Derived from *China's Statistical Year Book 1992, 1996.*

Differentiated taxes were used to implement industrial policy, i.e., the commercial sector was more heavily taxed than industry; tax rates for heavy industry were lower than those for light industry. Price was maintained stable by means of price control and other monetary policy. Having curbed the superinflation caused by civil war in the initial period after founding of the PRC, the price was maintained stable nearly throughout 30 years. For example, the average annual rate of inflation in the 1951-1980 period was only 0.9%. The People's Bank of China has extended all it's branches down to county and township levels, received deposits from every household, and almost served as the accountant for the Ministry of Finance. The Ministry of Finance allocated the financial resources according to the universal plan worked out by the State Planning Commission. This institutional arrangement also explained the lack of development of a modern banking sector and modern public finance system in the pre-reform era. But at the initial stage of establishment of the central planning system in the PRC, it was flexible because of the existence of different forms of ownership in the economy. Pricing policy was also viewed to be a major instrument of trade policy. Faced with shortages in 1955, the purchasing prices of swine were hiked, the purchasing prices of grain were raised by 157.7% between 1950-1955, showing that the pricing policy was somewhat flexible in the First Five-Year Plan period.

3. Development Planning in the Period between 1957-1980

(1) Period Covered

This period covered the time between the Second Five-Year Plan (1958-1962), the adjustment period (1963-1965), the Third and Fourth Five-Year Plan period (1966-1970 and 1971-1975), which include the period of "cultural revolution" (1966-1976) and the major part of the Fifth Five-Year Plan period (1976-1980).

(2) The Second Five-Year Plan, the Great Leap Forward[2] and the Adjustment Period

In Sept. 1956, a suggestion regarding the the Second Five-Year Plan was put forward at the Eighth Party National Congress. The target suggested was: by the year 1962, the gross value of industrial and agricultural output

---

2. See Appendix 1.

would be increased by 75% compared to 1957, the steel production would reach 10.5-12 million tons. These targets were modified several times in this period. For example, it was announced in the official document of the Enlarged Politburo Conference in 1958 that the steel production would reach 10.7 million tons by the year 1958, i.e., the amount of production would double that of 1957, which was projected to be 5.35 million tons. And then came the period of Great Leap Forward and three-year period of adjustment. The development in this period was effected greatly by political events, about which there are already many books and papers available (please refer to Reference 8). Two lessons are important: the first is, the growth target must be correctly assessed; and the second, there must be a sound planning process, including its approval and modification.

(3) The Third and Fourth Five-Year Planning period (1966-1975). This is also the period of "cultural revolution", therefore both the two Five-Year Plans were only in outline. But some generalizations of public policies implemented in this period can be summed up as follows:

i. Heavy industry continued to play a leading role. The share of heavy industry in total industrial production during the Third and Fourth Five-Year Plan period rose to 54.5% and 52.1% respectively, a further increase of 6.1% and 3.1% as compared to that at the end of 1957.

ii. There was further increase of the share of state-owned enterprise. The basic policy in this period was to further expand the state ownership, weaken the collective ownership and abolish the private ownership system. It can be seen from statistics that even the number of individual workers was reduced from 8.83 million down to 0.15 million in 1978.

In contrast with the policies implemented before 1978, a rapid increase of individual workers was evidenced in 1979, from 0.32 million to 17 million in the urban area (cities and townships), and to 33.1 million in 1996. Comparison of these figures can serve a better understanding of the change of policies before and after the launch of economic reform drive.

iii. Location policy. Industrial policy after the Third Five-Year Plan period emphasized local self-sufficiency, which resulted in hundreds of prefectures being involved in wide-ranging production activities.

iv. Foreign Trade Policy. Due to the absence of diplomatic relations with many Western countries as well as the trade embargo imposed by them, China had only established foreign trade relations with the former Soviet Union and other Eastern European countries. After the normalization of international relations in the 1970's, China's export/GNP and import/GNP is only 4.5% and 4.7% respectively in 1978. While in 1995, these two ratios rose to 20.3% and 15.8% respectively. This also serves to illustrate the impact of the open policy on foreign trade since the launch of reform and opening-up drive in late 1978.

(4) The Fifth Five-Year Planning Period (1976-1980)

The content of the Fifth Five-Year Plan was not well worked out due to the transition from political upheaval to the normalization of political, social and economic order of China. There was also inconsistency and discontinuity of planning program. In the beginning of 1978, a 10-year development program was announced. This ten-year development program was too ambitious that it was difficult to be coped with the available financial resources. According to this program, it was planned to use a total amount investment on capital construction equivalent to the sum of investment of the previous 28 years; 120 large projects were to be constructed or to be continued from 1978-1985; the targeted output of grain was 400 million tons, and the steel output would reach 60 million tons[3] by the year 1985. And there was a serious disproportion of investment on heavy and light industries in 1978, with the share of investment of heavy and light industries being 50.9% and 6.1% respectively. The Third Plenary Session of Eleventh Party Central Committee was held in late 1978. A series of corrective measures on development were adopted. These measures include: accelerating the development of agriculture and light industry; the procurement price of agricultural products was to go up by 30.8% in 1979 and 1980, thus mobilizing the initiative of the farmers to raise agricultural production. Encouragement was given to the development of light industry to better satisfy the needs of the people in general. The distribution of national income was also adjusted to reduce the rate of investment (from 36.5% to 31.6%) and to increase the rate of consumption (from 63.5% to 68.4%).

---

3. The output of steel reached 400 million tons by the year 1984. In 1985, it was 46.7 million tons, and in 1990 it was 62.1 million tons.

2.03 Major Achievement and Features of Development Planning in the Pre-reform Era

It has been mentioned in 2.01 that there are two main objectives in development planning. Despite the political upheaval in the three decades, the two main objectives were achieved.

1. Achievement in Industrialization

Table II-5 presents the growth of industrial products of different branches of the industry in real terms, which serve to illustrate the achievement in the efforts for industrialization in the implementation of development planning.

Table II-5 Growth of Industrial Products in
Different Branches of Industry

Serial No.	Name of Products	Units	1952	1980	Average Growth Rate Per Year (%)
1	Pig iron	million tons	1.93	38.02	11.2
	Steel	million tons	1.35	37.12	12.5
2	Electricity	bil. KWH	7.3	300.6	14.2
3	Crude coal	million tons	66	620	8.3
4	Crude oil	million tons	0.44	105.95	21.6
5	Chemical fertilizer	10^3 tons	39	12,320	22.8
	Caustic soda	10^3 tons	79	1,923	12
	Plastics	10^3 tons	2	898	24.3
6	Power generating equipment	MW	6	4,193	26.3
	Mining equipment	10^3 tons	1.8	163	17.4
	Machine tools	10^3 units	13.7	134.0	8.4
	Internal combustion engines	10^3 hp	40	25,390	25.9
7	Cement	million tons	2.86	79.86	12.6
	Plate glass	million std cases	2.13	27.71	9.5
8	Timber	million cu. meters	11.20	53.59	5.7
9	Sugar	10^3 tons	451	2,570	6.4
	Salt	10^3 tons	4,945	17,280	4.5
	Tobacco	10^4 cases	265	1,520	6.4
	Wine	10^4 tons	23	368.5	10.4
10	Cotton yarn	10^3 tons	656	2,930	5.4
	Cotton cloth	bil. m	3.83	13.47	4.6
	Woolen piece goods	million m	4.23	101	11.9

2. Elimination of the Worst Aspect of Poverty

Although China has a high share of people in poverty according to the recent international standard (US$1 per day per capita), China has achieved its target to eliminate the worst aspect of poverty. The following quotation of a report on China from the World Bank serves as an objective assessment of the achievement of the objectives of development in the pre-reform era.

"... Since the average income in China is low, a large minority of the population is very poor. The people, however, have a much higher standard of living than those at similar income levels elsewhere. They all have work; their food supply is guaranteed; most of their children are at school; and the great majority have access to basic health care. Life expectancy — whose dependence on many other economic and social variables makes it probably the best single indicator of the extent of real poverty — is on average in China outstandingly high for a low-income country; even in the poorest province, it is not far below the average for middle-income countries."

Part III   Evolution of National Development Planning of China (1981-Present Day)

3.01 Introduction

It is mentioned in previous part that China had followed the Soviet model of development planning and used method of implementation through administrative means. Although the targets of development were achieved, there were nevertheless several drawbacks. The planning process is non-transparent, and frequently over-ambitious targets were set and as a result several of the plans were underfulfilled, such as the plan in the period of Great Leap Forward and the 10-Year Development Program in the Fifth Five-Year Planning period. It had been described in the overview that there was rich of international experience on development planning which can be taken for reference to improve China's planning system. Therefore, reform of the planning system, the role of the plan and its implementation were clearly defined in the second official document on reform issued on Nov. 14, 1993 at the 14th National Congress of the Chinese Communist Party. It was stated in article 17 of the document that "The plan sets forth the objectives and tasks for national economic and social development and the necessary coordinated economic policies; the central bank whose primary objective is to stabilize currency value, regulates the aggregate money supply and maintains balance of international payments; the fiscal departments regulate the economic structure and social distribution primarily by budgeting and taxation".

Many improvements have been witnessed in the planning system since the launch of reform drive. Up to current, four more five-year plans were worked out and implemented, namely, the Sixth to the Ninth. The major features of planning in this phase are:

1. The name of the planning is changed from economic plan to national economic and social development plan, i.e., social development had been taken into consideration, and this is in accordance with the current global concept of development;

2. Since the Eighth Five-Year Plan, the name and content of the plan has been changed to five-year plan and 10-year long-term program, indicating better coordination in evaluating the target of medium-term development within the long-term context;

3. The planning system has gradually been reformed from mandatory to indicative, from administrative to policy guidance. There was a section of major policies and measures for every sector of the economy since the Seventh Five-Year Plan. And there was a gradual shift to emphasize the means of market mechamim from the Sixth to Ninth Five-Year Plan;

4. Modern tools are employed, mathematical modeling, computer simulation and both qualitative and quantitative analysis are emphasized;

5. Coordination between macro and micro, national and regional aspects are taken into consideration. Feasibility study, cost-benefit analysis of projects, improvement of regional plans and its coordination within national plans are taken place in this period.

6. There is improvement of the planning process, including the process of approval by the National People's Congress.

7. There are various agencies, including international organizations, that study for the improvement of planning in China.

3.02 Evolution of Development Planning of China Since the Launch of Economic Reform (1981-Now)

1. The Sixth Five-Year Plan (1981-1985)

This plan has a broader coverage than the past ones. It was divided into five parts and thirty-six chapters. Part one dealt with the basic tasks and comprehensive index in six chapters; Part II focused on sectoral development plans (13 chapters); Part III was devoted to regional economic development plans (five chapters); Part IV was on scientific research and educational development plans (four chapters); Part was about the plan for social development (seven chapters).

It should be pointed out that China had learned from the planning experience of Japan and the Republic of Korea and added a chapter on "national land development and rectification" in part III of the document. The establishment of special economic zones and utilization of foreign investment were listed in two separate sections in chapter 19 (foreign trade and foreign economic relations) of part II. Environmental protection was listed and became chapter 35 of part V.

2. The Seventh Five-Year Plan (1986-1990)

(1) The Seventh Five-Year Plan for National Economic and Social Development had a unique feature in that both the goals and policy measures of implementation were explicitly stated, particularly that related to the industrial policy and industrial sector. According to some Western economics, industrial policy is considered to be micro-policy, in the former central planned economies, however, it is taken as the major policy of the government to pursue industrialization. There is also different points of view on the exact meaning of "policy" in the planning documents and among Western scholars. A part of this planning document relating to "policy" was abstracted in (2), and some comments are given in (3). The major contents of this plan is shown in Box II-1.

(2) Investment structure and investment policy briefing made up for a part of chapter 39 titled "Adjustment of Investment Structure." There were four principles for the adjustment. The fourth principle stated the goals and policy measures.

With regard to the regional distribution of investment, key investment for technological rehabilitation, restructuring and expansion would be allocated to the Eastern region; key investment for new projects of energy and raw materials would be allocated to the Central region.

The major policies and measures for adjustment of the investment structure are:

The approval and determination of large and medium-sized projects of various regions and trades would be based on the direction of adjustment of investment structure;

The state shall utilize part of the financial resource within the budget and bank credits as guiding financial resource to absorb the financial resources of the localities and enterprises for undertaking the urgently needed projects of the state;

Box II-1
Contents of PRC's Seventh Five-Year Plan
Introduction

Part I   Major Tasks and Targets of Economic Development (5 chapters);

Part II   Industrial Structure and Industrial Policies (10 chapters) (within which, 5 sectors have explicit statements about major policy measures in section headlines);

Part III   Regional Economic Development Policies (7 chapters) (within which, 4 chapters have explicit statements of major policy measures in section headlines);

Part IV   Science and Technology Development and Policies (5 chapters) (within which, 1 chapter has explicit statement of development strategy);

Part V   Educational Development and Its Policies (5 chapters) (within which, 1 chapter has explicit statements of major policy measures in section headlines);

Part VI   Foreign Economic Trade and Technological Exchange (6 chapters. There is no ex plicit statement of policies in section headlines, content about the special economic zones, coastal opening cities and opening region form one chapter in this part);

Part VII   Investment Structure and Investment Policies (4 chapters) (There is no explicit statement of policies in section headlines);

Part VIII   Objectives and Tasks of Economic System Reform (4 chapters) (there is no explicit statement of policies in section headlines);

Part IX   People's Livelihood and Social Security (6 chapters) (there are three chapters with explicit statements of policies or measures in section headlines);

Part X   Construction of Socialist Spiritual Culture (4 chapters); and

Annex

Economic instruments such as grant, interest subsidies, interest rates and tax rates would be utilized to assist the construction of these projects of the state and bring under control redundant projects and blind construction.

(3) It should also be pointed out that there are inherent institutional weaknesses for the implementation of macro-economic policies in most of the transitional economies, because of the under development of the money market, capital market, legal and taxation system. These weaknesses were also shown in the policy aspects of the fiscal, financial part of the planning document of China since 80's. Although the general guideline given in the planning document remained correct, it took time for a detailed study to make appropriate use of the indirect economic means. A report of the World Bank points out, "The Seventh Five-Year Plan for 1986-1990 was prepared in elaborate detail, with many years of officials time put into its preparation. ... However, the plan did not include a policy framework to influence the achievement of those targets, nor, in general, any particular program for the use of indirect economic levers...."

3. The Eighth Five-Year Plan and Ten-Year Long-Term Development Program for National Economic and Social Development

Although this document was simpler than the previous Sixth and Seventh Five-Year Plans, its structure of contents was almost the same as the Seventh Five-Year Plan, except that science and technology were combined with education in the same part; the part on investment structure was not made an independent part. The major feature of the document is the inclusion of a ten-year long-term development program linked with the details of Eighth Five-Year Plan. Part one of this document focused the target of development of ten-year period and a guideline for the development of the economy, science and technology, education, people's livelihood, economic system reform, foreign economic relations, etc. The remaining eight parts dealt with various details of the Eighth Five-Year Plan. With the experience gained in the economic reform of previous decade, the content of economic restructuring was described in detail: the ownership structure, reform of enterprise system, development of the socialist market system, price reform, fiscal and taxation reform, financial system reform, wage and housing sector reform, social security system reform, reform of the planning system and investment system, strengthening the economic control system, etc.

It is emphasized in this document that the crucial role of planning should be gradually shifted to forecasting, planning, guidance and control of the overall social economic activity, to pointing out the correct direction of economic operation, to maintaining the overall balance of the economy, and coordinating the structure and relationship of various activities.

4. The Ninth Five-Year Plan (1996-2000) for National Economic and Social Development and the Outline of Long-Term Targets up to 2010

It can be seen from this document that there is further extension of the long-term perspective plan to fifteen years (1996-2010). The contents of this planning document was more or less the same as the previous planning documents. But two national strategies were stated. One was to group science and technology and education together in one part under the title "Strategy to Promote National Prosperity through Science and Education." The other was to group "protection and development of national land resources", "environment and ecological protection", "urban and rural construction", "culture", "health care" and "physical culture" together under the title "Implementation of Sustainable Development Strategy, Push Forward the Sound Development of All Social Affairs".

This document also emphasized two major transformations: "transformation of economic system from traditional planned economy system to the system of socialist market economy" and "transformation of the pattern of economic growth from extensive to intensive".

In this document, there was a part titled "Promote the Peaceful Unification of the Motherland," which was also one of the national target of the PRC.

It should be pointed out the present Chinese top leadership is seriously implementing the strategy of revival of the nation through science and education, and the recent serious calamity of flood has taught the public a serious lesson on the necessity to implement the strategy of sustainable development and ecological protection.

3.03 Transformation of Thinking in Approaches of Planning

1. General

China had learned the planning practice from the former Soviet Union in the first Five-Year Plan period. This planning practice was also adopted and learned by the local governments in the process of decentralization at the later stage of the period of planning. Then, political upheavals arose in the period of Great Leap Forward and the period of "cultural revolution". Due to long-term isolation from the international community and the political unrest at home, no much improvement had been seen in terms of planning technique and the planning institutions. Transformation of concept in planning approaches and practices only took place after the launch of the drive for economic reform and opening to the outside world. The major changes are summarized as follows.

2. Evolution of Concept in Planning Approaches

(1) Institutional change

The State Planning Commission had been the sole government agency for the preparation of long-term, medium-term and annual plans in the pre-reform era. The government had established the State Economic Commission in 1982 (now called the "State Economic and Trade Commission"), which was given the responsibility to monitor and coordinate economic and trade activiies annually, and to examine and approve projects of technological upgrading of existing enterprise. Several policy consultation organizations were also established in 1980-1981, including the Research Center for Rural Development[4], which gave the policy recommendations on rural economic reform, the Technical-Economic Research Center, which had done research on cost-benefit analysis of projects in the Western way, "China toward the Year 2000 Study", an experimental project in China that studies the long-term scenario based on qualitative and quantitative analysis, the strategy for long-term development and policy research for its implementation. (A brief introduction of this pioneering project and the figures showing research methodology are attached in appendix 2). This center has also coordinated closely with theState Planning Commission on the research of the application of industrial Policy, etc. The State planning Commission has changed the practice of planning to some extent. It had worked together with various institutions in changing the planning concept and methodology. It has also organized various research institutions to help in the planning

---

4. The former Technicall Economic Research Center, the Research Center for Rural Development and other two research centers — the Economic Research Center, the Price Research Center — were merged into one — the Development Rresearch Cennter of the State Council in 1989.

work, such as the Chinese Academy of Social Sciences, the Commission of Comprehensive Survey, various research centers of the State Council and various research centers of the ministries. It had also made its own information center to study the application of modeling technique; the Research Academy of Macro-economy was also established under its jurisdiction.

(2) Changing the role of the State Planning Commission and strengthening the institutions of indirect control, such as People's Bank in performing the role of the central bank, the Ministry of Finance in fiscal and budgetary control, and the Ministry of Foreign Trade and Foreign Economic Relations in execution of foreign trade policy. Before the launch of the economic reform, China had a mono-bank system, and the People's Bank almost served as the accountant of the Ministry of Finance, and the Ministry of Finance followed closely the target set up by the State Planning Commission. The reform and improvement of the banking system has improved the executing capacity of the People's Bank (as the central bank) on monetary control. The Ministry of Finance has also enhanced its power in fiscal policy and budgetary control.

(3) Improvement of Planning Foundation and Tools

China had adopted the MPS system of planning, its foundation of statistics was based on the MPS system, which was gradually changed to the SNA system in the 80's. Green accounting has been studied. The input-output method was experimented in Shanxi Province before the 80's. The first national I/O table was produced in 1981. The Technical-Economic Research Center had experimented with various planning models early in Shanxi Province with a project named "Comprehensive Planning of Energy and Heavy Chemical Base of Shanxi Province." Computer-aided modeling and application has grown popular in China's planning agencies and nearly all research institutions.

3.04 Evolution of the Planning Process

1. The Planning Process from 1953-1980

Theoretically, the preparation of the five-year plan was done by the State Planning Commission, which followed the guidelines and decision of the CPC Politburo. The draft plan was discussed at Party's National Congress; and the State Council submitted the plan to the National People's Congress for approval. Due to lack of experience in planning, the preparation of the First Five-Year Plan was initiated in 1952 and sent to the National People's Congress for approval in 1955 although it covered the 1953-57 period. The targets of the Second Five-Year Plan had also been revised several times in the CPC Politburo, including the revision during the period of the Great Leap Forward. It is mentioned before that the Third and Fourth Five-Year Plans were only in the outline form as they covered the period of the "cultural revolution". Therefore, the planning process, generally speaking, was not normal during this period. Some of the positive and negative experience have been summarized in Reference 7.

2. The Planning Process from 1981 Onward

This refers to the period covering the Sixth, Seventh, Eighth and Ninth Five-Year Plans. Several prominent features were evident in this period.

(1) The Planning Process, Especially the Process of Preparation and Approval Was Gradually Normalized

The period of Sixth Five-Year Plan ran from 1981 to 1985. The plan was sent to the National People's Congress in Nov. 1982 for approval. The policymaking process before the approval by the National People's Congress was largely the same as the pre-reform era. First, the CPC Politburo set the major guidelines and targets and sent them to the National Party's Congress. The State Council would be responsible for the organizational work for the preparation of the plan following the proposal from the Party. Since the Seven Five-Year Plan, the date of approval by the National People's Congress has been fixed to the beginning year of the five-year plan period. The Seventh, Eighth and the Ninth Five-Year Plans were approved by the National People's Congress in April 1986, March 1991 and March 1996 respectively.

(2) Correct policy making depends very much on the correct information supplied to the policy makers as well as the correct judgment of the policy makers. Many policy research institutions have been established since 1981. The former Tech-Economic Research Center (the current Development Research Center) of the State Council was established in 1981, and there are several hundred policy research institutions, academic and non-academic, at the central, provincial and even city levels now. These policy research institutions make policy studies and provide the necessary information as a

part of policymaking process.

(3) Expert groups were organized to draft the plan, the leadership of the Party would also pool opinions from representatives of various circles of life and make the final suggestion to the State Council. The following quotation from the report of Premier Li Peng to the Eighth National People's Congress on the "Ninth Five-Year Plan and Outline of Long-Term Program up to 2010" serves to explain this process clearly. "Suggestions with regards to the preparation of Ninth Five-Year Plan for National Economic and Social Development and Long-Term Program up to 2010 passed by the Fifth Plenary Session of the Fourteenth Party Central Committee mapped out fully the strategic objectives of the second step, and the guiding guidelines and major tasks.... The State Council prepared Ninth Five-Year Plan for National Economic and Socials Development and Long-Term Program (Draft) based upon the spirit of the suggestions, and exensively collected opinions from various circles. Now I report to the Congress on behalf of the State Council and ask all delegates for discussion and approval, and ask the Members of Chinese People's Political Consultative Commission to give their opinions".

3.05 Study of Chinese Development Experience Abroad

Development planning and development experience of China had long been a subject of concern among the international organizations and scholars. It is impossible to describe all them in detail. A very limited number of writings will be introduced here.

1. Reference 11, "Economic Development and Social Change in the People's Republic of China," had a complete review of China's development experience on political, social and economic aspects. Many official documents and papers from China were quoted, studied and analyzed in detail. Many development experiences of China, both positive and negative, had been well summed up.

2. Since the 80's, the World Bank send many missions to China. They have an ample study of the development experience of China. When the former Technical Economic Research Center initiated the project "China towards the year 2000" in 1982, the World Bank was carrying out a study project on China nearly in parallel with the above project. The World Bank project was titled "China: Long-Term Issue and Options"; it includes one main report

and five annexes, namely, the agricultural sector, the education system, Chinese development from international perspective, projection of growth through economic modeling and energy. These studies had not only summed up China's development experience in the past several decades since the founding of the PRC, they had also studied the development issues and actions up to the year 2000 (the official World Bank Publication of this study was in 1985). They have continued the study of China's development experience in their annual study *Current Economic Memorandum*. Recently they have completed the study *China 2020*.

3. Various organizations of the UN and OECD, and Japanese research institutions and scholars also have published a lot of studies on development experience of China.

Part IV Experience and Lessons of Development Planning in China

4.01 Introduction

It is described in part I that there are now extensive literature available on development planning and development economics. But successful planning for development is not a simple task. For the developing countries, sustained economic growth is the priority of concern at their current stage of development. But social-cultural factors are also important when they try to achieve take-off. And the modern concept of development includes a relatively balanced growth on sustainable development — social and economic development.[5] There is no universal principles of development that can be applied successfully to any specific country or region without an in-depth knowledge of the concrete conditions of that country or region. It is correctly pointed out in Reference 11 that "I see my investigation as a model for similar investigations of trends and developmental policies in Third World Countries (of which, of course, the People's Republic is one), help each individual country find a new and future-oriented outlook within the frame-

---

5. Definition adopted in Agenda 21 of Rio Dedaration on Environment and Development "Development today must not undermine the development and environment needs of present and future generationns".

work of the traditional heritage by employing traditional values for renewal and revitalization." The leery words of development planing from the above quotation are "new," "future oriented" "traditional heritage" and "renewal". In the following sections, the lessons and experience of development planning in China will be presented for reference.

4.02 Experience and Lessons of Development Planning in the Pre-reform Period (1950-1978)

1. The Chinese Experience from the Perspective of Development Policy Research

(1) Mobilization of the Population as Development Vehicle — Pursuit of an Egalitarian Development Strategy at Its Initial Period of Development

Within the framework of orthodox development theory, it is the entrepreneurs and the elites to whom the innovative function (Joseph Schumpter) is assigned. The Chinese leadership, on the contrary, has repeatedly made the attempt to instill appropriate attitude in the masses, to consider the mobilization and participation of the "masses" much more important than the efficient allocation of resources. At the meantime, an egalitarian development and basic needs approach is advocated. It has also been pointed that "Chinese economic development under Mao has been argued by some commentators to have played a role in the thinking about basic human needs strategies.... In 1977-1978, the World Bank picked up the concept of basic human needs from the ILO and pushed it hard. These development strategies are based upon the concrete condition of China by that time: China was much too poor to be able to tolerate grave inequality."[6] This egalitarian growth strategy is implemented at regional level.

The success of mobilization of the population as development vehicle is not only shown in various economic activities in the pre-reform era, it is also shown in counteracting the serious flooding disaster this year (1998).

Before 1978, social equality was emphasized rather than the pursuit of economic efficiency. If the criteria of social equality are used to evaluate the public social policy, it can be said that China had a very small Ginl coefficient before 1978, although the living standard on the whole is low by inter-

---

6. See Reference 12.

national standard, because China started from the historical background of a very much underdeveloped state in 1949. The result of this development effort implemented before 1978 was that, notwithstanding their low income share, the poorest people in China were far better off than their counterparts in most other developing countries[7].

The egalitarian development strategy implemented before 1978 was char-

Table IV-1   Comparison of Total Output of Society (1952-1978)
unit: 100 Million yuan (Index of growth with 1952 to be base year 100)

| Year | Total | Output | of | Society | | |
	Liaoning	Inner Mongolia	Shandong	Guangdong[8]	Guizhou[9]	Gansu
1952	76.2	15.61	69.82	49.92	12.69	16.78
	(100)	(100)	(100)	(100)	(100)	(100)
1978	483.7	109.76	445.01	350.31	87.95	125.21
	(775.6)	(525.21)	(614.18)	(541.1)	(487.9)	(612.66)

Source: *A Compilation of Historical Statistics of Provinces, Autonomous Regions and Municipalities Directly under the Central Government, 1949-1989*, China Statistical Publishing House, 1990.

acterized by a balanced regional development strategy with less emphasis on the location advantage; a full employment policy for the urban workers with a very low wage growth rate and also a low inflationary rate. There was also a social security system which covered a wide range of benefits for the urban workers. All able-bodied rural residents were assigned jobs on commune lands and in sideline industries in the commune system implemented before 1978 in rural areas, minimum per-capita grain ration and relief fund were allocated to orphans, disable and elder people. Table IV-1 shows the growth of output from 1952 to 1978 of six provinces selected from six regions, which shows the difference of growth of output of those regions is small, the only exception was Liaoning Province, its output index in 1978 compared to 1952 is the highest among the six provinces (or regions) under comparison. Because this province received the highest share of state

7. The World Bank : *China: Socialist Economic Development*, Washington D.C., 1982.
8. In 1996, the per-capita GDP of Guangdong and Guizhou is 7,973 yuan respectively.
9. *Ditto*.

investment to be the basis of heavy industry before 1978.

The figures in table IV-1 can also illustrate the negative effect of the egalitarian regional development strategy. It can be seen that Guangdong and Inner Mongolia nearly have the same growth rate of total output of society in the pre-reform period, due to the underutilization of the location advantages and the close-door policy implemented before 1978, the potential of development of Guangdong Province is suppressed. And since the launch of economic reform and opening to the outside world, the economic growth of Guangdong Province is very much accelerated, in 1996, its GDP is 651.9 billion yuan, which is 12 times of its total output in 1978. In 1996, the GDP of Guangdong Province is 6.6 times of Inner Mongolia by the same year. It shows the necessity to reform the development strategy in China's current stage of development. And the egalitarian regional development strategy implemented in the pre-reform era deserved its merits that the underdeveloped hinterland region had better growth of social development which is shown in table IV-2. But when development is up to a certain stage, the egalitarian regional development strategy should be modified, and a growth strategy based upon the comparative advantage and linkage to world trade should be emphasized. Although balanced de-

Table IV-2 Comparison of Growth Rate of Selected Social Indicators of Selected Provinces

Selected Social Indicators	Unit	Growth Rate (1952-1978)		Ratio (2)/(1)
		Guangdong Pro. (1)	Gansu Pro. (2)	
I. Health Care				
1. Number of Health Care Institutions	Unit	6.1	9.4	1.54
2. Number of Hospital Beds	bed	7.6	12.7	1.67
3. Number of Doctors/1,000 Person	person	2.0	7.5	3.75
II. Education (Number of Students in School)				
1. Number of Students in Higher Education	10⁴ Students	4.4	6.7	1.52
2. Number of Students in Middle School	10⁴ Students	11.9	14.3	1.20
3. Number of Students in Primary School	10⁴ Students	3.5	6.6	1.89

velopment should be adocated, but it is impossible to have a balanced regional development at all times. History shows that certain region may have higher growth than other regions. But it is necessary for the planners to have an awareness to keep equity of growth in mind.

Table IV-3 presents the annual rate of wages of state owned enterprises. The average wage growth rate from 1952-1978 is only 1.4%, but the arithmetic average of rate of inflation within this period is only 0.77%, the highest one is 16.2% (1961), the lowest one is -5.9% 1996). The wage difference among sectors is also low, in 1952 the ratio of highest average wage rate to lowest average wage rate is 1.76:1 (urban public utility: commerce) in 1978, it is 1.52:1 (construction to agriculture irrigation).

Table IV-3 Average Wage Rate of State Owned Enterprises (Yuan)

Sector / Year	Average wage/ year	Industry	Construction	Agriculture Irrigation	Transport postal	Commerce	Urban Public Utility	Science Education & Health	Finances Insurance	Institution
1952	446	515	564	375	583	360	634	368	458	376
1957	637	690	744	501	752	529	651	580	613	631
1962	592	652	705	392	702	494	631	542	559	626
1965	652	729	730	433	774	579	687	598	624	684
1970	609	661	650	419	709	553	660	555	588	678
1975	613	644	704	460	699	562	639	574	609	645
1978	644	683	748	492	733	587	652	582	643	662

Source: *Statistical Yearbook,1981,*China Statistical Publishing House, 1990.

(2) This low wage policy in the urban workers was an inherent part of the former Soviet model of industrialization which was mainly financed by peasants, i.e., in the drive to raise the rate of industrialization, while keeping prices stable by ensuring the supply of an adequate quantity of agricultural goods at fixed prices to the non-agricultural sector, plans have tended to discriminate against the rural producers. This has resulted a low personal saving of the population of China before the launch of economic reform. In 1978, the per-capita personal saving of Chinese in the banks is only 21.9 yuan, the per-capita saving of the urban people is 90.1 yuan, while the rural people is only 7.1 yuan. This explains how China can achieve a high growth rate of industrialization in the pre-reform period. The former Soviet model of industrialization has been called into question by recent research (Ellen

1975, Vas 1979), and China has taken an early move of its reform in the rural areas.

(3) Following of the Basic Rules for Development

The development was proceeded from the principle that the general lack of resources was not to be overcome by an inflationary policy. It had been described above that the average rate of inflation in the pre-reform period is only 0.77%. This principle is followed in current, when there is high inflationary pressure due to overheating of the economy in the year 1988 (rate of inflation 18.5%) and 1994 (21.7%), the government will respond with all means to curb down the rate of inflation, while a part of other developing countries generally regard inflationary tendencies as normal sideeffect of growth.

(4) The Priority of Agricultural Development

China placed increasing emphasis on the agricultural sector from learning of negative lessons in former Soviet experience of development planning. The former Chairman Mao had given priority of sectoral development in the order of agriculture, light industry and heavy industry early in 1956 (*On Ten Great Relationships*). China had taken basic measures in guaranteeing and increasing the yield per hectare through the expansion of irrigated land and its protection against floods. Millions of people were employed following the principle of mobilization of the population as development vehicle, to carry out hydraulic projects, although insufficient planning often led to severe damage of the environment, e.g., salinization of the soil, deforestation, and lowering of the water table. China had also improved its agricultural production through the introduction of high-yield seed, multiple harvest and mechanized equipment. The expansion of fertilizer production was given highest priority; in 1957 China ranked the 33rd in the production of fertilizer among the world, while in 1978 the rank is raised to the 3rd among the world. The commune system of socialized agriculture had developed rural infrastructure and rural management system, which not only served political and social needs, but foster economic support systems, such as input supply and marketing. It had also served to foster social aims, such as preventive medicine and universal education, it had also diversified the rural sector from being a peasant agriculture to a basis of rural industrialization. In short, the development of the agricultural sector has provided a reasonable physical, marketing and human infrastructure, but without incentives. All these factors provide a basis of the intuition of successful agricultural sector reform in the later period.

(5) The Development of Rural Small-scale Industry and the Employment of Technology Conforming to Development

The contribution of town and village enterprise in economic development in the period of reform is well known internationally, the so-called TVEs has a share of around more than 30% of gross value of industrial output and employ more than 100 million of labor force. But this success had been derived from foundations laid through the development policy before the 80's. Five small industrial sectors were advocated in the regime of the commune system, i.e., small coal mine, small machinery plant, small fertilizer plant, small cement plant and small hydro-powers. These small plants may be not economic or inefficient due to their small scale. But this development policy and activity have trained the local cadres, technicians and workers. This creation of human resources have prepared the foundation of growth of TVEs in the reform period. This unique development policy of involvement of broad rural industrialization is conformed to the basic principle of mobilization of the "masses" to be development vehicle. On the aspect of technology, China had advocated the concept of "walk on two legs", i.e., both modern advanced technology and traditional technology should be used to adapt to local conditions. It is commented in Reference 11 that "Coupled with the support of small-scale industries, and especially since 1958, China has made simultaneous use of native, traditional as well as modern production processes. Traditional, labor intensive methods were employed in every area where they could make an effective contribution to development; at the same time, the development of innovations "from the inside" was encouraged, and adjusted to local conditions."

(6) Centralization and Decentralization of Development Planning — An Issue Requires Further Exploration

China's industrialization and development process have been effected greatly by the swing between centralized and decentralized development planning and the allocation of fiscal resources. Early in April 1955, the former Chairman Mao considered to decentralize the existing planning structure as well as a part of fiscal power down to regional level. He stated that when considering "contradictions between the central government and the regions," it was also necessary "to consider... How to arouse the enthusiasm of the regions by central authorities." Under this framework of decentralization, a fair portion of the power of various ministries of the central government were reassigned to provinces and autonomous regions. Decentralization was temporarily abandoned following the failure of the Great Leap Forward. During the period of "cultural revolution" (1966-1975), the provinces and regions once again gained increasing influence in terms of planning local production, financing and distribution of investment. Table II-4 can illustrate the impact of centralization and decentralization of fiscal power. China had further decentralized its investment planning and fiscal power during the current period of economic reform. Decentralization has the advantage that the local government is more knowledgeable on the local conditions, especially for a country with a size as China, but it has also been pointed out correctly by observation from abroad that "Reversing the resulting decline in revenues will be crucial as China proceeds with reform, and as government takes on its full set of social obligations from enterprises." Reform of the extra-budget and collection of fees to normal budgetary process is one of the major aspects of reform in current government agenda. This is an issue requires further exploration.

2. Major Issues of Development Planning in the Pre-reform Era

The major issues faced by China on development planning is well summed up by former Chairman Mao in his famous speech on the "ten great relationships". His speech is also quoted in item "development planning" in dictionary of economics published abroad. In his discussion of ten relationships, four of them are political questions with a mainly Chinese orientation. The six other relations are recognized by Western economists that involve mainly questions of economic strategy and have appeared in many different contexts. Six of them will be described: maintenance of balance was crucial in the relationships between: (1) agriculture, light industry and heavy industry; (2) industry in the coastal regions and in the interior; (3) civil investment and defense construction; (4) the state, the units of production and the actual producers; (5) the central and local authorities; and (6) China and the foreign countries.

4.03 Experience and Lessons of Development Planning from 1979-Current

It had been described in a previous part that the reform of the planning system is one major item on the reform agenda. The evolution of the four Five-Year Plans in this period have been described in part III. Hereunder, several major features will be pointed out.

1. There is transformation from an egalitarian growth strategy to a strategy based upon the comparative advantage and competitive advantage.

Since the launch of economic reform and opening to the outside world, different regions can realize fully their comparative advantages of various aspects. Some regions enjoy a very rapid economic growth rate. From 1979-1990, the average national growth rate is around 9.1%, while seven provinces, including Zhejiang, Guangdong, Fujian, Jiangsu and Shandong, have a growth rate higher than national average. The regional income disparity can be expressed in different indicator. Fig 4.1 shows the change of ratio of per-capita GDP of richest province and poorest province. It shows that there is increase of regional disparity since 1991. Although there is increase of regional disparity of growth between the regions, but as a whole, the wealth of the people is improved. This fact can be shown from the large increase of per-capita savings in the urban and rural areas as shown in table IV-4. It shows that in 1978, the per-capita income of Chinese is only 21.9 yuan in 1978, it becomes 3,147.6 yuan in 1996. The growth rate of per-capita savings in the urban area in this period is 28.8%, while in the rural area, it is 30.

Table IV-4

Item	Year	1978	1996
I	Total National Population 10⁴	96,259	122,389
	Total Savings 100 mil. yuan	210.6	38,520.8
	Per-capita Saving yuan	21.9	3,147.6
II	Urban and Township Population 10⁴	17,245	35,950
	Savings 100 mil yuan	154.9	308,502
	Per-capita Savings yuan	90.1	8,581.4
III	Rural Population 10⁴	79,014	86,439
	Savings 100 mil. yuan	55.7	7,670.7
	Per-capita Savings yuan	7.05	887.8

8%. The growth rate of savings in the rural area is higher than that of urban. It shows the correct transformation strategy from egalitarian growth strategy to that "to let a part of the people to become rich first on the basis of honest hard work."

2. Basic Development Strategy of Modernization Is Outlined by Deng Xiaoping. The Strategic Objective and Steps Are Divided into Three Stages:

(1) Stage 1: Doubling GNP from 1981-1990 to solve the basic needs (enough food and cloth) of the people;

(2) Stage 2: Doubling GNP further from 1991-2000 to let the people to live a relatively better livelihood (in Chinese term "*Xiaokang*");

(3) Stage 3: The per-capita GNP will reach the level of middle developed countries, around 2030-2050, the people's livelihood will be relatively well-off, to realize basically modernization of China.

This basic development strategy is very pragmatic with full consideration of the huge amount of population and an in-depth understanding of various regions of China. But it is achievable. The achieved target of first stage in advance has convinced the people and the global society.

3. The development planning in this period is gradually shifted from traditional planning concept established before the 80's to the following features: Integration of economic system reform and development; the plan is prepared with an open economic system — concept based upon an analysis of the long-term global trend and domestic conditions; macro-economic stability is emphasized; two basic strategies are emphasized: the strategy of revival of the nation through science and education, and sustainable development strategy; promotion of coordinated regional development, and poverty alleviation is emphasized; promotion of opening to the outside world; and industrial policy is advocated.

4. Issues in Chinese Development Process

Issues and key aspects of development process are described in President Jiang's report to the 15th National Congress of the CPC. The process in this period includes these issues: to transform from a country with high share of population in agriculture with a natural and semi-natural economy to a country dominated with high degree of economic marketazation; transform China into a country with relatively developed science, technology, education and culture from a status with high share of illiterate and semi-illiterate population; transform China to a relatively rich wealth of all people from a status with a high share of poor population; gradually reduce the regional disparity from a status of very unbalanced regional economy and culture to a relatively matured socialist market system; build a socialist democratic system through reform and exploration; and to create a human resources with high spiritual culture.

V. Concluding Remarks

Development is a process. Development planning in China is still at a stage of learning by doing. Development planners of China are searching for an appropriate type of planning to meet the requirements of establishing a socialist market economy to adapt to the basic features of China.

REFERENCES

1. *The New Palgrave — A Dictionary of Economics,* edited by John Eeatrvell, Murrary Mileage and Peter Newsman, the Macmillan Press Limited, 1987.

2. *World Development Report 1983,* the World Bank.

3. *French Planning,* comment by Jean Mount. EDI Training Material 405/714, Aug. 1984, the World Bank.

4. *The Developing Economies and Japan,* by Saburo Okita, University of Tokyo Press, fifth printing, 1986.

5. *Development Planning — The Essentials of Economic Policy,* by W. Arthur Lewis, Harper & Row Publishers, New York, 1966.

6. *Selected Works of Zhou Enlai,* People's PUblishing House, 1980 (in Chinese).

7. *Retrospect of Several Important Decisions and Events by Po I-Po* (2 Volumes), CPC Central Committee Party School Publishing House, 1993 (in Chinese).

8. *Modern China Economic Dictionary,* chief editor: Ma Hong, China

Social Science Publishing House, 1982 (in Chinese).

9. *China: Socialist Economic Development, The Main Report,* March 10, 1982, the World Bank.

10. "Decision of the CPC Central Committee on Issues Concerning the Establishment of a Socialist Market Economic Structure" (Nov. 14 1993), "China Economic News" sponsored by Economic Daily, Beijing, EIA Holdings LTD., HongKong.

11. *Economic Development and Social Change in the People's Republic of China,* by Willy Kraus Springer-Verlag, 1982 (English language edition is an up-to-date revision and translation of the German edition by W. Kraus).

12. *The Postwar Evolution of Development Thinking,* by Charles P. Omen and Ganeeshan Wignaraja, Macmillan in Association with the OECD Development Center, 1991.

Appendix 1[10]

Great Leap Forward

The name given to the development policy launched in China at the end of 1957, which was intended to speed the development process by a 20 to 30 percent of industrial growth rate. The basis was a simultaneous development in all types of industry and agriculture, although the emphasis was on heavy industry where the scarce available capital was used and elsewhere there was large-scale substitution of labor for capital, and highly labour intensive techniques were implemented in small industries and agriculture. The success of this venture has been very difficult to assess because of other events which were coursing simultaneously. People's communes were established in 1958 and although they helped to get rural labor involved, they removed much of the incentive to work by taking away private land-owing and disrupting family life. Technical experts who were not given the respect due to them as Party officials took control. Between 1959 and 1961, various natural disasters occurred and Soviet experts left

---

10. From MIT Economic Dictionary.

in 1960. Many of these other occurrences, although not related to the implementation of labor-intensive techniques, blur and accurate assessment; and it is not possible to assume that the economic slump which followed was a result of the policy. However, one clear lesson was learnt, in that extensive use of labor-intensive techniques requires trained experts to guide it and not Party officials.

Appendix 2

Abstract of An Overall Introduction to the Study "China Towards the Year 2000"

1. Introduction

After ten years of turbulence during the "cultural revolution", the Eleventh Central Committee of the Communist Party of China (CPC) at its Third Plenary Session had brought order out of chaos. The Party and the nation had successfully shifted the focus of national strategies to four modernization's. A series of guidelines of economic and social development had been formulated by the Party and the government and achieved tremendous success that has raised the attention of the whole world. On this basis, it is necessary for China to study its prospects to the end of the century and after. Since the Autumn of 1982, the former Technical Economic Research Center of the State Council (now the Development Research Center of the State Council, Research Center for Economic Technological and Social Development of the State Council) had carried out a systematic research project with the contents and organization of this theme. This subject was accepted in 1982 as a key research project of the philosophy and social sciences during the Sixth Five-Year Plan period.

The research project was carried out with the objective of presenting a relatively clear, concrete and vivid scenario of the development of China's socialist economy, culture, science and technology, people's living and spiritual civilization through an overall and comprehensive study, through synthesis and analysis of the subjective and objective conditions, domestic and international environmental studies under the guidelines set up by the Twelfth

National Congress of the Communist Party of China. The research goal was to find out a relatively satisfactory development pattern through comparative study of different feasible ways in achieving the strategic objective of socialist construction and also to study the basis and decision for the realization of these objectives as well as the necessary policy system for its realization. An analytical study and evaluation of this policy system had been carried out. In short, the project of the research "China Towards the Year 2000" is to realize better the strategic goal set up by the Twelfth National Congress of the Communist Party of China; to supply a systematic reference with scientific basis for the decision making and policy making of the Party and the State Council; to provide an overall scenario for the development planning of sectors and regions. It is hoped that through this concrete scenario our people will be further encouraged to concert their efforts towards realizing the ambitious guidelines of the Party. In other words, the study "China Towards the Year 2000" is to find a way to achieve the socialist modernization process of the Chinese way. This project was highly recommended by former Premier Zhao. His message to the annual plan submitted by the Research Center in 1983; "China Toward the Year 2000" was that if this study was well researched it would be of a great significance. He said that it was necessary that efforts should be made to do a good job of it.

Headed by Ma Hong, a number of leaders from the State Planning Commission, State Economic Commission, State Science and Technology Commission, the Chinese Academy of Social Sciences and the former Technical Economic Research Center in the State Council formed a major leader group. They established a research team, including personnel from the Research Center, and the China Scientific and Technical Information Institute responsible for the organization and research work. The research received cooperation from scholars and administrative officials from various scientific research institutes, economic management departments, planning institutes and institutions of higher learning. This research project was divided into three hierarchical levels. More than 400 research fellows were involved into the first- and second-level studies. One hundred and eight S&T associations were involved in the third-level studies. Through more than two years of hard work, including collection of data, field survey, qualitative and quantitative analysis, synthesis and analysis, initial research results of the first-level studies were completed in May 1985.

The main results include one main report, twelve sub-reports and a collection of projection data. The tittles of these are: "Main Report — China Towards the Year 2000", "Population and Employment of China Towards the Year 2000", "Economy of China Towards the Year 2000", "Consumption of the People of China Towards the Year 2000", "Natural Resources of China Towards the Year 2000", "Energy of China Towards the Year 2000", "Agriculture of China Towards the Year 2000", "Science and Technology of China Towards the Year 2000", "Environment of China Towards the Year 2000", "Agriculture of China Towards the Year 2000", "Transportation System of China Towards the Year 2000", "International Environment of China Towards the Year 2000", "Macro-Economic Model Projections of China Towards the Year 2000". Besides the above mentioned main report and subreports that were the direct responsibility of each group leader, the second level reports of special topics were done by various ministries i.e., social life, culture, athletic and sports, broadcasting and television, communication, foreign trade, construction materials, oceanic development strategy, natural resources, railway transportation, highway transportation, ocean transportation, domestic waterway transportation, urban passenger transportation, civil aviation, pipeline transportation and health care system.

2. Figs Showing Research Methodology

Figure 1: Research Method for Complex Problems

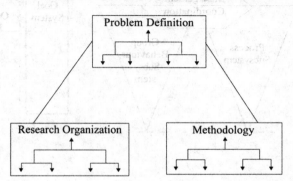

Figure 3: The Interrelated Elements in the Research Objective

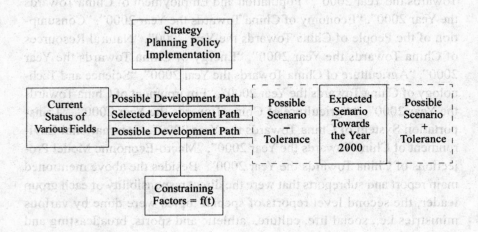

Figure 4: An Integrated System View Organization

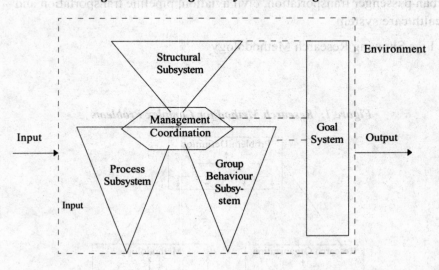

Figure 2. Organization of the Research Report "China Towards The Year 2000"

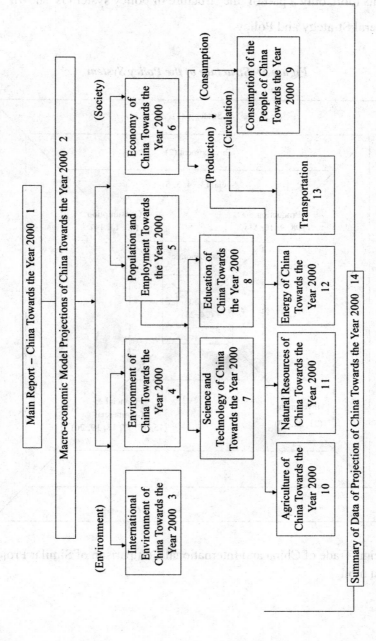

Note: Terms within blocks are titles of the report. Terms inside brackets show the category only.

3. Scenario of China Towards the Year 2000

Contents moil, only a part of the structure of policy system is shown

4. General Strategy and Policy

Figure 5: Structure of the Policy System

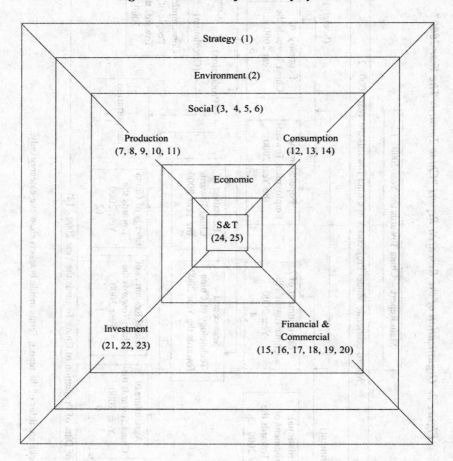

Strategy (1)

Environment (2)

Social (3, 4, 5, 6)

Production (7, 8, 9, 10, 11)

Consumption (12, 13, 14)

Economic

S&T (24, 25)

Investment (21, 22, 23)

Financial & Commercial (15, 16, 17, 18, 19, 20)

5. Foreign Trade of China and International Comparison of Similar Projects

Content moil

3. Redefining Regional Development Strategy — The Chinese Experience — Toward a Framework of Study of Regional Development Strategy of China

Most features of regional development analysis are related to the persisting and even increasing regional differentials in the course of national development. There are a lot of established theories, the early empirical work by Willamson, the structuralism economic hypothesis, the growth pole theory, the Faini's hypothesis on increasing returns to scales, the use of regional input-output table and shift share analysis. Due to the complexity of development process, grand theorizing about regional development has diminished in favor of studies of particular features of the process.

China is now in the process of transition from a former central planned economy to a socialist market economy. China is now at the primary stage of socialism. It is pointed out by President Jiang Zemin that "It is a stage in which a society with very uneven economic and cultural development among regions will become one in which the gap will be gradually narrowed, with some regions becoming developed first." There are many features unique to China which will effect the stage of regional development of different parts of China.

China is a member country of the UN, a member of the global society. There are many important decisions and events happened in the world in the last decade of the 20th Century, the Rio Declaration on Environment and Development by the Earth Summit in Rio de Janeiro in 1992, the World Summit for Social Development in Copenhagen, Denmark in 1995. The recent financial turmoil in Asia that erupted in mid-1997 is already apparent that the crisis and its likely effects are more severe than they initially appeared.

Both the external and internal conditions are so complex to have their impacts on redefining the regional development strategy of China. Therefore, the intention of this paper will focus on the particular features of regional development process of China. A brief retrospect of regional development of China will be given (historical retrospect), the new regional development strategy will be defined within the context of globalization and multipolarization (an opening system approach) with issues (issue-oriented) unique to different regions of China taken into consideration.

This paper will be divided into three parts and an appendix. The appendix is also an integral part of this paper, it is an abstract of an international study on global future scenario based on several theoretical assumptions. A part of the views expressed in the appendix is abstracted in part I of this main text.

Part I Perspective of the Global Development

1.01 Introduction

It had been proved by history, especially the contemporary history that no country can be developed successfully and efficiently in isolation. This human history proves one of the key concepts of general system theory that "Biological and social systems are inherently open systems". A country being an open system must exchange information, energy and material with their environments, natural or international. The regional development strategy should be studied within national and global context. Therefore, an overview of selective perspectives of trend of global development related to national and regional development strategy will be briefed in the beginning.

1.02 Globalization and Structural Change

1. Structural change has been a pervasive trend in all economies. It is evident that the information revolution will continue to boost productivity across the economy. There will be further change of the information-dependent tertiary sector, such as finance, mass media, and wholesale and retail trade. There may be a surge of major technology breakthroughs, including bio-

technology and micro-electronic mechanical system, which will begin to create entire new industries in coming decades.

2. There is also pervasive trend of organizational structural change, for example contract manufacturers manage much of the supply chain, companies can slash inventory and distribution costs and get access to market quickly. Business that were once organized along geographical lines are now reorienting themselves according to markets, or products, or processes — or all of the above in complex matrices.

3. There has been an acceleration of globalization over the last decade with emerging economies and non-OECD economies being a driving force through increasing integration of global economic activities. But such economic integration does involve adjustment costs, especially for countries with large amount of low-skilled workers and industries with low competitiveness

4.A "New Global Age" would provide a strong boost to standards of living the world over, it would also improve capacities to deal with issues on environment, urbanization and social aspects.

1.03   Four Scenarios of the World Economy Around 2015-2020

It is difficult to do exact projection of the future economic development of the global socially. Four scenarios of the world economy until 2015 had been done by a research project of OECD (with reference to Appendix 1). These four scenarios will provide a general reference of the world economy and its impact on national and regional development.

1. Global Shift   In this scenario, there is a real shift in economic activities from the Atlantic to the Pacific Basin. The dynamics of technological change, vigorous entrepreneurship, incentives and market competition are essential driving forces behind this scenario. Entire new industries will spring up and in some cases, old ones will be revived. This process is enhanced further in regions where trade liberalization occurs. America's business sector will be subjected to recovery of productivity growth and competitiveness. Japan will once again tackles various internal and external challenges with great flexibility. The Japanese economy may be forced to become gradually more open due to a labor shortage. The rise of the dynamic Asian Economies also continues. China, India and Latin America where approximately 50 percent of the world population will live around 2015, they will increasingly participate in the highly dynamic economic development enjoyed by the entire Asia-Pacific. There is relative decline in Western Europe in this scenario due to it appears ill-prepared in light of the innovative and competitive capabilities emanating from the Asia-pacific region. And European bias towards security, stability, and risk-averse behavior prevails once again. This has also significant negative repercussions for economic development in Africa and Central Europe. The effect of recent Asian currency crisis will not effect the long-term growth potential of effected countries. Asia will be kept to be a dynamic region.

2. European Renaissance   In this scenario, the Western Europe develops very favorably. The EMU is launched. The European process of integration is an important stimulus toward the strengthening of incentive structure on the Western European product and labor markets. And there is also a far-reaching process of reform of the Western European Welfare State. There will be a combination of the European tradition of social equity, apparent from the socio-economic aims of low unemployment and fair income distribution, with an increased sensitivity to economic incentive. Prosperous economic development leads to a relatively open economic bloc. By 2015 the European Community encompasses all of Europe, but may be with the exception of the Soviet Union. The process of transformation of the Soviet Union will proceed successfully that the economy begins to show significant growth around 2000. The growth of the US economy is not optimistic in this scenario. Fortress America is in the making. Protectionism stretches out farther. The economic development of the strong Asian economies, Japan and the dynamic Asian region is blurred by the problems of the US; the DAEs in particular are handicapped in their growth aspirations due to technological protectionism.

3. Global Crisis   Many assumptions are made in this scenario. The stagnation of growth of the USA and Europe, the rise of the Far East ensures a continuous deepening of tensions on trade between East and West. The global crisis scenario assumes a serious worldwide crisis in the field of world food supply due to simultaneous natural disasters happened in several large countries. The agricultural crisis will be interpreted by many as decisive evidence of lasting deterioration of agricultural land, and for this reason be considered an echo-shock. Others associate it with the greenhouse effect. A deep economic recession is set in motion by the shock of global crisis. It is necessary to have a scenario on "crisis", history taught us that the growth of the global society is not a smooth process. The recent Asian currency crisis is one, the flooding disaster in China and in part of the Asian region is another, although these crises have not created a global repercussion to such an extent to become a global crisis.

4. Balanced Growth   The revived and ever stronger striving toward sustainable economic development combined with continuos strong technological dynamics, constitutes the dominating forces of the balanced growth scenario. In this scenario, the weak points of the major industrial countries will be corrected from this new paradigm. The US reduces the government deficit and improves education and infrastructure. That is exactly the current effort of US government and achieved in several aspects. The Western Europe strengthens incentive structure and Japan opens up to the world economy. Reform process continue in the Soviet Union, China and India. Growth in this scenario is due to specialization, dynamic economies of scale and also because more competitive market structure-stimulated innovation led to a rapid diffusion of the rich technological potential. In this scenario, it is assumed that it helps to crack the strong internal, growth-impeding factors in Africa, Latin America and other regions. The virtuous cycle lends powerful support to the "market economies in the making" in the Central Europe and the former Society Union. Economic development spreads across the globe and assumes what may be called a strong multipolar character. This is also the Chinese view of the trend of change of the world "Globalization and Multipolarization". In this scenario, there is the realization of an international treaty toward reducing greenhouse gas emission, i.e., the Climate Convention 1994 will be implemented globally and seriously.

These above four scenarios provide a description of possible global environment which is the external condition of the national and regional development. Many concepts included in the above four scenarios are useful reference in the consideration of the basis of regional development policy. There are many conflicting factors to be considered, social equity, technological change, market competition, cultural tradition etc. The derivation of these four scenarios was based on a theoretical framework, which is attached in Appendix 1.

Part II Regional Development of China — A Retrospect

2.01 Introduction

The study of regional development strategy is a complex subject due to influence of many factors. There is no formula for success of a specific regional development strategy. It depends strongly on time and space. A retrospect of the historical experience and identification of the issues may be a useful method of approach in explaining "Redefining Regional Development Strategy" in Part III. There are many abundant literature on regional development of China both at home and abroad. A recommendation of selective readings is listed in the references. The retrospect given here must be very brief. It is divided into two periods, China's regional development strategy in pre-reform period and regional development after 1979 and up to 1995.

2.02 Regional Development of China in the Pre-reform Era (1950-1979)

In the pre-reform period, China had not studied the regional development on a very scientific basis. The classification of region is geograplrically and administratively in sense, the classification of these regions is more or less an inheritage of six military organizational regime during the later period of civil war. The six administrative regions are: the Northeastern, the Northern, the Eastern, the Central-Southern, the Northwestern, and the Southwestern.

The regional development in the national development plan was centered around three concepts: First, an egalitarian concept of regional development over national economic policy was promoted. The inland region had higher growth rate of social and economic indicators, Table 2.1 and 2.2 will illustrate this clearly; second, various efforts were made to change the spatial pattern between coastal and inland regions; third, regional development strategy was highly influenced by defense consideration, for example, the so-called "third line region" had absorbed around two fifths of all state investments during the "cultural revolution" period; the investment return is of minor consideration, and self-sufficient regional development strategy was pursued. Every province should be self-sufficient, complete industrial basis was established, including small coal mine, small iron and steel plant, small non-ferrous mine, small fertilizer plant, small cement plant and machinery plant. These are to support the agricultural development. It seems to be not cost-effective, without taking economy of scale into account. But it creates the root of development of TVEs which contributed to the high economic growth in the period of reform.

For Table 2.1, please refer to Table IV-2 of "Paper 2" of Part I.

2.03 Region Development of China after 1979

China has taken the regional development to be part of national economic development planning since the launch of economic reform and opening to the outside world. There is also evolution of the concept of regional development in this period. The experience of regional development in China will be briefed in the following.

1. Evolution of Classification of Regions

Table 2.2 Comparison of Economic Growth Rate of Selected Provinces
Unit: 100 million RMB

Province	Guangdong		Gansu	
Item	1952	1978	1952	1978
Total Output of Society	42.92	350.31	16.78	125.21
Agriculture	19.35	100.46	8.93	22.45
Industry	16.9	243.03	4.57	90.95
Tertiary	6.67	49.94	3.29	12.23
Output Index 1952=100	100	541.1	100	612.66
Growth Rate Output 1952-1978	6.7%		7.2%	

Proper classification of regions is useful in designing appropriate policies for regional development. In the regional economic development plan of the Sixth Five-Year Plan period (1981-1985), this classification of regions was very traditional. They were simply classified into coastal, inland and minority regions. Regional cooperation was advocated to promote the regional development within national context. In the Seventh Five-Year Plan period (1986-1990), the official document classified the regions into Eastern, Central and Western. Special economic zones, coastal open cities and open regions are also included in the Seventh Five-Year Plan. But they are not classified in the section of regional development of this official document. They were put in the part of "Foreign Trade and Foreign Economic Relations". In the Ninth Five-Year Plan, China kept the three regional classification formed in the Seventh Five-Year Plan. But a new concept of "seven economic regions" was further formed. This new concept of regional classification was a breakthrough of traditional classification of regions based upon administration and it focused more on economic relationship both domestic and abroad. It will be described in Part III of this paper.

2. Evolution of Regional Development Strategy

There is evolution of regional development strategy in this period. In the Seventh Five-Year Plan period, networking of economic regions and hierarchy of different ranks of economic regions were also devised. The economic regions of the first rank include five: the Shanghai economic region; Northeastern region; the energy-based region; southeastern region with four provinces, and the Beijing, Tianjin and Tangshan region. The economic regions of the second rank consisted of the capital city of every province and the port cities. The hierarchy of the networking of third-rank economic regions refers to the regions centered around provincially administrated cities. This integrated growth pole and network concept of regional development was incorporated in the Seventh Five-Year plan. And the approach of gradually open policy in the promotion of foreign trade and investment was another aspect of the regional development strategy in the Seventh Five-Year Plan. Special economic zones, coastal open cities and opening regions were planned and implemented. The Pudong zone of Shanghai was opened in 1990. And there was further opening of the capital of every province, major cities along the Yangtze River and coastal cities in the Eighth Five-Year Planning period.

2.04 Major Experiences and Lessons in Regional Development Strategy of China Before 1995

1. In the pre-reform era, there was no systematic study on classification of regions and regional development strategy. Egalitarian growth strategy is pursued. Social equity is emphasized rather than economic efficiency. Regional disparity derived from old China before 1949 was reduced, but the growth potential of certain regions was not fully tapped. This is shown from

the rapid growth of Jiangsu, Zhejiang, and Guangdong since the launch of economic reform. But their average annual economic growth rate from 1952 to 1978 was even lower than the national average (See Table 2.3 below).

Table 2.3 Comparison of Growth Rate of GNP (1952-1978)

	National Average	Jiangsu Province	Zhejiang Province	Guangdong Province
Growth Rate of GNP %	6.1	5.2	5.8	5.2

Source: *Compilation of Historical Statistical Materials (1949-1989),* State Statistics Bureau,1990.

2. Successful Experience of SEZs — Strengthening of Linkage of Trade and Investment to Outside World

The four special economic zones (Shengzhen, Zhuhai, Shantou and Xianmen) had an average annual growth rate of GDP around 32.8%, and an average annual growth rate of external trade around 25.5% from 1980 to 1994. The share of total pledged FDI of Guangdong Province from 1979-1991 was 43.4% of national total. Fujian Province ranked the second with a share of 9.2% of national total. This is one type of regional development strategy with external orientation.

3. Successful Experience of Jiangsu and Zhejiang Provinces — Domestic oriented Strategy and Growth of TVEs

Jiangsu and Zhejiang were the most developed regions of China before 1949. They were the major regions for modern industries at that time, such as spinning, machinery and commerce, due to relatively high levels of education and better skilled human resources in commerce. In the First Five-Year Plan period, none of the key industrial projects was allocated to them. They grew at 5.6% and 5.7% respectively from 1952 to 1978, which is lower than the national average growth rate of 6%. Their economic potential was fully tapped through domestic investment and trade since the launch of economic reform. The gross value of output of TVEs in Jiangsu and Zhejiang provinces was 14.3% and 8.6% of the share of national total respectively, ranking the first and the third of China in 1991. Their share of FDI was 3.4% and 1.5% of national total respectively in the 1979-1991 period. In 1995, the value of external trade of Guangdong Province was 7.6 and 10.3 times of Jiangsu and Zhejiang, but the GDP of these two provinces was 89.2% and 62% of that of

Guangdong, i.e., these two provinces had a domestic-oriented development strategy in general. This shows regional development can also be promoted through promotion of domestic trade and investment on the basis of sound human resources under the market mechanism. Table 2. 4 shows the structure of domestic trade of Zhejiang Province. It has better terms of trade with other regions.

Table 2.4 Net Rate of Import and Export of Major Sectors

Sector	Rate of import %	Sector	Rate of Export
Agriculture	5.5	Machinery manufacturing	20.7
Steel and non-ferrous industry	61.7	Electronic industry	13.2
Coal or coking industry	87.8	Chemical pharmaceutical Industry	33.5
Petroleum Processing	40.3	Rubber and Plastic manufacturing	48.7
Electric Power Industry	19.6	Textile Industry	27.2
Chemical fiber industry	58.3	Agrofood Industry	21.7
		Paper making and cultural products	30.9

2.05 Emerging Issues of Regional Development Strategy of China since the Launch of Economic Reform

Although China has been successful in its market-oriented reform, there are two emerging issues which should be carefully attended in considering and redefining the regional development strategy.

1. The gap in per-capita GDP has expanded as shown in Fig 2.1 and 2.2. Fig 2.1 shows the trend of change in the gap of per-capita GDP between the richest and poorest region, which increased from 2,500 yuan in 1980 to 7,400 yuan in 1995, calculated on the constant price of 1980. Fig 2.2 shows the ratio of per-capita GDP between the richest and poorest region. Viewing the development process as a whole, the gap kept nearly the same in 1980 and 1995. But it has been on the rise since 1990. This growth of regional disparity is a sort of market failure and should be

corrected with public policy. Yet, there is also issue of insufficient capacity of public finance due to decentralization of fiscal power in the process of reform.

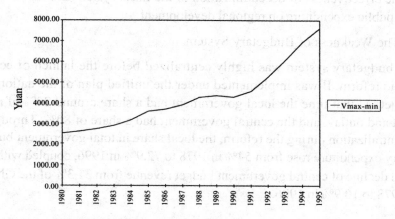

Fig 2.1 Variation of Per Capita GDP of Richest and Poorest Province

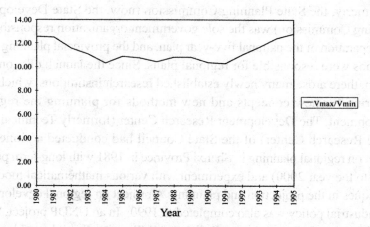

Fig 2.2 Ratio of Per- Capita GDP of Richest and Poorest Province

2. Change of Fiscal Relationship between the Central and Local Governments in the Process of Decentralization

(1) Decentralization has been one major aspect of China's reform, which

includes fiscal decentralization. But, whether local government are more or less likely than the central government to respond to local preferences depends also on the strength of various incentives and on how political decisions are made. The political process and system surely produce influence on the effectiveness of decentralization of the fiscal system and the necessary public expenditure on regional development.

(2) The Weakness of Budgetary System

The budgetary system was highly centralized before the launch of economic reform. It was implemented under the unified plan of the national budget. At that time the local government had a share around 20% of receipt and outlay, and the central government had a share of 80%. Through decentralization during the reform, the local share in total government budgetary expenditure rose from 54% in 1978 to 72.9% in 1996, coupled with a rapid decline of central government budget revenue from 31.3% of the GNP in 1978 to 10.9% in 1996.

2.06 Evolution of Research Institution and Research Methodology on Regional Development Strategy

1. Formerly, the State Planning Commission (now, the State Development Planning Commission) was the sole government organization responsible for the preparation of the national five-year plan, and the provincial planning commissions were responsible for regional plans. Since the launch of economic reform, there arose many newly established research institutions, which kept exploring for new concepts and new methods for planning the regional development. The Development Research Center (formerly Technical Economic Research Center) of the State Council had conducted a pioneering project on regional planning in Shanxi Province in 1981 with long-term projections (to the year 2000) and experiment with various mathematical modeling techniques in the projection and planning. A project on regional development and industrial policy was also completed in 1990. In an UNDP project, "Integrated Economic Development Policies and Planning," conducted by DRC from 1989-1993, one volume was on regional development, in which the classification of regions was studied. There is another joint research, involving Professor Ichimura and using regional I/O technique. The Development Research Center had recently also completed a project, "China's Coordinated Regional Development Strategy Towards 21st Century".

2. The Geographic Research Institute under the Chinese Academy of Sciences also engaged in regional development study. Recently, it published a report titled "1997 China: Regional Development Report". In addition, the Territorial Planning Institute, the Macro-Economic Research Academy, the State Economic Information Center under the State Development Commission also have studied regional development strategy in qualitative and quantitative aspects. The Academy of Social Sciences, including its central and local branches, also engaged in regional development studies. The governments at different levels have consulted the research achievements of the above-mentioned institutions in drafting the national and provincial development plans to be submitted to the people's congresses at different levels for approval. With regard to the central government, it is the CPC Central Committee Politburo that sets the major guidelines and targets for planning to be approved by the Party's National Congress. The government drafts the plan on the basis of the guidelines. The planning process and approval procedure have been normalized in recent years.

Part III Redefining Regional Development Strategy Towards 21st Century

3.01 Introduction

Sum up the development experience of China in the past half century, with the current and future domestic development to be the basis, and in adaptation to the trend of globalization and pervasive structural change of a national economy, there is need to redefining the regional development strategy towards the 21st century. It is difficult to define a development strategy with a very long term. The Chinese government has prepared the Ninth Five-Year Plan and Outline of Long-Term Target of 2010, there are also some research studies on China by the Year 2020 from domestic and international organizations. Therefore, the time span of regional development strategy towards the 21st century will be focused in the period up to around 2020. In this part, a conceptual framework of basis of redefining regional development strategy will be described first, and an explanation of those basic concepts will be followed. Some micro-case studies will be abbreviated to explain further those concepts.

3.02 Toward a Conceptual Framework of Redefining the Regional Development Strategy of China Towards 21st Century

Redefining the regional development strategy is established based on following:

1. The regional development strategy will be considered within the framework of national development strategy. Two basic strategies are proposed by the Party and the Chinese government in the official document — "Implement the Strategies of Developing the Country by Relying on Science and Education", and "Achieving Sustainable Development". These two basic strategies are in line with the basic concepts of two World Summit in the 90's, one on sustainable development and the other on social development. These strategies are also adaptable to the trend of global scenario, the dynamics of technological change will be one of the essential driving forces in the coming Century. This trend should be carefully assesed with the recent IMF-World Bank annual meetings focused on "Knowledge for Development" and the advocation of OECD on "knowledge-based economies", etc.

2. Coordinated regional economic development is emphasized. There is reclassification of the regions based upon the successful experiences of opening to the outside world and development of the domestic market. The seven regions classified in the Ninth Five-Year Plan and Outline of Long-Term Target of 2010 are based upon an open economy and market-oriented reform concept to strengthen further the process of integration of global economic activity on the one side and develop further the linkage of domestic market on the other. The new classification of regions is a breakthrough of traditional concept of Chinese regional development based on administrative regions. This new classification is based on economic criteria and linkage of economic activities both at home and abroad.

3. A Combination of System Orientation and Issue Orientation

The size of China is so large that a unified system concept (two basic strategies for example) must be supplemented with special issue of specific region, for example, there is a part of poverty region in China, there is also the region with declining industries such as the northeastern region of China. The issue happened in northeastern region of China is not new from international experience, it is the experience of Western Europe that "... the United

Kingdom containing mining and industrial areas that had received aid from domestic sources over many years, and Western part of Denmark having unemployment problems.... A Community Fund for regional investment and a Regional Development Committee were duly recommended as components of the proposed Common Regional policy."[1] This were also the issues in the US that "Much of the recent debate on regional growth and decline in the United States has focused on federal spending and other public policies that have allegedly 'favored' certain regions or states at the expense of others.... But regional growth and decline can be better understood in the context of structural change within a dynamic economic system — that system being the United States as a whole".[2] With industrialization process implemented around half century, with the structural change to be a pervasive trend in all economies, China is facing the problem that had been faced by developed countries. Therefore, it is necessary to redefine the regional development strategy within this new context.

4. Keep the Basic Condition of China in Mind

Although China had spent an effort of half a century in industrialization and development, and become a leading producer of quantity of several industrial products, such as textile, iron and steel, cement, TV set, etc. But the share of value of output of agriculture in GDP, especially the share of the labor force in agriculture still played an important role. This can be seen from international comparison of Table 3.1. This basic condition will effect the consideration of development strategy in many aspects.

5. Changing of Economic Actors in Development

In the regime of a former central planned economy, the major economic actor is the government, but in the transition toward a socialist market economy, there will be changing role of the government and the emergence of new economic actors. The government will reduce its role to be an economic actor, its major role should be focused on the establishment and implementation of the legal system, social aspects and intervention in the area of market failure. The government should perform its proper role for co-ordination and provision of an enabling environment for S&T development and business operations. This role of co-ordination is not unique for China to be

---

1. Reference 7.
2. Reference 8.

a transitional economy, this is also common in Western developed countries. (Please refer to Appendix — The Coordination Perspective)

Table 3.1 International Comparison of Selected Economic Indicators (1995)

	China	USA	Germany	France	Japan	South Korea	India
Total Population (millions)	1200.2	263.1	81.9	58.1	125.2	44.9	929.4
Urban Population (% of total)	35	76	87	73	78	81	35
Per-papita GDP (U.S.D.)	620	26980	27510	24990	39640	9700	340
Land for Cropland, Permanent Pasture (% of Total Land) 1994	53	47	49	54	14	22	61
Agriculture Value Added (%)	21	2		2	2	7	29
Labor Force in Agriculture (%) 1990	70	3	6	5	7	18	64

6. On the Other Side, Creation of the Capacity for the Participation at Grassroot Level Is Also Important

These five aspects will be elaborated in detail in the following section.

3.03 Regional Development Strategy of China Towards the 21st Century

1. Implementation of Sustainable Development — A Basic Strategy

(1) Although environmental protection had been determined to be one of the basic national policies in the 80's, the policy against pollution and other legislation has been weak. The "sustainable development strategy" is raised in China's Ninth Five-Year Plan, *China: Agenda 21* and the document of the 15th CPC National Congress. It was emphasized in President Jiang's speech to the 15th CPC National Congress that "As a populous country relatively short of natural resources, China must implement a sustainable development strategy in the modernization drive." Economizing on natural resources, overall planning for the improvement of land resources; rigor-

ously enforce laws governing the management and protection of land, water, forests, minerals and seas; institute a system of using natural resources with payment; strengthen the control of environmental pollution; improvement of the ecological environment by planting trees and grassland; conservation of water and soil and preventing and controlling desertification — all these were emphasized in above-mentioned report.

(2) The recent serious flood calamity of the Yangtze River and in Northeastern region have sounded a true warning to officials and the public at large. Therefore, implementation of sustainable development has become a national awareness. Efforts to create the forest and grassland are being intensified, and the quality of air is being reported in large municipalities. Means and measures have been adopted to control waste gas discharged from automobiles in large municipalities. It can be predicted that peoople will become more serious in implementing this strategy at different regions.

(3) Box 3-1 is a very brief abstract of a UNDP project, "Support for Sustainable Development of the Yellow River Delta," which can illustrate the effort to implement sustainable development at the regional level.

Box 3-1
Abstract of "Support for Sustainable Development of the Yellow River Delta"

1. Background of the Project

This project was the first program supported by UNDP and the Netherlands Government after the promulgation of the white book *China's Agenda 21* in 1994. The main contents of the project are to prepare for the large scale investment activities in the YRD. The aim of the project is three:

(1) To strengthen the study, analysis, planning and coordinating capacity of local institutions;

(2) To support the implementation of China's Agenda 21 Projects, harnessing the Yellow River course, developing agriculture and industries, conserving the national environment of urban development, optimizing utilization of land and water resources, etc. (A comprehensive preliminary planning)

(3) To promote the exchange of views and collaboration among officials at central, provincial and local levels, and also among central research institutions, universities and foreign experts.

2. Research output

One main report, three sub-reports (economic development report, water resource and its utilization report, environmental protection and pollution control report). There are also a series specific reports, planning and implementation of GIS of YRD; study of environmental system of YRD; transportation planning of YRD; I/O analysis; sustainable development industrial planning; optimal management of water resources, land use and regional planning; flood disaster risk analysis of YRD; mathematical model of sedimentation of YRD; current status, trend and strategy on environment of YRD.

3. Abstract of Executive Summary of Main Report

(1) Current Situation of YRD

(2) Object of sustainable development and criteria system

There are four objects of this study: (a) Economic Development; (b) Environmental quality including preservation of wetland; (c) Social Development (d) Safety (this is a unique object as the object of study is delta area of the Yellow River)

(3) Precondition of sustainable development of YRD

This includes the study of alternative schemes of harnessing the river course, analysis of available water resource and water pricing, prevention of various environmental hazards is also studied.

(4) Sustainable socio-economic development

A conceptual framework of scenario analysis is done: the first scenario is pursuit of maximum profit in marketization; the second is to use input-output analysis to identify competitive sectors; the third scenario is to take environmental quality to be priority concern; the fourth scenario is to take social development to be priority concern. There are many factors of social development, only increase of employment is considered in this research project.

Several qualitative conclusions are derived from this conceptual model.

Sustainable agricultural, industrial, tertiary sectoral development and urban-rural development are studied.

(5) Policy recommendation and institutional development

2. Implementing the Strategy of Developing the Country by Relying on Science and Education

(1) Major concepts of strategy in the official documents include the following:

Recognition of the impact of the future development of science and technology, particularly high technology on overall national strength, this is in line with the global trend towards the 21st century;

Policies on science are: selective approach, i.e., highlight key areas and refraining from doing other things; strengthening basic research and research in high technology, the pace of application of high technology on production should be accelerated; import policy should focus on high technology as priority, focus should be put on improvement of innovative capability; improvement of management systems of science, technology and education to promote their integration with the national and regional economy; to establish a closer linkage among scientific research institutes, institutions of higher learning and enterprises in production; protection of intellectual property rights should be strengthened and to create an incentive system; and actively bring in intellectual resources from overseas.

It is planned in China's Ninth Five-Year Plan and the Outline of Long-Term Target by the Year 2000 that all children should be able to receive nine-year compulsory education and illiteracy should be basically eliminated. It is pointed out in "Human Development Report 1997" that the increase of income disparity between the rich coastal regions and poor interior regions of China is due to the fact that "there was a weakening in the public sector after the central government transferred part of the responsibility for education and public health to local governments, as they were not priorities for local governments". It is expected that the local governments follow the line of this strategy in the regional development.

(2) Case Study of Implementation of This Strategy

There are around 25 provinces and municipalities where high technology development zones were set up. Some are efficient while others were not. For example, the gross value of output per enterprise in Shanghai is 36.8 million yuan in 1996, while it is only 3.6 million for enterprises of HTDZ of Lanzhhou. An in-depth study of regional development strategy related to the establishment of HTDZ or Science Park can be further studied. Box 3-2 is a brief introduction of Shanghai (ZJ) Hi-Tech Park.

Box 3-2
Brief Introduction of Shanghai (ZJ) Hi-Tech Park

1. General

Shanghai (ZJ) Hi-Tech Park is located in the middle of Pudong, the "dragoon head" for Chinese economic development. This is a 21-century establishment facing modern technopol in integrating scientific research, education, industry, dwelling and entertainment functions.

2. General Layout

ZJ Hi-Tech Park has a planned area of 17 km². It's planning is as follows:

(1) Hi-Tech Industry District

This district is devoted to two industrial bases, the State Bio-Tech Pharmaceutical Base (Shanghai) and State Microelectronics Industry Base. It is expected that these two bases will promote the new economic leading sector of Shanghai. This will be described further in 3.

(2) Scientific Research and Education District

This is committed to provide an ideal venue for the exchange of high-level intellects and scientific information, and it is going to gradually bring in the universities, national key labs, research institutes and engineering centers.

(3) It is intended to establish appropriate financing mechanism for the commercialization of research results of hi-tech, whether a venture capital system can be established is under consideration.

(4) Scientific Commercial and Residential District   This is to provide a high-level comfortable residential area with perfect public facilities and community environment.

3. Hi-Tech Industry District

(1) State Bio-Tech and Pharmaceutical Base (Shanghai) in ZJ. This Base is actively attracting both the domestic and overseas bio-pharmaceutical enterprises and R&D facilities, explore the technology innovation and commercialization system so as to improve the R&D and commercialization capability of the bio-tech and pharmaceutical industry and the international compatibility of the enterprise.

(2) State Microelectronics and Information Industry Base. The Shanghai Municipality has the comparative advantage in developing the information industry in China. The State Microelectronics and Information Industry Base in Shanghai (ZJ) will concentrate a group of modern microelectronics and information enterprises with a strong capability of R&D and technology innovation, and also a crowd of international intellectual force by taking advantage of agglomeration effect, and create huge-size enterprise groups for information communication and cooperation.

4. Scientific Research and Education District

This will bring in state open labs, engineering center and research institutions. Also it will cooperate with the domestic famous universities to establish universities in the Park and cooperate with the hi-tech tenants to establish key labs.

5. Current Situation

Up to the end of 1997, Shanghai (ZJ) Hi-Tech Park has established 39 projects with a total investment of 790 million USD. The lease of 900,000 m² land has been fulfilled. Over 40 projects has been allocated in the incubator, 19 projects have been under construction and 16 projects have become operational. The total output value has reached 2.1 billion yuan.

3. Coordinated Regional Economic Development

(1) China has reclassified the country into seven regions based on their relationship with domestic and outside linkage, based on their natural endowment as well as comparative and competitive advantages.

The seven regions and the planning for them are as follows:

1. The Yangtze River (Changjiang) Delta and river zone. This zone has such

advantages as river-sea link, well developed agriculture, solid industrial foundation and relatively high technological level, coupled with the opportunities brought about by the development and opening-up of Pudong and the Three Gorges project, a comprehensive economic belt with east-west and north-south linkage will gradually take shape, with large and medium cities along the Changjiang as its backbone.

2. The Bohai rim zone.With such advantages as well-developed communications, proximity to large and medium cities, a concentration of qualified scientific and technological personnel and rich coal, iron and oil resources, and propelled by the development of pillar industries and the construction of energy bases and communications lines, a comprehensive economic sphere will be formed around Bohai, primarily covering the Liaoning Peninsula, the Shandong Peninsula, Beijing, Shandong, Hebei and large and medium coastal cities.

3. The Southeast coastal zone. With such advantages as being close to Hongkong, Macao and Taiwan and a high degree and large scale of opening to the outside world, the areas primarily covering the Zhujiang Delta and southern and eastern Fujian where foreign exchange-earning agriculture, capital and technology-intensive foreign-funded enterprises and high value-added foreign exchange-earning industries will be further developed , it will become an economic zone with a well-developed export-oriented economy.

4. The zone covering part of southwest and southern provinces. With such advantages as sea, river and border access and rich agricultural, forestry, water, mineral and tourism resources, with the construction of cross-border communication lines and the opening up of water, power and mineral resources as a foundation and with reliance on the technological strength of national defense industries, the area will be developed as China's important energy, non-ferrous metals, phosphonium and sulfur production bases, as well as tropical and subtropical agriculture and tourism base.

5. The northeastern zone. With such advantages as well-developed communications, a complete system of heavy and chemical industries and rich land and energy resources and through accelerated transformation of the old industrial bases, opening-up and development of the Tumenjiang area, comprehensive development of agricultural resources, and development of advanced processing, the area will emerge as the nation's important base for heavy and chemical industries and agriculture.

6. The central zone. With such advantages as well-developed agriculture, a relatively sound industrial foundation and convenient communications, together with major railway lines between Gansu and Shanghai, Beijing and Kowloon, Beijing and Guangzhou, the area will become a new economic belt with important agricultural, raw material and machinery industrial base.

7. The northwestern zone. With such advantages as connections with East and Central Asia, rich in agricultural, animal husbandry, energy and mineral resources and military enterprises, and following the accelerated hydroelectric power and communications construction and opening-up of resources brought about by the Asia-Europe Continental Bridge, the area will become the nation's important base for cotton and livestock products, the petrochemical industry, energy and non-ferrous metals.

(2) Classification of Regions and Regional Development Strategy

Although there is new concepts on the classification of regions, some of which have been described above, new polices related to these regions have not yet been clearly identified. In the official document of China's Ninth Five-Year Plan and the Outline of Long-Term Target Towards the Year 2010, the description of policies is based on the classification of the Seventh Five-Year Plan, i.e., China is to be classified into eastern, central and western regions. The major policies and measures described for those regions are as follows.

The eastern region should utilize its locational advantages to strengthen further its linkage to the outside world, utilize more foreign investment and other factors of production, export-oriented strategy should be further promoted. Technology-intensive and resource-saving technology should be adopted. Reform should be deepended to ensure economic efficiency and quality. It should play a demonstrative role for the whole country.

The central and western region should utilize fully their natural and energy resources, to build more infrastructure projects such as transportation, communication as well as water conservancy ones. It should open up further and accelerate development by making use of market forces. Table 3.2 and 3.3 show the provinces and municipalities included in this two different types of classification of the regions.

4. Issue-Oriented — The Sectoral Specific Issue Development Strategy

Agricultural sector is the priority concern of China due to its importance to the country as explained in 3.02-4. Emphasis is put on the agricultural sector throughout all the planning documents and the Party's documents related to development strategy. The following is the recent strategy for the agricultural sector and related regional development.

1. The household contract responsibility system with remuneration linked to output should be kept stable. It is also written in the recent Land Management Law of the PRC that the contracts should be kept stable for 30 years, if there is the necessity to make adjustment for an individual contractor, it is necessary to get agreement from more than two thirdths of the members of the villagers' committee and report to and obtain approval from agricultural administrative departments of the township and county governments.

The two-tier operation system that combines unified management with indi-

Table 3.2 Regional Classification in China's Ninth Five-Year Plan

Name of Seven Regions	Area Covered	Share of National Total (%)		
		Land	Population	GDP
The Bohai Rim Zone	Beijing, Tianjin, Liaoning, Shandong, Shanxi, Inner Mongolia, Hebei	12	30	26
The Yangtze River Delta and Riverine Zone	Fourteen major municipalities in the Delta and 28 municipalities along the Yangtze River	3	14	20
Southeastern Coastal Zone	Fujian, Guangdong and southern coastal area of Zhejiang Province	3	8	
Northeastern Region	Liaoning, Jilin, Heilongjiang, four leagues (cities) of Inner Mongolia	13	10	11
Central Region	Henan, Hubei, Hunan, Anhui, Jiangxi	9	26	19
Northwestern Region	Shaanxi, Gansu, Qinghai, Ningxia, Xinjiang, three leagues (cities) in west Inner Mongolia	36	7	
Some Southwestern and Southern Provinces	Sichuan, Guizhou, Yunnan, Guangxi, Hainan and three cities in western of Guangdong	15	20	

Source: Reference 16.

vidual management should be kept, to gradually boost the strength of the collective economy.

Table 3.3 Regional Classification in China (Classification of Three Regions)

Name of Region	Area Covered
Eastern	Liaoning, Hebei, Tianjin, Beijing, Shandong, Jiangsu, Shanghai, Zhejiang, Fujian, Guangdong, Guangxi, Hainan
Central	Heilongjiang, Jilin, Inner Mongolia, Shanxi, Henan, Anhui, Hubei, Hunan, Jiangxi
Western	Shaanxi, Gansu, Ningxia, Sichuan, Yunnan, Guizhou, Qinghai, Xinjiang, Tibet

2. Market-orientated reform of the agricultural sector should be promoted, i. e., the procurement and sales system of agricultural products should be reformed, to encourage the farmers to enter the circulation system, to cultivate the commodity market and factor market of agriculture.

3. To encourage the application of modern science and technology to promote the production of the agricultural sector.

4. Development of TVEs should be further encouraged so as to provide a channel of transfer of surplus rural labor force to high value-added sector.

5. Small town and cities are major focus in the urbanization process of rural development.

6. Economic system reform should be matched properly with political system reform. It is necessary to expand democracy at the grassroots level of the rural area. Three basic measures to implement democratic system at the village level are advocated:

(1) The direct election system should be implemented in the villagers' committee;

(2) Important events related to village people should be decided through the approval of meetings of villagers or their representatives;

(3) The management system at the village level should be transparent to the rural public.

This is a very important procedure to establish the democratic system of

China, a bottom-up approach under central leadership.

6. Issue Oriented — The Regional Specific Issue of Regional Development at Current Stage

The launch of the agricultural sector reform in late 1978 had improved the farmers' income by a big margin. Absolute poverty in rural areas declined rapidly, from 260 million people in 1978 to around 96 million in 1985, and declined further, to 80 million in 1992. A new poverty alleviation program for the rural areas was instituted by the central government in 1994. It is named

Table 3.4 Distribution of 18 Extensively Poor Regions of China

No. of Regions	Poor Regions (geographical Features)	Provinces and Regions Involved	No. of Poor Counties
2	Yemeni mountains	Shandong	9
	South-Western and North-Eastern Part of Fujian	Fujian, Zhejiang and Guangdong	23
7	Nuluerhu mountain region	Liaoning, Inner Mongolia, Hebei	18
	Taihang mountain region	Shanxi, Hebei	25
	Luliang mountain region	Shanxi	21
	Qinling-Daba mountain region	Sichuan, Shaanxi, Hubei, Henan	68
	Wuling mountain region	Sichuan, Hunan, Hebei, Guizhou	40
	Dabie mountain region	Hubei, Henan, Anhui	27
	Jinggang mountain region and Southern Jiangxi	Jiangxi, Hunan	34
9	Dingxi dryland	Gansu	27
	Xihaigu region	Ningxia	8
	Northen Shaanxi	Shaanxi, Gansu	27
	Tibet		27
	Sourtheastern part of Yunnan	Yunnan	19
	Hengduan mountain region	Yunnan	13
	Jiuwan mountain region	Guangxi, Guizhou	17
	Wumeng mountain region	Sichuan, Yunnan, Guizhou	32
	Northwestern part of Guizhou	Guizhou	29

Sources: *Outline of Economic Development in China's Poor Areas,* Office of the Leading Group of Economic Development in Poor Areas, the State Council, Agricultural Publishing House, 1989.

the Eight-Seven Poverty Alleviation Program, i.e., to alleviate 80 million of people from poverty within seven years. The people in poverty is regionally specific. They concentrate in 18 extensively poor regions of China, which are listed in Table 3.4. For details, see Reference 12, a publication of UNCRD for its 25th anniversary, and also Paper 14 of this book.

7. Public-Private Partnership in Regional Development

Since the launch of the economic reform, China started to encourage the development of various types of ownership system. It is described in Reference 1 that "The non-public sector is an important component of China's socialist market economy. We should continue to encourage and guide the non-public sector comprising self-employed and private businesses to facilitate their sound development." This will not only promote the development of the national economy, but also promote the development of the regional economy.

UNCRD, DRC and the "Brilliant Cause" had jointly sponsored an international forum titled "The Role of the Private Sector in Poverty Alleviation through Social Efforts and Balanced Regional Development" on July 1-2 in Beijing, China. Box 3-3 is a brief description of "Brilliant Cause", which shows the redefining of China's regional development strategy by changing the role of the economic actors.

Box 3-3
Brilliant Cause Program — Public-Private Partnership
in Regional Development

The Chinese government had launched the national "Eight-Seven Poverty Alleviation Program in 1994, targeted at providing the basic needs of food and clothing for 80 million poor people within seven years. The Leading Group of Economic Development in Poor Areas (LGEDPA) was established by the State Council in 1986, the Poor Area Development Office (DADO) was established under LGEDPA to take care of the day-to-day work. Nearly all ministries were involved in this program.

1. The Launch of the "Brilliant Cause" Program and Its Achievements

At the second meeting of the Seventh Standing Committee of the All-China Federation of Industry and Commerce, ten non-public sector entrepreneurs put forward a proposal titled "Let's All Join in the Brilliant Cause of Poverty Eradication." This proposal was accepted and got wide support. In the past four years since the launch of the "Brilliant Cause" Program till June 30, 1997, 2,296 non-public sector entrepreneurs had joined the project of the "Brilliant Cause" Program, and the number of projects undertaken reached 2,731, with more than 5 billion yuan of investment and training around 255.6 thousand person-times. Some 47,100 poor people had got rid off poverty through the implementation of this program.

2. Types of Project Investment

Investment in this project are of many forms. The investment activity can be broadly classified into the following nine types (descriptions will be given to some types of poverty alleviation activities). The nine types of investment are:

(1) Agricultural development;

(2) Resource development;

(3) Chain-plant was located in poverty-stricken regions to manufacture the products of the same brands as produced by the parent plants;

(4) Integration of production activity of agriculture, industry and trade, agricultural and industrial production bases are set up in poor regions, the products are sold in both domestic and foreign markets;

(5) Development through relocation of population in difficult regions;

(6) Market-driven development (refer to 3.04);

(7) Export of Labor Force. Labor mobility and emigration from poverty-stricken regions are an effective means for the alleviation of poverty. The "Brilliant Cause" Shenzhen City Branch, collaborating with the Municipal Bureau of Labor and Municipal Economic Commission and with the support from local labor departments of the poverty-stricken regions, had imported a large amount of rural labor force from Guizhou and Jiangxi provinces, employed in non-public enterprises in Shenzhen.

(8) Development through training;

(9) Grant for public benefit.

3.04 Market-Driven Type of Poverty Alleviation

In the implementation of various types of investment development, it is found that market-driven investment produced very good results. Seventeen markets were organized, coordinated and constructed in the "Brilliant Cause"Program. Seven markets had been established (3 in Inner-Mongolia, 1 in Shanghai, 2 in Shenzhen, and 1 in Jiangxi); three markets are under construction (1 in Shenzhen and 2 in Jiangxi); seven markets are being planned (1 in Shenyang, 1 in Jingdezhen, 1 in Jujiang, 1 in Nanchang , 2 in Guangdong Province and 1 in Guizhou Province). The locations of those markets varied; some are located directly in the poverty-stricken regions of central and western China, such as the Brilliant Grand Market in southern Jiangxi, the special market of Mihao Peach of Guizhou; some are established in developed coastal regions to develop trade relations with the central and western regions aided with preferential policies to facilitate the entry of their products into the market of the developed regions. For example, the Shanghai Brilliant Small and Miscellaneous Goods Wholesale Market plays sush a role. All "Brilliant Cause" markets are established with the aim to allevate poverty by providing the channels for the circulation of products. Commerce, wholesale and retail services can absorb a fairly large amount of labor with low capital input. It will also provide a favorable condition for the "reemployment" program, currently implemented in China in the reform of the SOEs.

2. Unique Meaning and Role of "Market-Driven Type" of Poverty Alleviation

People in poverty are mainly distributed in remote mountainous regions of central and western China. Most of the people in poverty live in rural areas with unfavorable natural environment, backward means of production, simple economic structure and small scale of market. Thus, "market-driven poverty alleviation" plays the following unique roles.

(1) It is favorable to break the closed status of the natural economy, to upgrade the awareness of local officials and people regarding commodity transaction and trade.

(2) It is favorable to promote regional economy, push forward the development of the tertiary sector, promote the reasonable transfer of surplus rural labor force and reemployment of urban off-job workers and staffs. The growth of the market can surely promote the prosperity of regional economy.

Concluding Remarks

Regional development is a pervasive dynamic theme of study. Different countries differ in stages of development and adopt different policies. China is redefining itself. There is need in redefining the regional development strategy. The previous description can only present a birds'-eye view of this subject. This regional development strategy has to be proved correct through its implementation. In a rapidly changing global environment and human society, doing and adaptation are the basic strategy to ensure success.

Appendix

Theoretical Framework of Perspective on Economic Development

(Abstracted from "Scanning the Future: A Long-term Scenario Study of the World Economy 1990-2015" by Andre de Jong and Gerrit Zalm, Central Planning Bureau, the Netherlands)

1. Three perspectives on economic development are studied. These three perspectives provided the basis in deriving the four scenarios given in 1.03. These three perspectives have different theoretical basis.

(1) The equilibrium perspective   This is based on the neoclassical theory. The basis of thought is a well-functioning price mechanism which co-ordinates the decision of various economic subject. The level of prosperity hinges on the production factors available: natural resources, availability and quality of labor supply, and size of capital stock.

(2) The co-ordination perspective   This is based primarily on the views of Keynes, i.e., rational behavior on a micro level can lead to significant unbalances on the macro-level. Balanced economic development can be promoted by stabilizing exceptionally volatile expectations, the pursuit of private interests alone may fail to bring about stable economic development, some degree of co-operation and co-ordination is required. Government can play an important positive role.

(3) The Free Market perspevtice   This is based on the Neo-Austrian school of economic theory, this perspective states that growth is never painless. There will always be winner's and losers, and both the will to win and the fear of losing drive to a significant degree the dynamics of a market economy. Entrepreneurs play an important role in this perspective.

REFERENCES

1.   "Holding High the Great Banner of Deng Xiaoping Theory for an All-round Advancement of the Cause of Building Socialism with Chinese

Characteristics into the 21st Century," report delivered at the 15th National Congress of the Communist Party of China on Sept. 12, 1997 by Jiang Zemin. *Selected Documents of the 15th CPC National Congress*, New Star Publishers, 1997.

2. *Business Week,* August 24-31, 1998. *The 21st Century Economy,* the Mcgrew-Hill Companies.

3. *The World in 2020* , OECD, 1997.

4. *Long-Term Prospects for the World Economy,* OECD, 1992.

5. *The New Palgrave Dictionary of Economics,* Vol. 4, edited by John Eatwell, Murray Milgate and Peter Neuman, the Macmillan Press Limited, 1987.

6. "Prospect for and Issues on the Chinese Economy in Transition", Wang Huijiong and Li Shantong, collected in *Challenges of Transformation and Transition from Centrally Planned to Market Economies* , UNCRD and DRC, *Research Report,* Series No. 26, UNCRD, July 1998.

7. *Regional Development in Western Europe,* edited by Hugh D. Glont, John Wiley & Sons, 1975.

8. *Regional Growth and Decline in the United States,* second edition, Bernard L. Weinstein, Harold T. Gross and John Rees Praeger, Special Studies Praeger Scientific 1978 and 1985 by Preaeger publisher.

9. Major References on Regional Studies of China

9-1. *China's New Spatial Economy Heading towards 2020,* edited by Godfrey Linge, Hongkong: Oxford University Press.

9-2. *China's Spatial Economy: Recent Developments and Reforms,* edited by G.J.R. Linge and D.K. Forbes, Hong Kong: Oxford University Press, 1990.

9-3. "Regional Development for Developing Countries — The Chinese Experience," Wang Huijiong, in *Current Issues in Regional Economic Development and International Co-opperation,* UNCRD, March 1997.

9-4. *China: Regional Coordinated Development Strategy Towards 21st Century,* Task Force of Project, DRC Economic Science Publisher,

Sept. 1997 (in Chinese).

9-5. *Economic Development Reform and Policy,* Vol. 3 (*China: Regional Economic Study*), UNDP Project, DRC Social Science Literature publisher, 1994 (in Chinese).

9-6. *Zhongguo Diqu Fazhany yu Chanye Zhengce,* chief editor: Ma Hong, Fang Weizhong, China Fiscal Economic Publisher, 1990 (in Chinese).

9-7. *1997 China Regional Development Report,* Lu Dadao, Xun Fengxuan, et al. Commercial Publishing House, 1997 (in Chinese).

4. Two Decades of Experience of Policy Modeling of DRC[*]

I. Introduction

Development Research Center of the State Council was established in the early 80's. It was one of the products of economic reform and opening to the outside world of China in the late 70's. The role of this center is to provide policy consultative service for the government. Therefore, the study and application of mathematical model in our work focused very much on policy analysis. We must confess that China is a late comer in modern economic science as well as in themes of economic models for policy analysis. Our center had tried with full effort to catch up and bridge the gap in this field with the contributions from all our collaborators in this development process. It should also be emphasized in the very beginning of this paper that there are technical difficulties to get exact results from economic mathematical modeling; this issue can be seen clearly from the criticism given by Keynes to the pioneering research of macroeconomic model of Tinbergen in that there were problems of miss clarification, multi-collinearity functional forms, dynamic specification, structural stability, and the difficulties associated with the measurement of theoretical variables, etc. The crucial issue in China is that mathematical economic models should be based on certain economic theory, while the transitional economics of the former central planned economy to a market-oriented economy is a new field in economic study.

In spite of these facts, we have recognized that "Mathematical models are an important tool of forecasting and policy analysis, and it is unlikely that they will be discarded in the future. The challenge is to recognize their limi-

---

[*] The author and co-authors of this paper are Huijiong Wang, Boxi Li and Shantong Li.

tations and to work towards turning them into a more reliable and effective tool. There seems to be no alternatives." That is exactly why our center focused our efforts on the work in the past two decades.

This paper will be divided into two parts: the first part will give a brief retrospect of the policy modeling projects that had been done by us within the context of the economic situation of China at different stages of economic reform. This will give a general picture of evolution of policy modeling in China. And the second part will summarize the lessons and experiences. Brief concluding remarks are given at the end.

II. A Retrospect of Policy Modeling of DRC

Policy modeling work of DRC can be roughly divided into two periods based on the broad context of progress of economic reform as well as the experience of our staffs.

2.01 First Period (1982-1990)

In this period, China was at the initial stage of economic reform and opening-up, the planning system was undergoing changes and reform.

1. Initial Period of Application of Mathematical Modeling in Policy Analysis

(1) The first pioneering effort to the application of mathematical modeling in policy analysis was incorporated in the project of "Comprehensive Planning of Shanxi Province". This project was assigned by the central government, it was to study the long-term development planning of Shanxi Province. This represents a natural process of development of policy analysis described by Chenery that "the earliest form of policy analysis in underdeveloped countries was typically described as 'development planning', since one of its purposes was to assess the consistency of policy instruments and objectives. This term is perhaps unfortunate, since it is afterall taken to imply greater government control of economic activity." In fact, it is well known globally that a gradual approach had been adopted by China in the process of reform and opening. Therefore, in the project of "Comprehensive Planning of Shanxi Province", China hadn't implemented the reform of the planning system in the initial period. The concept of

planning was still traditional in sense, and the only available policy instrument was "investment allocation".

But this pioneering project implemented in Shanxi Province from Feb. 1982-June 1983 has two unique features: first, the planning period was extended to cover 20 years (1981-2000) compared to the past practice of 5-year planning period; second, our center had the privilege to organize various government organizations, research institutions and academic people to work together in such a national key project. There are around 1,400 people involved in this project. We tried to experiment policy analysis with new techniques in this project. A wide variety of modeling exercises were experimented in this project. There are around 100 people involved in the exercise of policy modeling. A total of 26 models were prepared. The scope of study covered very broad areas: the comprehensive planning of Shanxi Province, investment on coal sector, electric industrial planning, water resource utilization, optimal plantation, population model, environmental projection and planning, education planning and projection, investment on science and research, input and output of light industry, output projection of electronic industry, etc. The techniques used include input-output, econometrics, state sector differential equation, linear programming, multiple goal programming, decision analysis, etc.

(2) The result was finally edited into a book titled *Compilation of Economic Mathematical Models of Comprehensive Planing of Shanxi Province*. This pioneering project represents a very nascent stage of policy modeling of the DRC. But we have attained the purpose to get acquaintance to the application of various mathematical tools to the economic policy analysis, a team and organizational relationship has also been created among the researchers. An appendix with the brief introduction of seven mathematical tools are included in the above publication. In spite of the traditional concept of planning, the important types of interaction among the policy variables (objectives and instruments) and the constraints on the economic system of Shanxi Province had been correctly identified in the specification of the planning model.

(3) Although a nascent stage in economic mathematical modeling, we came to understand the key of economic mathematical modeling is an interdisciplinary study between economics, mathematics and the real world. The scholars involved in the Task-Oriented Transient Organization have dif-

ferent backgrounds, automation, economics, mathematics and others. Therefore, it is commented in the "Preface" of the above-mentioned book that "Economic modeling and mathematical 'model' are two fashionable terms in China. Model is designed through abstraction and simplification of the system of real world. Economic modeling is a simplified abstraction of economic activity. It can be in the form of a flow chart, statistical table, bar chart, hydraulic model to simulate economic system that had once been used abroad; but they were short-lived. Mathematical model to represent the economic system became widely adopted both domestically and abroad. It should been emphasized that our 'model' is a combination of economic activity and mathematical means. The precondition to design a relatively useful model is a detailed objective observation of economic phenomena, with appropriate analysis and synthesis to understand clearly the interrelationship among the variables of various economic activities, to compare this with established theory and express these relationships with appropriate mathematics."

(4) Project Evaluation

The question of how to allocate investment and other scarce resources among sectors and projects was also an urgent issue of development policy of China with governmental investment allocation playing a dominant role. Our center had proposed to the State Planning Commission the application of "Feasibility Study of Industrial Projects". We had organized a meeting of national scale, and a book had also been published (Reference 2).

2. Second Period of Policy Modeling of DRC

(1)China Toward the Year 2000

A pioneering project of strategic planning of China.

With the experience gained in the development planning at provincial level, we had got aware of the weakness of traditional Soviet model of the planning system which became inappropriate in current stage of China's development. This point was also correctly summarized in a recent IMF report that "In the case of Russia and China, at the outset predominantly agrarian economies where the majority of citizens were illiterate, the transformation to an industrialized and educated society was achieved roughly within a generation. However, once these economies entered intermediate or higher stages of development and resource allocation choices became more complicated was unable to cope." Therefore, in the national priority project of "China Toward the Year 2000," initiated in 1983 and completed in 1985, a strategic development planning was developed which is totally different from the traditional model of Soviet planning. This study includes a main report and 13 sub-reports. Two of these sub-reports are: "Macro-Economic Model Projections of China Toward the Year 2000" and "Summary of Data of China Toward the Year 2000". This has been descilbed briefly in Appendix 2 in paper 2 of this book.

(2) China: Economic Development and Modeling

Fourteen models had been prepared in the project, which covered the study of development strategy and policy analysis, macro-economic model with application of econometrics, macro-economic model based upon production function and analysis of TFP, population and coordinated economic development planning model, quantitative analysis of economic structures, reproduction of two major sectors, long-term trend of development model, application of system dynamics, long-term trend of development model, China's social economic development model, medium- and long-term macro-economic model, education planning mathematical model, energy system planning and decision model, energy demand model, China's environmental projection model, production structure plantation model, etc. The number of people involved in this sub-report is around 100. The collection of these models are openly published in 1990 (See Reference 3). This project represents the policy modeling with collaboration of people of different organizations at the national level. The mathematical tools used are the same as the first project described in 1-(1). In addition, system dynamics and recursive programming have been added. This effort of modeling exercise had got the first-class national award of application of mathematical modeling in the national exhibition of computer application.

(3) Unique Features of This Project

(a) Through learning and doing on policy analysis, 25 policy recommendations had been made to decision makers through this research. All these policy recommendations, reviewed today, seem to be correct. But not all of them had been adopted by the decision makers. Just quote one example. We had recommended that "An enterprise should be established to be an entity closely bound up with the destinies of the state, collectives and Individuals." This recommendation implicitly suggested that a new system of share company can be implemented to fit the interests of various actors of the economy. But it was not the right time to adopt this policy recommendation by the government in the year 1985. It should also be emphasized that not all policy recommendations were derived from the modeling system. These policy recommendations were derived through a systematic analysis and abstract from all sub-reports. For example, housing reform had also been recommended in that time. But implementation of this policy was initiated only recently.

(b) There is improvement in the consideration of the policy planning in this project compared to the initial period. For example, the features pointed out by Chenery that "The logic of policy planning leads to distinctions among social objectives, constraints and policy instruments. A feasible program is then defined by a set of values for the policy instruments that satisfies the specified objectives and does not exceed the predetermined constraints." Broad policy instruments have been considered in this modeling exercise, for example, several conditions of balance had been incorporated in the model of "Development Strategy and Policy Analysis", i.e., optimum balance between supply and demand, the factors of production, balance of payments, fiscal balance, and balance of credit, although all these are theoretical in sense, anyhow, this is more or less an improvement with sole consideration on investment allocation. And also in the model of "Population and Coordinated Economic Development Planning Model", four major systems with sets of criteria were established, the economic system, the ecological system, population and resource system and social system. This model had implicitly a broad perspective of sustainable development, which became the theme of the World Summit in 1992 in Rio De Janeiro.

(c) International Comparison Adopted in This Modeling Exercise

(4) Regional Development Strategy and Regional Industrial Policy

Through the experience of policy modeling in a decade, we felt that China is too large that study at the national level would result in insufficient consideration of the diversity of different regions. Therefore, we launched another national project, "Regional Development Strategy and Regional Industrial Policy," in late 80's. Nearly every province had included a chapter of I/O analysis in their study. Therefore, we have pushed forward further the development planning supported by mathematical modeling in every province. It should also be emphasized that a decade had been passed since the implementation of reform and opening-up policy, therefore, there bound to be gradual change in concept of planning as compared to the initial period.

2.02 Policy Modelling of DRC in the 90's

Through the gradual approach of economic reform and opening-up, China had already created certain features and factors of market mechanism in the 80's: the establishment of four SEZs in 1980, the opening of 14 coastal cities in the mid of 80's and the further opening of the delta area of Yangtze River, Pearl River, etc. The decentralization of decision making process to different levels of government, the booming of the TVEs also had promoted greatly the formation of market mechanism. The official announcement that "The target of economic restructuring is to establish a socialist market economy" in the 90's had accelerated further the formation and improvement of the market mechanism. Therefore, there was certain shift of focus of the policy modelling of the DRC in the 90's.

1. To Keep the Trait of Studying the Macro-economic Modelling Through Organized Research

Our center had carried out the project through organized research. In view of the experience gained in the 80's, we kept on this trait and published "collection of models" in 1993 and 1999 (Reference 9, 10).

(1) In the publication *China: Applied Macro-economic Models 1993*, 19 models have been collected, the technique applied was generally the same as that used in the 80's. Integer programming was added in this exercise. In consideration that the application of model in the past generally focused on medium- and long-term goals. A model with quarterly forecasting was also added. And there are three models which covered new areas of application in this publication, i.e., the quarterly macro-econometric model of the People's Bank of China, China's macro-fiscal model and a model of scheme of reform of pension system.

Some new concepts from abroad were also described in chapter 1 of that publication. It is seen that through a decade of efforts in the application of mathematical modelling, some scholars and professionals have mastered a variety of sophisticated techniques, especially so for many scholars from fields other than applied policy research. It seems that there was the need to have some institutional organizations to work specifically on model evaluation, so that there would be continuity to keep improvement to a specific type of model rather than to work on application of various mathematics with several feasible models in application to proper issue. These ideas had also emerged in the West. "Models must meet multiple criteria which are often in conflict. They should be relevant in the sense that they ought to be capable of answering the questions for which they are constructed. They should be consistent with the accounting and/or theoretical structure within which they operate. They should provide adequate representations of the aspects of reality with which they are concerned."[1]

These criteria of model evaluation can be found in Hendry and Richard (1982) and McAleer and others (1985), although our concern on model evaluation is slightly different from them.

(2) In the publication *China: Applied Macro-Economic Models 1999*, 13 models were collected. The new area of application includes "Model of International Balance of Payments and Money Supply", "Demand of Money, Modelling and Projection of Money Supply", "Modelling of Analysis and Projection of Chinese Agricultural Policy", "System Dynamics of Infrastructure", and "Regional Water Resource Planning and Coordinated Economic Development". It can be seen from the titles of those papers collected the policy concern in this period. Indirect instruments, such as monetary policy, exchange rate policy, have become important policy instruments rather than direct control through mandatory planning.

There are three new types of models added, i.e., "China Macroeconometric Modelling in Link Project of UN", "China: Multisectoral Development Analysis Model" and "DRC CGE Model". These latter two models were developed in our center through international assistance from Inforum model of Professor Clopper Almon and Professor David Roland-Holst, Dominique

---

1. From reference.

vander Mensbrugghe of OECD Development Center and Dr. Sebastien Dessus and Wang Zhi.

Emphasis in this publication is given once more to the continuity of improvement of the existing model with the evolution of IMF Multimode Mark III to be example. Attention is also given to the application of scenario analysis in explorations of long-term prospective.

2. Microeconometrics

To be a governmental organization to provide policy consultation services, we always keep our eyes open to the trend of the global society. We notice that emphasis on the use of micro-data in the analysis of the economic problems had been pioneered by Ruggles in 1956 on the development of a micro-based social accounting framework and the work of Orcutt and his colleagues. We have learned the use of microanalytic simulation models of policy analysis from Urban Research Institute and experimented in the area of social security system reform in Shandong Province (Refer to Reference 11).

3. Recent Achievement

The very recent achievement of policy modelling is the application of CGE model to study the impact of China's accession to WTO. This project was carried out in 1997-1998. Two models are used in this analysis. The first one is a country model of China, including 41 sectors and 10 representative households (5 rural and 5 urban) with major focus on the evolution of the impact of China's domestic economy under different trade policies. The second model is a 17-region one, with 19 sectoral recursive dynamic models on world trade and production. The period of study covers 1995-2010. Useful and pragmatic conclusions and policy recommendations are derived from this project. The result of study has attracted wide attention domestically and internationally. It has been quoted into reference in the recent IMF publication, *China: Competing in the Global Economy*. There are a few studies on this important theme of policy study, this project has not only the impact at the national and global levels. Nevertheless, it is also a major concern at sectoral and even enterprise levels.

2.03 A Summary of Features of Policy Modelling of DRC in the Past Two Decades

Table 2.1 Policy Modeling of DRC in Past Two Decades

Demand Side	Supply Side	
Economic Background of Major Concern of Decision Makers	Policy Researchers	Type of Modeling

80's
Central Planning Economy
Policy Goal:
  Economic Growth
  Elimination of Bottlenecks
Policy Measures and Instrument
  Investment Allocation
  Industrial Policy
	• To study the feasibility of quadrupling of GDP in 20 years
	• Major bottlenecks:
	  Infrastructure
	  Energy
	• Development Planning with high, medium and low scenario
	• Investment allocation
	• Preliminary study of strategy and policy
	• Understand with analysis of components of supply and demand
		• I/O
		• Macroeconometric model
		• System dynamics
		• Programming model etc.

90's
Socialist Market Economy
Policy Goal:
Economic Growth
  Control of Inflation
  Provide More Employment Opportunity
  Fiscal Balance
  Balance of Payments
  Income Distribution and Social Issues
Policy Instrument:
  Fiscal Policy Including Taxation and Tariff
	• Improved focus on strategic planning
	• Long-term prospective exploration
	• Medium-term projection
	• Short-term forecasting
	• Policy analysis
		• I/O
		• Macroeconometric model
		• experimentation of microsimulation models
		• System dynamics
		• CGE
		• Programming models etc.

III. Lessons and Experiences

3.01 Introduction

It is not the purpose of this paper to give theories and details of policy modelling, only a brief summary is made on the history of policy modelling of our center. It should be emphasized that there are many governmental and academic research institutions that contributed very much to the development of macroeconometric modelling, mathematical modelling with various applications and theoretical study. It is also not our intention to be involved in theoretical debate either on economic theory, or on the feasibility of appropriate mathematical tools, etc. It is mentioned in the beginning of this paper that policy modelling requires an interdisciplinary study of economics, mathematics, and policy making process in a real world. It is not simply the application of mathematics to the real world, an in-depth knowledge is required of various disciplines of social science, the history of evolution, the knowledge of the real world, the features of various mathematical tools, etc. This brief history of policy modelling of DRC presented an overview of the learning process of our center in working in the world of economy during transition of China. Some lessons and experiences will be briefed in 3.02.

3.02 Lessons and Experiences of Policy Modelling of DRC

1. In policy modelling, we advocate the "combination of quantitative and qualitative analysis," it can be seen from the description in part II of this paper that all 25 policy recommendations seem0 to be correct if reviewed today. But not all of them are derived from the policy modelling. Because the real world is too complicated to be explained completely with a single school of economic theory. It is correctly pointed out that "The ambiguity in testing Theories, known as the Duhem-Quine thesis, is not confined to econometrics and arises whenever theories are conjunctions of hypothesis (on this, see for example Cross, 1982). The problem is , however, especially serious in econometrics because theory is far less developed in economics than it is in the natural science."

2. International and domestic cooperation and exchange of information are crucial in an emerging knowledge based economy. Because the issues of the real world is so complex, while the number of researchers of China are very much limited, therefore, organized research or the form of ToTos (Task oriented, transient organizations) are adopted by our center through these two decades.

The relatively successful modelling in the 90's is due also to international collaboration with OECD Development Center, Harvard University, the World Bank, ADB, modelling group of Inforum, ADBI and many others.

3. Although many models have experimented in our center, but the critical role of the modeler is to select the appropriate technique best adapted to the issue under investigation. We should emphasize once more that the best choice is not the sophistication of mathematics.

4. Policy modelling researcher should also focus on the presentation of his results to the decision makers, a simple, straightforward expression should be designed to make the policy recommendations to be acceptable by the decision makers.

Concluding Remarks

The history of the mankind is undergoing rapid change in the process of globalization and multipolarization. The global society and economic activity are increasingly characterized by rapid changes and uncertainty. These raise new challenges to modeler. A keen awareness should be given to these. Continuous effort should be paid to policy modelling as a part of the effort of the mankind to make a better society through continuous learning and doing.

REFERENCES

1. *Compilation of Economic Mathematical Models of Comprehensive Planning of Shanxi Province* (in Chinese for internal use), edited by Technical Economic Research Center of the State Council, Planning Commission of Shanxi Province, chief editors: Wang Huijiong, Tian Jiesan, deputy chief editors: Zhang Shouyi, Zheng Daxian (Note: Zhang Shouyi is also the head of editing section), publish in 1984.

2. *Feasibility Study of Industrial Projects* (in Chinese), edited by Technical Economic Research Center of the State Council.

3. *Zhongguo Jingji de Fazhan yu Moxing* (in Chinese), edited by Economic, Technological and Social Development Center of the State Council, chief editor: Li Boxi, deputy chief editors: Li Shantong, Pang

Banxuan, China Fiscal and Economic Press, 1990.

4. *Asian and Pacific Economy Towards the Year 2000,* edited by Fu-Chen Lo, APDC (English version). There are seven papers related to China towards the year 2000 project in this book, one of which is titled "Overall Quantitative Analysis of China's Economy Towards the Year 2000)." It describes policy modelling of that project.

5. "The Evolution of Development Planning," Hollis B. Chenery, Development Discussion Paper, No. 158 HIID, Nov. 1983.

6. "Econometrics" by M. Hashem Pesaran, in *The New Palgrave, A Dictionary of Economics,* Vol. 2, dited by John Eatwell, Murray Milgate and Peter Neuman, the Macmillan Press Limited, 1987.

7. "Mathematical Economics" by Gerard Debreau, in *The New Palgrave, A Dictionary of Economics*, Vol. 3, edited by John Eatwell, Murray Milgate and Peter Neuman, the Macmillan Press Limited, 1987.

8. *Zhangguo Diqu Fazhan yu Chanye Zhengce* (in Chinese), edited by Ma Hong, Fang Weizhong, China Fiscal and Economic Press, 1990.

9. *China: Applied Macroeconomic Models 1993* (in Chinese), chief editors: Wang Huijiong, Li Boxi and Li Shantong, China's Fiscal and Financial Press, 1993.

10. *China: Applied Macroeconomic Models 1999* (in Chinese), chief editors: Wang Huijiong, Li Boxi and Li Shantong, China's Fiscal and Financial Press, 1999.

11. *Microanalytic Simulation Model and Its Application*, Li Shantong and Gou Jialing, Machine-Building Industry Press, 1999.

12. *WTO: China and the World* (In Chinese), Li Shantong, Wang Zhi, Thai Fan and Xu Lin, China's Development Press, 2000.

13. *A History of Macroeconometric Model Building,* Ronald G. Bodkin, Lawrence R. Klein and Kanta Maruah, Edward Elgar Publishing Limited, 1991.

14. *Applied Methods for Trade Policy Analysis: An Overview,* Joseph F. Francois and Kenneh A. Reinert.

15. *China: Competing in the Global Economy,* edited by Wanda Tseng and Markus Rodlauer, IMF, 2003.

Part II

Development of Science and Technology of China

Part II

Development of Science and Technology of China

5. Chinese Experience of Technological Independence

The research objective of this study is to present China's experience in attempting to meet its target of "self-reliance." The research was carried out at both macro and micro levels. Special attention is given to S&T policy, which is centred around the following: (a) the role of government; (b) the socio-economic background to S&T policy; (c) planning and coordination of S&T policy with respect to socio-economic development; and (d) policies to encourage the efficient use of inputs to the S&T system, e.g., financial and human resources.

The Chinese study used a systems approach. The S&T system, economic system, social system and international system were studied as interrelated parts of an integrated whole. The system is a dynamic one, which changes with geographical location and time (fig. 1). We started by reviewing the past, and moved on to analysing the past and current status of S&T and its prospects for the future (fig. 2). The S&T system was analysed according to a life-cycle concept (fig. 3).

Historical Perspective

China has carried out a socialist transformation and construction of the economy since 1949. The characteristic features of the Chinese socio-economic system can be defined with reference to such factors as ownership, decision-making, motivation, information, and coordination structure. The patterns of past socio-economic development in terms of these basic features are described below.

The Completion of Basic Socialist Transformation, 1949-1956

Following the three years of economic rehabilitation from 1949 to 1952, China initiated and established a relatively flexible central planning system. The first Five-Year Plan for national economic development was carried out between 1953 and 1957. An initial basis for socialist industrialization, involving the construction of 694 "above-norm" projects (including 153 major ones), was planned and completed.

Between 1953 and 1956, the annual average increase in the gross output value of industry was 19.6 per cent and of agriculture 4.8 percent. During that period, more than 110 large industrial enterprises were completed, mostly in heavy industry. This laid the groundwork for Chinese socialist industrialization. The value of the industrial out-put of the state-owned enterprises reached around 53 percent, and that of the collectively owned 19 percent, in the year 1957. The remaining industrial enterprises were in the category of either joint state/private ownership or private ownership.

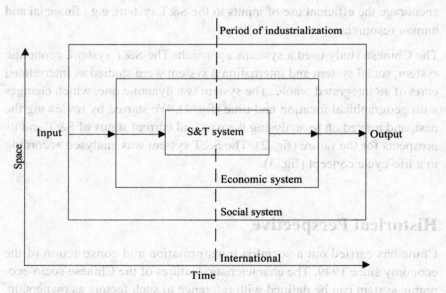

Fig. 1. System in time and space phase

Planning in that period was relatively flexible, the scope for control was limited to minor parts of the state-owned enterprises, important materials, and projects. Indirect control of the cooperative, individual, private capitalist and state capitalist economy was through proper economic policies, the pricing system, taxation, and the credit system.

In the agriculture sector, the Agrarian Reform Law of the PRC was promulgated in June 1950. After the land reform, the agricultural production system was changed in three stages: the mutual aid team; the elementary agricultural producers' cooperative; and the advanced agricultural producers' cooperative.

Pattern of Socio-economic Development from 1956-1977

China undertook full-scale socialist construction in the period from 1956-1966. Between 1956 and 1966, fixed assets in industry grew four times in the value while national income increased by 58 percent in terms of comparable prices and by 34 percent in terms of per-capita amount. From 1966 to 1976, the ten-year "cultural revolution" brought China its biggest setback since 1949; but, in spite of this, China as a whole still had a relatively high rate of economic growth in that period. The grain output rose from 193 million tons in 1956 to 282.73 million tons in 1977. Also in this period, crude steel output rose from 4.45 million to 23.74 million tons, coal from 11 million to 93.6 million tons, chemical fertilizers from 0.133 million to 7.238 million tons, machine tools from 25,928 to 198,700 sets, and cotton cloth from 5.770 billion to 10.151 billion metres.

The aim of the ownership system of that period was to strengthen the state-owned economic system and weaken the collectively owned system. Private ownership had almost been abolished. In rural areas, the rural commune economy was established. In the commercial sector, the sales of state-owned enterprises reached over 90 percent during this period. The commodity circulation system suffered considerably.

The ambit of mandatory planning in the coordination system was increased after 1956, while in the period of the "Great Leap Forward" (1958-1960), planning control was decentralized to the provincial level. Owing to the lack of effective macro-control, the economic system did not function efficiently. Central planning was once again emphasized in the adjustment period of 1963-1965, but, because the planning system was again disrupted in the period of the "cultural revolution", there were no improvements or modifications in the conception or practice of planning at that time. In particular, the information flow was weakened.

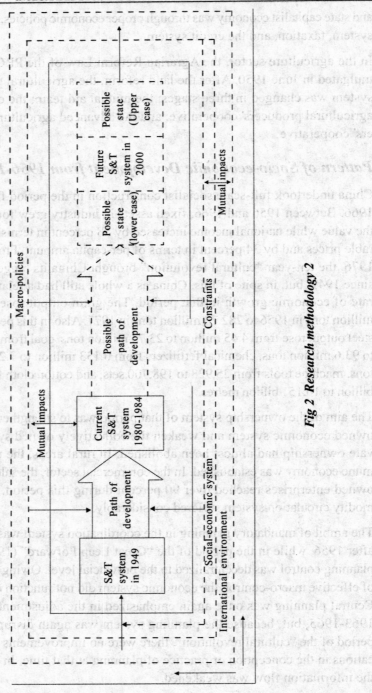

Fig 2 Research methodology 2

The New Pattern of Socio-economic Development after 1978

Since 1977 there has been intense discussion in China about the pattern of economic development. Reform was initiated first in the rural areas by the introduction of the "production responsibility system." The system of contracted responsibility for production, with remuneration linked to output, greatly strengthened the performance of the agricultural sector. Furthermore, a variety of rural activities was encouraged, especially the development of rural enterprises. In 1985, the gross value of the industrial output of rural enterprises ran at around 30 percent of the gross industrial output of the whole nation.

China pressed ahead with its rural reforms, and the rural economy moved towards specialization, large-scale commodity production, and modernization. As a result of the success of this reform, and of a series of experimental reforms in selected areas of the urban economy, a document on the "Decision on Reform of the Economic Structure" was adopted by the Twelfth Central Committee of the Communist Party of China at its Third Plenary Session. Emphasis was placed on the fact that "invigorating enterprises is the key to restructuring the national economy."

Stress was also placed on removing obstacles in the way of the development of the collective economy and the individual economy in cities and rural towns and the creation of conditions for their development, which gave them the protection of the law. The scope of mandatory planning was reduced and guidance planning was extended step by step. Certain farm and sideline products, small articles for daily use, and labour services in the service and repair trades were subjected to market regulation. This new pattern of socio-economic growth was rapid. For example, in 1985, grain production was 370 million tons and coal production, 620 million tons.

China's development strategies and policies from the 1960s to the 1980s were directed toward two main objectives:

Industrialization

Before the 1980s, the importance of developing a heavy industrial base was particularly emphasized. Before 1977, this development effort resulted in the creation of almost the entire range of modern industries. China was now

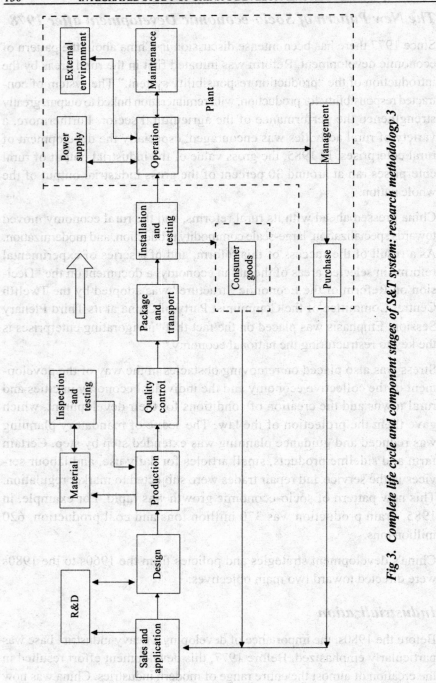

Fig 3. Complete life cycle and component stages of S&T system: research methodology 3

nearly self-sufficient in those industries making capital equipment. This objective was achieved through high investment expenditure and a massive infusion of centrally mobilized resources. Consequently, consumption grew more slowly than income. But, after the economic reforms of 1977, government policies on consumption aimed not only at ensuring a more rapid improvement in living standards, but also at narrowing the differential between heavy and light industry.

Poverty Reduction

The second major development objective was the elimination of the worst aspects of poverty. Owing to the past pattern of development, there was a general absence of individual incomes from property. The income share of the richer group was small; and as a fundamental policy objective the low-income groups had their basic needs satisfied. Formerly the food supply was also guaranteed through a mixture of state rationing and collective self-insurance. The great majority also had access to basic health care, education, and family-planning services. Consequently, life expectancy was raised from 37.7 in 1960-1965 to 64.2 in 1975-1982. The life expectancy at birth of males and females in 1984 was respectively 68 and 70.

The main economic policies in the 1980s and the relationship between the main social and economic policies and the S&T policies are listed Qualitatively in Table 1.

Figure 4 shows the pattern of growth of the Chinese economy by sector from the 1950s to the 1980s, as well as the trends after 1978.

The growth rates for the main agricultural and industrial outputs are also shown in Table 1. The figure clearly demonstrates the socio-economic development pattern and its impact on the agricultural and industrial sectors.

Table 1. Output of selected agricultural and industrial sectors showing the effect of socio-economic development pattern and policies

	1960	1964	Growth rate(%)	1965	1977	Growth rate(%)	1978	1985	Growth rate(%)
Agricultural sector									
Grain (10⁴ tons)	14,350	18,750	6.91	19,453	28,273	3.16	30,477	37,911	3.17
Cotton (10⁴ tons)	106.3	166.3	11.84	209.8	204.9	-0.20	216.7	414.7	9.72
Oil-bearing crops	194.1	336.8	14.77	362.8	401.7	0.86	521.8	1,578.4	17.13
Industrial sector									
Cotton cloth (10⁸ tons)	54.5	47.1	-3.58	62.8	101.5	4.08	110.3	146.7	4.16
Crude steel (10⁴ tons)	1,866	964	-15.22	1,223	2,374	5.68	3,178	4,679	5.68
Chemical fertilizers (10⁴ tons)	40.5	100.8	25.60	172.6	723.8	12.69	869.3	1,322.2	6.17
Crude oil (10⁴ tons)	520	848	13.01	1,131	9,364	19.26	10,405	12,409	2.64
Coal (10⁸ tons)	3.97	2.15	-14.21	2.32	5.50	7.46	6.18	8.72	5.04
Electricity generation (10⁸ kwh)	594	560	-1.46	676	2,234	10.47	2,566	4,107	6.95
Bicycles (10⁴)	176.5	170.5	-0.86	183.8	742.7	12.34	854.0	3,227.7	20.92
Television sets (10⁴)	0.79	0.21	-28.20	2.44	28.46	41.55	51.73	1,667.66	64.24

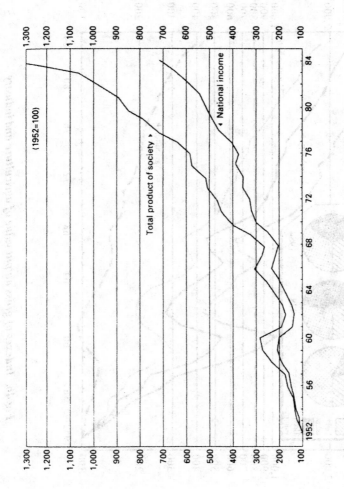

Fig 4a. Indexes of total product of society and national income

Source: *China Statistics Year Book 1985.*

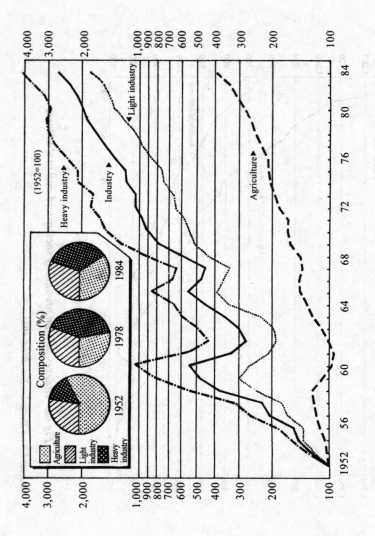

Fig 4b. Indexes of gross output value of agriculture and industry

Source: *China Statistics Yearbook 1985.*

The growth rate in the agricultural sector from the 1960s to 1977 was relatively slow, owing to the lack of scope for the expansion of cultivated land and also to excessive governmental intervention in the application of the misguided "grain first" policy. From the figures for the rate of growth of grain, cotton, etc., in Table 1, the effects of the socio-economic development pattern and policy are self-explanatory The rate of multiple cropping had been increased to an average of 1.5, and traditional labour-intensive cultivation techniques had been refined by extensive improvements in modern irrigation (Table 2).

Table 2. Degree of michanization, electrification, farmland under irrigation and amount of chemical fertilizer used in Chinese agricultural sector

Item	1952	1957	1965	1977	1980
Mechanically tilled land area					
In (10^4 ha)	13.6	263.6	1,557.9	3,841.0	4,099.0
% of total arable land (%)	0.1	2.4	15.0	38.7	41.3
Irrigated area (10^4 ha)	1,945.9	2,733.9	3,305.5	4,499.9	4,488.8
% of arable land	18.5	24.4	31.9	45.3	45
with mechanical and					
electrical irrigation	31.7	120.2	809.3	2,434.9	2,523.1
E letricity consumption					
in rural area (10^8 kWh)	0.5	1.4	37.1	221.9	320.8
Chemical fertilizers					
utilized	7.8	37.3	194.2	648.0	1,269.4

Since the Second Five-Year Plan emphasized the government's policy of promoting the growth of industry, the amount of inputs — capital, labour, and materials — was greatly increased with respect to the output. The growth rate of the industrial sector was consequently high between the 1960s and 1977.

The status and role of S&T at various stages of development is demonstrated by the following three factors:

The growth of S&T personnel and the education

1.The growth of S&T personnel and the education system (Tables 3 and 4).

2 Major achievements of S&T events from the 1960s to the 1980s:

Tale 3. Natural scientific and technological personnel in state-owned units (unit: 10^4 persons)

Item	1952	1978	1980	1981	1982	1983	1984	1985
Engineering	16.4 (38.6)[a]	157.1 (36.1)	186.2 (35.3)	207.7 (36.4)	235.4 (37.6)	280.2 (40.9)	316.2 (42.4)	340.4 (43.6)
Agriculture	1.5 (3.5)	29.4 (6.8)	31.1 (5.9)	32.8 (5.7)	36.2 (5.8)	40.5 (5.9)	43.5 (5.8)	45.1 (5.8)
Public health	12.6 (29.6)	127.6 (29.4)	153.3 (29.0)	168.0 (29.4)	180.7 (28.8)	193.4 (28.2)	207.8 (27.8)	216.1 (27.6)
Scientific research	0.8 (1.9)	31.8 (7.1)	32.3 (6.1)	33.8 (5.9)	37.2 (5.9)	32.8 (4.8)	33.5 (4.5)	33.6 (4.3)
Teaching	11.2 (26.4)	89.4 (20.6)	125.0 (23.7)	129.1 (22.6)	136.9 (21.9)	138.3 (20.2)	145.6 (19.5)	146.5 (18.7)
Total	42.5	434.5	527.6	571.4	626.4	685.2	746.6	781.7
Teachnical personnel per 10,000 population (individuals)	7.4	45.7	53.7	57.4	62.0	67.1	72.5	74.7
Technical personnel, staff and workers per 10,000 population (individuals)	269.0	593.3	657.9	682.5	725.8	781.2	864.4	869.5

[a] Source: Figure in parentheses are percentages of total.

Table 4. Development of education system

	Number of schools			Number of students (ten thousand)		
	1949	1980	Factor increase of 1980 over1949	1949	1980	Factor increase of 1980 over1949
Institutions of higher learning	205	675	3.3	11.7	114.37	9.8
Secondary specialized schools	1,171	3,069	2.6	22.9	124.34	5.4
Ordinary middle schools	4,045	118,377	29	103	5,508.08	53.5
Primary schools	346,800	917,316	2.6	2,439	1,462.96	6
Kindergartens	1,300	170,419	131	1.3	1,150.77	88.5

— October 1964: The first successful test of an atomic bomb;

— September 1965: Synthesis of insulin...;

— October 1966: Successful guided atomic missile test;

— 1966-1967: Comprehensive survey team comprising 30 different disciplines carries out systematic survey in regions above 7,000 metres on Mount Qomalangma;

— June 1967: Test of H-bomb;

— April 1970: First Chinese earth satellite (173 kg in weight) launched;

— September to December 1979: Optical fibre communication system established and tested for operation in Shanghai, Beijmg, and Wuhan;

— October 1979: Liver cancer diagnosis at an early stage through radio-rocket electrophoresis with autoradiography.

3. Programme effort   This was one of the Chinese S&T successes directed by the central government, in which resources were concentrated on large specific projects. However, for a large variety of products this had to be supplemented by the technology market, ie., market orientation should be the crucial factor to promote their development.

National Factor Endowments

Natural Material Resources

The basic physical resources of China — natural resources and existing production capabilities for important products — are shown in Tables 5 and 6.

Table 5. Feature of some selected Chinese natural resources

Item	Unit	China	India	Japan	World average
Arable land	Ha	115-133 million	173	-	-
Arable land	Ha/capita	0.1	0.2	0.03	0.35
Forest covering	%	12	22.7	67.9	31.3
Grassland	Ha	224 million	11 million	0.6 million	-
Annual stream flow (water resources)	m³	2,614.4 billion	-	-	47,000 billion
Annual stream flow per capita	m³/capita	2,563	-	-	10,800
Hydropower resources	10 million kW	6.76	-	-	-
Proved coal reserves	10⁹ tons	737.1a	121.36a	-	-
Iron ore reserves	10⁹ tons	47.20	22.4	-	-

ᵃ Source: *Statistical Yearbook of China 1985.*

Table 6a.   Output of main industrial products

	Output in 1980	Output in 1985	Factor increase of 1980 over 1949
Coal(10^6 tons)	620	872	18.4
Crude oil (10^6 tons)	105,95	124.90	882
Electricity (10^6 kWh)	300,600	410.700	69
Steel (10^6 tons)	37,12	46.79	231
Machine tools	134,000	121,000	82
Chenical fertilizers (10^6 tons)	12.32	13.22	2,160
Cotton yarn (10^6 tons)	2.93	3.53	8
Sugar (10^6 tons)	2.57	4.51	11.8
Wristwatches (units)	22.67	54.47	
TV sets (units)	2.49	16.67	
Radios (units)	30.04	16.00	

Table 6b.   Output of main farm products (10^6 tons)

	Output in 1980	Output in 1985	Factor increase of 1980 over 1949
Grain	320,56	379.11	1.8
Cotton	2,707	4.147	5.1
Edible oil	7,691	15.784	2.0
Pork, mutton, beef	12,055	17.607	4.4
Aquatic products	4,5	7.05	9.0

Although China has a fair amount of natural resources, in per-capita terms they are low, and unevenly distributed. A proper locational policy for industry is necessary in order to manage correctly the country's transportation and resource distribution problems. China world ranking for certain products is shown in table 7.

Human Resources

China is rich in human resources. Her population was 1.045 billion in 1985. The educational level of the population has improved, but figures on a percentage basis still fall short of those of other countries, particularly the gross enrolment ratio in higher education.

China's factor endowments vary widely between regions. At the initial stage

Table 7. **World ranking in production capability of**
selected products in 1985

Item	World ranking
Grain	2
Cotton	1
Meat	2
Steel	4
Coal	2
Crude oil	6
Electricity generation	5
Value added (industrial)	
Value added (agricultural)	1

of development, <u>human resources and socio-cultural factors play a more critical role than natural factor endowments</u>. But factor endowments are also important as a potential source of development.

After 1949, with the emphasis on local self-sufficiency rather than specialization, the comparative advantages of different regions were not fully explored. A comparative study between Shanghai (a formerly relatively developed metropolis) and the Northwest region (which was underdeveloped before 1949) was carried out and this illustrates some of the problems.

Shanghai was a large metropolis before 1949. It had begun to develop modern industry in 1865, when the Jiangnan Bureau of Manufacture was established. By the time of the First World War there were more than 100 enterprises. The first electric power plant was constructed in 1882, and the Shanghai-Nanjing and the Shanghai-Hanchow railways were completed in 1908 and 1909 respectively. Banking and financial services were also developed in the early twentieth century. Therefore, although Shanghai had hardly any mineral resources, its industrial output was quite high owing to its skilled labor force, convenient transportation, and sociocultural factors: before 1949, there were around 200,000 privately owned enterprises and a total number of employees of 428,000, constituting respectively 36.01 percent and 26.06 percent of the total for the whole nation.

The Northwest region of China comprises five provinces: Shaanxi, Gansu,

Ningxia, Qinghai and Xinjiang. Here, many minorities live together. Lying on China's northwest border, it forms an arid and semi-arid belt. Its area is vast and its population sparse, but it is resource-rich (Table 8). Historically, it was the birthplace of Chinese culture and the place where occidental and oriental civilizations once converged. Nonetheless, communication and transportation in this region are poor, with some places difficult to access. Furthermore, the ecological environment is quite fragile. Although huge strides have been made in economic and social progress since 1949, the region's level of development is comparatively low.

Table 8. Natural resources and factor cndowments in Northwest region, 1985

Item	Shaanxi	Gansu	Ningxia	Qinghai	Xinjiang
Population (10^3)	30,020	24,410	4,150	4,070	13,610
Mineral resources					
No. of types	86	66	99	59	115
Major resources	Molybdenum, mercury,asbestos,coal	Nickelm, platinum	Coal, gypsum	Lithium, potassium salt, magnesium salt, sulphur, cobalt	Coal, pertoleum
Grassland (10^3 ha)		13,330		33,450	50,000
Arable land (10^3 ha)	4,113	2.26[a]	933	588	9,330

a. Ha per capita available.

Table 8 shows the natural factor endowments of the Northwest region, and Table 9 is selected data for comparative purposes. It can be seen that the Northwest is rich in natural resources, but also that its gross value of industrial output (GVIAO) is far behind that of Shanghai. Table 8 also shows the economies of scale and comparative advantages of Shanghai and the region, and reveals that different areas (provinces or municipalities) have nearly the same industrial structure. While the efforts made by different provinces and regions towards "self-reliance" are evident, it is also clear that the comparative advantages of the regions have not been fully explored.

Agricultural Sector

Through their long experience of farming, the Chinese have developed a whole series of traditional methods with intensive cultivation as the key link. Internal upheavals and warfare in the first half of the twentieth century weakened the limited development of agricultural services and led to the widespread destruction of the rural infrastructure. After liberation, a socialist managerial system was adopted in China's countryside and remuneration by workpoints was popularized. The collective economy of China's agriculture for years was affected by an over concentration of managerial powers and a unitary form of operation, both of which dampened peasant enthusiasm. But considerable development of irrigation and drainage systems to regulate the water supply, the provision of chemical fertilizers by the government, and the very high input of labour promoted agricultural growth. The rural reform also stimulated exceptionally rapid growth in agricultural production. Rural incomes and food consumption rose as a result of rapidly rising yields.

Industrial Sector

Nearly the entire range of modern industry has now been set up with much emphasis on the manufacture of capital equipment. In the past three decades, China has manufactured much new equipment unaided. In almost every industry, through self-reliance, plants large and small have been created. Special efforts have been made to spread manufacturing to backward regions. Meanwhile, industrial research institutes and the more advanced factories have striven to make new products and to master new technologies.

As a result, a solid foundation of engineering experience and a wide range of technical capabilities have been established. But owing to the rigidity of the economic and S&T system, advances have been made mainly through extensive growth. Technological self-reliance was sought not just at the national level, but also in individual ministries, provinces, localities, and even enterprises. The result of this was a wasteful allocation of scarce resources and slowness in product innovation and utility improvement.

The links between industry and agriculture were weakened in the past by the "grain first" policy. Cash crops were neglected for a relatively long period and this affected the development of agrofood and other agro-related industries. The linkage was unilateral in the past, industries providing the major inputs to agriculture, such as chemical fertilizers, diesel oil, farm machinery, etc., while the agricultural sector only provided primary prod-

Table 9. Selected data for comparison

Item	Shanghai	Shaanxi	Gansu	Ningxia	Qinghai	Xinjiang
GVIAO (1985)a	89.2	25.6	16.1	3.3	3.1	12.4
GVIAO (1985)a	2.3	6.8	4.2	1.0	1.0	4.9
GVIAO (1985)a	86.9	18.8	11.9	2.3	2.1	7.5
Major sector output (enetrprise unit numbers/ value outprt $\times 10^6$ yuan)						
Mineral mining (all types)	4/4	704/777	492/980	121/387	61/68	457/124
Agro. food	754/3764	1599/1517	675/808	215/206	162/224	1243/1122
Textiles	844/14648	393/3082	120/556	46/135	20/152	309/1273
Handicrafts	155/816	163/49	117/51	20/6	36/19	110/26
Chemical engineering	433/5745	415/847	183/1110	64/101	29/96	101/182
Building materials and non-mining manufactures	566/1768	1744/780	625/469	210/110	174/108	828/417
Metal processing	1034/11834	1004/957	608/2360	188/249	85/251	268/197
Machine-building	1586/11279	1178/2559	481/947	141/336	142/227	417/393
Electronics and communications manufacture	135/2357	6/132	4,100	1/9	-	3/38

a. Ha per capita available.

ucts — the basic food for industrial workers.

There were 7,816,680 scientific and technical personnel at the end of 1985. The design capability of a country is an important measure of S&T capability. Science's impact on society is mediated through those professions concerned with design and construction. In 1981, there were 2,654 design institutes with more than 346,000 staff, and the construction industry's manpower had increased to more than 5 million. China had also established a large R&D force.

Theoretically, the country had already established a scientific and technological capability. Yet, industrial technology in China generally lagged behind that of the industrialized and newly industrializing countries. The current status of S&T and its rigid structure were derived from two sources: first, the Soviet model of S&T, inherited from the institutions and organizations that were set up in the First Five-Year Plan period, and, second, that derived from the political environment of the "cultural revolution" period. Modification of the Soviet-derived rigid structure took great effort and time, while the effect of the "cultural revolution" created an S&T gap with advanced countries, which also would take time to close.

Before 1949, there were just over 600 persons engaged in scientific research. Furthermore, research that was closely linked with production was practically non-existent. Yet, during more than 35 years of effort, through ups and downs, R&D has played an important role in China's socio-economic development. R&D institutions were unable to realize their potential fully owing to the lack of horizontal linkages, the overcentralization of R&D forces in the Chinese Academy of Sciences, the existence of different ministries, and the segregation of the civilian and defence sectors. Moreover, the traditional organization of R&D in China put too much emphasis on "technology-push" rather than on responding to demand. Consequently, exploitation of the technology market was proposed in the reform of the S&T management system.

There are six types of R&D institutions, as follows:

1. The Chinese Academy of Sciences. This has at present around 154 institutes under its organization.

2. Ministerial and provincial research units. These are scientific research organizations that function under various ministries of the State Council or those at the local level. For example, the Ministry of Water Resources and Electric Power has eight research institutes: the Electric Power Research Institute in Beijing; the Institute of Water Conservancy and Hydroelectric Power Research Institute in Beijing, which is jointly governed by the Chinese Academy of Sciences and the ministry; the Xi'an Thermal Power Engineering Research Institute; the Nanjing Automation Research Institute; the Electric Power Construction Research Institute; and the Nanjing Hydraulic Research Institute and Scientific and Technical Information Institute.

Another example is the railways. The Railway Ministry established the China Academy of Railway Science in 1950. This consists of 10 research institutes: Railway Transportation; Locomotive and Rolling Stock; Railway Engineering; Signalling and Communication; Metals and Chemistry; Computer Technology; Technical Information; Standards and Metrology; and Southwest and Northwest regions.

3. The university sphere Research organizations in colleges and universi-

ties amount to around 1,400 with 30,000 S&T personnel.

4. The factory research sorce These are research organizations run by factories and mines. Their main concerns are project-connected.

5. Research force in national defence   These are research organizations of national defence. The role of R&D in atomic research achievements, as well as in rockets and satellites, is well known.

6. The Chinese Academy of Social Sciences (CASS). This had 31 research institutes and 2,431 researchers in 1985.

In China, it should also be noted that there are very few private R&D institutions.

Table 10. Distrnbution of institutions and S&T personnel

	No. of institutions	Total no. of workers and staff	Personnel engaged in S&T activities		
			Total	Scientists and engineers	Other S&T personnel
Subordinate to departments under the State Coundil	622	266,412	204,370	93,026	36,787
Subordinate to provinces, autonomous regions, and municipalities directly under the central government	3.946	434,354	313,146	105,850	75,385
Subordinate to the Chenese Acadcmy of Sciences	122	69,650	58,220	32,174	8,828
Total	4,690	770,416	575,736	231,050	121,000

Table 10 gives the distribution of S&T personnel and institutions under the various authorities.

Case-studies in the Different Economic Sectors

Seven sectors in the economy were chosen for research. The rationale for the choice of these sectors is given in Fig. 5. The case-studies focused on the agricultural sector, the light industry sector (textile and agrofood), the infrastructure sector (electric power), the heavy industry sector (iron and steel, machine-building, and machine tools) and the electronics. Two illustrative case-studies are described in detail here, one on the agrofood sector and the other on the steel industry.

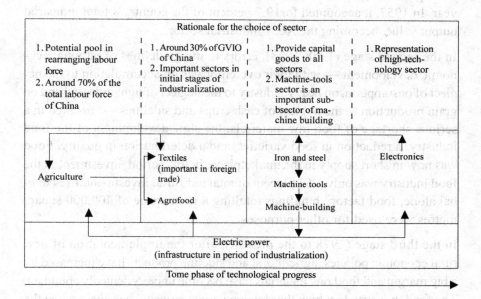

Fig. 5. Rationale for the choice of sectors

Food sector

Before its liberation in 1949, China did not have a fully fledged food industry. In the large cities there were only a few enterprises engaged in food processing, vegetable-oil pressing, livestock-slaughtering and cigarette making, while in the rural areas there were only manual workshops. The country's food industry altogether numbered 1,379 enterprises with a total of 100,000 employees. Less than one-fourth of these enterprises operated with machine power and hired more than 500 workers.

For China, therefore, food processing is a new branch of industry. During the past three decades or so, the food industry has undergone three stages of development.

During the first stage (1949-1957), the industry received 37 percent of the country's total industrial investment. Under the principle of cooperation between urban and rural areas and between industry and agriculture, many food processing workshops were set up both in the cities and in rural areas. During these eight years, the food industry grew at a rate of 13.2 percent a year. In 1957, it accounted for19.7 percent of the country's total industrial output value, becoming the No. 1 industrial sector.

In the second stage (1958-1978), errors in the guidelines of national economic development — with their overemphasis on accumulation to the neglect of onsumption, on heavy industry to the neglect of light industry, and on grain production to the neglect of cash crops and sidelines — resulted in a serious shortage of food raw materials, the slow development of the food industry, a reduction in food varieties, and a deterioration in quality. Food was now in short supply in the marketplace. In this period, investment in the food industry was only 1.53 percent of total industrial investment. In Shanghai alone, food factory buildings totalling a floor space of 400,000 square metres were used for other purposes.

In the third stage (1978 to the present), after the implementation of new rural economic policies, agricultural and sideline products have increased by a big margin and food raw materials have become unprecedentedly abundant. The food industry, to which the state now gives priority, has again taken the road of vigorous development. Investment in the industry constituted 2.96 percent of the country's total industrial investment in 1980, 4.3 percent in 1981, and 5.4 percent in 1982 and continues to rise. The momentum of development in rural townships is even greater. From 1979 to 1982, the output value of the food industry increased by an annual average of 10.4 percent. This was accompanied by an increase in food variety and a marked easing of food shortages in the marketplace. By 1983, the food industry had diversified into 24 separate trades. There were more than 60,000 state-owned enterprises with 2.5 million employees, producing 6 billion yuan in output value. The food processing sector led other industries in contributing tax revenue to the state. Food exports earned US$3.5 billion.

Total output value registered an increase of 13.2 percent during the First Five-Year Plan period (1953-1957); a decrease of 1.7 percent during the Second Five-Year Plan period (1958-1962); and increases of 11.4 percent from 1963 to 1965, 2.4 percent for the Third Five-Year Plan period (1965-

1969), 8.4 percent for the Fourth Five-Year Plan period (1970-1975), and 9.3 percent for the 1979-1983 period.

Self-reliance in science and technology. The food industry suffered from various restrictions and developed slowly and so cannot be expected to have made much technical head-way. Technical progress in the field was negligible during the 20 years from 1958 to 1978. The present and future direction of the food industry is to achieve high-speed development on the basis of enlarged reproduction. The strategy aims to make up for the long neglect by means of a sudden take-off. Therefore technical development is still directed towards popularizing existing techniques, with the import and development of new and sophisticated technologies taking second place. This trend is best illustrated by the proliferation of township food enterprises applying low-level techniques.

Though China's food industry has undergone unprecedented development in recent years, it is still very backward. The country's total output of farm products is in fact quite large, but the per-capita amount is small and cannot be increased quickly. China is a success agriculturally. With less than 7 percent of the world's cultivated land, it feeds nearly one-fourth of the global population. However, in comparison with that of other countries the speed of development is slow.

Furthermore, China's average per-unit area yield is lower than the world's highest, though it comes up to the world average. The per-capita output of various kinds of food, particularly milk, is also lower than the world average.

At present, the output value of the food industry in developed countries is usually greater than that of agriculture. It is 169 percent, for example, in the United States and 232 percent in Japan. In China, the output value of the food industry is only one-third that of agriculture.

In the cooking process used by Chinese families, the discard rate is 20-30 percent for vegetables, 30-40 percent for fish, and 20 percent for chicken and ducks. If the food industry is technically advanced enough, these leftovers can possibly be processed into food, or into feedstuffs, which can again be turned into food in the form of livestock or poultry. Because of a low capability in storage, processing, and transportation, a large amount of grain has to be stored in farmers' homes. This alone leads, because of insect pests, to a waste of 15 billion kg, or 8 percent of the stored amount. China annually produces 8 million tons of fruits, but can store and keep only

5.3 percent of them, resulting usually in a waste of 5-25 percent. The wastage rate of vegetables is also 25 percent. Similarly, the processing ability for aquatic products is less than 10 percent of the output, causing an annual loss of 1 billion yuan. A lack of processing capacity for potatoes leaves 2.5-5 billion kg rotten, with a value of 0.5-1 billion yuan. The loss rate for grain products processed by traditional methods is 2 percent greater than grain processed by machines. In 1980, however, grain processed by machines made up only 28.6 percent of the total, and as a result some 5 billion kg of grain was wasted. Compared with the traditional pressing technique in edible oil extraction, the soaking method gives a 5 percent increase in output, but only 13 percent of oil-bearing seeds are now processed by the soaking method, leading to a loss of 350 million kg of vegetable oil.

This inadequate production capability is closely connected with the low level of investment in the industry. The food industry in Shanghai, for example, has given 9.8 billion yuan to the state over the past 30 years, compared with only 50 million yuan invested by the state in food enterprises during the same period. As a result of the lack of investment, food factories have to operate with out-of-date equipment, which often breaks down. At present, with the situation in rural areas getting much better and offering greatly increased amounts of farm products, shortfalls have been replaced by overabundance. The consequent stockpiling of farm products calls for an urgent, large-scale development of the food industry.

There is no difficulty in developing suitable technologies in the fields of storage, transportation, and primary processing. What is needed is investment funds and the popularization of technologies. Because the accumulation of funds needs time, low-level and even primitive techniques will continue to exist for some time yet.

A surplus of certain farming products cannot by itself meet the demands of the food industry. A large-scale food industry needs large-scale, regional raw materials and a supply base that is guaranteed by the cultivation of suitable varieties. In other countries, food enterprises usually have their own farms or have long-term contracts with farmers. The enterprises decide what to plant, how much, and when, and even dictate the kind of fertilizer to be used and the time of harvest. For example, in the United States, the state of Florida is a producer of oranges, the state of California of peaches, and the state of Hawaii of pineapples; in Japan, the counties of Ehimi and Shizona yield great amounts of tangerines, while Hokkaido is a producer of asparagus. Such specialized economic zones make it possible to set up large-scale, highly efficient and highly mechanized canned-food factories, wineries, and sugar-making factories.

China lacks adequate raw material bases. Structurally, the food industry is characterized by scattered raw material supply bases and small-scale operations. In terms of economic relationships, the practice in China is the direct opposite of that in other countries: here it is the farms or farmers that run food enterprises, instead of vice versa. The existing supply bases, like the green bean base near Nanjing, now face serious difficulties. Many food factories, set up on the basis of "doing whatever is available," simply cannot expand in scale and become highly efficient.

The comprehensive use of raw materials, in effect, increases their quantity. Technical treatment immediately after the harvest and timely industrial processing can prevent the decay of grain and reduce losses. Modern processing technologies can turn inedible ingredients of grains into edibles or materials of higher value. Technologies for the comprehensive use of raw materials are as yet far from being developed in China. Neither is enough attention paid to the resources of waste products. Waste matter and leftovers from the country's gourmet powder factories, sugar refining factories, butcheries, and breweries alone are enough to feed 4 billion chicken each year. Some countries in the world have developed unique food processing industries for export-based on imported raw materials combined with advanced technologies. Denmark's fruit jams, the Netherlands' cocoa and Switzerland's instant coffee, for example, are all products made from imported raw materials. China has yet to build such industries.

In order to create an industrialized food industry and raise economic efficiency, large-scale raw material bases must be set up in China, and varieties of food crops suitable for industrialized processing cultivated. To demonstrate the distance yet to be covered, we could cite the example of potatoes. Potatoes processed for their starch in some countries contain 22-24 percent of starch, and some new varieties reach a figure as high as 28 percent. In China, however, the starch content is only 12-20 percent.

At this stage in the development of the country's food technology, China has engaged in a series of programs including directional breeding, technical guidance and services, the popularization of fine crop strains, pricing policy, long-term purchase contracts, and regional planning.

Since the shortage of food resources is an important factor limiting the development of China's food industry, continuing neglect of the establishment of raw material supply bases will only perpetuate this shortage. This in turn will restrict the development of a modern food industry. On the other hand, with advanced technologies we can enlarge the sources of food raw materials through comprehensive utilization, high-tech processing, and the development of a sector which processes raw materials for export.

Except for the consumption of food grains, which is higher in China than in other countries, the per-capita consumption of other foods is quite low. And except for sugar, which has a 90 percent commodity rate, the rate for market-oriented foods in China is generally low: 14.25 percent for grains, 43.7 percent for pigs, 1.95 percent for beef cattle, 6.1 percent for mutton, and 53. 1 percent for cooking oil.

The present low level of consumption offers great potential for the development of the food industry. Food science and technology, therefore, have considerable market prospects. For instance, there is stockpiling of such starch-containing products as maize, potatoes, and cassava in some part of the country, while elsewhere starch, noodles, and vermicelli are in short supply. This can be avoided through proper utilization of the industry. The extremely low level of commercialized food products demonstrates that the food industry is facing challenges from a natural economy and from traditional consumption patterns. A solution to this problem depends on sustained economic development and greatly improved living standards.

China's food industry is not complete. This is reflected in a weakness in the supply of basic raw and accessory materials for the flour, oil, protein, sugar, and food additive industries.

The flour industry in the United States turns out about 100 varieties of flour. In Japan, 64 varieties of flour are used for making bread. China has only two; a coarse type and a fine type. In cooking oil, there are dozens of varieties, and these, hydrogenized to varying degrees, can be mixed to make hundreds of varieties. In Japan, for example, cooking oils number more than 200. In China, however, there are only two types; unprocessed raw oil, which dominates the market, and a small amount of second-grade oil.

There is as yet no protein industry in China. Every year, the 2 million tons of cottonseed cakes and 1 million tons of rapeseed cakes, as well as peanut and sesame cakes — all by-products of oil pressing — are mostly used as animal feed and manure.

Maize, a source of sugar after sugar-cane and beet, is a staple crop in China. Glucose, maltose, levulose, top-levoluse syrup and other raw materials needed by the food industry can be produced from maize starch. But China has not fully utilized maize. The starch industry remains at a simple level and is still confined to turning out one product raw starch. Starch reprocessing is very limited and no development has been made toward making denatured starch and starch derivatives. Of the starch used overseas, only 30 percent is raw starch, and 70 percent is reprocessed starch. The number of starch derivatives exceeds 100.

Food additives including trace elements, microbial elements, pigments, germicides, thickeners, emulsifiers, and special condiments are very important in raising food quality. They are widely used overseas. In China, there are fewer varieties and their output is small. "Grandma Bean Curd," a popular dish from Sichuan Province, has become one of the main soft-can foods in Japan simply because a special condiment with the flavour of "Grandma Bean Curd" has been developed and mass-produced there.

In short, because of the rough and simple processing of farm products in China, food raw materials are not fully and rationally utilized.

In the meantime, it is difficult to turn out high-increment products owing to the shortage of necessary food raw materials — particularly of special basic ingredients — that results from an absence of intensive processing.

The food industry in the United States developed 9,747 new products between 1970 and 1979. In Japan, there are more than 300 kinds of bread and over 1,400 types of canned food. Products on foreign markets include cholesterol-free, sugar-free, and salt-free foods, low-caloric food, and low-sodium food, as well as high-energy, high-protein, and high-cellulose foods. There is also food for the young, the aged, and athletes, and foods with various kinds of local flavours.

Although an increasing number of new food products have come into being in China in recent years, those foods sold in volume have remained the same as before. Baby food and fast food have not as yet established a reputation. Many new products often disappear shortly after their introduction.

Decades of neglect in the food industry have resulted in a huge gap between supply and demand; and the development of basic raw and accessory materials and new products is largely out of the question. Coordination among specialized enterprises does not yet exist in China, owing to defects in the economic structure as well as to China's traditions in the food-processing sector. A large number of newly established enterprises are gearing their production directly to the consumer market, while the basic materials industry gets little attention. As a result, the limited number of food scientists and technicians have not been able to devote themselves to strengthening the foundations of the food industry.

Food equipment manufacturing is a backwater of China's industry, receiving little attention and developing at a slow pace. Except for the canned-food, dairy, soft drinks, grain-processing and oil-pressing industries, whose equipment is partially provided by specialized factories, the old factories in other fields have to depend on their own repair and spare-parts workshops for new equipment. It was not until 1978 that industries began studying the problem and started manufacturing food-related equipment.

The present situation can be described as one of a weak foundation, low technological standards, and a lack of sophistication in equipment. The development of equipment that carries out intensive processing and permits a comprehensive utilization of raw materials has only just started. China's food-equipment manufacturing industry is backward. Canned food production in China, for example, is a sector with a relatively high level of mechanization: each worker produces 4.7 tons of canned food a year. But this is only one-fortysixth of what a worker in the United States produces. The efficiency of Chinese machines for making bottles is only one-tenth that of those made overseas. China-made machines can pack only one-quarter the amount of candies packed by similar machines.

China is capable of making small renovations to simple separate machines or production lines and gradually copying them. In 1980 the Baiyun Rice and Flour Products Factory in Guangzhou introduced a fast-noodle production line. Within a year, the factory was able to pay off the foreign investment of US$280,000. The factory renovated the "irrational" parts of the production line, raising its efficiency as well as the quality of fried noodles. Moreover, all the spare parts that are susceptible to wear and tear can be substituted by those made in China. In 1983, China's first fast-noodle production line was successfully trial produced, passed appraisal, and was put into operation in Tianjin. The production line cost only 270,000 yuan. A renovation was made on the production line later, changing de-watering through frying into de-watering through steaming. The change gave birth to a steamed fast-noodle production line. By July 1985, 60 steamed fast-noodle production lines made by the Renmin Machinery Factory of Guangzhou had been installed and put into operation in many cities. In the food industry, there are a good many facilities of this kind which can be manufactured by unspecialized factories. However, despite the fact that China has the ability to do this, repeated imports of the same technology are still a common practice. Up until now, about 40 fast-noodle production lines have been bought. By the end of 1983, foreign investment used by China's food industry for introducing advanced technologies amounted to over US$100 million.

The New Sugar Refinery in Jilin Province was a major project in the First Five-Year Plan period (1953-1958). All the facilities and technology were supplied by Poland. The refinery was designed to treat 1,000 tons of beet per day. Technical renovations and the addition of equipment increased the refinery's capacity to 1,500 tons by 1980. The technical level and economic efficiency of the refinery have always been counted as high in China, yet its equipment and technology, in fact, belong to 1940s Poland. In 1983, the refinery introduced from Denmark a cleaning technology, seven key pieces of sugar-refining equipment, and six control systems. These facilities, after some technical transformations, can treat 3,000 tons of beet per day.

The equipment in the above example is typical of that currently used in the food industry. Thirty years ago, China built part of its food industry with imported equipment. Factories operating with such equipment have given the best performance during these 30 years. Now China's food industry is 30 to 40 years behind the developed countries, and it therefore has to continue importing advanced equipment to catch up.

Food factories can make small renovations to existing machines, and specialized equipment manufacturing factories have the ability to copy and improve simple machines, but they are unable to manufacture highly efficient, technically advanced equipment in complete sets, let alone develop new models of machines. This is because the latter are closely related to the general level of the technology employed by the food industry and the scale of that industry. There will be no demand for highly efficient equipment without the existence of large scale enterprises.

Packaging is an indispensable part of high-grade, high-increment products. Food and food-packaging industries promote each other. China still has to import many packing materials and containers. To some extent, foreign countries can even influence our food production and export by controlling the export of packaging materials to China. China's export foods still face the problem of "first-rate materials, second-rate quality, third-rate packaging, and fourth-rate price," giving poor economic results.

With regard to glass containers, the trend overseas is toward lighter and thinner types strengthened by chemical processes. Improved sealing technology has given rise to various kinds of push-turn covers and plastic-metal composite caps. We still use old-type caps that are difficult to open, in spite of repeated complaints from consumers.

Overseas tin-plate making has developed from double cold rolling to continuous casting, and from electroplating to organic polyester coating. China imports large amounts of material for tin plate. Can-making overseas has developed from double reeling to deep punching, three-segment connecting, and welding. These technologies are still not used in China, and only a few sample machines have been imported. Owing to an inability to control lead penetration in the welding process, Chinese-made cans face the danger of being squeezed out of the international market.

The development of compound material for plastic packaging takes place even more quickly overseas. The appearance of plastic tins is due to the invention of compound materials able to withstand high temperatures. Different layers of this material play complementary functions, resulting in an ideal packaging material for food. In China, the quality of the paper, aluminium foil, and plastic used for compound packing materials is not yet up to standard. The so-called "soft packaging," with only one layer of plastic, that is seen on the market does not meet hygienic requirements.

In general, the cost of packaging does not exceed 10 percent of the total cost of production in foreign countries; the cost for ordinary food varieties may come to only to 3-4 percent of the total. The main way to cut down on packaging costs is to set up highly centralized packaging materials and containers enterprises. Some such enterprises overseas have developed into multinational corporations. Packaging materials in China, owing to price hikes for raw materials, can account for 30-40 percent of the total production cost of food, adding to the burden on consumers and hindering the development of packed food.

The more intensively food is processed, the more coordination among specialized departments is needed. This is one of the weakest links in China's managerial system and economic structure. Food technology is subject to packaging technology, which in turn is subject to the materials industry.

Some of China's food products are comparable with, or even better than, those overseas. The quality gap in the final product is often due not to technology per se, but to raw and accessory materials, packaging, equipment, factory conditions, and circulation links.

It must be admitted, however, that the technology in most factories is backward. This reflects a weakness in the development of technology which is based upon experience rather than a systematic study of mechanisms. Consequently, some operational processes cannot be flexibly adapted or modified to guarantee the quality of products. This indicates an inadequacy in technological personnel, which hampers the popularization of more mature technologies.

In our push for the industrialization of traditional foods, the research and development of technology is also crucial. Technology should not be just a means of expanding traditional methods; it involves different, modern methods which can nevertheless be based on the mechanisms of the old. China's traditional method of making bean curd is worth studying. It is now not as advanced as those available overseas because of a shortage of technical personnel and research means.

The starch industry demonstrates the backwardness of the technology. In foreign countries, a closed process is used, which needs less water, discharges less waste water, employs technologically advanced equipment, and is highly efficient. The advantages of the new production method are a high rate of starch collection, high quality, and a better comprehensive utilization. The utilization rate of maize reaches 99 percent. However, in China, the open process is still used. It needs large quantities of water, discharges too much waste, causes pollution, has a low rate of starch collection, and produces starch of low quality. Additionally, many exploitable resources are wasted in those small factories with a low utilization rate.

Production of 500 kg of starch from potatoes, for example, involves a waste of 80 kg of protein.

In other countries, raw materials are processed at multiple levels, which results in their complete utilization. For instance, in processing kelp Japan makes some 60 different kinds of pickles. Even the water used for boiling kelp is made into a soft-packed food. In China kelp is merely dried in the sun before being marketed, which involves no technology at all. The existing technology is not widely applied, and this sometimes causes big technological gaps between factories in China. This phenomenon, not limited to the food industry, is due to an economy of shortages and a lack of competition caused by underdeveloped commodity production. As a result, technically backward enterprises have the "right of existence" and similar factories still continue to be built. There is not enough motivation to raise comprehensive economic efficiency, nor is there pressure to do so.

Up to now, China has not had a short- or long-term plan for training technical personnel for its food industry. A very limited number of students are being trained in the country's universities and colleges to become technicians and food industry administrators. In the light industrial sector, which has the biggest number of trainees, only 2,682 persons were trained in institutions of higher education during the Sixth Five-Year Plan period. During the same period, about the same number were trained in secondary technical schools. If the situation remains unchanged, there will be only one technician for every two food factories by the end of this century.

In the 60,000 state-owned food enterprises, technical personnel make up less than 1 percent of all staff and workers. Technicians with a college education are very scarce. The 300,000 collectively owned enterprises have their own comprehensive food research institutes. Three provinces and autonomous regions have no food research institutes of any kind. Most of the existing research organizations deal with the primary processing of grain and edible oil.

Take the starch industry, for example. Many countries have set up national research institutes. There is the Northern Agriculture Research Center in the United States and the National Grain and Potatoprocessing Research Centre in Germany. Companies or factories dealing with starch or starch sugar, as well as some universities, have setup their own research institutes.

There is not a single research body in China's starch industry, nor do universities and colleges offer courses related to starch production.

We can also make comparisons with Japan. From central to local departments and to enterprises, Japan's food industry has an established system of research institutes. Located in the science city, Tsukuba, is the state-run general food research institute, which operates under the jurisdiction of the Ministry of Agriculture, Forestry, and Aquatic Products Industry and has about 100 senior researchers. Every county has a food research institute with 10-40 researchers. Most of the food enterprises have their own research and development department with researchers accounting for 20-40 percent of the total workforce. All the research institutes have a rational division of work and cooperate with one another, avoiding repetition and waste. The research budget of Japan's scientific research food industry in 1980 reached about 1 billion Renminbi (RMB). Japan also has a complete educational system to train qualified personnel for the food industry. Many universities have courses in food disciplines, while some big enterprises have set up training schools and food colleges offering two-year courses.

The lack of scientific and technological personnel is normally a major factor affecting self-reliance in science and technology. This problem is more serious, however, in China's neglected food industry. A way out lies in reforming the economic structure to allow researchers and technicians in the food industry to develop their talent to the full by occupying proper posts. China's old administrative system makes impossible a rational distribution of technical and research personnel. The latter face all sorts of possible technical problems in individual factories. Meanwhile, the technical personnel in research institutes often have to study basic problems in a state of isolation. This results in a failure to pool research personnel for major projects, which could have offered a way of solving the problem of the general shortage of personnel.

Further development of food science and technology, and of the food industry itself, cannot be assured if necessary measures are not taken in macro-management. What is needed is a feasible program for the development of the food industry, including programs for different trade lines and a science and technology development plan. At present, food production is scattered throughout a dozen or so economic sectors, including light industry, commerce, agriculture, animal husbandry, fishery, and land reclamation. As a result, it is even more difficult to make a coordinated and feasible general plan for the industry.

Second, there must be a definitive policy for the industry. Whether it is categorized as being closer to agriculture — providing basic food for the people — or to industry — offering high-grade consumer goods will determine its scope. Overseas, canned food is a low- or medium-grade consumer good, while in China it is regarded as high-grade. Many agricultural products are developed because of price subsidies. The food industry often has to use raw materials at a negotiated price because of a shortage of allocated, low-priced materials. Price gaps put factories producing industrial foods at a disadvantage, compared with those producing primary agricultural foods. High tax rates have hindered the development of some food products. For instance, the tax rate for maltose and glucose is as high as 30 percent.

Coordination among specialized enterprises is essential to the development of large-scale socialized production. Coordination among various fields, and links between production and trade, are especially needed in the food industry, particularly by enterprises doing intensive processing. An absence of socialized coordination necessitates the maintenance of a workshop production method. China's economic mode, structure, and management system have forced enterprises to try to do everything themselves, regardless of their scale. The food industry is no exception. Overseas, canned food factories do not produce their own cans. In Japan, for example, all empty cans are provided by three specialized factories. All the cans have brand names printed or pasted on, so that the canned food factories have only to do the packing. A production line making a single type of can helps standardize the product and makes it easier to employ advanced automation facilities. In China, however, all the 700 canned food enterprises make their own containers.

There is an even larger gap between China and developed countries in micro-management. In Japan, one yen of fixed assets in the food industry can give an annual output value of 35 yen, while in China one yuan generates only 3.7 yuan, one-tenth of Japan's output.

Iron and Steel

Iron and steel is a traditional industry. China had already mastered the problems of production, construction, and design capability. The present problem is insufficient production capability, leading to an increase in the importation of steel in recent years. For example, steel imports were 12,300,000 tons in 1984 and 20,030,000 tons in 1985. To illustrate the problems in the industry, a micro case-study of the Capital Iron and Steel Corporation, an enterprise following the overall economic contract responsibility system, is presented.

The Beijing-based Capital Iron and Steel Corporation (CISC) is an iron and steel complex whose activities include mining and iron-ore dressing. CISC's predecessor was the Shijingshan Ironworks, which was established in 1919 and produced only iron before 1949. The aggregate output of iron for 30 years was a mere 286,200 tons. The plant was rebuilt since founding of the PRC. Now CISC mines and dresses 14 million tons of iron ore, turns out three million tons of iron and 2.7 million tons of steel, and rolls half a million tons of steel. The corporation now markets more than 200 brands of steel products. There are 14 categories and more than 100 varieties. CISC made a profit of 430 million yuan in 1983.

The overall economic contract responsibility system for the enterprise has two major components. First, the enterprise promises, by contract, to fulfil the tasks and targets stipulated by the state on the basis of increasing its profit turnover to the state by an annual rate of 6 percent, while the state gives a corresponding degree of autonomy, as well as economic benefits, to the enterprise. Second, under the responsibility system adopted by the corporation, responsibilities are spelt out for executives of the corporation, plants, and mines, as well as for workers in workshops and grassroots units. Their work performance is strictly vetted and rewards and punishments are handed out.

The economic reforms have brought changes in both the internal and external conditions of the enterprise's technical work. Under the old system, most of the profits and depreciation fees had to be turned over to the state. No funds were available for technological development, technical items had to be approved by the authorities concerned, and any technological progress made few gains for the enterprise. Now, CISC returns a greater amount of profits, and uses its own money to raise the technological level of its plants.

Within the corporation, a technical responsibility system links the interests of managers, technicians, and employees to technical progress in their respective fields. This motivates all to engage in technical innovation and to achieve good results. Practice has proved that the economic reform has promoted and accelerated the technological progress of the enterprise. From 1978 to 1984, CISC, using its own capital, achieved good results by adopting a set of new technologies in the main production system. In 1984, of the 70 major comparable indexes in terms of technical level and economic efficiency in the metallurgical industry, CISC was among the top 35. In iron-smelting and converting, some technologies have reached an international level. The profits of the enterprise have grown by 20 percent annually for six consecutive years.

Technical management is primarily the responsibility of the corporation's technical department. Its main task is to make technology development plans, organize for and coordinate the implementation of the plans, and conduct the day-to-day management of technical work. The department is under the direct supervision of the deputy manager of production and technology and the chief engineer. Specific research and design projects are initiated by the Design Institute and the Research Department for Computers, Control Equipment, and Instruments. There are corresponding technical sections and technicians in plants, mines, workshops, teams and groups. Thus, a four-level technical management system is created, from the Technical Department down to the work groups.

Technical management work consists mainly of implementing technical planning, technical-specialized planning, technical quotas, regulations and standards, technical analysis, and technical measurements.

Technical planning is an important integral part of the corporation's production development planning, and oversees technical principles, quotas, measurement, trial production of new products, and scientific research. It is also concerned with reducing energy consumption, improving quality, developing scientific information, and popularizing science and technology. An annual and a long-term plan is worked out.

On the basis of this technical planning, a technical-specialized plan is made by the Technical Department from initial plans sent by plants, institutes, and centres in order to meet the requirements of scientific research and to exploit new products. The Technical Department controls technical quotas, measurements and standards.

The technical analysis keeps abreast of developments in production and technology, determining what affects output and quality. Technical renovation upgrades old enterprises, with a consequent increase in benefits. Until the end of 1978, the development of CISC took place mainly through new construction; after that, the focus of its technical work was on technical renovation. The enterprises had limited funds and old equipment on which fresh investments would have little effect. CISC selected, designed, and evaluated items for renovation, taking several measures designed to tap the potential of the enterprise and to increase output, develop new products, improve quality, lower energy consumption, find new ways of saving energy — such as tackling waste gas, waste water, and industrial residue in a comprehensive way — and protect the environment. Some concrete examples of these improvements are given below.

Tapping Potential to Increase Production

The steel plant originally had three 30-ton converters, with a designed capacity of 600,000 tons. By using new types of furnace lining, enlarging the furnace volume, prolonging the furnace lifetime, and applying composite blowing, the plant reduced consumption and shortened steel-making time. Consequently, annual output in 1984 climbed to 1.67 million tons. The 1985 production was expected to reach 1.8 million tons, 300 percent of the designed capacity.

Developing New Products and Improving Quality

Measures were taken to improve the quality in every aspect of mining, sintering, steel-making, and steel rolling. Through the application of a computer-controlled production process, the concentrate grade was raised from 62 to 68.3 percent, the qualified rate of sintering jumped from 76.6 to 97.5 percent, and the leftover rate for cutting steel billet was lowered from 3-3.5 percent to 1-1.5 percent. In 1984 alone, more than 140 new products with 418 kinds of specifications were developed.

Reducing Energy Consumption

The iron and steel industry accounts for about 13 percent of the total energy consumption of the national economy. In the iron and steel complexes, the process of steel-making takes 45 percent of the total energy consumption; with sintering and coking, it amounts to about 70 percent. So the Capital Steel Plant centred its energy-saving efforts on the iron system, first attempting to lower the coke ratio. Using new techniques for emitting coal powder, the furnace coking ratio was cut from 455 to 412 kg, with an annual profit of 16 million yuan. This was only one-third of the investment. After the renovation of the furnace and the heating furnace, which use converter-coking coal-gas mixed supply steel rolling, the diffusion rate of gas produced by four converters declined from 17.9 to 8 percent, the utilization rate was raised, and pollution decreased. The pressure difference was also used to generate power and hot water for heating purposes.

Environmental Protection and Comprehensive Treatment of Waste gas, Waste Water, and Industrial Residue

Environmental protection is a key aspect of technical innovation in the complex. In fact, environmental protection also saves energy, increasing production and improving work conditions. For instance, the technical renovation of the sintering machine of No.2 blast furnace is just such an item with additional benefits. In recent years, the Capital Steel Plant has focused its work on raising the water recycling rate and reducing the waste water discharge and dust concentration in gases. More than ten synthetical treatment programmes were carried out, all with obvious effect. The phenol contained in the waste water discharge declined from 8-10 mg/1 to 0.04-0. 06 mg/1. In the sintering workshop, where dust smoke is a serious hazard, the dust concentration in the gases declined from 1,000 mg/cubic metre to 100-150 mg/cubic metre; the dust concentration of gases in 90 percent of the workshops is less than 10 mg/cubic metre, up to international standards.

As an major enterprise in a developing country, the Capital Steel Plant should aim to learn from the most advanced enterprises in the world, relying on its own abilities and improving itself step by step. By adhering to this principle in renovating its No. 2 converter, the plant achieved the comprehensive objective of high output, low energy consumption, environmental protection, and automation of production.

The old No. 2 blast furnace of the Capital Steel Plant was made in Japan in 1929. It was moved to Beijing from Pusan, Korea, in 1941. The blast furnace body is of the steel belt type, with a single-bell furnace crown and horizontal raw material feeding. It was still very old fashioned after several major repairs. The furnace coke ratio was as high as 600 kg, combined fuel was 700 kg, the coefficient of use was 1.4 tons per cubic metre per day, and the pollution was heavy. In 1978, the plant decided to carry out major repairs on the converter. Considering the time that the repair would take — eight to ten years — and the fact that China was at least ten years behind the world level in converter technology, it was decided instead to perform a comprehensive technical innovation.

The innovation began in 1978 and was completed by 1979. The renovated No.2 converter adopted 37 items of new technology, including a blast furnace with bell-less top, injection of coal dust as fuel into the blast furnace and crown-burning hot gas furnace, and other environmental protection measures. The furnace volume was enlarged from 500 to 1,327 cubic metres. In 1984, an imported programmed controller and other computer systems were installed. The material supply, coal injection, and the main body of the blast furnace were automatically controlled. The renovation proved to be effective. The technical and economic targets approached international levels. The total investment was recouped within 19 months.

An overall survey of the Capital Steel Plant had shown that the plant lagged far behind advanced international levels in respect of the technical equipment in every system. The mastering of advanced foreign technology, therefore, was always a key task for the plant.

The technical information network is the chief organization for obtaining foreign technical information. A chief engineer is in charge of the network, which is run by the technology department. The designing institute of the information office is the backbone of this information network. Subordinate plants and sections are responsible for collecting information in their own speciality. Every information unit puts forward a comprehensive information summary data to the technical department every six months. This serves as a basis for scheduling technical design and keeping up with, and surpassing, advanced levels both at home and abroad. An annual session of the information network is held every October to exchange experiences and discuss the plan for the following year. The network solves important scientific and technological problems faced by the enterprises.

The "importation office," which supervises the import of technology, is also an important information service. The network attends to purely technical information, while the "importation office" deals with the analysis of prices and commercial information. Consultative arrangements with foreign companies and experts, overseas investigations, and attendance at conferences and exhibitions are also channels for obtaining information.

The direct import of foreign techniques is an effective way to improve the technical level of an enterprise. The process of technical importation includes collecting and analysing information, choosing and evaluating techniques, negotiation on import items, importing, installing, and testing. In this way the managerial and technical ability of the enterprise is improved.

Between 1981 and May 1985, the Capital Steel Plant imported 122 technical items, of which 15 brought obvious benefits; the volume of business amounted to US$100 million. To ensure correct technical importation and digestion, the Capital Steel Plant set up an "importation office," which organized the import of technology, and collected, analysed, and sorted out the information. It was ensured that the technology was up-to-date and appropriate for the plant. Stress was laid on the importation of instruments, control systems, and equipment that would rapidly improve the technical level and reasonable use of resources. Investigations were conducted to compare different technologies before importation so that both advanced technology and a reasonable price was guaranteed. Attention was paid first to absorbing and then to transferring the imported technology.

Technical innovation in old enterprises is closely related to the dissemination of technology. The lack of knowledge of new technology is an important factor that delays its spread. Awareness of existing technical systems is a prerequisite for technical innovation. A major factor influencing the effectiveness of technical work is its organization and systems. In this lies the significance of the economic reform and economic responsibility in the Capital Steel Plant.

The analysis of the Capital Steel Plant shows that self-reliance in technology means relying on the development of the state's, enterprise's, or scientific research units' own resources — that is, their knowledge, equipment, organization, personnel, and investment. Self- reliance results from the combined effects of organization, absorption of information, technology development, policy-making, and policy implementation. It is not an individual ability, but an itegrated one.

Exogenous Sources for Technological Progress and Self-reliance

As members of modern society we live in an interdependent world. Owing to the rapid development of transportation and communications, distances have become shorter and the degree of interdependence has increased. There are interdependencies between regions and nations as well as between provinces and regions within a country.

It is not easy to identify the feasibility for S&T interdependence in specific areas and sectors. Only general observations can be made.

The sectors highlighted in the case-studies were: agriculture; light industry (textiles and agrofood); infrastructure (electric power); heavy industry (iron and steel, machine-building and machine tools); and high technology (electronics), not all of them are quoted in this case studies. Economically, China has a static comparative advantage in the agriculture, agrofood, and textile sectors. It is therefore possible in these sectors to cooperate well with exogenous sources in order to achieve technological progress.

A full range of production, R&D, and design capability has been built up in nearly every sector of economic activity in China. It is now necessary to strengthen the horizontal linkages and to emphasize the interdependence between sectors and activity components for mutual technological progress. Owing to the prolonged closed-door policy in the past, industrial technology in China has generally lagged behind that of industrialized and newly industrializing countries. Even in the traditional agrofood sector, it is still necessary to draw on exogenous sources in the drive for technological progress.

Cooperation with the outside world does not mean abandoning self-reliance. Interdependence and self-reliance are complementary; self-reliance should still be emphasized, because in terms of S&T the developed countries have a comparative advantage. Many sophisticated technologies are part and parcel of the military R&D of developed nations and so governments impose controls and restrictions on them, mandating an emphasis on self-reliance among less developed nations. Developed countries, for their part, reap the benefit of "job creation" in their economies when they engage in technology transfer.

Past technology transfer can be roughly divided into three periods.

First in the 1950s, China adopted a "follower's" strategy, importing technology from the Soviet Union and other Eastern European countries. This transfer was in the form of both hardware and software, and complete sets of equipment and processes were imported. Emphasis was laid on the capital goods production sector. Technology transfer also took the form of complete sets of technical drawings and documents and the services of expert technical assistance in planning, design, construction, testing, and the operation and maintenance of various types of industrial plants. The establishment of research organizations was also assisted by foreign experts.

Second, in the 1960s, after the Sino-Soviet conflict had come into the open,

China imported technology and equipment on a small scale from Japan and the Western European countries. Priorities were placed on metallurgy, chemical fibre, petroleum, chemical engineering, textile machinery, mining equipment, electronics, and precision machines. This importation of technology supplemented the technological capability already established in the 1950s, and promoted S&T self-reliance in textiles, machine-building and machine tools, and electronics. Self-reliance and the process of "walking on two legs" were emphasized during this period.

In the period 1956-1967, a 12-year S&T development programme was carried out. This provided China with a technological capability in nuclear energy, jet technology, computers, automation, semi-conductors, and radio electronics. The success of the program was due not only to the coordination of different sectors, but also to the coordination between different regions, particularly with the relatively developed regions such as Shanghai. In this period widespread development of small- and medium-scale labour-intensive industries in the countryside was also initiated.

Third, in the 1970s, after she had had her United Nations seat restored in 1971, China imported technology and complete plants from a variety of non-Communist sources and on a larger scale than ever before. This had a strong positive impact on the productive capability of several industrial sectors, such as chemical fertilizers and chemical fibres. But the absorption of this technology remained a problem, owing to the rigidity of the existing S&T system.

Since the announcement of the basic policy of "opening to the outside world", China has started transferring technology from abroad on a larger scale, adopting various means and forms. Steps such as the encouragement of foreign investment (such as joint ventures, cooperative ventures, direct investment, and leasing) and the establishment of special economic zones (SEZ), including the 14 cities and the three deltas along the coastal area, all involved certain amounts of technology transfer. Whether China can benefit further from this policy or not depends on the establishment of a proper system of related policies, which will be mentioned later.

The effort to achieve technological progress based on exogenous sources and "self-reliance" is best described in the following quotation from a Western expert:

While the realization of the concept of "walking on two legs" has differed in degree from phase to phase and according to the political line prevalent at the moment, it has never been subject to any real basic doubt. Traditionally, labour-intensive methods were employed in every area where they could make an effective contribution to development; ... on the other hand, China did not seal itself off completely from large worldwide technological developments. China was aware that its level of performance in certain technological fields was limited and therefore made some effort, in fields important to development, to catch up with international standards.

Table 11. Innovation by source
(international esperience) (percentage)

Country/region	Year	Innovation source	
		Government and university	**Enterprise**
USA	1953-73	5	80
Europe	1982 (report)		70

The proper selection of the right type of technology is the key to upgrading technology. In the past, China had swung between the extremes of importing turnkey plants and relying wholly on domestic R&D. And the traditional organization of R&D in China involved a top-down technology push. This approach was successful in limited cases but international experience has proved that individual enterprises play a much more active role in innovation, as shown in Table 11. This is also demonstrated by the case-study example of the Capital Iron and Steel Corporation, which was one of the first groups to experiment with the new economic system. It had more autonomous decision-making power than the enterprises had previously and S&T played an increasing role in the promotion of its production and profits. Clearly, there is a need to push the economic reforms further.

The segregation of sectors in the past has seriously affected the utilization of exogenous sources in a broader sense. Domestic sectors and regions were isolated from each other, as was the defence sector from the civil sector. Major advantages can be gained by breaking down these barriers

Central government agencies and ministries, with their research institutes and superior resources, have played a dominant role in determining what innovations are needed. This top-down "technology-push" approach to innovations was effective in large program efforts, such as those in the period 1956-1967. But it failed to meet the needs of a wide variety of commodities. Large enterprises such as the Capital Iron and Steel Corporation can solve such problems alone. But for the industrial system as a whole, responding to the demands of users is important in promoting the self-reliance capability of R&D. This is the idea behind developing a technology market, as suggested in the S&T management system reform. But it is necessary to have a broader perspective of market orientaton.

A Desirable Path and a Strategy for S&T Development

China has announced the "Decision of the Central Committee of the Communist Party of China on the Reform of the Science and Technology Management System," which is an official document outlining the new strategy for S&T development. One should mention here that the S&T system is a subsystem of the economic system. The economic reform should provide a suitable environment for the current S&T development strategy. The aim of the economic reform is to establish a dynamic socialist economic structure (including the establishment of an organizational structure for the S&T system). The planning system (including the S&T planning system) will be reformed so that the law of value is consciously applied in developing a socialist commodity economy.

In the economic sphere, special emphasis is placed on invigorating enterprises and establishing various forms of economic responsibility. The parallel in S&T is the reform of its funding system. The reform of the economic management system includes separation of the functions of government and enterprises, promotion of a new generation of cadres, and the continual expansion of foreign and domestic economic and technological exchanges. China will no longer isolate herself from the economic and technological world. It has been realized that the S&T system of the industrialized countries evolved organically with the rest of their socio-economic systems.

The current strategy for the S&T system, outlined in the "Decision on the Reform of the S&T Management System," contains two basic elements. First, the reform is based upon general guidelines which specify that "science and technology must serve economic development, economic development must rely on science and technology." The three main aspects of this are reforms of the operating mechanism, organizational structure, and the S&T personnel system.

Second, the reform of the operating mechanism of the S&T system entails the reform of the funding system and the planning system, and the exploitation of the technology market. The reform should overcome the defect of relying purely on administrative methods in science and technology management.

In the past, the government allocated research funds unconditionally to research institutes according to the number of staff, and was indifferent to the economic aspects of the research community. Under the reformed system, for a given period of time funds provided by central and local departments for S&T will increase gradually, at a rate higher than the growth in state revenue, in order to encourage the development of S&T activities in general.

For basic research and some applied research, funds will be provided through research foundations. But for research institutions engaged in technology development activities, it is planned that government contributions for current expenditure will be gradually reduced and abolished. Banks will be actively encouraged to provide loans for scientific and technological work, and to supervise and control the use of such operating funds.

Research institutions engaged in such important public matters as medicine, public health, labor protection, family planning, the prevention and control of natural calamities, environmental sciences, and other social sciences, as well as institutions providing certain scientific and technological services, will continue to receive state funds in accordance with existing block funding practice.

The commercialization of technological achievements and the exploitation of the technology market will be arranged to suit the development of the socialist commodity economy. It is realized that technology plays an increasingly important role in the creation of the value of commodities, and more and more technologies have become intellectual commodities in their own right. The intellectual industry has now emerged as a new trade. The technology market will therefore constitute an essential component of China's socialist commodity market.

The exploitation of technology covers seven main points and includes actively developing diverse forms of trade in technological achievements, technological job contracting, technical convey and other services. Furthermore, the establishment of different kinds of business institutions dealing with technological commodities will be appropriately supported. Various measures will be taken to encourage enterprises to use new technologies and to improve their economic ability to satisfy buyers' demands. Statutes and regulations will be formulated to protect the legitimate rights and interests of buyers sellers and intermediaries. The ownership of intellectual property will be protected by the state through patent laws and other relevant statutes. The market prices of technological achievements will be determined through negotiations between sellers and buyers with no restrictions imposed by the state. All income from transfers of technology achievements will, for the present, be exempted from taxation. Technology development units and enterprises may reward personnel directly engaged in such development with a portion of the income from technological transfers. And units responsible for technological achievements may set up joint ventures with enterprises by contributing shares in the form of technologies.

Research projects having national priority will remain under the control of state planning, while other activities conducted by scientific and technological institutes will be managed by means of economic levers and market regulation, in order to enable these institutes to develop through internal impetus and to imbue them with vitality.

The reform of the organizational structure will change the situation whereby a disproportionately large number of research institutes are detached from enterprises; where coordination is lacking between research, design, education, and production; where the defence and civilian sectors are separated from each other; and where barriers are erected between various departments and regions.

The organizational structural reforms will be focused on strengthening the enterprises' ability to absorb and develop technology, and on strengthening the intermediate links in a complete life-cycle production system, as shown in Figure 3. Emphasis is placed on encouraging partnership between research, educational, and design institutions on the one hand and production units on the other. Some of the detailed suggestions are as follows. The institutes of higher learning and research institutes under the Chinese Academy of Sciences, the central ministries, and local authorities will be encouraged to set up various forms of partnership with enterprises and design units on a voluntary and mutually beneficial basis. Some of the partnerships may gradually become economic entities. Some research institutes may develop on their own into enterprises of a research-production type or become joint technology development departments for small and medium-sized enterprises. Large, key enterprises would gradually improve their own technology development departments or research institutes. Defence research institutes would create a military-civilian partnership. While ensuring the fulfilment of national defence assignments, they would serve economic construction, accelerate the transfer of technology from the military to the civilian sector, and engage energetically in research and development programs for civilian products. Collectives and individuals would set up research or technical services on their own. Local governments would exercise control over them and give them guidance and assistance. Institutes in this category would be profit-orientated.

The objective of the reform of the personnel system is to create a situation favourable to the emergence of a large number of talented people who can put their specialized knowledge to good use.

"The proper person in the proper position" is the optimum way to utilize human resources. The older generation of China's S&T specialists will be encouraged to continue to play their role in training qualified personnel and directing research, in writing books, and in acting as consultants to promote various public activities. A great number of accomplished and vigorous young and middle-aged people will be assigned to key academic and technological posts. Scientists and engineers in their forties and fifties will be able to contribute their full share as a bridge between the older and younger generations. Young talents will be nurtured.

In solving the serious "ageing problem" in the leading bodies of many research institutes, measures will be taken to train different types of scientific and technological managers, a new breed which possesses both modern scientific and technological knowledge and management skills.

Mobility of personnel will be encouraged. Competent people will no longer be made to sit idle and waste their talents. Appropriate S&T policies and preferential measures will be adopted to encourage S&T personnel to work in small and medium-sized cities, in the countryside, and in regions with communities of minorities. Research and design institutes and universities will gradually experiment with recruiting personnel by invitation so as to break the so-called "iron bowl."

Active efforts will be made to improve the working and living conditions of scientific and technological personnel. The principle of "from each according to his ability, to each according to his work" will be earnestly adhered to in order to oppose egalitarianism. Rational remuneration for scientists and engineers will be gradually introduced. A system of honours and material rewards will be instituted.

The management system in agricultural science and technology will be reformed so as to serve the restructuring of the rural economy and to facilitate its conversion to specialization, commercialization, and modernization. In vigorously promoting technology development, efforts in applied research will be redoubled and basic research will be guaranteed a steady and continuous growth. Opening to the outside world and establishing contact with other countries is a basic, long-term policy for China's scientific and technological development. Within this field, the utmost will be done to integrate foreign trade with technology and industrial production, and greater importance will be attached to importing patented technology, technical know-how, and software. More channels will be opened to expand various forms of international cooperation in development, design, and manufacture. Certain domestic research and development work will be closely related to imports in order to absorb advanced imported technology. A policy of active support will also be adopted for technology development projects with promising international prospects so as to promote the ability of Chinese commodities to enter the world market. Active efforts will also be made to expand international academic exchanges.

The basic function of S&T in the coming decade is not to try to catch up with the advanced countries. S&T should first play its role in industrialization and serve the development of traditional industries and of technological rehabilitation. The industrialization process to be carried out will rest on the new S&T-based technological revolution.

In R&D institutes reforms will be carried out to strengthen the horizontal linkages between the universities, research institutes, and enterprises, between domestic regions, and between China and the external world.

R&D will have three functions. These are, first, to carry out strategically important basic research and applied research for selected areas of long-term importance, and, second, to develop and carry out a "technological complex" strategy, according to which priority will be given to the development of traditional technology (special imortance being attached to energy, transportation, and the supply of raw materials, which are the bottlenecks in present economic development). Other priorities are the development of high technologies (with electronics and information technology as the guiding technology) and the reform of traditional industries and technologies, which will be combined with high technologies.

Thirdly, a "Sparks Program" for the rural areas, where more than 75 percent of the population live, will be carried out. Whether S&T can be effectively utilized in the industrialization process of rural areas depends on the socio-cultural pattern of the regions. Guidance from the government plays a very important role in promoting this process. The "Sparks Program" is sponsored by the State Science and Technology Commission, which entrusts scientists and engineers with the job of designing simple and low-cost equipment with a high economic efficiency for rural use.

The S&T system must adapt to the structural changes of a dynamic society, and therefore human resource inputs must adapt to the dynamic changes of the S&T and economic system. China's present stock of educated manpower has an unusual composition. The proportion of the population with primary education is high, but the number of people with advanced educational qualifications is small (Table 12).

This unusual structure has dual implications. It is favourable to grassroots participation for self-reliance in S&T and economic growth. As the World Bank points out: "Widespread basic education in some East Asian economies has helped achieve both usually high output per unit of physical capital and, unusually, equal sharing of the benefits of rapid development."

Yet, on the other hand, this type of educated manpower structure is unfavourable to the development of self-reliance in S&T, because a minimum number of highly educated people is required to promote the development of S&T. The present S&T specialized personnel structure in the national economy (Table 13) is insufficient and could hamper growth even in the traditional sector.

In order to compare the relative intensity of specialized personnel employed in different branches of the national economy, a notion of "equivalent density" of specialized personnel has been adopted. This is defined as the percentage of the number of employees. A college graduate is taken as unity, while one who has completed graduate education, short-cycle higher education, or specialized secondary education is assigned an equivalent value of 2, 0.6, or 0.2 respectively.

Table 12. Education attainment of population, by age and sex
(percentages)

Country and age-group	Percentage of persons who have completed at least							
	Primary school		Lower secondary school		Upper secondary school		Post-secondary school	
	Male	Female	Male	Female	Male	Female	Male	Female
China								
15+ (total)	79.1	51.1	42.9	26.0	13.3	8.3	1.0	0.3
15-24	95.1	82.2	71.0	53.6	23.5	17.8	0.1	0.1
25-34	88.8	61.9	48.0	26.4	13.4	7.6	0.8	0.4
35+	63.2	24.6	21.5	7.5	6.4	2.4	1.6	0.5
India								
15+ (total)	37.2	14.7	21.3	7.1	10.3	3.0	1.6	0.4
15-24	53.6	27.4	35.5	15.1	15.6	6.4	1.2	0.7
25-34	39.4	14.4	23.4	6.5	13.1	3.1	2.7	0.7
35+	26.4	7.1	12.0	2.4	5.9	0.9	1.3	0.2
Republic of Korea								
15+ (total)	82.3	66.3	44.5	22.4	23.7	8.9	6.2	1.6
15-24	97.5	95.9	55.9	39.3	23.2	13.1	1.6	1.5
25-34	94.9	85.7	57.9	29.6	37.2	14.2	11.7	3.4
35+	63.7	37.7	28.2	8.2	16.3	3.6	6.6	0.7

Source: *China*, World Bank Country Economic Report, 1982.

Educational reforms entitled "Decision on the Organization and Management of the Educational System" were announced in 1985. The basic purpose of the reform was to produce more skilled, high-quality manpower. There would be nine-year compulsory schooling. The structure of secondary education would be readjusted and vigorous development of vocational technical education undertaken. The system of college admission, recruitment planning, and placement of graduates would be reformed and the autonomy of higher education institutions would be extended. The supervision and guidance of education would be strengthened, so as to ensure successful implementation.

Besides these five main steps, a multi-level and efficient system of higher education would be built up in order to remedy the shortage of highly educated manpower.

Social capacity in adapting new and existing technology is important in the management of S&T development. China already had a socio-infrastructure in planning; the problem was how to improve the planning system, i.e., to reduce the scope of mandatory planning and to improve indicative planning.

The long-term national development goal was to catch up with the developed countries by 2050 while maintaining a socialist system in which the benefits of prosperity are widely shared, avoiding polarization. Another goal for the year 2000 was to improve living standard and eliminate poverty, quadrupling the gross value of industrial and agricultural output (GVIAO) between 1980 and 2000 and increasing per-capita national income from about $300 to $800. The leaders of the government have emphasized repeatedly the role of S&T in achieving these goals.

The strategy for development towards S&T self-reliance was, as explained earlier, to create a self-perpetuating mechanism for the S&T system through economic reform and the supportive socio-cultural infrastructure. Both self-reliance and the transfer of technology from abroad will be emphasized, taking into account latecomers' ability to borrow. In the modern interdependent world, it is feasible for latecomers to adopt a "follower's" strategy but at the same time to increase their capacity to innovate and to adapt new technologies.

Because of different levels of development in different regions and different sectors, different strategies and S&T development policies will be adopted.

The resource allocation for science and technology R&D in China is roughly 1 percent of its GDP. This is low in comparison with the R&D expenditure of many of the developed countries, such as the USA, United Kingdom, Germany, and Switzerland, where R&D expenditure generally exceeds 2 percent of their GDP. Around 70 percent of this outlay is allocated to development, while the remaining 30 percent is divided between basic and applied research. The resource allocation for S&T and between sectors is entirely determined by the government according to its choice of priority sectors.

Table 13. Percentage of specialized personnel in different sectors

Sector	%	Sector	%
Space	15.7	Weaponry	2.9
Shipbuilding	11.4	Building materials	1.99
Nuclear	10.5	Coal mining	1.87
Civil aviation	8.3	Urban and rural construction and environmental protection	1.83
Electronics	7.3		
Petrochemicals	7.4		
Water conservancy and power generation	6.2	Textile	1.58
Railways	4.6	Highway and water transportation	1.48
Non-ferrous metallurgy	4.4	Silk industry	1.36
Petroleum	4.3	Light industry	0.96
Ferrous metallurgy	4.2	Retail and wholesale trades	0.73
Chemical	3.8	Finance, banking, and insurance	3.4
Post and telecommunications	3.8		
Machine-building	3.6	Jurisprudence and public security	4.9
Automotive industry	3.5		

a: Survey carried out by the Ministry of Education from the statistical returns of 72 central departments.

Nearly all R&D systems in the past were publicly owned. R&D management, in the words of one Western scientist, was such that despite a very elaborate structure of R&D functioning relatively well in China in the context of developing countries, the Chinese still do not have what may be called a systematic effort to build or utilize R&D management expertise on modern lines... that can be explained as a necessary consequence of not having so far developed general management education and training on a system basis....

This point has now drawn the attention of the Chinese government, and reforms are being undertaken. But difficulties could arise because many components are involved in this reform, and, in the transitional period, interaction between the old system components and those of the new system has to be taken into consideration.

6. Technology Innovation and Enterprise Management and a Case Study in China

1. Introduction

The global economy is now undergoing rapid industrial and economic change. Every nation, state and enterprise is competing in an international and domestic market for economic profits and prosperity. And technology innovation is playing a very important role in these efforts. A central theme in this paper will be our focus on the essential role of enterprise management in promoting technological innovation.

Schumpeter proposed distinctions among: 'inventions', derived under laboratory conditions, and the diffusion of innovations, which often includes modifications in what is being diffused. These three form a common thread in effecting technical change.

Technological innovation may be promoted both at macro and micro levels. There are many official reports dealing with technological innovation at the national level.

For example, OECD has published a series of innovation policy reviews to enable its member countries to appraise the extent to which the institutions and mechanisms which influence such developments in various fields are properly fulfilling their roles. In fact, the technology innovation capacity of an enterprise is greatly affected by the innovation policy of the government. It is the role of the government to devise explicit policies and programs to assist enterprises in technological innovation through establishing domestic technology institutions that provide education, training, standards setting, R&D consulting and financing services.

However, the focus of this paper will be the role of enterprise management in promoting technological innovation. It will be presented in three parts: Section 2 is a review of some basic concepts; Section 3 presents a case study of technology innovation in the Capital Iron and Steel Corporation; Section 4 summarizes an on-going research project for the World Bank involving some recent explorations of the mechanisms of technology innovation.

2. A Framework of Technology Innovation and Enterprise Management Concepts

The discussion will begin with some basic concepts of technology innovation and enterprise management, including some suggested new elements.

Concept (1)

As shown in Figure 1, the management of technology innovation involves interactions between technology innovation and enterprise management. Technology innovation is a process which is initiated by demand-pull and technology information push, and which must be well managed if it is to be developed effectively. On the other hand, the technology innovation process must also affect the enterprise structure and its management processes if these two are to be effectively adapted to each other.

Figure 1 Basic conceptual framework connecting technology innovation processes and enterprise management

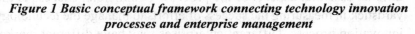

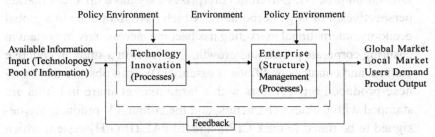

Concept (2)

Technology innovation is the process by which industry generates new and improved products and production processes. This process can be divided into three phases, as shown in Figure 2. Effective management of technology innovation must cover each of these, as will be explained.

Figure 2 Technology innovation process

Phase I	Phase II	Phase III
1) Information Searching	1) (Research)	1) Marketing Planning
2) Goal Setting	2) Development	2) Market penetration
3) Project Identification	3) Design, engineering, testing	Market information collection
4) Project Selection	4) Production	3) Market development Market information collection
		4) Market maintaining & shifting

Note: ▨ overlap of phases

(a) Management of technology innovation is different from the management of invention because there is already a large pool of reserve technology available in a modern information society. The key objective of most enterprises is to search for, and to get access to, available information and certain types of technology which have prospective commercial value and which match the internal capabilities of the enterprise.

(b) Market research, market penetration and market development are additional essential aspects of the process. Commercial success is the yardstick in measuring the success of efforts to manage the technology innovation process. Different enterprises may have different market perspectives. For large corporations which have to operate in a global economy, international marketing has become increasingly important in ensuring corporate profits and growth. In this effort a study of concrete cultural and country conditions is essential. We can observe that Japanese-produced refrigerators with a large market share in China are stamped with Chinese characters, and the colour TV products are designed to be tuned to the CCIR standard PAL (B/G/H) system which may be adopted in many countries and, therefore, may gain more market share than the same type of colour TV sets produced in other developed countries. This commercial success is not derived from the basic invention, but from simple innovations designed to ensure adaptation to global market requirements. Even for small enterprises, there may be large market opportunities uncovered by effective market research during the innovation process.

(c) Although design is a very important element in the innovation process, this capability is often weak in many enterprises, especially in developing countries. This point is made clear by the following sentences quoted from a German publication of illustrative purposes (it also holds true for enterprises in the USA and other competitive enterprises):

"Whether it be the limousine with the 'good star' on its bonnet, or the dull black ball-point pen .... there is confidence in the goods produced in the Federal Republic with respect to technological innovation.... If German industry's ability to export has been steadily on the increase within the last few years, in spite of *Time* stating that the image of German craftsmanship had lost some of its former sparkle, then this is mainly due to design. It should also be emphasized here that 'Forms in engineering design' are important, because they are highly cost effective."

Concept (3)

Effective management of product innovation requires management of the complete production process life-cycle. Figure 3 shows this concept. It should be pointed out that Americans discovered the principle of Total Quality Control, but it was the Japanese who diffused and improved the TQC process, which represents an important type of innovation. It should also be emphasized that there are opportunities for innovative developments in every component stage of the complete process.

Figure 3 Complete production life-cycle process

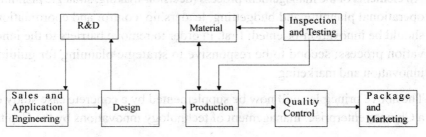

Concept (4)

Innovation in production processes need not be revolutionary in nature: every minor improvement may be beneficial. It is the accumulation of quantitative modifications which will cause a qualitative change. Chinese enterprise management encourages 'rationalization proposals' to help advance innovation processes.

Concept (5)

For the enterprise to be responsive to technology innovations, it should be structured to enhance the flow of technical and market information into the research, development and design departments. Research and development departments are important for large corporations and MNC (multinational corporations) with long-term strategic planning and development perspectives. But the structure of the enterprise should also provide strong links with local and global marketing, to ensure that innovations move forward effectively to commercial success.

Concept (6)

Technology innovation is mainly accomplished through the creativity and initiative of human resources. Therefore, the staffing of the enterprise must provide for the several key functions necessary to achieve successful innovation. In a modern global information society, technology development will continue to occur aggressively outside a country's border. Hence, cooperative means to monitor, develop or acquire technology worldwide will become increasingly important for large corporations, and accordingly the structure of the enterprise must be adapted to this need.

Concept (7)

All elements of the management process (decision-making, strategic planning, operational planning and budgetting, leadership, control and coordination) should be innovation-oriented: first, in order to remove barriers to the innovation process; second to be responsive to strategic planning for guiding innovation and marketing.

The above principles will now be supplemented by a concrete case study of a Chinese enterprise: management of technology innovations by the Capital

Iron and Steel Corporation, which is one of the frontrunners in the economic reform of Chinese enterprises.

3. A Case Study of Technology Innovation and Enterprise Management in China: Capital Iron and Steel Corporation

3.1 General Background

The Capital Iron and Steel Corporation (CISC) is an iron and steel complex including mining, ore dressing and process metallurgy. This corporation was established in 1919 and produced only iron before 1949. Now it mines and dresses around 14 million tons of iron ore annually, produces around three million tons of iron and steel, and rolls half a million tons of steel.

It was one of the first groups of enterprises to implement enterprise reforms. Before the reform, all state-owned enterprises had to submit most of their profits and depreciation to the state. There were no financial resources available for technology innovation through autonomous decisions by the enterprises themselves. As a stage of enterprise reform, full retention of the profits by the state was replaced by the taxation of profits and by after-tax profit retention by enterprises. Enterprises are allowed to arrange technology innovations by themselves, although some large projects still have to be approved by various levels of government. CISC has not only improved the quality and quantity of its production, but it has also invested in, and operated, a variety of different economic activities, some in the tertiary sector, and it has even invested abroad including an iron mine in Peru.

3.2 Enterprise Structure Related to Technology Innovation

As mentioned earlier, the enterprise structure and management processes include the management of technology innovations, as shown in Figure 4.

The technology innovation process is managed through plans prepared by the Technical Department and carried out through four hierarchical levels: the technical department level; the plant and mine level; the workshop level; and the working group level. The Technical Department is also responsible for operating a technical information network together with the information office of the Research Design Institute. Technical organizations and technicians at different levels are responsible for collecting related special technical information and for preparing a comprehensive information summary for the Technical Department every half year.

Technology innovation is promoted by rational proposals from the workers and staffs. The Corporation issues a weekly publication, *Trends*, which records and analyses the rational proposals related both to production processes and to commercial management. The Corporation not only relies on the internal Research and Design Institute for promotion of technology innovation process, but it has also established extensive collaborative relationships with universities, colleges and specific scientific and technological institutions.

As mentioned earlier, the staffing of the enterprise must provide for several key functions necessary to achieve successful innovation. The Education and Training Department of CISC is responsible for providing continuous education and training for the staff and workers. Because the opening to the outside world and the importation of foreign technology and equipment play a crucial role in the technology innovation process, the weakness of the foreign language capability of the staff became a barrier to the technology innovation process. As a result, the Education and Training Department offered training courses in foreign languages and specific courses on metallurgical technologies. In addition, general training is also provided for the great majority of workers.

3.2.1 Technical Planning

Technical planning is an integral part of the strategic development planning of CISC. Its preparation is based on the long-term development and production perspectives of the enterprise, on trends in international and domestic advanced metallurgical technologies, and on various other indices. Technical goals and production goals are set up and cross-checked by the design department for technical and economic feasibility. And finally, it is to be approved by the Planning Department of the Corporation.

Special technical plans are also prepared for short-term technology innovation processes, along with plans for implementation of later stages after approval of the master technical plan.

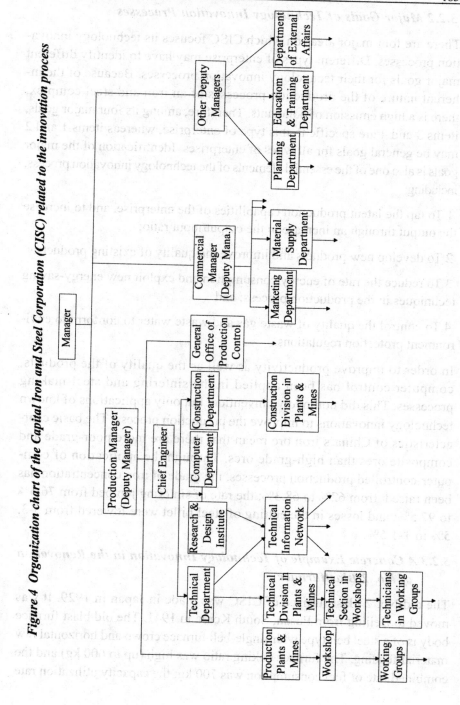

Figure 4 Organization chart of the Capital Iron and Steel Corporation (CISC) related to the innovation process

3.2.2 Major Goals of Technology Innovation Processes

There are four major areas on which CISC focuses its technology innovation processes. Different types of enterprise may have to identify different major goals for their technology innovation processes. Because of the inherent nature of the production processes of an iron and steel complex, there is a high emission of pollutants. Therefore, among its four major goals, items 3 and 4 are specific to this type of enterprise, whereas items 1 and 2 may be general goals for all types of enterprises. Identification of the major goals is also one of the essential elements of the technology innovation process, including:

1 To tap the latent production capabilities of the enterprise, and to increase the output through an increase in the output/input ratio;

2 To develop new products and improve the quality of existing products;

3 To reduce the rate of energy consumption and exploit new energy-saving techniques in the production process; and

4 To control the quality of waste gas and waste water to conform to environment protection regulations.

In order to improve productivity as well as the quality of the products, computer control has been applied in the sintering and steel-making processes. This did not involve invention, but only applications of known technology innovations to improve the production process. The basic characteristics of China's iron ore mean that there are more poor-grade and composite ores than high-grade ores. Through the application of computer-controlled production processes, the grade of iron concentration has been raised from 62% to 68.3%; the rate of sintering jumped from 76.6% to 97.5%; and losses in the cutting of steel billet were lowered from 3-3.5% to 1-1.5%.

3.2.3 A Concrete Example of Technology Innovation in the Renovation of No. 2 Blastfurnace

The old No. 2 blast furnace of CISC was made in Japan in 1929. It was moved to Beijing from Pusan, South Korea in 1941. The old blast furnace body is of a steel belt type with single-bell furnace crown and horizontal raw material feeding. The furnace coking ratio was high (up to 600 kg) and the combined rate of fuel consumption was 700 kg; the capacity utilization rate was 1.4 tons per cubic metre of furnace volume per day; and pollutant discharges were serious. CISC determined to carry out a renovation of this furnace through technology innovation. The renovated No. 2 blast furnace was completed within two years and 37 items of available modern technology were adopted after detailed evaluation and selection. These included a bell-less top; injection of pulverized fuel into the blast furnace so that the furnace coking ratio was brought down to 412 kg; the furnace volume was enlarged from 500 cubic metres to 1,327 cubic metres; and computer control was also applied. As a result, the quantity and quality of production were greatly improved through this renovation process.

3.2.4 Concluding Remarks about the Technology Innovation Processes of CISC

Very recently, CISC summarized its experiences with technology innovations to renovate traditional industries and existing enterprises. These summaries, although derived from Chinese state-owned enterprises, may also provide some hints for public enterprises in other countries. The major findings were as follows:

1 The state should create an economic environment in traditional industrial sectors to provide incentives and capabilities for enterprises to launch technology innovation processes. Reduction of tax burdens so that more profit after tax would be retained by the enterprise would provide sufficient resources for financing technology innovations in such enterprises.

2 The enterprise should have autonomous power to make investment decisions. Past Chinese practices in gaining approval for technology renovation projects are inappropriate.

3 The foundation of successful technology innovation involves mobilizing the initiatives and creativity of vast numbers of employees.

4 Correct guidelines and methods are essential to achieve the modernization of traditional industry. The favourable results of CISC were due to basing the technology renovation on a full analysis of the features of the enterprise itself and adopting a comprehensive program of production and renovation with the key project.

4. Current Research Trend in Promotion of Technology Innovation Process: a Case Example of an Ongoing Joint Research Project with the World Bank

4.1 The Appropriate Application of Universal Principles Depends on Specific Conditions

As was mentioned in Section 1, much of the literature dealing with technology innovation and enterprise management is already available, and both the principles of technology innovation and the general theory of enterprise management are well established. After 15 years of research at Massachusetts Institute of Technology and elsewhere on the problems of managing industrial research and development and the technological innovation process, it was concluded that "Effective corporate innovation requires the planned integration of staffing, structure and strategy." This conclusion restates existing theory that the essential elements of management are: planning (including strategy), organizing (including enterprise structure), staffing, leading and controlling. This view was preceded by four traditional theories: scientific management; administrative management theory; the bureautic model; the theory of the firm in microeconomics. After a century of evolution in management theory, we are now in the phase of systems and contingency concepts where traditional theories are still useful. Accordingly, there may well be some universal principles in technology innovation and enterprise management, but the successful application of such principles would seem to depend on the detailed analysis of the external and internal conditions of any given enterprise as will be clarified by the Chinese enterprise case study below.

As a framework for analysing conditions in specific countries, it is necessary to analyse both broad social conditions and local conditions. There have been several forms of social control over enterprises as well as changing relationships between enterprises and governments since the latter part of the 19th century. The four major forms of social control have been: competition in the marketplace; government regulation — the influences of other external groups; the growing professionalism of management. After 1890, there was an increasing influence by government regulation and control and a decreasing share of market control over enterprises in most Western countries. But in recent decades, there has been an increasing liberalization of government controls' in many Western countries; and there has also been an increasing inclination to rely on competition and market mechanisms in China and in some Eastern European countries. This trend will form an external environment within which the relationship between technology and enterprise management will undergo further changes.

4.2　A New Exploration of Technology Innovations

Although technology innovation and enterprise management are well established subjects, there is a need to explore new elements and relationships which can further improve the technology innovation process. Accordingly, a joint research project was organized recently by several Chinese institutions (including our Development Research Centre of the State Council) together with the World Bank to study the institutional and policy priorities needed to promote technology innovation in industry. It is hoped that the following simple description will provide a useful conclusion to this paper in the form of an introduction to this program to develop further insights into future technology innovation potentials.

4.2.1 Background to This Project

Post World War II history has demonstrated that some industrial dynamic countries in Asia, such as Japan, the Republic of Korea and Singapore, and in Europe, such as Germany and Holland have succeeded in building effective 'technology cultures'. As a result, these countries are now setting the pace of technical change. The purpose of this project is to determine how technology can be financed in micro applications and what broader policies institutions and programs would be needed to foster more rapid and broader technological development. International financial institutions, as well as top-down studies of Chinese national science and technology policies in the past, have recognize that there has been only very limited success in promoting effective use by industry of the technological resources available to the government as well as in forging link between the two. Accordingly, it is necessary to study further the 'technology cultures — of some successful countries as well as any differences in their institutional, educational and cultural characteristics. It is hoped that comparative studies of successful and less successful countries may provide some new useful insights and guides to the more effective promotion of technology innovation.

4.2.2 Method

To begin this study, two types of questionnaires have been prepared one for industrial firms and one for technology institutions. Several sectors of industrial firms and several types of technology institutions will be surveyed by sending them these questionnaires.

The questionnaires will address the following key issues.

1 Under what circumstances and structures do different institutions seem to function more effectively? There is a Technopolis in Japan and Science Parks in universities in Western countries, as well as central, provincial and other research institutions in China. Which can function most effectively? What kinds of activities do they tend to perform better?

2 Within what sorts of industrial structures do individual firms seem to provide more effective contributions and to cooperate most effectively with others?

3 In what sorts of technology areas (e.g., related to their science foci) do particular kinds of firms and other institutions tend to respond to such programs — and to what specific kinds of projects? How could the responsiveness of various types of firms influence the results of such programs?

This survey will be done in several countries in East Asia, in South Asia, in Western Europe and in Eastern Europe. It is hoped that the research will suggest some macropolicies for encouraging and increasing the effectiveness of technology innovations.

5. Conclusion

Technology innovation has played a dominant role in economic development. Enterprise management is also playing an increasing role in modern economic development. Improvements in technology innovation and in enterprise management can make major contributions to the prosperity of the global economy.

Bibliography

Goldman, M., "Research proposal for a study of institutional and policy priorities for technology development in industry," World Bank.

Kast, F.E. and Rosenzwerg, J.E., *Organization and Management*, McGraw-Hill Inc., 1979.

Koontz, H., *Essentials of Management*, McGraw-Hill Inc., 1979.

Innovation, prepared by the editors of *Technology Review* with the assistance of Myron J. Excelbert and the MIT Alumni Center of New York.

Innovation Policy, France, OECD, 1986 .

Sheth, J. and Ashghi, A., *Global Marketing Perspectives*, South-Western Publishing Co., 1989.

Tosi, H.L. and Can-oil, S.J., *Management* (second edition), John Wiley &Sons, 1982.

Self-Reliance in Science and Technology: China as a case study, a research project for UNU, 1987, principal investigators Wang Huijiong & Li Boxi.

Walcoff, C., Ouelletle, R.P. and Cheremisinoff, P.N., *Techniques for Managing Technological Innovation*, Ann Arbor Science, 1983.

7. Some Issues of Technology Management in China — A Challenge Towards the 21st Century

I. Introduction

China has achieved an impressive economic performance since the launch of economic reform and opening to the outside world in the late 70's. The growth rate of GDP averaged 9.3% from 1980 to 1990, and it is around 12% from 1991 to 1995. This rapid economic growth is also accompanied by rapid structural change as well as rapid growth of the external sector. The share of primary, secondary and tertiary sector in GDP has been changed from 30.4%:49%:20.6% in 1980 to 19.7:49:31.3 in 1995. The growth of the external sector is also impressive, it enjoys a growth rate of 11.7% from 1980 to 1990, and an average growth rate of 19.5% from 1991-1995. The structure of goods for export is also undergoing changes. The share of primary and manufactured goods in export has been changed from 50.3%:49.7% in 1980 to 14.4%:85.6% in 1995.

In 1995, China produced 18.4 billions meters of cloth, 445.6 millions tons of cement, 34.7 million units of TV set (within which 19.6 million units are colored TV sets), the amount of which ranked the first among the world. China produced 92.9 million tons of crude steel, 986.1 billion kwh of electricity which may be ranked the second or third of the world. And China has a 67.9% share of intra-Asian FDI flow, a share of 58.9% of FDI flow from the world to Asia. All these are overwhelming figures, but there is also other side of the coin, Chinese total social investment in 1995 is 194.5 billion yuan (which is around 23.4 billion USD. If an exchange rate of 8.3 yuan to 1 USD is used) which is 33.7% of GDP of the same year, the total labor force in 1995 is 689.1 million, 27% of which is engaged in urban economic activities. Therefore, this high economic growth and performance is contributed largely by high capital and labor input. How much is the contribution of technology? And it is a well known fact that science and technology are essential factors of growth of a modern economy. Because the global products and trade are changed gradually from labor intensive to capital intensive and to knowledge intensive. This is the point we are going to analyze in this paper first through presentation and analysis of some economic facts and explore the issues of technology management in China. This will be a major challenge to China toward the 21st century if a long-term sustainable growth of development is to be pursued.

II. Analysis of Some Economic Facts Related to Technology Management

It should be pointed out that the high economic growth of China in the past seventeen years have brought about enormous economic expansion in quantity, but there is still a large room for improvement in economic quality. That's why it is emphasized once more in China's recent Ninth Five-Year Plan and Outline of Long-Term Target Towards 2010 that "...We must bring about a vigorous change in the mode of economic growth and treat the improvement of economic returns as the central task of our economic work. We must rely on economic restructuring to enable an enterprise operating mechanism conducive to economizing resources, reducing cost and increasing economic returns, a technological advance mechanism conducive to independent innovation and an economic operation mechanism conducive to fair competition on the market and optimized distribution of resources to evolve". This statement is quoted to provide a background of analysis of the topic of this paper. Let's analyze several facts:

1. China has created a capability in production of lot of consumer's durables, but she has not created very much an innovative capability in a competitive market.

China's high growth rate of external sector is accompanied by both a high growth rate of import and export. The production capability of consumer's durables of China is formed through large amount of redundant importation of production lines, therefore, the economy of scale is not competitive.

China has imported around 120 production lines of TV sets and around 100 production lines of refrigerators in the eightieth. But the concentration ratio of production is quite low which is shown in Table 1.

Table 1   Comparison of Concentration Ratio CR4 of Some Consumer's Durables

	Refrigerator CR4(%)	TV set CR 4(%)	Bicycle CR4(%)
China 1988	26.1	19.8	23
Japan 1980	73	59	42

Note: 1 Concentration Ratio CR4(%) is the percentage of a market's sales accounted for by 4 of the largest firms in that market.

2 Source: *Industrial Organization and Effective Competition*, chief editors: Wang Huijiong & Chan Xiaohong, China Economic Publishing House, 1991.

With the above background, it can also be seen that although China produces the highest number of TV sets in the world, there is high growth rate of import of consumer's durables from abroad which is shown in Table 2. This shows the demand of the urban household for new models of products which can not be met by domestic production system. The import of production lines cannot create the capability to produce new models of products. And also the small scale of production has failed in price competition in the domestic market because the producers have no means to reduce the price of product as shown in Table 3.

Table 2 Relative Growth Rate of Import of Consumer's Durables of China
(With the preceding year=100%)

Unit: %

Item	1991	1992	1993	1994	1995
Color TV set	100.7	149.1	377.7	198.8	99.4
Electric refrigerator	50.4	72.7	291.8	154.0	146.0
Telephone set	112.4	183.2	210.7	176.7	99.4
Video camera	121.7	138.6	142.1	67.1	163.3

Source: Summarized from "Custom Statistics" of respective years.

Table 3 Producers Price Index of Consumer's Durables
(with preceding year=100% base year 1987=100%)

	1988	1989	1990	1991	1992	1993	1994	1995
Index	106.0	133.6	99.3	96.5	101.7	108.8	108.4	105.2

Source: *China Statistical Yearbook 1994,* and *A Statistical Survey of China*, China Statistical
Publishing House, 1996.

The success of economic reform has improved greatly the living standard of the urban and rural household. There is tremendous demand on the consumer's durables. Figures 1 and 2 show the growth of consumer's durables owned by urban and rural household. Enterprises in the Chinese economy should have the capability to forecast the demand and utilize the technological resources to produce to meet the demand. But the perfor-

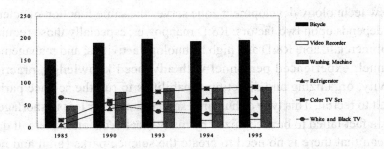

Fig. 1 The growth of consumer's durables owned by 100 urban household

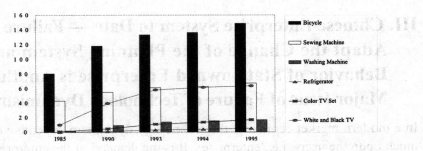

Fig. 2 The growth of consumer's durables owned by 100 rural household

Source: *A Statistical Survey of China*, China Statistical Publishing House, 1996.

mance of the enterprises is disappointing in this aspect. The failure to coordinate the importation of redundant production lines illustrates the weakness of macro-management of technology. And the weakness in forecasting the market demand and competition for new product illustrates the weakness in micro-management of technology. The micro-management of technology related very much to the major economic actor of the market, i.e., the enterprises. We shall discuss the Chinese enterprise system in "III" of this paper.

2. China has created around 52 high and new technology development zones with preferential policies to attract high and new technology investors, but its performance is not up to expectation.

This illustrates the issue in macro-technology management. International experience shows that the success of the science park in China (the high and new technology development zone serves the same function of science park) depends upon two factors: R&D manpower, especially those required for commercializable R&D and high technology activities; and management personnel: experienced personnel with advanced knowledge, practical creativity, organizing and directing capabilities to run the science park is difficult to recruit. This type of human resource is more or less in shortage in China, a fact failed to be recognized by many local decision makers. It does not mean that there is no need to create the science parks (high and new technology development zones), the issue is too many that have been created. The human resource available cannot cope with the number of science parks created.

III. Chinese Enterprise System to Date — Failure to Adapt the Change of the Planning System and Behavior of State-owned Enterprise is Another Major Issue of Failure of Technology Dynamism

In a modern market economy, the technology dynamism depends very much upon the users, i.e., enterprises. It is the demand of the enterprises in active use of technology and innovation of technology so as to improve its competitiveness in the domestic and global market. For the state-owned enterprises at different levels in a transitional economy, they are the major recipients of the investment allocated by the state or province, seeking expansion rather than improvement of current production through technological innovation, while innovation is an important means for an enterprise to improve its competitive position over rival suppliers by enhancing its product differentiation advantages and for improving market performance. But China at its current transition from a former central planned economy to a socialist market economy is facing the challenge to establish an appropriate market structure which may be a more conducive innovation to offer better incentives and resources for undertaking research and development. Besides, the very much traditional allocation of investment by the state becomes a major obstacle for improvement of current product and process. It is interesting to note that the state allocation of investment in China is divided into two categories: one is called capital construction, which is allocated to new investment projects, and the other is called technological rehabilitation, which is allocated to existing enterprises for the improvement of products and production processes. These two types of investment are authorized by two different state commissions: the former is authorized by the State Planning Commission, the latter is authorized by the State Economic and Trade Commission. But this division of power of approval has accentuated the trend that the local government and enterprises list the projects of capital construction into the category of technological rehabilitation for easy approval. This type of investment system has resulted in duplication of import of production lines and equipment by enterprises without serious effort to improve the products and processes through reliance on technology. The performance of the Chinese enterprise system can be shown through Figs. 3, 4 and 5. The major facts will be briefed below:

1. Since the launch of the economic reform, change has taken place in the structure of ownership system. Formerly, the structure of Chinese enterprise system is dominated by the state-owned enterprise. Currently, various forms of ownership coexist. The current structure of enterprise system is shown in Table 4.

It should be pointed out that from the official statement, both state-owned enterprises and collectively owned enterprises are considered to be in the category of public ownership system. The arbitrary division into two groups

Table 4   Enterprises and Gross Value of Output of Industry by Ownership

	Items	1990	1991	1992	1993	1994
I	Number of Enterprises (10000) Group 1	795.78	807.96	861.21	991.16	1001.71
I-1	State-owned Enterprises Group 2	10.44	10.47	10.33	10.47	10.22
I-2	Collective-owned enterprises (4-categories)	166.85	157.72	164.06	180.36	186.30
I-3	Individual-owned enterprises (2-categories)	617.60	638.67	685.40	797.10	800.74
I-4	Other ownership enterprises	0.88	1.08	1.42	3.21	4.45
II	Gross Value of Output of Industry (100,000,000 yuan) Group 1	23,924.36	28,248.01	37,065.71	52,691.99	76,909.46
II-1	State-owned Enterprises Group-2	13,063.75	14,954.58	17,824.15	22,724.67	26,200.84
II-2	Collective-owned enterprises	8,522.73	10,084.75	14,101.19	20,213.21	31,434.04
II-3	Individual-owned enterprises	1,290.30	1,609.10	2,506.80	4,402.05	8,853.23
II-4	Other ownership enterprises	1,047.56	1,599.58	2,633.58	5,352.06	10,421.35

Source: *China Statistical Yearbook 1995,* China Statistical Publishing House.

here is for convenience to study the performance of them to find out major problems.

2. The state-owned enterprises take the dominant share of the total societal investment which is shown in Figure 3. In the Chinese statistical system,

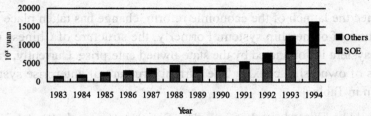

Fig. 3 Total social investment and SOE investment (10^8 Yuan)

(Total Societal Investmetn=others+SOE)

there is no available statistics on R&D spending of different institutions, but it is shown in Japanese statistics that in 1993, the annual R&D spending of industry has a share of 72.3% of national total, the research institute has a share of 14.3%, and the university has a share of 13.4%, while in China, the state-owned enterprises invest heavily for new expansion without a detailed record of R&D spending. The weakness of statistics is also an issue on both macro-technology and micro-technology management.

3. Fig. 4 shows the declined contribution of employment of state-owned enterprises while the town and village enterprises have a high growth rate of the employment. In fact, the town and village enterprises are generally in shortage of technological manpower. Their survival depends very much upon their market orientation. They are more technology-demanding. But their support from appropriate institutions are not sufficient. There is room for improvement in macro-management of technology to support those TVEs. Of course, we should not over exaggerat the truth, sometimes, some TVEs

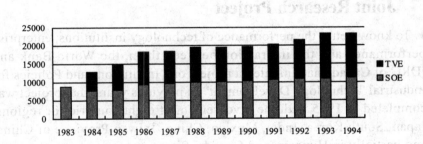

Fig. 4 Growth of employment of SOE and TVE (10^4)

may be also protected by the local authorities in local market — an imperfect market in transitional economy.

4. Fig. 5 shows the declined share of gross value of industrial output of state owned enterprises. It should be emphasized once more that the enterprise is the major client of technology. Anyhow, it is worthwhile to take a part of Schumpeter's theory into consideration, the key to economic growth is the innovative entrepreneur who takes risks and introduces new technologies to stimulate economic activity, replacing old technologies by the process of creative destruction. We cannot expect a stagnated enterprise to have technological dynamism.

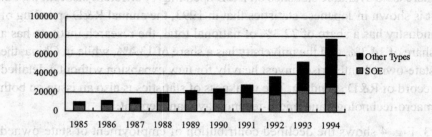

Fig. 5 Growth of gross value of industrial output (10^8 Yuan)

IV. Interaction of Enterprise and Technology Support Institutions-A Case Study of China of International Joint Research Project

1. To know better the performance of technology institutions, enterprise performance and the interaction between them, the World Bank and IDRC of Canada had initiated a project on "Institutions and Policies for Industrial Technology Development" in previous years, that project was completed in 1995 with the involvement of eight countries or regions, Japan, South Korea, India, Mexico, China, Taiwan Province of China, and partially in Hungary and Canada. Six sectors of industry were selected for study based upon their characteristics related to science and technology intensity, industrial structure, economies of scale, young or matured industry, etc. These six sectors identified for study are textile, foundry, machine tool, polymer, autoparts and software. Country teams used the same form of inquiry sheet to survey enterprises (about 18 interviews in each sector plus a random mailed survey) and technological institution. Our center and NRCSTD[1] had participated this project. The major aspect of the survey will be abstracted which will reveal the macro and micro aspects of technology issues. Table 5 is a summary of

---

1. NRCSTD is abbreviation of National Research Center of Science and Technology Development which is an institution belonged to State Science and Technology Commission.

the response of enterprises to government policies. Number 1 to 5 represents the rank of importance of preference. The larger the number, the higher its rank of importance.

Table 5   Response of Sectors to the Rank of Preference of
Government Policy — China Case Study

Government Policy \ Sector	Textile Sector	Foundry Sector	Machine Tool	Polymer Sector	Autoparts	Software Sector
1. Fiscal policy, tax exemption and reduction	4	4	4	4	4	4
2. Fiscal allocation of resources	4	4	4	4	4	4
3. Specific technical credit	4	4	4	4	4	4
4. Training	3	3	3	3	3	3
5. Government purchasing	3	3	3	3	3	3
6. Standard and Testing	3	3	3	3	3	3
7. Market protection	3	4	4	4	4	4
8. Export incentive	4	4	4	3	3	4

Note: All figures has been rounded without decimal.

It is interesting to note the expectation of enterprises, they generally have a high expectation on the policy from the government rather than reliance on the market or improvement of its competitiveness in the market through better skill of staffs through training, or some forms of protection of the market. They give high rank of preference in relying upon government, a traditional enterprise behavior of a former central planned economy. The response on training can be highly in contrast with the Japanese practice. The Japanese has the view that "...OJT (on-the-job training) enables frequent technological innovations"[2] since it can cope flexibly as well as speedily with changes in circumstances. Japanese firms pay huge amounts for education and training... the total amount spent on in-house training in Japan including the costs of OJT opportunities, add up to the equivalent of 3.3% of the GNP."

2. There is need for the improvement of performance of technological insti-

---

2. From reference

tutions — a problem area of technology management.

Table 6 is abstracted from our survey of textile enterprises to see their evaluation of various forms of technological institutions of the textile sector, this will provide a general view of current situation of Chinese technological institutions.

Table 6 Response of Evaluation of Various Forms of Technological Institutions of the Textile Industry through mail survey of 35 Enterprises

(unit: Times)

Types of Institution / Problems	Central Technological Institution	Provincial or Local T.I.	University or College	Consulting Company	Association	Academic Association	Research Association	In House T.I.	Frequency Total
Too high charge	8	5	2	2	5	4	-	1	27
Cannot solve practical problems	6	2	2	1	3	1		4	19
No response in time to give solutions	2	5	-	-	-	1	-	12	20
Shortage of qualified personnel	1	5	14	-	1	1	-	8	30
Bureaucracy	2	3	6	1	-	-	-	1	13
Frequent change of persons	4	3	4	-	-	-	-	3	14
Intellectual property rights	1	-	-	2	-	-	-	2	5
Difficult to collaborate	2	3	-	-	1	1	1	3	11
Frequency Total	26	26	28	6	10	8	1	34	139

Analysis of figures will give some issues of current technology management in China, an economy in transition. High complaints on inhouse technology institution of delay in response (12/20), intellectual property rights (2/5), shortage of qualified personnel (8/30) cannot solve practical problems (4/19) and difficult to collaborate (3/11) are issues happened within enterprises, showing micro-technology management features. Most of them belong to personnel management, work discipline, etc. These issues should and ought to be solved by enterprises themselves through improvement of technological management or personnel management, or through strengthening on-the-job training. But it is interesting to note the fact in Table 5 that previously the enterprises give a low rank of preference of training to government policy. This enterprise behavior will be a challenge in China's economic reform.

V. Issues of Technology Management in China — Summary and Some Theoretical Explorations

1. In the previous sections, the issues of technology management are presented through economic facts, the current performance of Chinese enterprises and a micro-case study of "Institutions and Policies for Industrial Technology Management". Hereunder, the major issues of both macro-technology and micro-technology management will be summarized as follows:

A. Issues of Macro-Technology Management

(1) In a modern world of increasing interdependence, no country can do all researches (basic and applied) and development activities solely within itself. It is well known that cross boarder cooperative research and development activities are popular currently. The latecomers must have an appropriate policy and regulation in effective transfer of technology to catch up and develop their own innovative capability. The current technology management in China is not quite effective in that aspect.

(2) There is no isolated technology policy, from the policy perspective, the technology policy should be designed within the context of national development strategy and economic policy. China has advocated industry policy in the recent decade. She has also paid attention to the environmental issues which can be shown from the official document "China Agenda 21" authorized by the State Council in 1994. There are some coordinations of technology and environmental policies. But a more close coordination of industrial policy, technology policy, environmental policy, foreign direct investment policy, energy policy and others is necessary. Giving the more than 50 ministries at the central level, and traditional compartmentalization of the ad-

ministrative operation, this becomes a major obstacle in macro-technology management. For example, development of automobile is emphasized in China's industrial policy. But there is the need to have close collaboration in study on the environmental issue, the issues of road and parking place in urban planning, and the energy policy issue because China has a dominant energy resource of coal rather than crude oil.

(3) The large number of technology institutions of China is not a sufficient condition for the promotion of industrial technology. The current macro-technology management should facilitate to create an environment to link the activity of technology institutions to meet the needs of production enterprises.

B. Issues of Micro-Technology Management

(1) The Chinese technological institutions are mostly established by various ministries and bureaus at the central and provincial levels. Formerly, they received financial allocations from those ministries and bureaus. Therefore, they had no tradition to be market-oriented: the management style was bureautic as shown in Table 6, the frequency of response of "bureaucracy" is 13 out of total 139 and "frequency of not response in time," 20/139. The Chinese science and technology management system reform had been implemented to cut and reduce financial support from the government and force the TIS to face the market. But their behavior has not been changed greatly. Because the nature of a separate entity of technology institutions without linking to enterprises has not related very much to the problems faced by the enterprises. And also a part of the researchers generally have no field or working experience at the factory level. Therefore, the high frequency of complaints on "shortage of qualified personnel" 30/139 and "cannot solve practical problems" with a frequency of response 19/139 as shown in Table 6. This is a personnel management problem.

(2) It should be pointed out that in many Western countries, it is now also advocated to force the public research institutions to face the market. A Canadian researcher has expressed the opinion that they face the same difficulties in market operation in the terminal conference of the World Bank project mentioned above. He thinks there should be at least two divisions in a research institution, one the market division and the other the research

division, because the character of a researcher is not well adapted to look for the market. This is critical for micro-technological management reform for all economies to change the public technological institutions to market orientation.

(3) For the R&D institutions within the enterprises, it can be found from the previous analysis that the state-owned enterprises of China are not competitive currently as described in III-2, 3, 4. And the in-house technology institutions are complained with a frequency of 34 of their weakness in performance as shown in Table 6. The complaint on intellectual property rights is a new issue of enterprise management in China. But all other complaints are related to the management problem of goal and value system of the technology institutions from the systems concept of management. The micro-technology management of R&D system in corporate management should develop the goal and value system within the context of the corporation. The functional areas should be developed within R&D institutions to fulfill the long-term and short-term goal of the corporation, i. e., profitability, growth, market share and product quality. But these functional areas have not been well established in the micro-technology management in China. These goals of corporation are new to the in-house technology institutions in the transition from the former central planned economy to a socialist market economy.

2. Some Theoretical Explorations

(1) Technology management is not the management of technology of a product or a process, there are many interfaces linking technology management to other management aspects: the management of the enterprise, the marketing management, the labor or personnel management, the production management, etc. In a broader context, it is the interaction of macro- and micro-technology, the interaction of various elements in a social economic system which determines the efficiency of technology management. We cannot expect to have an economic system with the tradition of extensive growth that can change to a new culture of intensive growth over night. The systems concept of management focuses on the life-cycle management which had been described in Reference 1. And it also involves the concept of management on inter-face, i.e., the impact of the broader system in which the sub-system works. This concept is expressed in Figure 6. This diagram and systems concept of management

will not be elaborated in detail here. This has been described in detail in Paper 5 of this part. In brief, the systems concept of management recognizes the interaction and mutual impact between the technology system (including management system) and economic system (including enterprise system, market system, planning system, etc.), the interaction between the economic and social systems (including the belief system, political system, cultural system, education system, etc.) and these systems also have mutual interaction with international system. These systems change over space. Therefore, the MNCs have to take care of the aspect of cross-cultural management. These systems are also changing over time, i.e., a dynamic concept rather than a static concept of management should be focused.

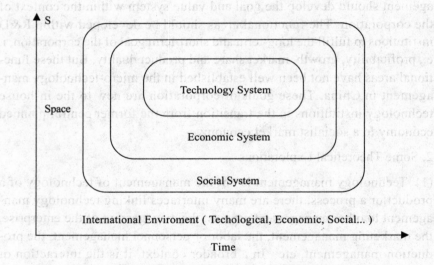

Fig. 6 System concept of management

(2) The impact of institutional effect

Since technology management system functions within the economic management system. Therefore, the reform of the technology management system is effected greatly by the reform of economic system. In many transitional economies, traditional economic theory is taken as the basis of reform, "getting the price right" and "letting the market force to take care everything". But there is also other schools of thought of economic theory, the "institutionalism". The term "institution" refers to the norms, roles, and structures developed by people to organize and guide their individual or joint activities. Based upon "institutionalism", economic systems change with time; technology constantly forges ahead, while society usually lags behind in adjusting to technological progress. We shall not apply blindly this school of thought, and we shall not also apply blindly the economic doctrine of laissez-fair. In Chinese situation, the technology has not forged ahead, but globally, the technology has forged ahead. Therefore, the on-going economic reform process has effected the reform of macro- and micro-technology management. There is certain analogy between social system, economic system and mechanical system, the "inertia". The larger the mass (size of country and population) the larger the inertia. That is the basic reason for the relatively successful economic system reform in China through a gradual approach. The concluding remarks of my paper is that, whether China can overcome the technology management issues described depends very much on the depth and breadth of the reform of the economic system. This is a major challenge towards the 21st century. This depends on how the complex social systems engineering is designed and implemented.

REFERENCES

1. *International Journal of Technology Management,* 1994, Vol. 8, Nos. 1/2, guest editor: Bela Gold Inderscience Enterprises Ltd, Geneva.

2. *Technical Progress of Enterprise: Policy and Institution,* chief editors: Wang Huijiong and Xu Shaoxiang, China Development Press, 1996 (in Chinese).

3. *Technological Independence-The Asian Experience,* edited by Saneh Chamarik and Susantha Goonatilake, UNU Press, 1994. (The author is the leading contributor for Chapter 2: "China").

4. "Transitional Corporations and Technology Transfer," UN, 1994.

5. "Evaluation Results 1992", the World Bank, 1994.

6. *Economic Theory,* Prof. Dr. M.A.G.Van Meerhaeghe Stenfert, Ko-

rean Pub. Co., 1980.

7. *Management Handbook,* Paul Mali, Ph. D. CMC, Editor-in-chief, John Wiley and Sons, 1982.

8. *Industrial Organization and Effective Competition*, chief editors: Wang Huijiong and Chen Xiaohong, China Economic Publighing House, 1991.

9. *China Statistics Yearbook 1994,* China Statistical Publishing House.

10. *A Statistical Study of China 1996,* China Statistical Publishing House.

Part III

Economic Development and Reform of China

Part III

Economic Development and Reform of China

8. Industrialization and Economic Reform in China

I. Overview

1.01   China has seen great economic progress in past four decades. Before 1949, the Chinese economy was dominated by the agricultural sector. Industrial sector was at its infant stage. Poverty was prevailing in urban and rural areas. The life expectancy of the people at birth was only around 40 years. Since the founding of the PRC, great efforts have been spent in industrialization and poverty elimination. The result of these efforts can be illustrated by quoting several remarks from reports of some international agencies. On the industrialization aspect, "China is the largest producer of manufactured goods in the developing world, and ranks as sixth largest contributor to world manufacturing value added (MVA). ... China possesses one of the most diversified industrial structures in the world. She is the world's largest producer of cotton yarn and textiles, third largest producer of cement and sulphuric acid, and ranks among the top six of the production of steel."[1] On the elimination of the worst aspect of poverty, it is pointed out by World Development Report 1990 that "In China, which accounts for a quarter of the developing world's people, life expectancy reached 69 in 1985." The life expectancy birth (year) is 70 in 1989.

1.02 The achievements of Chinese industrial economic strategy is shown in table 1.1 which lists change of rank of quantity of production among the world of major industrial products.

In order to understand better how achievements are realized and the strength, weakness and potential of the Chinese economy and its interdependence

---

1. *The People's Republic of China,* UNIDO, Dec. 2, 1985. The quoted statement is based upon statistics of 1984. The recent statistics is shown in Table 1.1

with that of the world. I shall explain China's industrial economic strategy into several stages in the following sections.

**Table 1.1 China's Rank of Quantity of Production of
Selected Products Among the World**

Item / Year	1949	1957	1965	1978	1980	1985	1988	1989
Steel	26	9	8	5	4	4	4	4
Coal	9	5	5	3	2	2	2	1
Crude Oil	27	23	12	8	6	4	4	6
Electricity generation	25	13	9	7	6	4	4	4
Cement		8	8	4	3	1	1	1
Chemical fertilizer		33	8	3	3	3	3	3
Chemical fiber		26		7	5	5	4	4
Cloth		3	3	1	1	1	1	1
Sugar			8	8	10	6	6	6
Television set				8	5	1	1	1

II. China's Industrialization in the Pre-reform Era (1949-1978)

2.01 China's industrial economic strategy — General

China's industrial economic strategy can be divided broadly into two periods, the period before 1979 and the period after. The year 1979 can be considered to be the year of turning point of change of approach of industrial economic strategy. From 1949-1978, or in the pre-reform period, economic industrial strategy is mainly inward oriented, and it has two major features, one is to carry out the transformation of the ownership system of production into public ownership, the other is to rely central planning system as the major mechanism in planning and implementation of the industrial economic strategy.

The industrial economic situation and policy in this period can also be described by several sub-periods.

2.02 Industrialization in the period of 1949-1957

China industrial economic strategy from 1949-1957 is characterized by the following features:

1. Heavy industry — the priority sector in industrialization process   Following three years of economic rehabilitation from 1949 to 1952, China had initiated and established a central planning system. The industrial policy in the First Five-Year Plan period (1953-1957) is characterized by the model of an accelerated build-up of heavy industry. The proportion of heavy industry in terms of gross value of industrial output rose from 37.3% in 1953 to 48.4% in 1957. The share of light industry was greatly reduced as shown is Table 2.1. An initial base of industrialization was established in that period through the construction of 694 above-norm projects (including 156 major ones). Averaged annual growth rate of industry and agriculture in that period were 18% and 4.8% respectively.

Table 2.1 Change of share of goods in production

Year	% Share of producer goods	% Share of consumer gods
1953	37.3	62.7
1954	38.5	61.5
1955	41.7	58.3
1956	45.4	54.5
1957	48.4	51.6

* Source: *China Statistics Year Book 1984*, China Statistics Press.

2. Trade Policy — Socialist transformation of all commercial sector was conducted, and self reliance was pursued. Central planned economy is characterized by a material allocation system of the state. The commercial sector is responsible only for the agricultural products and other consumer goods. In the traditional MPS system of the former Soviet model, the commercial sector is considered to be non-productive, its development is of minor concern. Unlike the industrialization process carried out in 18th and 19th centuries in the West and the industrialization process of NIE's after World War II, industrial development is featured also with an active trade development, either domestic or external trade. The trade policy of China in the pre-reform period had imposed a negative effect to the industrialization process. Table 2.2 shows the change of share of total trade turnover in percentage of different types of firms from 1950 to 1957. And Table 2.3 shows that the

retail service, catering and other services had been declined in this period.

Table 2.2   Transformation of Ownship System of Commercial Sector before 1957 (% of Total)

Year	State Firms in %	State capitalist and Cooperative Firms	Private
1950	14.9	0.1	85.0
1953	49.7	0.4	49.0
1954	69.0	5.4	25.6
1955	67.6	14.6	17.8
1956	68.3	27.5	4.2
1957	65.7	31.5	2.7

Source: *Economic Development and Social Change in PRC*, Willy Kraus, Springer-Verlag, 1979.

Table 2.3   Some Facts of Chinese Commercial Service 1952-1957

Year	No. of Firms of Retail Service 10,000 units	No. of Restaurants 10,000 units	Other Services 10,000 units	No. of Persons Employed in retail Service 10,000	No. of Persons Employed in Restaurants 10,000
1952	420	85	45	709.5	145
1957	195	47	28	568.9	115.5

For the external trade, it has been historically small relative to total economic activity, reflecting the large country /size of China and its diversified resource endowments. In the above-mentioned period, the expansion of foreign trade had been further constrained due to the absence of diplomatic relations with many Western countries. There was only barter trade between China and the former U.S.S.R. and Eastern European countries. There is technology acquisition from them through the import of complete plants and equipment. It should be pointed out that technology acquisition by that period was successful. Because importation of technology included hardware and software. Complete sets of drawings were provided. Foreign experts came to China, including those in designing, construction, testing, operation and maintenance links. R&D institutions were also set up following the former Soviet model. It is estimated that the contribution of total merchandise trade to growth of GNP was around 0.9 percent from 1952-1957.

3. Institutions for Implementation of Industrial Economic Strategy

(1) The Central Planning System

China had adopted a Soviet-type central planning model to promote the development of the economy in the 50's, because China was influenced by the apparently impressive development of the former Soviet Union at that time. Moreover, the former Soviet Union was the only major country China could turn to for assistance. In line with the Soviet model, high rates of capital investment were emphasized, with priority given to heavy industry. The agricultural sector was used to support industrialization by means of setting its prices that favoured industry over agriculture. The State Planning Commission was established in 1952. It set up a system of central economic planning — the medium term five-year plan and the annual plan. The plans were consisted of several parts, a production plan, material allocation plan, a wage and labour plan, etc. The planning bureau in each province and county prepares a similar local plan. The central plan was implemented through mandatory purchases and allocations of key products. Goods regarded as of national importance were around 1,000 in number, which were initially allocated at the national level among provinces and centrally controlled organizations. Beneath the general planning umbrella, responsibility for commodity flow was divided among several agencies according to the nature of the goods concerned. Most of industrial producer's goods were allocated by the State Material Supply Bureau, the Ministry of Commerce was responsible for consumer goods and services, etc. Each of these agencies had subordinates or counterpart units at the provincial and county level. Therefore, there was a strong vertical chain of action, but the horizontal connection was weak.

(2) The Budget and the Banking System

The principal instrument of financial control over the economy was the state budget. It was decided in 1950 to strictly centralize all matters of economy and finance, including the administration of revenues and decisions. Accordingly, the share of the expenditure of the central government from 1950 to the end of the First Five-year Plan period was predominant (see Table 2.4). Differential taxes were used to implement industrial policy, i.e., commerce was more heavily taxed than industry, with the tax rates for heavy industry being lower than those for light industry, etc. In the pre-reform period, enterprises had generally been obliged to remit virtually all their profits to the state, and the enterprise profits were nearly the most important source of revenue of the state budget. This is shown in Table 2.5. Table 2.6 is prepared to show the change of share of expenditare between the central and local governments for comparative study. This will give a better understanding of section 2.03(5) followed.

**Table 2.4 Share of the Central Government and
Local Administrations of State Expenditure 1950-1957** (in percent)

	1950	1951	1952	1953	1954	1955	1956	1957
Central government	74.20	74.72	71.08	75.84	74.90	75.93	71.05	70.78
Local government	25.80	28.28	28.92	24.16	25.10	24.07	28.59	29.22

Source: *Economic Development and Social Changes in the PRC,* Willy Kraus, Springer-Verlag, 1979.

Table 2.5   State Budget Revenue Income in Item (Selected Year)

unit: 100 million yuan

Year	Tax	Enterprise Income	Debt Income	Income from Energy and Transportatiom Constructiom Fund	Other	Subsidies for enterprise at loss
1953	119.67	76.69	9.62		16.88	
1957	154.89	144.18	6.99		4.13	
1960	203.65	265.84			2.80	
1963	164.31	172.68			5.26	
1966	221.96	333.32			3.43	
1971	312.56	428.40			3.77	
1976	407.96	333.06			30.56	
1981	629.89	353.68	73.08		32.81	
1984	947.35	276.77	77.34	122.45	77.95	
1985	2040.79	43.75	89.85	146.79	52.24	
* 1990	2821.86	78.30	375.45	185.08	430.74	578.88

Source: *China Statistics yearbook 1991,* China Statistics Press.
* In 1985, China changed the profit remittance system to taxation.

Table 2.6 Share of the Central Govemment and Local Administratioms of State Expenditure in Ddifferent Periods

Year or period	Income	Budget Revenue Central	Local	Expenditure	Budegt Central	Local
Ist Five-Year Plan period	1,354.9	615.2	739.7	1,345.7	997.3	348.4
2nd Five-Year Plan period	2,116.6	480.4	1,636.2	2,288.7	1101.6	1,187.1
1963-1965	1,215.1	335.8	879.3	1,205.0	718.9	486.1
3rd Five-Year Plan period	2,529.1	790.1	1,738.9	2,518.5	1,538.0	980.5
4th Five-Year Plan period	3,919.7	576.4	3,343.3	3,919.4	2,125.2	2,657.2
5th Five-Year Plan period	4,960.7	774.5	4,186.1	5,247.4	2,590.2	2,657.2
6th Five-Year Plan period	6,830.7	2,087.6	4,743.1	6,952.0	3,395.1	3,556.8
7th Five-Year Plan period	13,517.7	5,341.4	8,176.2	13,978.3	5,532.6	8,445.7
1986	2,260.3	916.7	1,343.6	2,330.8	962.3	1,368.6
1989	2,947.9	1,105.5	1,842.4	3,040.2	1,105.2	1,935.0
1990	3,312.6	1,367.9	1,944.7	3,452.2	1,372.8	2,079.4

China's banks in this period were essentially administrative organs facilitating and supervising the implementation of decisions pertaining to the allocation of real resources. The role of the banking system vis-a-vis enterprises was to provide the amount of credit needed to comply with government administrative directives and to audit payments to ensure that funds were used for their earmarked purposes. Until the late 1970s, the Chinese financial system was virtually a monobank system, modeled on that of the former Soviet Union, under which all financial transactions are handled by one bank, and there is a virtual absence of nonbank financial institutions and markets. The principal institution was the People's Bank of China which handled all domestic industrial and commercial credit operations, most rural credits, and served as the major supervisory agency for the few other financial institutions that existed. In addition, the People's

Construction Bank of China acted as fiscal agent for budgetary transfers to the enterprises in support of capital construction investments; the Agricultural Bank of China as a lender to the rural sector and supervisor of rural credit cooperatives.

(3) Regional Development Strategy and Locational Policy

The regional development strategy was more or less egalitarian and locational policy was defense-oriented for industrial siting. Nearly all important projects were located in northeastern part and hinterland. The cities along the coastal areas were of minor concern. Interprovincial differences in per-capita industrial output have narrowed somewhat mainly because growth has deliberately been kept below the national average in the old industrial centres (Shanghai, Tianjin and other cities along the coastal) and above the national average in the interior and border provinces and the new capital Beijing. This was more or less a negative aspect of the economic industrial strategy in that period because the comparative advantage of coastal areas could be fully realized.

2.03 Industrial Economic Strategy in the Period from 1958-1978

In order to avoid a lengthy discussion, we arbitrary makes the classification of this period, which covers the period of the Second Five-Year Plan (including the period of Great Leap Forward from 1958-60), the Adjustment Period (1963-1965), the Third and the Fourth Five-Year Plans (1966-70, 1971-75), and part of the fifth Five-Year Plan (1976-80). The industrial economic strategy is characterized by the following features:

1. Heavy Industry Continued to Play the Leading Role

Although Chairman Mao had assigned an order of priority at the end of the First Five-Year Plan period in sectoral development, i.e., agriculture — light industry — heavy industry, this guideline had not been followed in this period. The gross value of output of heavy industry and light industry in 1979 was 98.5 and 22.8 times that of 1949. Steel industry was given top priority of concern in the period of the Great Leap Forward and defense industry was very much emphasized during "cultural revolution". In the Third and Fourth five-Year Plans, the share of investment in heavy industry was 54.5% and 52.1% respectively, which were 15.8% and 13.4% higher than in the First

Five-Year Plan.

2. The basic policy on ownership system was to strengthen further the state ownership system, the collective ownership system shrunk in share, the private ownership system was nearly at the margin of abolishment. This can be illustrated from the data of employees in Table 2.7.

Table 2.7   Number of Eemployees of Different Types of Ownership

(10,000 persons)

Year	State-owned Enterprises	Collectively Owned Enterprises	Individual Labor in Urban Areas
1957	2,103	650	104
1962	3,309	1,012	216
1965	3,738	1,227	171
1970	4,792	1,424	96
1975	6,426	1,772	24
1980	7,451	2,048	15

3. Trade Policy

Domestic trade remained stagnant as shown in Table 2.8, while the external sector had a high growth rate in the 70's as shown in Table 2. 9. The 1960s was a decade of severe foreign exchange constraints, the main effect of the severe shortage of foreign exchange in the 1960s was to reduce machinery and equipment imports and an import substitution strategy was pursued. Foreign exchange constraints eased significantly in the 1970s as China resumed her position in the UN, appearance of a surplus of crude oil and the growing export capability of domestic industries. The early 1970s saw the resumption of technology acquisition from abroad. In contrast to the 1950s when the objective was to build up a broad range of heavy industries, the import program in the 1970s focused on acquiring a domestic capability to manufacture intermediate goods, especially chemical fertilizer, synthetic fibers, other petrochemical products, chemicals and high quality steel products.

Table 2.8 Some Figures of Commercial Activity

Item of service units (10000)	End of 1957	End of 1965	End of 1978	End of 1983
1. Retail Commercial Service	159.3	88.1	104.8	478.7
(1) State owned	52.1	34.6	35.7	60.6
(2) Collectively owned	101.9	24.9	58.3	74.0
(3) Individual	41.9	28.6	10.8	344.1
2. Restaurant owned	47.0	21.7	11.7	87.7
(1) State owned	4.0	3.8	5.4	5.5
(2) Collectively	31.2	7.2	2.7	11.5
(3) Individual	11.8	10.7	3.6	70.4

Table 2.9 Growth of Foreign Trade

Period	Exports/mports (current $)		Export/ Imports (Current price)-La		Growth of total merchandise trade/growth of GNP
	Average Annual Growth		Rate Over Period in %		
1950-60	12.2	13.2	9.7	10.7	0.9 (1952-57)
1961-70	4.0	4.2	2.6	2.8	0.3 (1957-79)
1971-79	23.0	27.0	9.8	13.8	2.0

"International price index," compiled by the World Bank.

Source: Ministry of Foreign Trade, "China: Socialist Economic Development", the main Report
of the World Bank, 1981.

4. Science and Technology Policy

As a whole, China emphasized the role of science and technology in the development process, in the realization of industrial economic strategy. One of China's successful experiences in science and technology policy is the S&T program directed by the central government, in which resource can be concentrated to achieve specific large projects. For example, China had implemented a 12-year S&T Development Program from 1956-1967,in which eight sectors of strategic importance were listed, nuclear energy, jet technology, electronic computer, automation, semi-conductor and radio electronics. Achievements of this program has laid the foundation of the first successful test of atomic bomb in Oct. 1964, and the launching of first

Chinese artificial earth satellite in April 1970; and China had mastered available production technology of a full range of products, improving and modifying them to suit local conditions despite prolonged international isolation. But technological self-reliance had been sough at the national, ministerial, provincial and local levels, and even in the enterprises (many of which, for example, manufacture their own machinery). This had been extremely wasteful of both physical capital and human resources. There was no linkage between the civilian sector and the defense sector. In addition, the linkage between scientific research and technological application was weak due to many institutional problems.

5. Institutions for Implementation of Industrial Economic Strategy

(1) Planning System Swings between Centralization and Decentralization

China's industrial policy and industrial structure are affected greatly by swing of centralization and decentralization of the planning system. Early in April 25, 1956 Chairman Mao thought it was necessary to decentralize the existing planning structure. Starting from the "contradiction between the centre and the regions," he stated that it was necessary "to consider... how to raise the enthusiasm of the regions by allowing them to run more projects under the unified plan of the centre." Within the framework of the decentralization measures of 1957, large portions of activities were taken away from the central government ministries and reassigned to the provinces. This decentralization reform also had a profound effect on the entire finance system (see Table 2.6). The State Council decree of Nov. 15, 1957 established the financial autonomy of the local authority. The efforts of decentralization were practised until the time when they were abandoned after the failure of the policy of Great Leap Forward. Recentralization began in 1961. And once again, the provinces had gained increasing influence in the planning of local production, financing and distribution of investment in the period of "cultural revolution". This background explains two important facts. The first is that China has not established a very rigid and perfect central planning system as the former Soviet Union had. This is of very much help for the reform carried out in the 80s. The second is the unique feature of dualism of a widespread pattern of vertical integration on the one side and identical industrial structure of different provinces on the other. Example of the former were the ministries of building materials, chemical and metallurgical industry, which had their own mining operations; and nearly all ministries had their own machine-building enterprises supplying at least some of their own needs for machinery. For the later, Table 2.10 shows clearly identical industrial structure of typical provinces which can explain the inefficient economic performance resulted from local self-sufficiency of each province due to "decentralization" and self-reliance policy for the provinces in the pre-reform period.

Table 2.10 Dispersion of Production Activities among and Within Provinces in 1982

Production Activity	No. of Provinces Involved in Activity (out of 29)	No. of Prefectures or Municipalities		
		Jiangsu (out of 14)	Hubei (out of 14)	Gansu (out of 13)
Food grain	29	14	14	13
Cotton	21	11	2	3
Coal 27	9	7	3	
Cement	29	14	14	13
Pig Iron	27	9	3	2
Steel	28	13	8	4
Steel Production	28	14	7	4
Fertilizers	28	14	12	6
Machine tools	28	13	9	2
Cloth28	14	14	4	
Bicycles	26	12	6	1
Sewing machines	24	12	8	0
Watches	24	11	8	0

Source: *China: Long Term Issues and Options,* World Bank, Country Economic Report, 1985.

(2) Regional Development Strategy and Locational Policy

Because the swing of centralization and decentralization, the emphasis of local self-sufficiency in industrial policy and the neglect of trade, all provinces and hundreds prefectures were involved in a wide range of production activities, and more or less a balanced regional development strategy is pursued. The locational policy was hinterland oriented, especially so in the Third and Fourth Five-Year Plan period.

III. China's Industrial Economic Strategy in the 80's — The Period of Economic Reform

3.01 Introduction

China has achieved great economic progress from 50's to 70's as remarked by an international agency that "Not withstanding these twists and turns, which have engendered some dramatic economic fluctuations, there has been substantial progress toward the two main objectives (industrialization and elimination of poverty). Industrialization has been very rapid, largely as the result of an unusually high rate of investment, virtually all of which has been financed by domestic savings. The share of industry in GDP (around 40%) is currently similar to the average for the middle income developing countries. And China's most remarkable achievement during the past three decades has been to make low-income groups far better off in terms of basic needs than their counterparts in most other poor countries."[2] But through three decades of experience in economic development, China realized that the economic gains came at a very high cost in terms of extensive use of productive factors, i.e., high investment and large labor input.

Because China had followed the Soviet model in planning and administration, public sector-led development strategy dominated and private sector was near the brink of abolishment. The government rather than the market had played a major role in resource allocation. A semi-closed economy prior to 1979 could not be adapted to the rapidly changing conditions of the international economy. Therefore, reform and opening-up have been promulgated as two basic national policies since the Third Plenum of the Eleventh Party Central Committee in 1978.

3.02 Major Aspects of Economic Reform

It is difficult to understand China's industrial economic strategies in the 80's and thereafter without an apprehension of the aspects of economic reform, because there are many interrelated aspects. The major aspects of economic reform since the late 70's include agricultural reform, reform of the system of

---

2. From World Bank Report: *China: Socialist Economic Development,* the main report, June 1981.

microeconomic decision, reform of the price system of the external trade, reform of the wage system and the labour market, fiscal reform, banking and financial system reform. The critical aspect of the above are: starting with the household responsibility system in the agricultural sector, the approach taken in the 80's involves a dispersal of decision-making powers as well as control over resources to lower ranked economic units such as provinces and enterprises. Importance is also attached to expanding consumption possibilities so as to restore incentives. Reform program also sought to multiply trade links and establish channels through which Chinese producers can obtain foreign technology. The reform is also attempting to break down the severe compartmentalization resulted from the hierarchical vertical structure of enterprise relationships with their supervising ministries under pre-reform central planning, establishment of horizontal links of enterprises across sectors are encouraged. With a view of the above-mentioned aspects of economic reform, China's major economic industrial strategy will be described below.

3.03 Industrial Economic Strategy: Restructuring of Industry to Promote Efficiency and Change of Attitude toward Trade

Restructuring of industry is realized from several fronts:

1. Targeting Policy to Heavy Industry Is Changed

In the document of the Sixth Five-year Plan (1981-1985), it was mentioned in the basic tasks that "it is necessary to increase the production of agricultural products, light industry and textile industry and other daily consumer goods with full efforts to adapt to the demands of society, ... It is necessary to adjust the aim of products ... so that the production of producer's goods will be more or less in match with the production of consumer goods." The growth of consumer goods was also emphasized in the Seventh Five-Year Plan (1986-1990). Table 3.1 shows the change of shares of heavy and light industries in different periods.

2. Trade Policy

As noted by Adam Smith, the development of industry is likely to be severely handicapped if it is deprived of the ability to trade widely. Learning experience from the past, economic reform has involved liberalization of government control over domestic trade sector and change of affitude toward trade.

Table 3.1   Change of Shares of Heavy and Light Industrial Sectors in Different Periods

Period	Year	Light Industry	Heavy Industry
Recovery Period	1950	70.7	29.3
	1952	64.5	35.3
1st Five-Year Plan Period	1953	62.7	37.3
	1957	55.0	45.0
2nd Five-Year Plan Period	1958	46.4	53.6
	1962	47.2	52.8
Adjustment Period	1963	44.8	55.2
	1965	51.6	48.4
3rd Five-Year Plan Period	1966	49.0	51.0
	1970	46.2	53.8
4th Five-Year Plan Period	1971	43.0	57.0
	1975	44.1	55.9
5th Five-Year Plan Period	1976	44.2	55.8
	1980	47.2	52.8
6th Five-Year Plan Period	1981	51.5	48.5
	1985	47.4	52.6
7th Five-Year Plan Period	1986	47.6	52.4
	1989	48.9	51.1
	1990	49.5	50.5

Source: *Zhongguo Gongye Jingji Tongji Nianjian 1990*, China Statistics Press.

Table 3.2   Share of Output by Industrial Sectors

	1952	1957	1965	1978	1985	1987
Metallurgy	5.9(5)	9.3(4)	10.7(5)	8.7(5)	8.0(5)	8.0(5)
Power	1.3(10)	1.4(10)	3.1(7)	3.8(7)	3.3(8)	3.1(8)
Coal & Coke	2.4(8)	2.3(8)	2.6(10)	2.8(10)	2.3(9)	2.2(9)
Petroleum	0.5(11)	0.9(11)	3.2(6)	5.5(6)	4.5(6)	4.2(7)
Chemical Industry	4.8(6)	8.2(5)	12.9(4)	12.4(3)	11.2(4)	11.8(3)
Machinery	11.4(3)	18.2(2)	22.3(1)	27.3(1)	26.9(1)	28.0(1)
Building Materials	3.0(7)	3.3(7)	2.8(9)	3.6(8)	4.2(7)	4.5(6)
Forest	6.5(4)	5.4(5)	2.9(8)	1.8(9)	1.6(10)	1.5(11)
Food Processing	24.1(2)	19.6(1)	12.6(3)	11.1(4)	11.5(3)	11.1(4)
Textile	27.5(1)	18.2(2)	15.8(2)	12.5(2)	15.3(2)	18.1(2)
Paper Making	2.2(9)	2.3(8)	1.8(11)	1.3(11)	1.3(11)	2.1(10)

Source: *China Toward the Year 2000*, Wang Huijiong and Li Poxi, New World Press, 1990.
Note: Number in the bracket of Table 3.2 is ranking in terms of share of output.

(1) Domestic Trade   Private traders have been encouraged in marketing and transportation, during 1984-85, about three fourths of small state enterprises in commercial sector was contracted or leased to collectives and individuals.

Procurement and marketing procedures for agricultural commodities have unfolded outside of the central plan, and the state allocated around 837 category I[3] and II products in 1980. But the amount and scope of material allocation have been reduced. For example, the amount of central allocation of four key materials, i.e., steel, coal, timber and cement, are 74%, 58%, 81% and 35% respectively in 1980, and it was reduced to 50%, 42%, 24% and 10% in 1988. The local governments increased their shares in allocation and the enterprises increased theirs too through self marketing. But China's trade system remains inefficient. Interregional flows of goods are still subject to restrictions, reflecting local governments' control over the distribution of goods that remain subject to mandatory planning.

(2) External Trade   The opening of China's economy to the international market is a reform that rivals the transformation of agriculture. The growth rate of foreign trade from 1981 to 1989 was 12.3%, the growth rate of export and import were 11.4% and 13.1% respectively. In 1989 and 1990, external trade amounted to 30% of GDP as against 14% in 1981. Prior to 1978, China's foreign trade was handled exclusively by 12 state-owned foreign trade corporations organized along product lines. Levels of exports and imports each year were controlled by the central planning system, administered by the Ministry of Foreign Trade (MFT and later MOFERT). By conducting trade through the FTCs, the tradeable goods sector of the domestic economy was insulated from the rest of the world. The government started to reform the foreign trade system in 1978. Control over trade has been decentralized. The enterprises have been provided greater resources as incentives and given more decision-making authority and responsibility for their financial performance. The structure of the plan was revised to consist of two parts: the command plan estab-

---

3. China has three categories of producer goods. The goods in Category I were under unified distribution and subject to balancing by the State Material Supply Bureau. Category II goods were special products allocated by the central industrial ministries responsible for their production. Anyhow, China allocated fewer goods centrally than the former USSR. In 1980, China allocated 837 category I and II products as compared with about 65,000 in the USSR (of which about 50,000 were balanced and allocated by the ministries)

lishes mandatory quatas for the volume of exports and imports of key commodities, the guidance plan assigns targets for the value of exports and imports of certain products to local governments and FTCs. The foreign trading rights of domestic enterprises are increased, and the so-called agency system was also introduced in 1984.

3.04 Industrial Economic Strategy: Restructuring of Ownship System

Restructuring of economy is also realized through the reform of state enterprise and development of non state-owned economic entities.

Different forms of ownership are developed with public ownership remaining predominant. State enterprises have been given greater financial responsibility and granted increased freedom in determining their own operations. And since the late 1970s, China's rural industrialization and development have undergone a remarkable transformation. Private industrial activity and other non-agricultural activities are now permitted. Rural industry also has been benefited from tax advantage and since 1984, enhanced access to credit from the state banking system.

1. State Enterprise Reform

Table 3.3 Changes in the Share of Gross Value of Industrial Output (GVIO) by Ownership (%)

Serial No.	Year	Total	State-owned Enterprise	Collective-owned Enterprise	Joint State-Private	Enterprise	Individual owned	Others
1	1949	100	26.2	0.5	1.6	48.7	23.0	
2	1950	100	32.7	0.8	2.1	38.1	26.3	
3	1951	100	34.5	1.3	3.0	38.4	22.8	
4	1952	100	41.5	3.3	4.0	30.6	20.6	
5	1953	100	43.0	3.9	4.5	29.3	19.3	
6	1954	100	47.1	5.3	9.8	19.9	17.9	
7	1955	100	51.3	7.6	13.1	13.2	14.8	
8	1956	100	54.5	17.1	27.2	0.04	1.2	
9	1957	100	53.8	19.0	26.3	0.1	1.8	
10	1958	100	90.1	9.9	0	0	0	

Source: *Chinese Statistics Almanac 1984.*

(1) China has not advocated privatization because there was nearly no private capital at all before 1979. It can be seen from Table 3.3 that state-owned enterprises had a share of 90.1 percent of the gross value of industrial output in 1965 and collectively owned enterprises accounted for 9.9 percent. It was not practical to implement privatization, instead, the strategy to foster the growth of different types of ownership, including the experimental operation of stock and bond markets, was adopted. Recently, an increasing number of China's most influential state-run commercial firms are undergoing a new round of stock-based restructuring as domestic reforms and development speed up.

(2) State enterprise reforms began in 1979 with experiments on profit retention system, which replaced the old system of 100 percent profit remittance. The "economic responsibility system" with five forms of profit retention was introduced in December 1981. In 1983, the government initiated a nationwide change from "profit transfer" to "income taxation." In 1984 "Provisional Regulations on Expansion of the State Enterprises' Autonomy" was announced.

The major contents are as follows:

(i) Greater autonomy in operational decisions such as production planning, product sales after fulfilment of planned targets.

(ii) Industrial output exceeding the planned output could be sold at prices within the range of 20 percent above or below state-prescribed prices.

(iii) Increased authority given to factory managers for purchasing of materials, utilization of financial resources, organization setup, personal and labour management, wage and bonus, etc.

(3) In 1985, bankruptcy law was drafted and experimented in selected industrial cities, but no major state-owned enterprises have been declared bankrupt. However, some forced mergers of weak enterprises with stronger ones have been reported.

(4) From 1985-87, there is gradual move towards "contract management responsibility system", the objective of this reform is to separate ownership from management authorities in the daily operation of the enterprises. There are several forms of contracts. They generally specify targets for the expected performance of the enterprises, quotas for output to be sold

at state-fixed prices, and obligations to the government mainly in the form of taxes. Leasing arrangements have also been promoted for small enterprises in the service sector. But the result of this was questioned due to "Agency" problem.

(5) The scope of mandatory planning has been reduced significantly, this promoted the market orientation of SOE. Fixed investment of the state enterprises financed by the state budget has declined sharply of its share from 60 percent of such investment in 1978 to 20 percent in 1987. The enterprises have been given greater responsibility for their own investment by utilization of the retained portion of their earnings. At the same time, the number of products that are allocated through the output plan of state has been declined from 188 items in pre-reform period to 11 items for consumer goods, and from 56 items in 1978 to 22 items at present for production goods now. But all of the petroleum and electricity output is virtually controlled by the central and local governments. This is also true for the railway transportation, because energy and transportation are now major constraints on industrial production. The central and local governments retain a strong influence over the economy.

(6) Regulation of Transformation of Operating Mechanism of SOE

In July 23, 1992, the State Council promulgated the "Regulations of Transformation of the Operation Mechanism of SOE" in order to push the SOEs to operate in markets, to increase their vitality, and make them independent legal persons to be responsible for profits and losses by themselves. This document is divided into 7 chapters and 54 articles. Some related informations are quoted in Box 3.1.

Box 3.1
Regulations of Transformation of the Operation
Mechanism of SOE

Chapter I General

There are 5 Articles.

Article 4: Based upon the principle of transformation of operating mechanism, strengthening control at macro-level and liberalizing control at micro-level, the government must change its role to reform the management style of enterprises, to cultivate and develop the market system, to establish and perfect the social security system, to implement the reform in planning, investment, public finance, taxation, finance, price, material supply, commerce, external trade, wages, personnel and labor management in package and in coordination.

Chapter II Rights of Enterprise Operation

There are 17 articles describing separately the rights in operation of assets, the rights of decisions of production operation, the rights in pricing products and services, the rights of sales of products, the rights of procurement of materials, the rights of imports and exports, the rights of decision in investments, the rights in handling the retained financial resources, the rights in alliance and take-over of other enterprises, the rights of employment and staff, the rights of personnel management, the rights of distribution of wages and bonus, the rights of setting up of internal organizations, the rights to refuse apportion (*tanpai*) of expenses. Only selected articles are abbreviated for their essential points as follows:

Article 7: To create conditions for the implementation of the stock-sharing system.

(Note: The State Reform and Restructuring Commission had announced "Some Opinions on Normalization of Stock-Sharing Limited Company").

Article 8: The Enterprise Enjoys the Rights of Decisions of Production Operation

The enterprises can make decisions of production operation by themselves, to produce products and to supply services for the society based upon the guidance of macro-economic planning of the state and the demand of the market.

The state, in case of necessity, has the right to issue mandatory plans to the enterprises. The enterprises have the right to refuse to implement mandatory plans of any department except the order that comes directly from the planning department of the State Council and provincial government, or the mandatory plans from relevant departments authorized by the planning department of the state and provincial government.

Article 10: The enterprises enjoy the rights of sales of products.

The enterprises can sold any product produced by themselves (outside the scope of mandatory planning) nationawide. Any department and procincial government is not allowed to enforce a blockade, or restriction or any other discriminative measures.

Article 12: The enterprises enjoy the rights of import and export.

The enterprises can select foreign trade agencies nationwide freely in import and export. They have the right to participate the negotiations with foreign partners.

Article 13: The enterprises enjoy the rights of investment decision.

The enterprises can engage in productive construction through retained profit and self-financing in accordance with the industrial policy of the state and sectoral and regional development plans. They can start project through self-determination if they can solve the conditions for construction and production by themselves. But they should report to the government for record and receive supervision.

Article 22: The rights of operation of the enterpsies are protected by the law,....

Chapter III The Duties of Enterprises to Be Responsible for Profit and Losses by Themselves

There are 8 articles dealing with the wage and bonus system of the enterprises, prize and penalty for the obligation of the enterprise leadership and enterprises of different system (contract responsibility or leasing), obligations in accounting and auditing, etc.

Chapter IV Change and Termination of Enterprises

There are 9 articles dealing with the various conditions of change of products, production, stop, production, mergers, separation, bankcruptcy and debt clearing, termination of an enterprise, etc.

Chapter V Relations between Enterprise and Government

There are 7 article dealing with the relations in assets between the enterprise and the government, the role of the government in macro-control and micro-guidance, the role of the government in development of the market, in improving the social security system, in supplying the public services, etc.

Article 41: The assets of the enterprises belong to the ownership of whole people, i.e., owned by the state. The State Council handles the rights of ownership of assets of the enterprises on behalf of the state.

Chapter VI Legal Responsibility

There are 3 articles dealing with the legal aspects separtely for the related departments of government if they interfere with the various rights given to the enterprises and for the enterprises if they fail to fulfill the various responsibilities, etc.

Chapter VII Accessional Regulations

5 articles ...

2. Rural Enterprise (TVE Town and Village Enterprise) Development

There has been a sharp increase in nonagricultural activities since the rural reforms in 1979. Restrictions on non-agricultural activities have been relaxed, a large number of township and village enterprises (TVE), other collective-owned or individual-owned enterprises were established or expanded in the countryside. In fact, the origin of TVE can be traced back to the industrial strategy of "walking on two legs" during the "Great Leap Forward" and the policy encouraging the development of "five small industries" in the commune and brigade economy in the late 50's and 60's. In 1978, the Third Plenum of the Eleventh Central Committee of the Chinese Communist Party declared that as long as the further development of rural enterprises is "in conformity with the principle of rational economic development, commune and brigade enterprise should gradually be engaged in the processing of all farm and side-line products that are suitable for rural processing. Urban factories should shift part of their processing of products and parts and components that are suitable for rural processing to commune and brigade enterprises and help equip the latter with necessary equipment and technology .... In addition, the state should adopt a policy of allowing tax breaks or tax exemptions for commune and brigade enterprises in the light of their situation." In 1981, a document was issued by the State Council to set up some policies for further encouragement of nonagricultural economy in cities and towns. It is mentioned in this document that "Due to the low productivity level and underdevelopment of commodity economy, it is a necessary consequence that there shall be coexistence of multi-economic elements and multi-operational modes in a definitely long historical period.... Every local government and the related departments of public finance, commerce, light industry and material supply, banking, industrial and commercial administration should promote seriously the development of individual non-agricultural economy of cities and towns and to give support and convenience in related areas of capital, sources of commodity supply, plant sites, taxation and market administration." In 1984 formal authority was given to rural localities to develop non-agricultural activities under different forms of ownership. All these polices and measures liberalized several factors which contributed greatly to the growth of TVE. First, there is enough supply of surplus labour, and labour is more efficiently utilized in agricultural production following the implementation of the responsibility system. Second, there is a sharp increase in credit provided to TVEs by the banks and there is also internal accumulation of funds from retained profits (generated in part by concessional tax treatment) of TVEs. Third, there is strong demand for goods produced by TVEs stemming from higher rural income due to rural reform, and also the factor of state enterprise reform which allowed these enterprises to procure inputs outside the plan. By 1991, output of TVEs had risen to 1,162 billion yuan, which is nearly 41.1% of the gross value of industrial output and the TVEs employed roughly 96 million workers (16.4% of the total labour force and 22.3% of rural labour force).

3. Development of Private Enterprises

(1) Although China does not advocate privatization from a practical mind, it does encourage the development of different types of ownership system. Consequently, private enterprises have played a very important role in the high growth rate of rural economy, as shown in the following Table 3.4[4], 3.5 and 3.6.

---

4. All these statistics are now available in *China TVE Yearbook*, published by China Agriculture Publishing House. Tables in this paper was quoted from old edition (Note by author, May 2003).

We can see from these tables that private enterprises in TVE had the highest growth rate in employment and in output from 1984 to 1991. The share of gross value of output of private enterprises in TVEs was 6.9 percent in 1984, while it increased to 27 percent in 1991. This demonstrates the high vitality of rural private enterprises. A joint research conducted by the World Bank and Chinese research institutes from 1985 to 1987 reports that the impression given by most case studies is that private enterprises have strict control over their property, enjoy autonomy in management, are responsible for their own profits and losses, are relatively efficient at decision making, and are economically efficient because their direct links between rewards and performance.

(2) Causes of Boom of Private Enterprises

The boom of the private enterprises is due to the social and economic preconditions brought about by the economic reform.

(i) Rural monetary accumulation

The rural reform has been conducive to rural monetary accumulation which provides funds for launching private enterprises. There are three sources of fund: The household savings; collective funds — including fixed assets and

Table 3.4   Composition of Town and Village Emterprises
(No. of units)   Unit: 10,000 units

Year	Total No. % share	Owned by Village (Former Commune) No. % Share	Owned by Hamlet (Former Brigade) No. % Share	Joint Venture No. % Share	Owned by Individual (Prival) No. % Share
1978	152.43 100	31.97 20.98	120.45 79.02		
1979	148.04 100	32.05 21.65	115.99 78.35		
1980	142.47 100	33.74 23.69	108.72 76.31		
1981	133.76 100	33.53 25.07	100.22 74.93		
1982	136.18 100	33.79 24.81	102.39 75.19		
1983	134.64 100	33.81 25.11	100.83 74.89		
1984	606.03 100	40.15 6.62	146.16 24.10	90.63 14.94	329.59 54.34
1985	1222.46 100	41.95 3.43	143.04 11.70	112.12 9.17	925.35 75.70
1986	1515.31 100	42.55 2.81	130.22 8.59	109.34 7.22	1233.20 81.38
1987	1750.25 100	42.01 2.40	116.27 6.64	118.91 6.79	1437.07 84.16
1988	1888.16 100	42.35 2.24	116.65 6.18	119.99 6.35	1609.18 85.22
1989	1888.63 100	40.57 2.17	113.00 6.05	106.94 5.72	1608.12 86.06
1990	1850.44 100	38.78 2.10	106.61 5.76	97.88 5.29	1607.17 86.85
1991	1908.88 100	38.16 2.00	106.01 5.56	84.86 4.45	1678.85 87.99
G.R.1984 -1991	17.8%	-1%	-4.7%	-1%	26.2%

Table 3.5 Composition of Town and Village Emterprises
(No. of workers and staffs)   10,000 persons

Year	Total No. % share	Owned by Village (Former Commune)		Owned by Hamlet (Former Brigade)		Owned by Joint-Venture		Owned by Individual (Private)	
		No.	% Share	No.	% Share	No.	% Share	No.	% Share
1978	2826.56 100	1257.62	44.49	1568.94	55.51				
1979	2909.34 100	1314.44	45.18	1594.80	54.82				
1980	2999.68 100	1393.82	46.47	1605.96	53.53				
1981	2969.56 100	1417.55	47.74	1552.01	53.26				
1982	3112.91 100	1495.00	48.03	1617.91	51.97				
1983	3234.64 100	1566.94	48.44	1667.69	51.56				
1984	5208.13 100	1879.17	36.08	2103.00	40.38	523.91	10.06	702.05	13.48
1985	6979.03 100	2111.36	30.25	2215.69	31.75	771.42	11.05	1880.57	26.96
1986	7957.14 100	2274.88	28.66	2266.40	28.55	834.10	10.51	2561.76	32.28
1987	8805.18 100	2397.45	27.23	2320.78	26.36	923.63	10.49	3163.32	35.93
1988	9545.46 100	2490.42	26.09	2403.52	25.18	976.59	10.23	3674.94	38.50
1989	9366.78 100	2383.57	25.42	2336.51	24.95	883.75	9.43	3762.90	40.17
1990	9264.75 100	2333.24	25.18	2259.27	24.39	814.34	8.79	3857.96	41.64
1991	9609.11 100	2431.01	25.30	2336.02	24.31	726.32	7.56	4115.76	42.83
GR1984 -1991	9.1%	3.75%		1.52%		4.78%		28.7%	

Table 3.6 Composition of Town and Village Emterprises
(in gross value of output)   Units: 10^9

Year	Total No. % share	Owned by Village (Former Commune)		Owned by Hamlet (Former Brigade)		Owned by Joint-Venture		Owned by Individual (Private)	
		No.	% Share	No.	% Share	No.	% Share	No.	% Share
1978	495.13 100	281.71	56.90	213.42	43.10				
1979	552.25 100	310.64	56.25	241.61	43.75				
1980	665.10 100	372.98	56.08	292.12	43.92				
1981	739.65 100	416.98	56.60	319.67	43.40				
1982	849.26 100	479.57	56.67	366.69	43.33				
1983	1007.87 100	572.72	56.82	435.15	43.18				
1984	1697.78 100	808.58	47.63	645.19	38.00	126.54	7.46	117.47	6.92
1985	2755.04 100	1160.59	42.13	913.05	33.14	245.00	8.89	436.41	15.84
1986	3583.28 100	1446.91	40.38	1109.39	30.96	314.14	8.77	712.84	19.89
1987	4945.59 100	1897.18	38.36	1460.45	29.53	446.23	9.02	1141.72	23.09
1988	7017.76 100	2666.96	38.00	2067.87	29.47	591.40	8.43	1691.54	24.10
1989	8401.82 100	3092.97	36.81	2489.29	29.63	682.03	8.12	2137.52	25.44
1990	9581.11 100	3431.61	35.82	2822.15	29.46	726.62	7.58	2600.72	27.14
1991	11621.69 100	4274.54	36.78	3445.28	29.65	755.47	6.50	3146.40	27.07
GR1984 -1991	31.63%	26.85%		27.0%		29.0%		59.9%	

floating capital that are now at the disposal of individuals who operate rural enterprises under contracts or lease agreements; and loans from banks and credit cooperatives as well as credit from local residents.

(ii) Labour supply

China has a huge stock of surplus labor in the agricultural sector. The abolition of the commune system has eliminated the restrictions that curbed the movement of labor force from agricultural to non-agricultural sectors and from one place to another. This provides ample supply of labor force for private enterprises.

(iii) Availability of technology and of technical and managerial personnel

The gradual commercialization of technology has offered private enterprises access to the technology market (a part of science and technology system reform). The prosperity of private enterprises depends more on the availability of managerial and technical talent. The technical and managerial personnel of private enterprises are former commune and brigade leaders, skilled craftsmen and educated youth, as well as former workers in state enterprises or town and village collective enterprises. It also depends upon the location of TVES. For example, the booming TVE nearby Shanghai or other municipalities is also benefited from the human resources of those municipalities, as shown in the "Sun Day Engineers".

(3) Provisional Regulation for Private Enterprises in PRC

In order to promote the further development of different types of ownership, the State Council of the PRC had promulgated "Provisional Regulations on Private Enterprises of the PRC" in June1988. It is divided into 8 chapters with 48 articles.

Article 2 states, "The private enterprises mean those economic organizations whose assets are private-owned, with employment of more than eight workers and in operation for profit." It mentions that "The private sector is a supplement to socialist public economy; the state protects the legal rights of private enterprises...." Chapter 2 is titled "Classification of Private Enterprises". In this chapter, three types of enterprises are classified, individual, partnership and limited company. It is also described in this chapter that "It is not allowed to issue stocks to the society" for the limited companies. From the above brief information, we can see that China has given legal rights for the development of private enterprises, further deregulation will depend upon further reform.

4. Other Types of Ownership System

In recent years, other types of ownership system enjoys the highest growth rate as shown in Table 3.7. Others in Table 3.7 include joint-ownership units and foreign-owned units. The former consists of joint ownership of state and collectives, state and individuals, collective and individuals and Chinese and foreign investors. The latter includes units owned by overseas Chinese, Chinese from Hongkong and Macao as well as foreign investors.

Foreign Direct Investment: It has been an experience of developing countries that foreign direct investment (FDI) produces a positive effect on economic development if it can be utilized properly. FDI is accompanied by a package of capital, technology and market access which tend to go to those manufacturing sector with potential comparative advantage. China has paid attention to the utilization of foreign investment and importation of advanced technology of strategic importance to accelerate the socialist modernization process. In 1975, it was announced that China would welcome foreign direct investment. In line with the announcement, special economic zones (SEZs) were established in 1980 as the major areas for direct investment. They were viewed as

Table 3.7　Gross Value of Industrial Output (GVIO) and Growth Rate by Types of Ownership

	GVIO 1989	Average Annual Growth Rate 1985-1989	GVIO 1990	Average Annual Growth Rate 1989-1990
Total	2201.7	22.7%	2385.1	8.3%
State-owned Enterprises	1234.3	18.3%	1300.8	5.3%
Non-state-owned, Subtotal	967.4	29.7%	1084.3	12.1%
Collectively Owned	785.8	26.0%	851.0	8.3%
Township Enterprises	219.4	30.3%	248.0	13.0%
Individually Owned	105.8	55.7%	129.5	22.4%
Others	75.8	59.5%	104.7	36.8%

experimental bases to provide China with experience in the management skills used in advanced market-oriented economies and exposure to advanced technologies and equipments. SEZs will also serve the function of diffusing these knowledge to the rest of the economy. Foreign investment-funded enterprises located in these zones were granted as incentives preferential tax and tariff

Table 3.8 Some Statistics Related to Use of Foreign Investment

Year	Total		Foreign Borrowing		FDI		Other	Inv.
	Project	Amount (US$10⁹)	Project	Amount (US$10⁹)	Project	Amount (US$10⁹)	Foreigners No. of Projects	Amount (US$10⁹)
Amount of Agreements Signed (Contract) in Utilizatiom of Foreign Investment								
1979-1990	29,693	1,020.78	644	568.33	29,049	403.60		48.85
1979-1982	949	205.48	27	135.49	922	60.10		9.89
1983	522	34.30	52	15.13	470	17.32		1.85
1984	1,894	47.91	38	19.16	1,856	26.51		2.24
1985	3,145	98.67	72	35.34	3,973	59.31		4.02
1986	1,551	117.37	53	84.07	1,498	28.34		4.96
1987	2,289	121.36	56	78.17	2,233	37.09		6.10
1988	6,063	160.04	118	98.13	5,945	52.97		8.94
1989	5,909	114.79	130	51.85	5,779	56.00		6.94
1990	7,371	120.86	98	50.99	7,273	65.96		3.90
Amount of Foreign Investment Utilized								
1979-1990		680.75		458.55		189.82		32.38
1979-1982		124.57		106.90		11.66		6.01
1983		19.81		10.65		6.36		2.80
1984		27.05		12.86		12.56		1.61
1985		46.47		26.88		16.61		2.98
1986		72.58		50.14		18.74		3.70
1987		84.52		58.05		23.14		3.33
1988		102.26		64.87		31.93		5.46
1989		100.59		62.86		33.93		3.81
1990		102.89		65.35		34.87		2.68

rates and tax holidays and exemptions. They were also provided somewhat great latitude in their operation than enterprises elsewhere in China. In 1984, 14 coastal cities and Hainan Island were permitted to offer tax incentives of such investment similar to those offered by the SEZs. That year, after the publication of speeches given by Mr. Deng Xiaoping on his tour of the southern part of China, more cities were opened to the outside world, which include the capital of every province, major cities along the Yangtze River, etc. Overtime, China has become less concerned about the ownership structure of foreign investment-funded enterprises, and completely foreign-owned firms have been established in China. To overcome some problems that had been faced by foreign firms, the State Council also issued draft regulations on direct investment in October 1986. The regulations provide FDI with reduction in land use fees, taxes, costs of certain inputs and labor costs. Approval and licensing procedures for foreign investment-funded enterprises were streamlined to a certain extent, and several mechanisms were also established in October 1986 to lessen complaints caused by the requirement that foreign investment enterprises must balance their foreign exchange accounts. For example, enterprises producing primarily for the domestic market were allowed to use domestic currency profits to buy goods to be exported; foreign exchange adjust centers were established where foreign investment enterprises with surplus foreign exchange could sell these funds to enterprises that need foreign exchange at market-determined rates. Through all these reform measures, the utilization of foreign investment have increased as shown in Table 3.8.

3.05 Institution for Implementation of Industrial Economic Strategy

1) Throughout the ten years of economic reform, China's economy has seen a mixed structure of central planning, market and bargaining mechanism. The scope of central planning is greatly reduced, but a fair part of the economy is still operated under the planning system. An incomplete market is in development but it is quite fragmented. Partial price reform has played a major role to provide production units with proper signals following which they make their decisions. Price adjustments began with large increases in consumer prices of nonstaple foods, and subsequently, a number of further price adjustments were made for grain, textiles, petroleum products, transport services, and major nonstaple foods,

such as eggs, pork and vegetables. Now, the price of most nonstaple foods has been liberalized, and the two-tier price system is now implemented for many products. This system was first introduced in the rural areas where farmers sold their output up to a quota amount to the state at negotiated prices or on the free markets, and later on, the two-tier price system was extended to cover a wide range of products.

2) Macro-economic management and reform of the banking system

China has not established a sound system of indirect control for macro-economic management when the direct means of control by central planning is gradually reduced. Since 1983, taxation on enterprise profits has been established as a replacement for the system of profit remittance that existed previously. Later on, the contract responsibility system was introduced in 1986, tax obligations of state enterprises have been set in the management contracts. And a contract system is also arranged between the central and local governments, and under this arrangement, the later contract to remit to the next higher level of government targeted amounts revenue. Revenue above these targets is retained by the local governments or shared with governments at higher levels.

As for the banking system, China has a mono-banking system in the pre-reform period. In 1984, the PBC was transformed into a separate central bank and a system of specialized banks was established. The specialized banks include: the Agricultural Bank of China (ABC), whose main role is to provide working capital to state agricultural supply and marketing units in rural areas, in 1984, ABC started to extend loans to collective township enterprises; the People's Construction Bank of China (PCBC), whose management was entrusted to the Ministry of Finance, whose principal function was to distribute funds from state budgetary appropriations to enterprises to be used in capital construction (a Chinese term, i.e., investment in new enterprises or major expansion of existing enterprises) and to supervise the use of funds, the funds for capital construction were provided as nonrepayable interest-free grants before 1979, since 1979, investment grants previously coming from the budget have been gradually replaced by loans, yet the PCBC has little decision-making power over budget-financed capital; the Bank of China, which is dominant in foreign exchange transactions and whose functions generally consists of settlement of trade and other foreign exchange accounts between local and foreign enterprises and banks, extension of credit to foreign trade enterprises, domestic and foreign currency deposits, joint venture investment abroad, issue of foreign currency denominated instruments such as bonds; and the Industrial and Commercial Bank of China, the largest bank in China whose principal functions include mobilization of individual and enterprise deposits in urban areas, provision of working capital for the state, collective and individual enterprises in urban areas, technical transformation lending for urban enterprises, payroll management and supervision and cash management for state and large collective enterprises. In addition, there are the Credit Cooperatives in both urban and rural areas. Urban Credit Cooperatives provide loans and payment service for individual and small-scale cooperative enterprises in urban areas, and the Rural Credit Cooperatives provide loans for all types of agricultural, industrial and commercial activities at the village level. A variety of non-banking financial institutions now exist in China due to the development of reform. There are now around 700 Trust and Investment Companies, more than 2,700 insurance companies, more than 50 Chinese insurance companies abroad, in addition to security companies and financial leasing companies. As with the banks, the non-banking financial institutions are principally state-owned. And the ability of the specialized banks to direct their activities remains circumscribed. Most of their lending has to be dictated by the government through the credit plan, non-planned lending has also been influenced by governmental pressures, particularly at the local level, to direct funding to particular enterprises.

3. Regional Development Strategy

In contrast with regional development strategy in the pre-reform period, coastal area development strategy has been pursued to promote economic growth since the Six Five-Year Plan period. It is stressed in the Six Five-Year Plan that: "It is necessary to utilize the current economic foundation of coastal areas, to tap fully its potential, so as to bring along further development of the economy of the hinterland..., actively expand foreign economic cooperation and trade, make full use of the comparative advantage of abundant labor force, higher processing technique and convenience in transportation, to develop import processing and export orientation production and trade. At the same time, it has been planned to utilize a part of foreign capital and import appropriate advanced technology." In the Seventh Five-Year Plan, a chapter titled "Special Economic Zones, Coastal

Open Cities and Open Regions" is added. The open regions refer to the delta areas of the Yangzi River, Zhujiang and southern part of Fujian Province. It is mentioned in this document that "A production structure of commerce-industry-agriculture should be formed gradually in the open regions of delta areas of Yangzi River, Zhujiang and southern part of Fujian. An earnest attitude should be adopted to deal with their technology import and technology upgradation, so as to increase their earnings of foreign exchange from export with full effort." These statements can briefly outline the industrial economic strategy in the 80's, i.e., opening to the outside world, importation of technology to improve the present production process, development strategy through export orientation. This strategy has brought along a growth rate of GDP averaged at 9.7% annually from 1980-1989. But serious inflation occurred in 1988 and 1989. This regional development strategy had increased also income disparity between the coastal and the hinterland areas. For example, the per-capita GDP of several coastal provinces, Liaoning, Guandong, Zhejiang and Jiangsu, in 1990 is 2,432, 2, 319, 2,007 and 1,942 yuan respectively, while that of Guizhou is only 779 yuan.

IV. Industrial Economic Strategy in the 90's and Recent Economic Reform Policy Measures and Issues

4.01 China's industrial economic strategy in the 90's can be better understood by abstracting some essential points of an official document, "Ten-Year Development Perspective of National Economy and Social Development", and some explanation will follow.

The development objective in the 90's is to quadruple the value of GDP of 1980 (in constant price) by the year 2000, on the basis that economic efficiency is greatly improved and the economic structure is optimized. In view with this target, the value of GDP calculated on the basis of the 1990 price will reach 3,110 billion yuan in the year 2000, the average annual growth rate in this decade will be 6%. The annual average growth rate of gross value of industrial and agricultural output is 6.1%, within which the annual growth rate of agriculture is 3.5% and that of industry, 6.8%.

4.02 Major Industrial Economic Strategy to Achieve the Target Prescribed in the Ten-Year Development Perspective

The industrial economic strategy to achieve the target set up in the Ten-Year Development Perspective can be summarized as follows:

1. Economic Restructuring Shall Be a Primary Concern

We can see from the previous sections that the path of China's industrialization of the four decades and that some problems have arisen in the economic structure.The foundation of agriculture is still weak, because the land area under cultivation has not increased, competition for water supply in some parts of China between agriculture, industry and human consumption will increase, the production gains required to feed newly increased population at high nutritional levels will have to come almost entirely from increased yields on cultivated land, development of basic industry and infrastructure lags behind economic growth. For example, China has railways totaling 53, 400 km in length, 1.03 million km of highways, 104,000 km waterways and 506,700 km of air ways in 1990, quite insufficient from international perspective. China's energy consumption per-capita (kilogram of oil equivalent) is 591 in 1989, while the figure for Italy is 2,721. The energy situation had long been a debate among Chinese experts, and it is also a problem observed by experts abroad. We can see from Table 4.1 that the growth of primary energy (except hydro power development) does not match

Table 4.1 Growth Rate of Energy Sector

Year	GDP		Crude Oil		Coal		Natural Gas		Hydro Power		Electricity	Total
	Value (100 mill. yuan)	Growth Rate %	Produ-ction (10⁴T)	Growth Rate %	Produ-ction (100 M.T.)	Growth Rate %	Produ-ction (100 MM³)	Growth Rate %	Produ-ction (100 M. KW.-Hr)	Growth Rate %	Produ-ction (100 M. KW.-Hr)	Growth Rate %
1980	4773.0		10122		6.22		127.4		655		3093	
1985	8567.6	11.56	12490	5.4%	8.72	8.8%	1129.3	0.3%	924	8.98%	4107	7.35%
1986	9696.3		13069		8.94		137.6		945		4495	
1990	17686.1	7.75	13831	1.43%	10.80	4.84%	152.9	2.69%	1267	7.61%	6212	8.42%

Note: 1) Calculation based upon *China Statistics Yearbook 1991*, Chinese Statistics Press.

2) Growth rates: average annual growth rates in the planned period.

3) Value of GDP is in current price, growth value is calculated on the basis of constant price.

with the growth of GDP. Further effort in the energy sector should be made. There are surplus capacities in the processing industry, along with the problems of low technical level and low degree of specialization. The tertiary sector cannot adapt to the needs of the economic growth and the lives of the people, too.

2. Major Economic Industrial Strategy

(1) To develop the agricultural sector with full effort, to promote the growth of agricultural sector with all areas, i.e., production of all types of crops, perfection of household responsibly system, to develop various forms of social services, and to promote agricultural growth through improvement of education and S&T input, etc.

(2) To strengthen the construction of basic industry and physical infrastructure and restructure and renovate the processing industry so as to improve the product quality and increase the variety of products, so as to increase the competitiveness of manufacturing sector.

(3) To promote the growth of the tertiary sector, including commerce, material supply, finance, insurance and tourism, so as to cope with economic restructuring and expand employment.

(4) Export-oriented strategy is further enhanced and deepened, the existing economic and technology development zones, coastal open cities and open zones should be further consolidated, development and opening of the Shanghai Pudong area should receive full attention, at the mean time, selected cities and regions along the boarder line of hinterland will be opened to the outside so as to promote the development of foreign trade and techno-economic exchange of these regions.

(5) The development of the electronic sector will be a priority. It will be taken as a leading sector to promote the economic restructuring and modernization of national economy.

(6) Actively and effectively utilize foreign investment. Foreign debt will be kept in a reasonable scale and with reasonable structure. Improve the environment for foreign investment, combine properly the utilization of foreign investment with upgradation of technology and rehabilitation of enterprises.

(7) Both planning and market shall be utilized as effective means to promote the economic development, restructure the economy and enhance the effi-

ciency and competitiveness of industrial production and products.

(8) Further reform will be conducted to enhance the production capability. Further reform will be introduced in ten aspects: improvement of the structure of ownership system with public ownership being predominant, enterprise reform, establishment of a socialist market system, price system reform, fiscal and taxation system reform, financial system reform, wage system reform, housing and social security system reform, planning and investment system reform, and strengthening the economic regulation system.

4.03 New economic reform policies have been adopted since Deng Xiaoping's call for fast economic development and opening wider to the outside world made during his southern China tour. China's economic development has sped up from its sluggish pace seen under the past austerity program and the enthusiasm of the people and government officials at different levels have been further triggered for furthering economic reform. Many economic measures have been adopted by the central to local governments. Some major points are described below.

1. Policies and Measures on Further Opening Up to the Outside World

(1) The strategy to open to the outside world has been strengthened in width and depth. In the past, cities open to the outside world were mainly in the coastal areas and the delta area of the Yangtze River, Pearl River, and the Minjiang River. This time, more cities are added to the list to include those port cities on the upper and middle reaches of the Yangtze River. Besides, by summing up the past experience to open up, the port cites are more closely linked to the economic centres of the related regions and can better benefit from open policy. Therefore, five port cities and four provincial capitals in five provinces — Anhui, Jiangxi, Henan, Hubei and Sichuan — are added. They Wuhu, Hefei, Jiujiang, Nanchang, Yueyang, Changsha, Wuhan, Chongqing and Chengdu. Also added are cities along the borders and inland provincial capitals, such as Manzhouli, Suifenhe, Heihe, Huichun, Dandong, Erenhot, Tacheng, Yining, Bole, Wulumuqi, Changchun, Huhhot, Shenyang, Harbin, Ruili, Wanding, Hekou, Pingxiang, Dongxing, Kunming and Nangning. Hance, the number of cities open to the outside world is greatly increased.

Also the scope allowed for foreign investment is also expanded for experimentation. Formally, foreign investment was only allowed in the industrial activities. Now, experiment has been made to introduce foreign investment in activities of the tertiary sector, such as finance, commerce, tourism and real estates.

(2) Policies for cities open to the outside world are very complicated. For cities in the border areas, detailed regulations are provided. But for all the provincial capitals, they are allowed to enjoy the preferential policies granted to the coastal cities. These policies and measures can be generalized into 10 major aspects:

i. The right to approve foreign investment projects

The right to give approval to foreign investment projects covers foreign investment production projects, on condition that they fulfil the requirements of China's industrial policies and no demand is raised for the government provide special assistance in construction and production and their export does not affect the existing quotas. But the right delegated to the cities cannot surpass that of the provinces. The concrete measures are to be determined by the provincial governments.

ii. Projects of technological upgradation of old enterprises, specially large and medium-sized SOEs.

The import tariff and product tax (or VA tax) are exempted for those imported instruments and equipments required by planned technological projects, which cannot be produced in China or whose supply cannot be guaranteed at present. This policy is effective up to the end of 1995 for the open cities in border areas and hinterland provincial capitals.

iii. Encouragement for development of export of agricultural and sideline products

The tariff and product tax (or VA tax) of imported processing equipment for the development of export of agricultural and sideline products can be exempted. This policy will be effective up to 1993 for coastal open cities. It will be effective up to 1995 for authorized open cities along the Yangtze River and hinterland provincial capitals that are opened.

iv. Encouragement of Foreign Investment

The rate of income tax on foreign-invested production enterprises shall be 24%; for foreign-invested technology- and knowledge-intensive projects, or projects with foreign investment over US$30 million, or project with longer periods for the recovery of investment or projects in energy, transportation, port and wharf, the tax rate will be 15% when authorized by State Administration of Taxation.

v. The import customs duty can be exempted for imported equipment used by foreign investment enterprises; the import duty of imported raw materials, parts and components for export production can also be exempted for foreign investment enterprises. The export duty and consolidated industrial and commercial tax can be exempted for product export. On products for domestic sales, taxes shall be levied in accordance with the relevant regulations.

vi. For foreign corporations, firms and other economic organizations that have not set up organizations in China but have incomes in the form of dividens, interest, rent, fees from royalties and other incomes earned in the open cities, the income tax rate will be 10% (for other cities, this rate is 20%).

vii. For qualified trade corporations at the municipal level, they can be granted the right to handle foreign trade with approval of the MOFERT.

viii. Based on the document "Provisional Regulations on Development and Operation of Blocks of Land by Foreign Investment", foreigners are allowed to invest in the operation and development of blocks of land.

ix. To simplify the examination and approval procedures for Chinese to go abroad for commercial activities. For people working in foreign trade enterprises that have the right to handle foreign trade, major staff in charge of trade activities of large and medium-sized enterprises, and Chinese employees handling sales in foreign investment enterprises, their procedures can also be simplified for them to make trips abroad. Once approval is given, it can be effective on more than one occasions.

x. In order to create a sound investment environment, a techno-economic development region can be established in each city, which receives relatively more foreign investment with the authorization of the State Council.

The ten policies above can be grouped into four categories: one is related to the expansion of the rights of open cities in foreign economic cooperation, including the right to approve foreign investment projects, the rightin in foreign trade, and the right to approve commercial peoples' trips abroad. The second is to support the opening cities to import advanced technologies and management expertise from abroad for reform of old enterprises and development of modern agriculture. The third is encouraging the use of foreign investment, the implementation of preferential policies for foreign investment enterprises. And the fourth is establishment of techno-economic zones in cities with necessary conditions upon approval by the State Council. The above is a summary of the main contents although each sentence is not as exact.

2. New Trends for Reform of External Trade

A. Import: preparation for the opening of the domestic market

(1) The import customs duty is lowered, with the duties on 256 types of commodities being lowered since last year. And in order to meet the requirement to restore its seat in GATT, China will continue to lower the import duties of certain commodities.

(2) The import commodity adjustment tax will be abolished this year;

(3) The list of 1,751 kinds of import substitution commodities has been abolished.

(4) 53 kinds of commodities are still administered through license, and 16 have been cancelled. The scope of import license adminstration will be reduced by two thirds within 2-3 years.

(5) Gradually abolish administrative authorization procedures for import licence. The administration office to authorize import of electro-mechanical equipment will be changed into a coordination office, and its main function will be to improve the coordination work for electro-mechanical equipment imports.

B. Export

(1) Abolish the mandatory planning for export and it will be replaced with a guidance plan.

(2) Liberalizing partially the administrative procedures for export commodities. Most commodities will be liberalized to be traded by different foreign trade enterprises at different levels (including the export activity of production enterprises), except for a few commodities of national priority with large amount of export (approximately 15 types) that will still be managed in a unified fashion through state-designated specialized corporations.

(3) Continue to decentralize the rights of foreign trade, including.

i. Commerce and material supply departments;

ii. Continuously expand the right of production enterprises that are qualitied to handle export;

iii. Continuously enlarge the right of foreign trade corporations in municipalities (prefecture) and countries where the necessary conditions are ripe to handle export.

iv. To grant the International Economic Engineering Corporation (responsible for export of labor service and contracts for engineering projects) with the right of foreign trade.

(4) Improve quota and license control and reduce appropriately the category of commodities under quota and license control. The above policies are suggested by the MOFERT, and they are waiting for the final authorization of the State Council. And the possible time for them to go into effect will be in 1993.

3. Further Liberalization of Price Control

4. Changing the Role of Planning in the National Economy

It is well known that mandatory planning played a key role in development and management of the economy of China in the past. And it is a focus of debate before Mr. Deng's speeches in his southern China inspection tour.

Now the State Planning Commission is going to change its role in national economy, to pay attention to the development of the market.

The new responsibilities of SPC will be: the study of economic strategy and planning, macroeconomic control of development, the nurturing of the market mechanism and the exercise of control over major projects and coordination.

The SPC will adjust its functions in eight aspects:

(1) Its former functions in micro-economic management will be changed to setting forth development strategies and issuing important guidelines and policies.

(2) Its role of enforcing direct administrative management will be replaced by indirect management, by setting economic policies and issuing regulations.

(3) SPC will direct, coordinate and control over the overall economic activi-

ties of the whole country, instead of engaging in specific economic activities of the state-owned enterprises and institutions.

(4) The management will focus on economic value, policy and forecasting instead of production and economic indices.

(5) SPC will shift its stress from industrial production and development to the entire national economy, covering production, marketing, distribution and consumption.

(6) SPC will give more regard to market development, instead of the former practice of heeding only supply but ignoring demand. In the future, emphasis will be placed on both demand and supply to develop a sound national market system.

(7) SPC will serve to balance national economic activities by using both national and foreign funds and resources.

(8) Centralized planning management will be substituted by macro-economic management to serve the needs of the enterprises and provide them with information and counselling.

4.04 Issues Related to Successful Implementation of China's Industrial Economic Strategy in the 90's

1. China has relied on central planning system and administrative means to a large extent to exercise control over the economy for nearly three decades and half. And China is going to rely on indirect means in economic management, i.e., to establish a system of macropolicy management. Whether China can establish the ability to conduct effective reforms in its monetary policy, fiscal policy and exchange rate policy and establish a rational price system will be crucial to the success of future reform efforts and the implementation of China's economic strategy in the 90's. Because effective monetary and fiscal policies exert a major influence on price stability, domestic savings, the volume of investment and the external balance, an effective exchange rate policy will contribute to promoting external trade and a rational price system will provide correct signal to the enterprises. Further institutional changes are needed to enhance the capacity of agencies at central and provincial levels for policy planning and implementation. Financial markets should be developed to maximize the effects of monetary measures.

2. The cyclic centralization and decentralization process has been a unique feature of the Chinese economy, ministerial self-sufficiency or departmentalism on the one side, and regionalism, i.e., each geographical planning unit tries to be self-contained, on the other side, development of a unified national market is faced with trade barriers among the provinces, <u>the fiscal contract system between central and local governments further accentuates the trend of regionalization. Great efforts and policy measures are required to establish a unified national market.</u>

3. China had established her state-owned enterprise system for four decades. But it is reported that one third of the SOEs are operating at a loss. Whether a successful enterprise reform can be conducted is a key issue in economic reform. In this aspect, we wish to learn from the experience of Brazil on how to properly managed public enterprises.

Conclusion

This paper presents briefly the industrialization process of China since the 50's. <u>A historical retrospect will help to understand the present and future prospect better</u>. Industrialization process for development and economic reform for furthering the development are two sides of the coin. China has achieved a rapid economic growth since the initiation of an economic reform. But issues are existed as pointed above. Anyhow there is bright prospect in the 90's in spite of the difficulties mentioned above.

9. Foreign Direct Investment Policies and Related Institutional-Building in China

Introduction

Since 1979, China has been a major participant in international capital market. Although by the end of 1994 China accumulated external debt of around US$92.8 billion, foreign direct investment (FDI) had been assuming greater importance in total foreign inflows. Indeed, since 1992 the amount of FDI inflow surpassed official development assistance from the bilateral and multilateral sources. China has put a strong emphasis on the promotion of FDI as an essential component of its economic reform.

China has achieved an impressive economic performance. Its growth rate averaged 9.4 percent in 1980-1989 and 10.4 percent in 1990-1994. There was also a rapid expansion of foreign trade. In 1978-1994, average annual import grew by 15.9 percent and export, by 17 percent. FDI played an important role in this rapid progress. In recent years, China has been among the largest recipient of FDI. In 1994 China absorbed US$34 billion of FDI, second only to the United States of America which received US$41 billion, out of a world total of US$204 billion. Although there are experiences unique to China, there are also general lessons to be learned which may be useful to other Asian and Pacific countries in their efforts to attract FDI, especially for those of the transitional economies in the ESCAP region.

The data and information in this country report are mainly based on official statistics and publications, especially those of the Bureau of Statistics and the Ministry of Foreign Trade and Economic Cooperation of China. It should be noted that foreign direct investment patterns are more difficult to analyse than trade, partly because governments do not report data on FDI in a consistent manner.

The study is organized into four sections. Section A illustrates the evolution of government policies and its impact on the regional and sectoral patterns of the FDI which is followed by a discussion on the key institutions in facilitating the FDI in Section B. Section C deals with FDI outflow. Some concluding observations are given in Section D.

A. Foreign Direct Investment Policies and Flows

1. Evolution of FDI Policies and Flows

Since late 1978, China followed a new development strategy which emphasized outward orientation and market-friendly policy reforms. The country began to actively utilize foreign investment to accelerate its reform and modernization processes. The policy evolution as regard foreign investment can be broadly divided into three stages:

(i) The initial stage (1979-1982)

In the initial period of attracting FDIs, China had no or little experience in dealing with foreign companies. Also, its legal system was unsuitable to facilitate business transactions with them. There were only a few FDI projects, consisting of 922 projects with total planned investment of around US$6 billion and actual amount invested of around US$1-2 billion. Policy change that facilitated FDI was launched in July 1979, when the Second Plenary Session of the Fifth People's Congress passed and announced the Law on Joint Ventures Using Chinese and Foreign Investment. Thereafter, the central government authorized the Guangdong and Fujian provincial governments to implement the special economic policies and related promotional measures to attract FDI. In line with this, four special economic zones (SEZs), Shengzhen, Zhuhai, Shantou and Xiamen, were established to implement the foreign investment promotion policies.

Initially, there were two major policy initiatives to promote FDI:

(a) FDI approval process

In this period, FDI approval were still tightly controlled, among others through a centralized authorization procedures which were quite cumbersome. Every project had to be submitted to the Foreign Investment Administrative Commission for approval from 1979/80. Two years later, the commission partially delegated the authorization process to the provincial and municipal agencies except for projects with planned investment of more than US$3 million.

(b) Preferential policies

The preferential treatment to FDI in this period was also limited. Income tax of a joint venture company was generally lower than other business enterprises, at 33 percent rate, with an exemption of this tax in the first year of operation and a reduction by one half, in the second year. There were no exemption or reduction on sales tax and import duty was still applied to the imported machineries and equipments.

(ii) The sustained growth stage (1983-1991)

In May 1983, after some successful experiences in the initial stage of economic opening, further liberalization in foreign investment was implemented by extending the geographical coverage of the SEZs. Since then fourteen additional port cities in the coastal areas were opened, which include Shanghai, Tianjin, Dalian and Guangzhou as well as the river delta areas of the Yangtze River, Zhujiang River (Pearl River) and the delta region of Southern Fujian. A set of foreign investment promotion policies was applied to these new SEZs. This includes granting preferential treatments, decentralization of authority for FDI application procedures and improved legal system related to foreign investment.

Further improvement on FDI incentives was made in 1986 with the promulgation of Regulations for Encouragement of Foreign Investment. Special preferential policies were granted to foreign investors which are export-oriented and/or use advanced technology. Guidelines were issued to influence the sectoral and regional distribution of FDI. In 1988, China broadened the regional scope of the special economic zones to the northern part of the coastal area, these are the Liaoning Peninsula, Shandong Peninsula and other municipalities and counties in that area. The Hainan Special Economic Zone was approved in 1988 and two years later the government started the opening of the Pudong area of Shanghai.

There has been a relatively rapid growth of FDI in 1987-1991 with the planned investment amounted to US$33.2 billion and the realized one was US$16.7 billion. In this period, the FDI share in production and export-oriented industries increased, whereas that in hotels and tourism-related sectors experienced a relative decline.

(iii) The high growth stage (1992-present)

Following a visit to southeast coastal region in January 1992 and witnessing FDI induced growth and prosperity in the area, Deng Xiaoping called for a bolder reform and opening. Subsequent economic reforms have moved faster. The State Council declared to open further six port cities along the Yangtze River, thirteen cities along the borders to Northeast Asia, Central Asia and Southeast Asia, and also eighteen capital cities of the provinces in the hinterland.

In effect, there has been a substantial change in FDI both in its breadth and depth. The planned FDI increased from US$58.1 billion in 1992 to US$91.9 billion in 1995; while figures for actual investment in the same period rose from US$11.0 billion to US$37.8 billion (see Table 1). And recently, it was announced by the director of the Office for Special Economic Zone that China will soon authorize more 'open cities' in the interior to promote economic growth and reduce the wealth gap between the prosperous eastern coastal areas and the underdeveloped interior.

Table1 Foreign direct investment, 1979-1995 (Billion US dollar)

Year	1979-1986	1987	1988	1989	1990	1991	1992	1993	1994	1995	Total
Number of projects	7,819	2,233	5,945	5,779	7,273	12,978	48,764	83,437	47,549	37,011	258,788
Pledged FDI	19.2	3.7	5.3	5.6	6.6	12.0	58.1	111.4	81.4	91.9	401.1
FDI actually utilized	6.6	2.3	3.2	3.4	3.4	4.4	11.0	27.5	33.8	37.8	137.2

Source: 1. Li Lanqing,ed., *Basic Knowledge of Utilization of Foreign Investment in China*, Central University of CCP Press, Chinese MOFTEC Press, April 1995.
2. *A Statistical Survey of China*, Chinese Statistical Publishing House, 1996.

2. Changes in Corporate Law

A series of law and regulations were promulgated to promote various forms of FDI venture. Some of the important ones are described below:

(i) Equity joint venture

Equity joint venture was the first type of foreign-funded enterprises established in China. Its establishment has been made possible by the "Law of the People's Republic of China on Joint Venture Using Chinese and Foreign Investment", promulgated in July 1979 by the National People's Congress. This legal business entity can be established by foreign corporations, firms and other economic organizations or individuals in partnership with Chinese corporations, firms or other organizations, approved by the government and located within the Chinese territory. Essentially, it is a limited liability company wherein profits and losses are allocated in proportion to equity shares of the foreign and Chinese partners. Generally, the foreign partner contributes technology, related machineries or equipments and foreign exchanges, whereas the Chinese partner usually contributes land, buildings and Chinese currency.

There were three other business legislation concerning the operation of equity joint ventures: (1) the "Regulations for the Implementation of the Law of the People's Republic of China on Joint Ventures Using Chinese and Foreign Investment", promulgated in 1983, provide more detail regulation on the structure of joint ventures, the organization of the board of directors and management and methods of equity shares calculation; (2) the "Provisions of the State Council of the People's Republic of China for the Encouragement of Foreign Investment" which improved the business environment for foreign investment; and (3) the "Resolution on Revision of the Law of the People's Republic of China on Sino-Foreign Joint Ventures" in 1990 which is an amendment to the 1979 law, responded to foreign investors' complaints. In particular, under the new law — in contrast with the previous one — it is no longer mandatory to have a Chinese partner as the chairman of the board of directors and this provision applies to any joint venture company.

(ii) Contractual joint venture

In Chinese term, the contractual joint venture is also commonly called the "Sino-foreign" cooperative managed enterprise. This form of foreign direct investment is simply an arrangement, between the Chinese and foreign partners to cooperate in a project or certain business activities, the terms and conditions specified in a contract. This form of FDI illustrates the gradual approach of China's reform and opening. In the beginning the Chinese government approved this form of FDI, especially when some of the first proposed foreign-funded projects required more flexibility in their financing and other arrangements than those provided under the equity joint venture law. Until April 1988, there was no law governing this sort of arrangement. The "Sino-Foreign Contractual Joint Venture Law of the People's Republic of China" was adopted in 1988 and it is essentially a codification of practices that had been carried out over the years.

The major difference between this form of FDI and the equity joint ventures is that profit (and loss) sharing is not necessarily proportional to the investment contribution (or equity) of each partner. Profit sharing as well as responsibilities for other business decisions are pre-determmed in the contract.

(iii) Wholly foreign-owned enterprise

This form of FDI refers to the enterprises located within Chinese territory with all capital invested by foreign corporations, firms, other economic organizations or individuals. In fact, several wholly foreign-owned enterprises were established prior to the promulgation of the "Law of People's Republic of China on Wholly Foreign Owned Enterprises" in April 1986, and the detailed rules for its the implementation were approved in October 1990. A wholly foreign-owned enterprise can be established subject to meeting at least one of the following conditions: (a) it uses advanced technology and equipment; (b) all (or most) of its products are exported.

This type of enterprise grew rapidly. By the end of 1994, the number of the wholly foreign-owned enterprises approved by the government totaled 46, 836 units, which was about one fifth of the total number of FDI companies, with an actual investment of US$20.3 billion, or about one fifth of the total actual flow of foreign direct investment.

(iv) Other forms of FDI

There have been other special regulations governing specific forms of FDI. Those include the-so-called "joint development" which applies to petroleum related ventures, financial institutions, build-operate-transfer (BOT) counter trade, leasing and so on. BOT projects, especially in infrastructure development, have been growing rapidly in the southeastern coastal area of China.

3. Special Economic Zones and Their Effects on FDI

As noted earlier, economic reform and opening in China proceeded gradually, beginning with the southeastern coastal area. Several locations in that area were designated as special economic zones (SEZs) in the late 1970s in order to bring in skills, technology and foreign management to China. This experiment resulted in the establishment of growth poles which has been further extended gradually to other areas in China.

Not surprisingly, the regional distribution of FDI has also been closely associated with this scheme and its extension to other areas in later years (Table 2). Thus,

Table 2 Regional Distribution of FDI, 1979-1992

Region	Number of FDI projects	Percentage shares	Pledged amount of FDI (US dollar million)	Percentage shares
Country's total	90,791	100	63,605	100
Coastal provinces and regions, within which:	76,620	84.4	52,253	82.9
Beijing municipality	3,694	4.1	2,950	4.6
Tianjin municipality	2,653	2.9	915	1.4
Hebei	2,077	2.3	735	1.2
Liaoning	3,683	4.1	2,492	3.9
Shanghai municipality	3,889	4.3	3,953	6.2
Jiangsu	9,520	10.4	3,034	4.8
Zhejiang	3,687	4.0	1,036	1.6
Fujian	7,943	8.8	6,253	9.8
Shandong	6,054	6.7	2,533	4.1
Guangxi Zhuang autonomous region	2,049	2.2	923	1.5
Hainan	3,055	3.4	1,512	2.3
Guangdong	28,316	31.2	26,414	41.5
Hinterland provinces and region, within which:	14,171	1,515	4,525	7.2
Hubei	1,829	2.0	528	0.8
Sichuan	2,474	2.7	513	0.8
Shanxi	630	0.6	109	1.7

Source: Liu Xiangdong, *Zhongguo Duiwai Jingji Maoyi Zhengce Zhinan*, Economic Management Press, 1992; *China Statistical Yearbook, 1993*, China Statistical Publishing House.

FDI was concentrated along the coastal region. Over 80 percent of the cumulative total of FDI during the period 1979-1992 was located in the coastal area, of which, Guangdong Province had a dominant share of 41.5 percent and Fujian Province, 9.8 percent.

The major features of the economic opening measures are discussed briefly:

(i) Special Preferential Policies Delegated to Guangdong and Fujian Provinces

In July 1979, the Central Committee of the Party and the State Council authorized local authorities in Guangdong and Fujian provinces to implement investment promotion policies. The delegation of (some) authority has empowered the provincial government to conduct their own economic affairs, which include certain regulatory functions in the area of trade, foreign investment, transfer of advanced technology, as well as the retention of a large part of tax revenue which was previously transferred to central government for local development purposes.

(ii) Establishment of Four Special Economic Zones

In August 1980, the People's Congress authorized the proposal of the State Council to Establish four special economic zones (SEZs) in Guangdong and Fujian provinces,[1] these are the Shenzhen, Zhuhai, Shantou and Xiamen areas.

Major features of policies implemented in the SEZs are:

(a) Coexistence of private and socialist public ownership system, the equity share of the foreign-funded enterprises in the SEZs can be higher than that in the hinterland;

(b) A market-oriented economy with some guidance from the state;

(c) Preferential treatments offered to foreign investors (see Appendix 1);

income tax rate reduced to 15 percent (note that the rate was 55 percent for the Chinese enterprises in general) and simplified procedures of entry and exit for foreign companies;

(d) Promotion of export orientation;

---

1. This proposal was advocated early in July 1979 by senior leadership and the decision was made by the Central Committee of Chinese Communist Party in 1979.

(e) Special authority granted to the local government. In some cases, the delegation of authority has been extended to include foreign economic relations, public security, customs, finance, foreign exchange, port, railway, post and communication, etc.

However, the SEZs have been subjected to some controls from the central government, particularly with respect to economic stabilization measures. For example, regional macroeconomic targeting was in effect and this included a ceiling on bank credit.

The SEZs are allowed to retain all new increments of fiscal revenue and foreign exchange income within a certain period and exemption of customs duty for imported materials used in the construction of fixed capital assets.

The four SEZs have been a great success. The actual amount of FDI into these four SEZs in 1980-1994 reached US$13.7 billion cumulatively or 144 percent of the national total. In 1991-1993. the actual amount of FDI in the three SEZs of Shenzhen, Zhuhai and Shantou in Guangdong Province was US$7.6 billion, US$3.7 billion and US$1.94 billion, respectively, or a corresponding share of their national total of 41.6 percent, 32.8 percent and 27.2 percent.

New industries established in the SEZs include electronics, light industry machinery, textile, food, construction material and chemical engineering and the value added share of the foreign companies exceeded one half of the total. There have been foreign investments in financial services also. Shenzen, for instance, is host to 16 foreign banks subsidiaries and 10 representative offices.

(iii) Further Extension of Special Economic Zones

Based on the success in promoting growth and trade through special economic zones, the scheme was further extended to other areas. The State Council decided to open fourteen industrial port cities of Tianjm, Shanghai, Dalian, Qinhuangdao, Yantai, Qingdao, Lianyungang Nantong, Ningbo, Wenzhou, Fuzhou, Guangzhou, Zhanjiang and Beihai to FDI. These cities have a better industrial base, relatively high level of technological capability and stronger science and technology related human resource skills. With population of no more than 8 percent of national total, their gross value of industrial production is more than 21 percent of national total. Hence, these areas have a competitive advantage in facilitating technology upgrading of existing enterprises through foreign capital and new technology.

In February 1985, the State Council further decided to open fifty-one municipalities and counties of delta areas of Pearl River, Yangtze River and Southern Fujian — Xiamen, Zhangzhou and Quanzhou. Again, since late 1980's the SEZs have been further extended to Eastern Liaomng Peninsula, Shandong Peninsula and other areas. The Shanghai Pudong New Zone is a large industrial scheme, intended to be the largest industrial, commercial and transport centre of international significance. The State Council decided that Pudong can implement certain similar policies of Economic Technological Development Zones and SEZs. For a summary of the regional economic opening see Table 3 below.

4. Sectoral Pattern of FDI

FDI in manufacturing was dominant, its share in total projects was 76.1 percent and in total pledged FDI, 56 percent (Table 4). Although the Government has put a priority in high and advanced technology related projects, labour-intensive projects dominated this sector. The average planned investment per manufacturing project amounted to only US$1 million, with short-term orientation and small- and medium-sized scale. Further, there was a decline in the average planned investment in 1989 whose average was lower than that of the preceding twelve years. This may be due to wider geographical coverage of economic opening as new cities or sub-regions, which were authorized to grant preferential policies for FDI, were quite aggressive and successful in inviting foreign investment into their area, including the small scale ones.[2]

There seemed to be a declining tendency of FDI in the tertiary sector. Unlike during the initial period, when the share of the tertiary sector's cumulative planned FDI reached almost two thirds of the total, the relative share of this sector declined to 27 percent in 1991. This was partly a result of government's increased restrictions on FDI in services. The relative share of FDI in the manufacturing sector jumped, so was also the case with real

---

2. It should also be mentioned here that the above trend may also be due to some changes in statistics. Prior to 1991, the offshore oil exploration is included in the manufacturing sector whereas thereafter a new item of geological survey is added separately.

Table 3 Regional Opening in China

Category I Coastal open regions	Category II Open cities along border (since Mardh 1992)	Category III Open cities along river and in hinterland (since July 1992)
Special economic zones Shenzhen, Zhuhai, Shantou, Xiamen (1980) Hainan Province (1988).	Heihe municipality Suifenhe municipality (Heilongjiang Province). Huichun municipality	1. Chongqing, Yunyang, Wuhan, Jiujiang, Wuhu.
Coastal open cities (April 1984) Tianjin, Shanghai, Dalian, Yantai, Qinhuangdao, Qingdao, Lianyungang, Nantong, Guangzhou, Zhanjiang.	(Jilin province). Manzhouli municipality Erenhot municipality (Inner Mongolia). Yining municipality; Bole municipality	2. Harbin, Changchun, Huhhot, Nanning, Urumqi, Kunming, Shijiazhuang, (seven capitals of provinces or autonomous regions along border, coastal areas)
Coastal economic open regions (February 1985) Yangtze River Delta; Pearl River Delta Southern Fujian: Xiamen, Zhangzhou, Quanzhou,	(Xinjiang Uygur Autonomous Region). Ruili municipality. Wanding municipality; Jukao municipality (Yunnan Province) Pingxiang municipality;	3. Taiyuan, Hefei, Nanchang, Zhengzhou, Changsha, Chengdu, Guiyang, Xi'an, Lanzhou, Xining, Yinchuan. (Eleven capitals of provinces
Coastal economic open regions (March 1988) a. Further expansion b. Opening of municipalities, counties and coastal cities of eastern Liaoning Peninsula, Shandong Peninsula, Bohai rim.	Dongxing township (Guangxi Zhuang Autonomous Region)	in hinterland.) 4. Shanghai Pudong New Zone (April 1990)
Coastal economic open regions includes now 260 municipalities and counties (their numbers in brackets below are up to June 1993) Hebei (14); Liaoning (21); Jiangsu (47); Zhejiang (34); Fujian (37); Shandong (31); Guangdong (57); Guangxi (6); Shanghai (6); Tianjin (5).		

Table 4 Sectoral Pattern of FDI,
1979-1994

Sector	Number	Share of total number of of projects (percent)	Pledged amount projects (US$ billion)	Share of total of FDI (percent)
Agriculture, forestry, husbandry,fishery	5 367	2.4	4.2	1.4
Industry	168 749	76.1	169.7	56.0
Tertiary sector	39 911	18.0	119.8	39.5
Others	7 691	3.5	9.3	3.1
Total	221 718	100.0	303.3	100.0

Source: Basic Knowledge of Utilization of FDI of China.

estates the share of which increased to 37.1 percent. It is noted that the latter has had some negative effects on the domestic economy as property prices rose sharply. Meanwhile, other tertiary sectors, such as health care, education, culture, art, scientific research, which had a low FDI share, are in need of more investment. Further, because there are serious weaknesses and problems with the financial sector, its liberalization has been slow and thus FDI in this sector has been negligible.

B. Key Government Institutions for Foreign Direct Investment

1. Administrative Hierarchy

The administrative system in China is complex and its structure, quite elaborate. For example, there are at the central government level not less than forty ministries or commissions, more than twelve cooperation bodies, five offices, thirteen additional administrations and bureaus and ten institutions. Further, almost all of these ministries have their corresponding administrative bureaus at the provincial level. A rather simplified chart of government offices related to FDI is illustrative of the cumbersome nature of the Chinese bureaucracy (Figs. 1 and 2).

In general, there are two major government institutions. The Ministry of Foreign Trade and Economic Cooperation (MOFTEC) and the State Planning Commission, involved in FDI matters. Their major responsibilities include the preparation of sectoral guidelines on FDI and simplification of the investment application procedures through decentralization of power to the

Figure III.1 Major institutions related to FDI

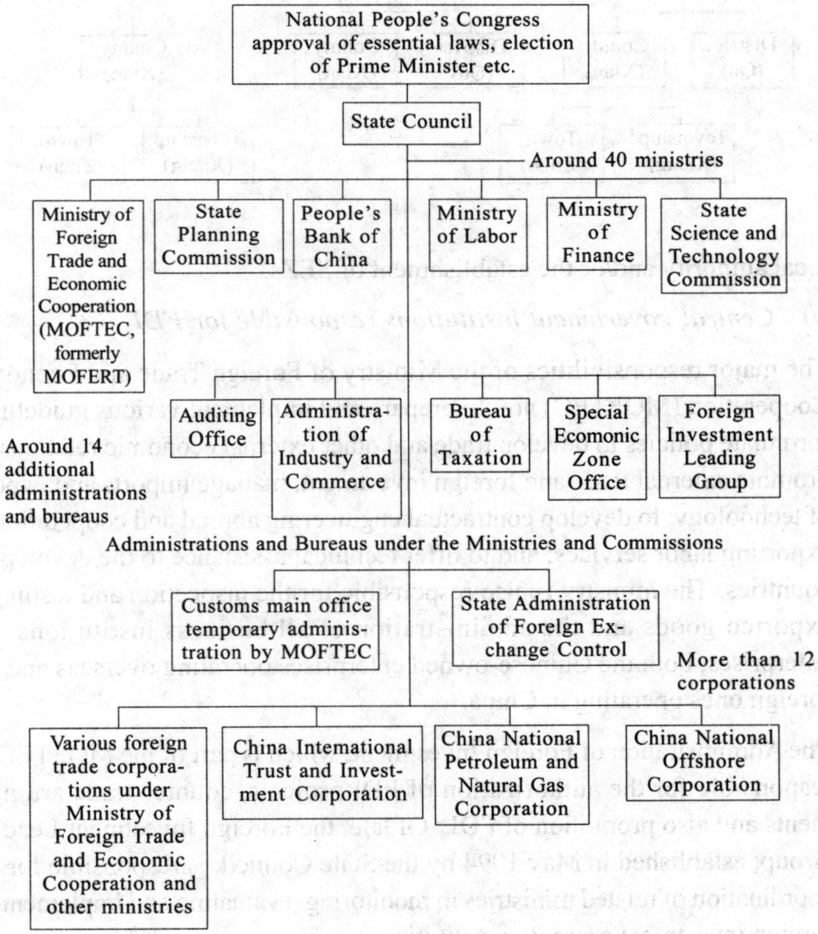

| National People's Congress |
| approval of essential laws, election of Prime Minister etc. |

State Council

Around 40 ministries

| Ministry of Foreign Trade and Economic Cooperation (MOFTEC, formerly MOFERT) | State Planning Commission | People's Bank of China | Ministry of Labor | Ministry of Finance | State Science and Technology Commission |

Around 14 additional administrations and bureaus

| Auditing Office | Administration of Industry and Commerce | Bureau of Taxation | Special Ecomonic Zone Office | Foreign Investment Leading Group |

Administrations and Bureaus under the Ministries and Commissions

| Customs main office temporary administration by MOFTEC | State Administration of Forelgn Exchange Control |

More than 12 corporations

| Various foreign trade corporations under Ministry of Foreign Trade and Economic Cooperation and other ministries | China Intemational Trust and Investment Corporation | China National Petroleum and Natural Gas Corporation | China National Offshore Corporation |

Figure 2 The Hierarchical Structuer of China's Administrative System

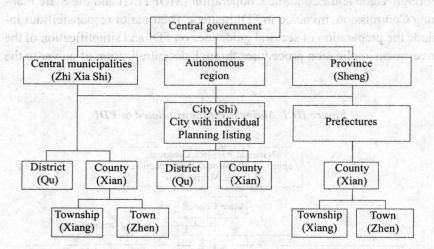

local authority and/or the establishment of SEZs.

(i)   Central government institutions responsible for FDI

The major responsibilities of the Ministry of Foreign Trade and Economic Cooperation (MOFTEC) are: to prepare and implement various guidelines, formulate policies to develop trade and other external economic relations; to promote external trade and foreign investment, manage imports and exports of technology; to develop contractual engineering abroad and cooperation in exporting labor services; and to offer technical assistance to the developing countries. The ministry is also responsible for the inspection and testing of exported goods and the administration of all business institutions and enterprises, both the Chinese-owned enterprises operating overseas and the foreign ones operating in China.

The Administration of Foreign Investment, which is part of the MOFTEC, is responsible for the authorization of FDI projects, counter-trade arrangements and also promotion of FDI. Of late, the Foreign Investment Leading Group, established in May 1994 by the State Council, is responsible for the coordination of related ministries in monitoring, evaluating and implementing foreign investment promotion activities.

Another related institution is the Administration of Industry and Commerce whose functions are to implement national economic policies, laws and regulations; to conduct study and draft laws, acts, and regulations related to industrial and commercial management; to determine the legal status of various industrial and commercial enterprises; and to supervise, manage or participate in the administration required for the functioning of market activities. An example of the latter is registration of the resident representative institutions of foreign enterprises, registration and protection of the domestic and foreign brands, trade mark, etc.

Every province, prefecture, city and county has a bureau or administration of industry and commerce. Generally, these institutions are also under the vertical administrative supervision from the central bureau.

Other central government institutions responsible for FDI are: (i) the State Planning Commission which is responsible to suggest the foreign investment targets and priorities, to coordinate the approval of special FDI projects (such as those which are above the sectoral quotas), to ensure an overall balance between sectors and regions in FDI targets; (ii) the Special Economic Zone Office which is responsible for evaluating FDI guidelines and policies and submit their recommendations to the State Council; (iii) Ministry of Finance, Auditing Office, State Administration of Foreign Exchange Control and the Customs Main Office; and the Ministry of Labor.

(ii) Local government institutions responsible for FDI

In every province, municipality, autonomous region and city, there exists a Foreign Economic Trade Commission (or bureau); these offices report directly to MOFTEC (at the central government level). However, there are regional variations, some local offices are authorized to represent MOFTEC. Thus local government institutions in certain areas have taken over the representation function. Although some of these institutions may have different names, but in their respective jurisdiction they perform the same tasks and responsibilities as those of the MOFTEC.

2. Authorization of FDI Projects

FDI in China should be examined and authorized by the Ministry of Foreign Trade and Economic Cooperation. Upon its approval, the ministry will issue a certificate of authorization. Recently, due to the rapid growth of FDI coupled with an accelerated pace of economic opening, the ministry was not able to cope with enormous administrative load. Hence, the power of authorization has been delegated to (some) local authorities.

The decentralization of the foreign investment approval began in Tianjin, Shanghai, Beijing, Guangdong, Fujian, Hainan, Liaoning, Hebei, Shandong, Jiangsu, Zhejiang and Guangxi areas. They were authorized to approve FDI projects with investment less than US$30 million, provided that these projects were productive and in accordance with the foreign investment guidelines and the state will not be required to invest in related/complementary construction and/or other facilitation requiring import.

At present, FDI approval has been delegated to other open provinces and autonomous regions along the border and along the Yangtze River. The recent FDI boom in these areas was partly explained by the decentralization. Generally, provinces and autonomous regions in the hinterland and the commissions, local offices of MOFTEC and Chinese Academy of Sciences have the power to approve FDI projects with investment under US$10 million.

3. Procedures for the Establishment of FDI Projects

In general there are several steps in the approval process for a newly established equity joint venture enterprise (Fig. 3). As shown, the approval process is quite complex. However, the process for other types of FDI is rather simpler.

For new capital construction projects, the State Planning Commission is responsible for the authorization of the project proposal and feasibility study; whereas for rehabilitation of existing enterprises, the State Economic and Trade Commission, is responsible.

MOFTEC is responsible for the authorization of all formal contracts for projects valued at above US$30 million. As a central governmental organization responsible for the administration and promotion of foreign investment and trade, it is also mandated as the chief organization responsible for devising and implementing policies and measures related to FDI promotion and regulation.

For projects involving local government-owned enterprises, the concerned local authority should prepare a reasonably complete project proposal. The proposal should justify its importance and outline its potential for receiving external assistance, financing (domestic or foreign sources) and projected sales (in the domestic and foreign market), etc. The proposal should be approved by a central government body (normally, the State Planning Commission), and then, upon its preliminary approval, subsequent procedures will be to follow steps 4 to 6, as illustrated in Fig. 3.

Figure 3 Procedures for Establishment of New Epuity Joint Venture Enterprise

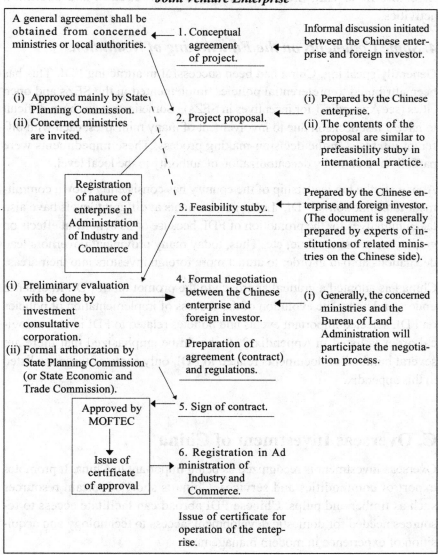

The Bank of China is involved in the process when foreign exchange is used for importation. Some local governments have established Foreign Investment Administrative Commission (or Bureau or Office) responsible the approval and administration of FDI. Some of them have a joint office to coordinate various local offices and bureaus for accelerating the approval process of foreign investment project and for assisting the foreign investors in solving the problems faced in production and operation activities.

4. Some Comments on the Functioning of Institutions

Generally speaking, China had been successful in attracting FDI. This has been attributed to preferential policies, implemented in the SEZs and open cities (see Appendix 1 for incentives in SEZs). Sometimes it has been difficult to have a fast decision due to involvement of many ministries, each with different interests, in the decision-making process. These impediments were partially overcome by decentralization of authority to the local level.

Above all, the top leadership of the country has consistently shown commitment to promotion of FDI. Local governments at different levels have also taken initiatives for the promotion of FDI, because of its beneficial effects on employment, tax revenue, etc. Thus, today many provincial governors lead delegations abroad in order to attract more foreign investors into their areas.

China has adopted a gradual approach to the promotion of FDI. In order to understand better the evolution of the process of implementation of policies on FDI, selected important events and policies related to FDI in chronological order is listed in Appendix 2. It should be emphasized that there are several hundred of documents related to FDI, only some of these are listed in this appendix.

C. Overseas Investment of China

Overseas investment is recognized as being important to China. It promotes export of commodities and services. China is short of certain resources such as timber and pulps. Chinese FDI abroad can facilitate access to resources needed for domestic development, access to technology and acquisition of experience in modem management.

Officially, the MOFTEC holds a position that China is not in a position to invest overseas in a large scale, the main focus is to attract FDI inflow. However, China is engaging in FDI in other countries. There are difficulties in estimating Chinese investment abroad as no systematic record is maintained. Official statistics showed that there were only 4,642 Chinese investment projects overseas with the total amount of US$5.24 billion. Such investment were undertaken by about 1,764 non-trading enterprises with total investment of US$1.76 billion and 2,878 trading enterprises with total investment of US$3. 48 billion. The geographical distribution of investment by the non-trading enterprises showed that an overwhelming proportion was invested in developed countries and a rather small proportion in the developing countries.

The Chinese investors have been engaged in a wide variety of business activities overseas. The major sectors include trading corporations such as the China Chemical Import and Export Corporation and the China Metallic Mineral Import and Export Corporation; non-trading enterprises include the Beijing Iron and Steel Corporation ("Shougang" which has five companies listed on the Hong Kong, China stock exchange and also owns a massive iron-ore mine in Peru); China Petrochemical Industrial Corporation; and various financial institutions in major international capital markets (mainly in Hong Kong, China).

As mentioned, there are difficulties in estimating the size of the Chinese FDI outflow as systematic records of this variable is scanty. However, the exceptionally large and negative signs of the "error and omissions" item in the balance of payment provides some indications of the unrecorded capital outflow. Indeed, the estimated "outward" investment has increased from US$3.2 billion in 1990 to US$17.8 billion in 1995 or, cumulatively, this amounted to a gross outflow of about US$55 billion for the period of 1990-1995,[3] calculated from IMF, International Financial statistics.

D. Concluding Observations

FDI flows are effected by the transnational corporations (TNCs). Hence it is necessary to observe the dynamic strategy of TNCs, from "simple inte-

---

3. This policy has been changed. Th Party and the government advocate "to go abroad", in parallel with "Induced inflow." (Author: May, 2003)

gration" to "complex integration", which allows them to coordinate a growing number of activities in a widening array of locations. Companies are arranging certain functions — research and development, procurement, accounting, data entry and processing, activities for specific products or product lines, such as component manufacturing and assembling — in a way that requires close links between parents and affiliates and firms linked via alliance. An understanding of this pattern is important so that recipient countries can adapt themselves to appropriate part of the overall value chain based upon their comparative advantages, specific strategy and policy for recipient countries.

Following its economic reform and opening, China has become the largest host developing economy to FDI. There are some lessons from Chinese experience. Firstly, there was a gradual approach to trade and investment liberalization and regional opening and decentralization. China's pace of liberalization varied across regions. It started from four special economic zones in coastal areas, extended to fourteen coastal cities and then farther extended to port cities along Yangtze River, the capital of every province and selected cities along its border. It should be recognized, however, that step-by-step approach in terms of opening up specific geographical areas to FDI may not be feasible in small countries. Secondly, some improvement in macroeconomic environment, establishment of physical and soft infrastructure as well as tax incentives and preferential policies are needed to promote FDI. Thirdly, industrial policies and guidelines for investment may be helpful to ensure that FDI conforms to national development strategies and objectives.

Appendix 1.
Incentives for FDI in Special Economic Zones

There is no unified data for incentives of foreign investment in special economic zones and fourteen open coastal cities. There are more than 38 official documents dealing with the preferential policies and measures applied to SEZs, fourteen open coastal cities, the Pudong New Zone in Shanghai and open cities along the Yangtze River and capitals of the provinces, etc. The open cities enjoy some of the preferential policies and measures applied to SEZs. The following table provides a general picture of the incentives covered.

Withholding tax	In the special economic zones there is no local surtax. Non-operating incomes (interest, royalties, license fees) are subject to a 20 percent withholding tax. However, this rate can be lowered to 10 percent or 0 percent for contracts involving advanced technology, technical data, technical training.
Equity joint venture	Income tax rate is set at 15 percent without any local surtax. Ventures commencing operations before 1985, or investing more than HK$5 million, using advanced technology, those having a long lead time, or considered as highly desirable, may apply for an exemption for the first three profit-making years or a reduction of 20-50 percent (Shenzhen); this exemption can extend to up to five years (Xiamen). Investors whose profits are reinvested for no less than five years can apply for a tax reduction/exemption on reinvested profits.
100 percent foreign owned companies	They are allowed in SEZs and ETDZs. They enjoy basically the same treatment as do Joint Ventures.
Accelerated depreciation	Faster depreciation rates can be granted to joint ventures inside the SEZ.
Remittance tax	No withholding tax.
Import tax	Investment goods and raw materials are exempt. Consumer goods can enjoy a reduction/exemption of import tax.
Export tax	No export tax levied on goods exported or delivered within the SEZs. However, goods delivered to the domestic market are subject to export tax, and to the repayment of import taxes that were not levied on the inputs incorporated.
Commercial and Industrial Consolidated Tax (CICT)	Construction or production imports; a reasonable amount of office suppplies; means of transportation imported by foreign enterprises

	for their own use; and food and beverages imported for tourists and restaurants can be exempt from CICT upon approval: - A 50 percent reduction of CICT available on imported high tax commodities; - If goods are manufactured mainly for export purposes, no CICT is levied at the factory level, except for a few types of commodities; - In Shenzhen, municipal authorities consider lowering the rate of CICT, when applicable.
Local taxes	No local surtax is levied on net income.
Personal tax	Income earned inside China will enjoy a 50 percent tax cut. After tax income can be freely remitted without any withholding tax. Furthermore, foreign employees enjoy reduction/exemption of import tax on daily life necessities.
Special conditions for overseas Chinese investors	In Xianmen, investors from Taiwan Province enjoy special preferential treatment in enterprise income tax. Furthemore, there is no income tax levied on foreign workers in any investment by overseas Chinese.
Industrial standardized buildings	The special Economic Zones' Development Companies provide standardized office space for investors.

Appendix 2.
Policies Related to FDI in China

Date	Item
1979	"Procedures for Processing, Assembling and Compensation Trade of Medium and Small Scale". Issued by the State Council.
1979	Preferential Policies to Foreign Investors in Guangdong and Fujian Province.
1979	"The Law of the PRC on Joint Ventures Using Chinese and

	Foreign Investment," abstracted to be "Law of Joint Venture Enterprise". Passed by the Fifth National People's Congress.
1979	"The Law of the PRC on Joint Ventures Using Chinese and Foreign Investment (Revised)". Passed by the Seventh National People's Congress.
1990	"Provisional Regulations on the Term of Joint Venture Enterprise." Approved by the State Council on September 30, 1990. Issued by the Ministry of Foreign Trade on October 20, 1990.
1990	"Regulations on Contract Operation on Joint Venture Enterprise Using Chinese and Foreign Investment". Issued by the Ministry of Foreign Trade, and the Administration of Industry and Commerce on September 13, 1990.
1980	Establishment of the four special economic zones. Authorized by the National People's Congress.
1983	"Guidelines on Promotion of Utilization of Foreign Investment". Issued by the State Council.
1983	"Notice on Implementation of 'Guidelines on Promotion of Utilization of Foreign Investment' by the Central Committee of CCP and the State Council". Issued by the Customs Office and the Ministry of Finance.
1983	Division of responsibility on foreign trade and foreign economic relations between the State Planning Commission, the State Economic Commission (now the State Economic and Trade Commission) and the MOFERT is clarified.
1983	"Provisional Method of Planning Management of Utilization of Foreign Investment". Issued by the State Economic and Trade Commission.
1984	Fourteen coastal cities opened through approval of "The Memo of conference of coastal open cities". Issued by the State Council.
1984	"Regulations on Land Use, Labor and Wage Management, Economic Contract, Enterprise Registration of Economic and Technology Development Zones of Dalian City" issued.
1985	Approval of "The Memo of Conference of Yanngtze River Delta, Peal River Delta and Southern Fujian Delta".
1985	"Some Aspects of Capital Registration and Share of Invest-

ment of Joint Venture Enterprises". Issued by the General Office of the State Council.

1985   "Provisional Regulations on Preferential Policies on Joint Venture Construction of Ports and Wharfs (Improvement of Management of Foreign Investment)." Issued by the State Council.

1986   Report "On the Work to Strengthen Utilization of Foreign Investment," jointly prepared by the MOFERT, the State Economic Commission and the State Planning Commission, and approved and issued by the State Council.

1986   "Regulationz on Further Improvement of the Production and Operation of Foreign Invested Enterprise". Issued by the State Council.

1986   "Regulations on Balance of Income and Expenditure of Foreign Exchange of Joint Venture Enterprises". Issued by the State Council.

1986   "Regulations on Encouragement of Foreign Investment".

1986   "Regulations of Autonomous Power on Employment, Wage Rate of Employees, Insurance and Welfare Cost of Foreign Invested Enterprises". Issued by the Ministry of Labor and Personnel.

1986   "Regulations on Financial Management of Joint Venture Enterprise, PRC". Issued by the Ministry of Finance.

1986   "Notice on the Issue of Certificate of Joint Venture, Contractual Joint Venture and Foreign Invested Enterprise". Issued by MOFERT, the State Administration of Industry and Commerce.

1987   "Notice on Strengthening Comprehensive Management to Promote the Business of Processing and Assembling with Components and Parts Supplied Abroad." Prepared by the State Customs Administration and issued by the General Office of the State Council.

1987   "Notice on Mastering the Favorable Opportunity to Promote Further the Business of Processing and Assembling of Contracted Material Supply". Issued by MOFERT.

1987   "Management of Products of Import Substitution of Chinese and Foreign Invested Joint Venture and Contractual Joint Venture Enterprises. Issued by the State Planning Commission.

1987   "Management of Products of Import Substitution of Chinese and Foreign Invested Joint Venture and Contractual Joint Venture Enterprise". Issued by the State Economic Commission.

1987   "Explanation of Item 5 of Implementation of Management of Machinery and Electric Products of Import Substitution of Chinese and Foreign Invested Joint Venture and Contractual Joint Venture Enterprises". Issued by the State Economic Commission.

1987   "Notice on Strict Examination of Qualification of Chinese Legal Persons in Chinese and Foreign Invested Joint Venture Enterprises". Issued by State Administration of Industry and Commerce.

1987   "Notice on Administration of the Chinese Cadre in Joint Venture Enterprises". Issued by the Ministry of Labor and Personnel.

1987   "Notice on "Regulations Concerning the Preparation and Approval of Feasibility Study of Foreign-Invested Projects" (Internal Experimental Implementation). Issued by the State Planning Commission and the Foreign Investment Leading Group Office of the State Council.

1987   Notice on "Provisional Regulations of Guidance of Foreign Investment". Prepared by the State Planning Commission and issued by the General Office of the State Council.

1995   "Provisional Regulations of Guidance of Foreign Investment". Prepared by the State Planning Commission and issued by the General Office of the State Council.

1995   "Directory of Industrial Sectors for Foreign Investment". Prepared by the State Planning Commission (Further Decentralize the Process of Approval). Issued by the General Office of the State Council.

1988   "Notice on Delegating Power to Provinces, Autonomous Regions, Municipalities Directly Under the Central Government, SEZs and Cities with Independent Planning Listing for Approval of Foreign-Invested Enterprises". Issued by the State Council.

1988   "Some Issues to Be Noticed on the Approval of Foreign Invested Enterprises". Issued by MOFERT.

1988   "Notice on Enlarging the Power of the Provinces, Autonomous

Regions, Cities with Independent Planning Listing of Hinterland Areas and Related Departments of the State Council for Approval of Foreign-Invested Enterprises". Issued by the State Council.

1988   "Notice to the Provinces, Autonomous Regions, Cities with Independent Planning Listing of Hinterland Areas and Related Departments of the State Council for Approval of Foreign Invested Enterprises," Issued by MOFERT.

1988   "Law on Sino-Foreign Contractual Joint Venture Enterprises". Passed by the Seventh National People's Congress and issued by Order of President of PRC.

1988   "Notice on Some Issues Regarding the Implementation of 'Regulations on Encouraging Investment from Compatriots in Taiwan".

1988   Further opening of the coastal areas: East Liaoning Peninsula Shandong Peninsula, Bohai Rim of Hebei Province, some coastal cities and counties of the Guangxi Zhuang Autonomous Region.

1989   "Regulations on Approval of Tax Rebate for Export Goods". Issued by State Administration of Taxation, the MOFTEC and the State Customs Administration.

1986   "Law on Foreign-Invested Enterprises of the PRC". Passed by the Sixth National People's Congress and issued by order of the president of PRC.

1990   "Detailed Regulations on Implementation of the "Law on Foreign-Invested Enterprises of the PRC". Approved by the State Council on October 28 and issued by order of the MOFTEC.

1991   "Notice on Explanation of Several Items in the 'Detailed Regulations on Implementation of the Law on Foreign-Invested Enterprises of the PRC'." Issued by the MOFTEC.

1991   "Notice on Opinions to Deal with Several Issues in Financial Management of Foreign-Invested Enterprise". Issued by the Ministry of Finance.

1991   "Notice on Some Issues Related to Accounting in Sino-Foreign Joint Venture Enterprises after the Implementation of Detailed Regulations on Income Tax Law of Foreign-Invested Enterprise and Wholy Foreign-Owned Enterprises". Issued by the Ministry of Finance.

1990	Opening of the Pudong zone in Shanghai.
1991	"Income Tax Law of Foreign-Invested Enterprises and Wholed Foreign-Owned Enterprises" is passed by the Seventh National People's Congress and issued by order of president of the PRC.
1991	Opening of portfolio investment-issue of shares.
1992	Opening of major cities along the Yangtze River and Border, and opening of the capital of every province.

10. Experience
with Tax Reform in China

Part I Introductory Part

1.01 Introduction

Tax and tariff system is a part of national fiscal system. In any economy, the primary role of fiscal system is to raise revenue to finance public expenditure. Based upon the theory of public finance, the role of tax is to be used to contribute to the budget revenue income of the government, in addition, it could be used to achieve three economic or social objectives, to influence resource allocation towards or away from certain activities, to move society towards a fairer distribution of income and wealth, and to promote economic stability. On the expenditure side, government should endeavour to improve cost efficiency in the satisfaction of public wants, while promoting growth and stability. Therefore, in studying this subject, the objectives of tax reform should be kept in mind, and it should be studied within the context of a national fiscal and budgetary system.

China had followed the Soviet model of a central planned economy since the establishment of PRC in 1949. China may have the same institutions and pattern of administration as Kyrgyzstan in those periods, which was characterized by the state ownership of the means of production; detailed quantitative governmental plans for enterprise inputs and outputs: foreign trade and financial plans that reflected the physical flows of the plans; bureautic bargaining over access to resources in the context of the plan targets; fixed prices to ease the planning process and the fulfillment of the plan as the main crieteria of enterprise efficiency. The fiscal system depended greatly on industry, especially the profits of state owed enterprises, and also taxes for government revenue. It was also the former Soviet model of industrialization that rapid industrialization process would be financed with savings extracted from the agricultural sector via the "price scissors". Through administrative prices that systematically discriminated against agricultural and raw material producers in favor of industry, surpluses from the agricultural and extractive sectors were transferred to the industrial sector. Therefore, in the years of the 70's before the launch of economic reform, industrial sector of China was the main source of government revenue, running from 66% to 69%, while the contribution from the agricultural sector ranged from 2.5% to 4.8%. Also, profit remittances came from the state-owned enterprises, the non-tax revenue, dominated the shares of governmental budget revenue income before the launch of economic reform.

In the pre-reform era, the government control over the activity of state-owned enterprises was exercised through sectoral ministries and the provincial governments. China, differed from the former Soviet model that several cycles of centralization and de-centralization had been implemented before the launch of economic reform, a part of the enterprises was also owned by the provincial and local governments. All sectoral ministries and provincial governments received directives from the former State Planning Commission (currently the State Development Planning Commission) and the Ministry of Finance concerning the amount of resources that their respective branches were compelled to channel to the budget.

The sectoral ministries at the central level and the sectoral bureaus at the provincial or local level were instructed to find ways of redistributing financial resources of the enterprises under their jurisdiction in a manner that would ensure the normal development of production, the financing of expenditures for the maintenance of the social infrastructure that were listed on the balance sheet of enterprises (mainly social benefits and services), and their contribution to the state budget of those amounts requested by the State Planning Commission and the Ministry of Finance.

The reform of fiscal system and tax of China are a complex process which involves many interrelated aspects, it is related to enterprise reform, price reform, social security system reform, inter-governmental fiscal relationship, debt management and other aspects. Therefore, only selected important related aspects can be described here. This paper will give a general discussion of governmental structure and current budgetary system of China in the beginning (1.02); evolution and reform of fiscal system of China will be given in part II. It is expected that with a brief retrospect of the fiscal system of China, it will provide a better understanding of the reform of the essential component of fiscal system, the tax reform of China; evolution and reform of system of tax with detail description of tax structure which will be presented in part III. China is in the transitional process from a former central planned economy to a socialist market economy, the reform process is "crossing the river by touching the stones", in spite of the fact that China had been successful to achieve a high economic growth rate averaged 9.7% in the past two decades through reform and opening. But there are also lessons in the exploration and implementation of reform, including tax reform in the past, major lessons of tax reform and future prospects will be given in part IV. A brief conclusion will be presented in part V. It is expected that the experience of tax reform described will provide some useful references for our neighboring country, Kyrgyzstan. It is also expected that Kyrgstan can achieve better results on tax reform through learning and integrating international experiences with the concrete conditions of their mother country.

1.02 Governmental Structure and Budgetary System

In March 22, 1994, the National People's Congress of China had approved the "Budget Law of the PRC". This law became effective since January 1, 1995. It is divided into 11 chapters and 79 articles. It is described in this law that "The state will implement a budgetary system that there should be budget for every level of government, the five levels of budget will be established for central government, the provinces, autonomous regions, directly administered municipalities; municipalities, autonomous prefectures with districts; counties, autonomous counties, municipalities without districts, municipal administered district; townships, ethnic townships and towns. The budget of various levels of government should be reviewed and approved by people's congresses of corresponding levels". The governmental structure is shown in Fig 1.1. Every level of budget should be balanced in outlays and receipts. A tax sharing system is currently implemented between the central and local governments which will be described further in part II and part III of this paper. It should be emphasized that this 5 levels of administration set up by the law in 1994 is different from the fiscal administration in the past.

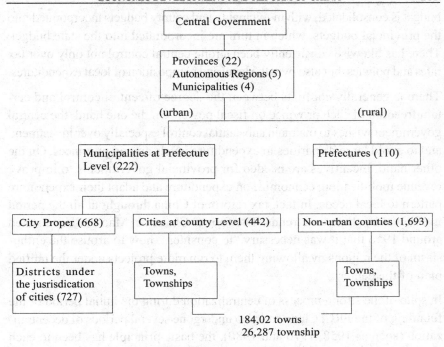

Fig 1.1 Government Structure of China

Note: 1. The above diagram and figures are quoted from *China Statistical Yearbook 1998*. The figures are by the end of 1997.

2. Taiwan Province is not included, Hong Kong Special Administrative Region is established in July 1, 1996. It is also not shown in this figure.

Part II   Evolution and Reform of Fiscal and Budgetary System of China

2.01 Major Features of Fiscal and Budgetary System in Pre-Reform Era

1. The principal instrument of financial control of the Chinese economy in the pre-reform era is the state budget, through which, about 30% of GDP flows. Provincial governments, autonomous regions, municipal and county governments, which have their own budgets, collect more than 80% of all revenues and carry out around 50% of all expenditures. In form, the state

budget is consolidated, with municipality and county budgets incorporated into the provincial budgets, which in turn are incorporated into the state budget. There has likewise consistently been strong central control not only over tax rates and policies, but also over the level and composition of local expenditures.

There is generally conflicts between the degree of central control and certain freedom of each province on fiscal power. On the one hand, the central government wishes to maintain substantial control especially over investment, and to avoid large disparities in expenditure levels among provinces. On the other hand, incentives are needed for provincial governments to improve revenue mobilization, economize on expenditure and adapt their expenditure pattern to local needs. In fact, tax reform of China throughout all the period is effected by these two trends. The former Chairman Mao had once stated around 1956 that it was necessary "to consider... how to arouse the enthusiasm of the regions by allowing them to run more projects under the unified plan of the center."

In spite of the strong process of centralization during the initial period of the founding of the PRC, China had also undergone several periods of decentralization (such as 1958, 1970 and 1980), the basic principle has been to each province to retain a predetermined proportion of the revenue it collects, which then determines its total expenditure, and to give the provincial government substantial freedom in deciding the composition of its expenditure. It should also be pointed out that these devolutions of fiscal authority have also generally been accompanied by a parallel devolution of authority over state enterprises.

There is another important feature of the Chinese budgetary system before the economic reform that there was much smaller share of revenue retained by rich industrialized provinces than poor, backward ones. In the very early stage of economic reform, 1980, for instance, the high-income municipalities of Shanghai, Beijing and Tianjin retained around 11%, 37% and 31% respectively of their revenues. Liaoning Province was relatively rich in that time, retained only about 50% of all revenues other than industrial and commercial taxes. While middle-income provinces, in contrast, retained a fixed proportion of industrial and commercial taxes and 100% of other revenues, and lower income provinces, including all the border provinces populated mostly by minorities, not only retained their revenues, but also received subsidies from the central government.

Another distinctive feature of the Chinese budget is that enterprise profits are the largest single source of revenue — partly because profit margins are high, but also because enterprises have generally been obliged to remit virtually all their profits to the state. The second biggest source of revenue is industrial and commercial tax, which accounts around three quarters of all tax receipts. Table 2.1 and 2.2 will give a general picture of fiscal income and the composition of source of revenue in the pre-reform period.

Table 2.1 Structure of Fiscal Income of China in the Pre-Reform Era.
(Selected Years) (With Total Fiscal Income=100%)

| Year | Enterprise Income | | Various Taxation Income | | | Debt Income | Other Income |
	Total (%)	Within which: Industrial Income (%)	Total (%)	Within which Industrial and Commercial tax (%)	Agricultural Tax (%)		
1950	13.4	6.8	75.1	36.2	29.3	4.6	6.9
1957	46.5	19.1	49.9	36.5	9.6	2.3	1.3
1962	46.6	27.1	51.7	39.8	7.3		1.7
1965	55.8	45.7	43.2	35.0	5.4		1.0
1970	57.2	42.3	42.4	35.0	4.8		0.4
1975	49.1	40.8	49.4	42.7	3.6		1.5
1978	51.0	39.3	46.3	40.3	2.5		2.7

Source: *China Statistical Yearbook 1984*, China Statistics Publishing House.

Table 2.2 Source of Revenue by Sector, PRC 1952-1978 (%) (Selected Years)

Year	Industry	Agriculture	Commerce	Transportation	Construction
1952	35.8	21.3	24.0	5.5	0.5
1957	50.3	13.1	24.1	8.5	0.5
1965	65.7	6.5	6.0	8.0	0.1
1970	67.2	4.8	11.5	6.8	-
1975	66.3	3.2	7.3	6.8	-
1978	67.7	2.5	11	6.5	0.2

Source: "People's Republic of China", by Christine P.W. Wang in *From Central Planned to Market Economies: the Asian Approach*, ADB, 1994.

2.02 Evolution of the Fiscal System

China had implemented a highly centralized political, economic and social system for a long time. Under this administrative structure, various levels of government under the central was treated as one level of administrative unit without detailed consideration of the independence of the budget operation, although the local governments also have their own outlays and receipts, but they only perform the function of local accountant in fulfilling the local expenditure and revenue income plan of the National Plan. This situation changes greatly since the launch of economic reform. The evolution of the fiscal system of China can be briefly outlined as follows:

1. The Period of Unified Outlay and Receipt (1950-1952)

Following the decades of inflation in the period of civil war (war of liberalization, in official term), Chinese government had spent a great effort to secure the monetary and financial stability that had been achieved, through a balanced budget. Since considerably more than 50% of investment expenditures were financed from the central government budget, the realization of industrialization measures presupposed a correspondingly rapid expansion of state revenues. All means and measures are used to establish a highly centralized fiscal system. At the national financial conference in February 1950, it was decided to strictly centralize all matters of economy and decisions on their use. The concrete features include the follows:

(1) All major receipts at various regions of China should be submitted to the Central Treasury in unification, they cannot be used without the order of allocation from the central government;

(2) All local outlays should be approved by the central government, these outlays will be allocated by the central government monthly;

(3) Budgetary system management is responsible solely by the central government, including tax system, the amount of management at various levels of fiscal systems, the wages, budget, auditing and accounting system were set up and implemented by the central government solely;

(4) The local governments were allowed to keep a very small share of fiscal resource to deal with the temporary requirement of rural development and urban construction.

(5) In March 1951, the central government of China determined to divide the fiscal revenue income and expenditure into three levels. The central fiscal system, the regional fiscal system[1], and the provincial (municipal) fiscal system. The division of revenue income was also determined roughly by that time. By the year 1951 China was mainly an agricultural economy, agricultural tax revenue or even the salt tax revenue were important revenue resources, and the government had not fully exercised its control over the enterprises and municipalities by that time. Therefore, it was determined that the central government revenue income will include agricultural tax, customs duty, salt tax, income of central operated enterprises, income of central administrative and judicial fees, debt income from domestic and abroad, income of state banks. The share of tax income between the central and local includes: commodity tax, industrial and commercial tax, stamp tax, trading tax, tax income of deposit interest, profit of monopolistic sales of tobacco and liquor. The income of regions and provinces include: slaughter tax, contract tax, real estate tax, special consumption tax, vehicle and ship tax, income of state-owned enterprises operated under regional level, income of administrative and judicial fees and others. By the year 1952, the central government had got in-depth control of the national economy, it is estimated by domestic study that the tax income of urban was around 44%, revenue income from the state-owned enterprise was around 23%, and the share of agricultural tax was declined its share to around 12%. There are also many studies on Chinese economy abroad, some tables are quoted in appendix for reference.

The extra-budgetary system was emerged by that period, it was a very small share of the income in order to give the local government a very limited freedom in using a minor resource, and also to avoid the trouble of submit this to the state treasury and reallocate it for local expenditure. By that time, the extra-budget revenue was generally composed of the surcharge of agricultural tax and miscellaneous fees of schools, etc.

It is important to notice the fact that in June 1952, it was announced to abolish the surcharge of agricultural tax from the local, all fiscal needs of the townships and towns will be supplied by the central. In November 1952, it

---

1. By that time, China was divided into six administrative regions, the Northeastern region (Liaoning, Jilin and Heilongjiang), the Eastern, the Northern, Southeastern, Northwestern and central. This level of fiscal management was abolished since Jan. 1, 1953.

was once emphasized by the central government that it was not allowed to collect surcharge of agricultural tax and miscellaneous fees. Therefore, it can be seen that extra-budgetary issue (which will be described in part IV of this paper) had a long historical background if there was not a clear classification of intergovernmental responsibility and power, and also a reasonable division of fiscal resources at different administrative levels. This is an issue that hardly can be avoided.

2. Period of Unified Leadership and Hierarchical Management (1953-1978)

China initiated the First Five-Year Plan since 1953. And the central government had got more experience on national management.

The principle of fiscal system set up by the central government in Aug. 1953 is: The fiscal system will be determined under the unified leadership and planning of the central government to set up the scope of responsibility and power, to implement hierarchical management. The fiscal management should be transformed from fiscal supply management to constructive fiscal management, it should correct the past wrong practice by focusing on small, receipt and administration rather than focusing on large, outlay and construction. The national budget was divided into three levels (central, provincial or municipal, and county). This budgetary system is implemented under the unified plan of the national budget, the scope of receipt and outlay is divided between the central and local government, generally, the local will have a share around 20%, while the central government will have a share around 80%.

The features in this periods are:

(1) Although there were three levels of budgetary system, but the local government below the central level had limited power in management. They cannot play an independent budgetary role at its level;

(2) The scope of expenditure of various budgetary levels was based on the division of responsibility and powers of the central and local governments. It also depended upon the relationship of attachment of enterprises, institutions (*shiyedanwei*) and various governmental organization;

(3) The legislative power in determination of main tax category, tax rate as well as power of adjustment, the power of tax reduction and exemption were centralized. In spite of the fact that the collection of the tax income

was responsible by the local government[2]. But the disposable revenue income of the local was determined by the central government. In order to mobilize the initiative of the local governments to collect taxable income, the central government allocated a proper share of the part of tax revenue income in excess of the planning target to the local; it is this deep rooted incentive structure evolved into various fiscal contract responsibility system in the period of reform in the 80's.

(4) The principle in setting up the local receipts was determined by its expenditure, if the local income was in excess of the local expenditure set up by the central government, the surplus fiscal income should be submitted to the central government; if there was insufficient revenue income to support the local expenditure, the deficit part will be complemented by the central government. Therefore, there was no incentive for the local governments to pursue a balanced budget;

(5) The target of receipt and outlay set up by the local governments was determined through the negotiation between the central and local governments. This negotiation was proceeded once every year, the so-called "determination once every year" (*yinianyidu*), sometimes, this negotiation was implemented once through several years, the so called "not to be changed in several years" (*jinnianbubian*).

(6) Although the fiscal system was divided into three levels, but the fiscal system at the basic county or city level had very limited management power. Under this three-level hierarchical system, the power of local public finance was highly concentrated at the provincial level in this period, the fiscal aspects at city and county level under the province was generally incorporated into the public finance at the provincial level, the unified system of receipt and outlay was still in effect in reality.

(7) Although China had implemented the central planning system in this period, it had undergone several cycles of centralized and decentralized planning in this period. In the period of Great Leap Forward (1958-1960), the planning system was more or less decentralized; there was centralization in the period of adjustment (1963-1965). This has also become the cause of

---

2. The central government had not established national bureau of tax to collect national tax before 1994., it relied upon the local government to collect all taxes.

expansion of extrabudget.

Table 2.3 and Table 2.4 are quoted from Reference 4, although these tables are quoted from studies abroad, but the informations contained checked fairly in close with available Chinese statistics. Table 2.3 can illustrate the centralization of governmental expenditure in the period from 1950 to 1957; Table 2.4 gives the relatively detailed information of state revenue income from various resources, the changing role of four major taxes (agricultural tax, salt tax, customs duty, industrial and business [commercial] taxes) can also be seen through analysis of these figures. Table 2.5 is quoted from the Chinese statistical yearbook which can illustrate the general fiscal situation of China from 1950-1978.

3. Period of Decentralization and Implementation of Contract Responsibility System (1978-1993)

China implemented the basic policy of economic reform and opening to the outside world since late 1978. The economic system reform was initiated in the rural area through the implementation of the contract responsibility system. This is a successful experience in the rural reform. But this was implemented later in all aspects without discrimination of the nature of them. Decentralization is another major feature of the reform and opening.

Decentralization is not new to China, nor has it been a continuous process. Between 1949 and 1978, the central-local relations in China had gone through two episodes of "sending down" and "taking up". The first wave of decentralization was initiated in 1957 and was followed soon after by recentralization. A second decentralization drive started in 1970 only to be reversed again. Decentralization pursued over the post-1978 period has been significantly different from previous occasions in two aspects:

Table 2.3 Share of the Central Government and Local Administrations of State Expenditures, 1950-1957 (in percent)

	1950	1951	1952	1953	1954	1955	1956	1957*
Central govt.	74.20	74.72	71.08	75.84	74.90	75.93	71.05	70.78
Local govt.	25.80	25.28	28.92	24.16	25.10	24.07	28.95	29.22

Source: Reference 4

Table 2.4 State Revenues, 1950-1957 (in million yuan)

	1950	1951	1952	1953	1954	1955	1956	1957
Tax yield								
Agricultural taxes	1,910	2,169	2,704	2,711	3,278	3,054	2,965	2,970
Salt tax	268	339	405	461	521	481	483	620
Customs	356	693	481	505	412	466	542	460
Industrial and commercial taxes	2,363	4,745	6,147	8,250	8,972	8,725	10,098	11,300
Private enterprises	1,910	3,312	3,458	3,422	2,872	1,671	640	240
Cooperatives			190	534	925	1,128	1,580	2,205
Joint state-private enterprises			184	265	422	556	1,580	2,855
State-run firms	435	1,433	2,315	4,029	4,753	5,370	6,298	6,000
Miscellaneous taxes	1	167	32	40	35	19		140
Total Tax Yield	**4,898**	**8,113**	**9,769**	**11,967**	**13,218**	**12,745**	**14,088**	**15,490**
State income from non tax sources								
Profits from state-run firms			4,653	6,369	8,457	9,404	11,414	11,363
Depreciations and other income from state-run firms	370	3,050	1,077	1,301	1,503	1,786	2,016	3,057
Income from foreign credits	244	625	1,305	438	884	1,657	117	23
Income from domestic bonds	260				836	619	607	650
Income from insurance business				52	70	84		27
Miscellaneous income	247	1,179	756	1,635	1,269	908	501	410
Total non-tax income	1,621	4,854	7,791	9,795	13,019	14,458	14,655	15,530
Total revenues	**6,519**	**12,967**	**17,560**	**21,762**	**26,237**	**27,203**	**28,743**	**31,020**
Growth per annum (%)		98.9	35.4	23.9	20.6	3.7	5.7	7.9

Source: Reference 4.

Table 2.5 State Fiscal income and Expenditure (unit: 100 million yuan)

Year	Total Income	Total Expenditure	Balance
1950	65.2	68.1	-2.9
1951	133.1	122.5	+10.6
1952	183.7	176.0	+7.7
1953	222.9	220.1	+2.8
1954	262.4	246.3	+16.1
1955	272.0	269.3	+2.7
1956	287.4	305.7	-18.3
1957	310.2	304.2	+6.0
1958	387.6	409.4	-21.8
1959	487.1	552.9	-65.8
1960	572.3	654.1	-81.8
1961	356.1	367.0	-10.9
1962	313.6	305.3	+8.3
1963	342.3	339.6	+2.7
1964	399.5	399.0	+0.5
1965	473.3	466.3	+7.0
1966	588.7	541.6	+17.1
1967	419.4	441.9	-22.5
1968	361.3	359.8	+1.5
1969	526.8	525.9	+0.9
1970	662.9	649.4	+13.5
1971	744.7	732.2	+12.5
1972	766.6	766.4	+0.2
1993	809.7	809.3	+0.4
1974	783.1	790.8	-7.7
1975	815.6	820.9	-5.3
1976	776.6	806.2	-29.6
1977	874.5	843.5	+31.0
1978	1,121.1	1,111.0	+10.1

Source: *Chinas Statistical Yearbook 1984,* China Statistics Publishing House.

First, the past decentralization was pursued to improve the delivery and supervision of the planning system, and decentralization since 1978, decision making authority has been devolved to lower levels of government in order to facilitate market reforms. The second, in the early years the objective was limited to administrative decentralization, since 1978 economic decentralization has also been pursued. Not only has decision-making authority been devolved to lower levels of government, but it has also shifted to certain extent, from governments at all levels to non-government economic agents, i.e., to enterprises, financial institutions and even to household. Although the trend toward decentralization since 1978 has enhanced the autonomy of subnational governments and enterprises quite significantly, this is a mixed blessing. It is healthy in that it helps ensure the permanency of a wide range of market reforms. By the same token, it also poses a problem in that it creates obstacles to those reforms that require local governments to cede some of their discretionary authority, and there is also the necessity to implement further in-depth reform of the enterprises. There is need continuously to improve the reform process which is still on going. The reform process related to tax reform in this period is characterized as follows:

1. With greater autonomy given to enterprises and local governments through decentralization, the central government's effectiveness in mobilizing resources and its role in financing investment and other expenditures has diminished. This shift is reflected in the trends in tax and non tax revenues mobilized by all levels of government in China, which have fallen from some 34% of GDP in 1978 to around 12.6% in 1993. This trend is shown in Fig. 2.1 as follows.

2. Shift in the Pattern of Revenue Generation

Before 1979, governmental revenue is derived by tapping sectoral surpluses through non tax means. Agricultural surpluses were tapped through price ceilings and procurement policies; egalitarian wage policy reduced surpluses in the urban household sector; and surpluses of enterprises were remitted to the budget. With respect to the tax policy, sectorally differentiated taxes were supposed to promote certain economic sectors, e.g., trade was more heavily taxed than industry. The tax rate for heavy industry were lower than those for light industry. But profit remittance played a major role in governmental revenue, indeed, until 1983, the bulk of government revenues, approximately 60%, was generated from the remittance of profits by state-owned enterprises to the government budget. In the early 1980's, this system began to be replaced, on an experimental basis, with taxation of enterprise profits in an attempt to provide state-owned enterprises with greater incentives for increasing efficiency. This experimental system featured, broadly, a statutory 55% enterprise tax rate (there was a separate tax for collectives and small enterprises) and an "adjustment tax" which was intended to tax away "excess profits". Since 1986, tax reforms have focused on a more general application to become "contract responsibility system". This was pushed forward to cover nearly all enterprises before 90's, this system aims to develop enterprise performance responsibility by establishing "clear" criteria for profitability and accountability. While contracts differ in their details, all establish a contract between government and enterprises determining profits or taxes to be remitted by the enterprise to the government. This contract system has introduced a significant element of discretion into the tax system, with contracts negotiated on an enterprise-by-enterprise basis by the Bureau of Finance of the government owning the enterprise. This system is abandoned in the 90's.

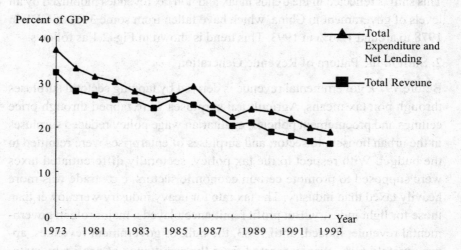

Fig 4.2 Goverment Budgetay Revemue and Expenditure as a Share of GDP, 1978-93

Percent of GDP

Source: Ministry of Finance.

3. Implementation of Fiscal Contract Responsibility System

It had been described previously that China's fiscal system is a unitary one. The central government directs expenditure policy and determines all aspects of tax policy. Beginning in 1980, experiments was implemented to move from the "big pot" system in which all revenue and expenditure authority was centralized to revenue sharing.

China had first experimented the fiscal contract responsibility system in the Jiangsu Province. The principle was to set up a definite ratio between the fiscal income submitted to the central treasury and the part retained by the province, this ratio is kept without change for four years.

After that, the central government had implemented four different forms of fiscal contract responsibility system (or revenue sharing system) to other provinces such as Liaoning and Sichuan provinces, etc. "Division of receipts and outlays" means to divide the scope of receipts and outlays of the central and local government based upon the attachment of administrative relationship of the entities. With regard to the outlays, all outlays belonged to the governmental organizations, institutions (*shiyedanwei*) and enterprises were classified into the central expenditure, while those outlays belonged to the local government organizations, institutions and enterprises were classified into the expenditure of the local government. (It can be seen that due to the unique system that the enterprises had to submit their profits to the government they attached, the share of profit submitted was the major source of the government revenue. For example, in the year 1977, the revenue income of the enterprises submitted is 46% of the total revenue income of the central government, this value reduced to 17.6% since the implementation of changing submit of profit into enterprise income tax effective from Jan. 1, 1983: this was reduced further down to 0.02% due to the further implementation of enterprise contract responsibility system in 1986, although a part of the enterprise income had been transformed into target submitted to the government in the contract. And at the same time, there was a rapid decline of the budget revenue income to be the share of GDP in the central government budget.

This revenue sharing system is very complex. Before 1988, the guiding principle is that local governments should retain enough revenue to cover a "basic level" of services and should turn the remainder over to the central government. The formulae differed in the details according to varying interpretations of what expenditures were considered sufficient to cover "basic level" of services, and by how much these expenditures should grow each year. The provinces and autonomous regions are classified into three groups: those allowed to retain only a fixed percentage of their tax collections; those entitled not only to keep all the tax collected, but also to receive an additional subsidy from the center (generally the autonomous region of the minorities belonged to this category); and those allowed to retain all the taxes collected net of a fixed lump-sum transfer to the central government (this had once applied to Guangdong province). This system is also complicated in time setting, for contracts with five autonomous regions, it was kept with no change for five years. For the three municipalities directly administered by the central government, namely, Shanghai, Beijing and Tianjin, a sharing of total amount was implemented, and the share was determined once every year.

Based upon this principle, the municipal and county governments also implemented the fiscal contract responsibility system with the provincial governments.

This system was changed since 1988 to a much more negotiated approach. Each province was allowed to retain revenues sufficient to cover its 1987 level of "basic expenditures". In addition, a province can retain a proportion of the incremental revenues above the 1987 level according to a renegotiated contract with the center. There were six different types of contracts across the various provinces, which in effect accorded the provinces a marginal retention rate. As a result, the share of the central government in total tax revenues has declined more sharply since 1989.

2.03 Normalization of Fiscal System (1994-)

The process of decentralization and implementation of contract responsibility system (enterprise contract responsibility system and fiscal contract responsibility system) have both its positive and negative effects. On the positive side, it promotes the process of marketization and mobilizes the initiatives of enterprises and local governments to a certain extent, but it also has its negative effects. The fiscal capability of the state is too much decentralized, the share of fiscal revenue income to GDP is reduced from 34% in 1978 to around 12.6% in 1993 (Refer to Fig. 2.1), it also induced a trend of local economic barrier and redundant investment among provinces and autonomous regions which is detrimental to the formation of a unified market. This is also one of the basic causes of high inflation in bust and boom cycle of the Chinese economy in the process of reform. There is also bureautic intervention from various governmental levels to enterprises under their jurisdiction. Therefore, there is also major reform of the fiscal system to be normalized.

1. Reform of the Central-Local Fiscal Relationship

There are four major reforms in the central local fiscal relationship.

(1) Three types of revenues are classified to be distributed between the central and local governments: fixed central government revenues, fixed local government revenues and shared revenues.

The fixed central government revenues include: all taxes and duties levied at customs, consumption tax, income tax on all central government enterprises, the business tax on railroads, bank headquarters and insurance company headquarters, etc.

The fixed local government revenue includes: business tax, income tax on all local government enterprises, personal income tax, urban and town land use tax, the urban construction and maintaineuce tax, real estate tax, vehical/ships tax, investment-oriented tax on fixed asessts, stamp tax, slaughter tax, agricultural land transformation tax, agricultural and husbandry tax, contract tax, etc.

The taxes (revenues) that are designated for sharing between the central and local governments include VA tax (75% share for central, 25% share for local), security trading stamp tax (50% each for central and local) and resource tax (within which, tax for off-shore oil belonged to the central government).

(2) Establish proper scope of outlays (fiscal expenditure) between the central and local governments based on the clarification of responsibility of administration.

(3) Implement reimbursement system of tax from the central to local governments. This is more or less a form of transfer payment, and it is also a compromising means in favor of local interests in the transition from the former fiscal contract responsibility system.

(4) Both central and local tax administration institutions are established to collect the respective category of tax. The sharing tax is collected by the central administrated tax institutions and return the local share to local governments.

2. Reform of Tax System

The major reform of tax system covers three aspects:

(1) Establish a new turnover tax system with value-added tax to be the dominant category, there is also reform of consumption tax and business tax. The reform of tax system is also implemented within the context of progress of legal system of China. Three regulations are promulgated by the State Council of China on Dec. 13, 1993 and are effective since Jan. 1, 1994. These three regulations are: "Provisional Regulations on Value-Added Tax, PRC"; "Provisional Regulations on Consumption Tax, PRC"; and "Provisional Regulations on Business Tax, PRC."

(2) Unify income tax system applied to enterprises of different ownership, a unified income tax rate of 33% is applied to all types of enterprises to create an environment of competition in equality. The "Provisional Regulations on Income Tax of Enterprises, PRC" is promulgated by the State Council on Dec. 13, 1993, and it is effective since Jan. 1, 1994. There is also reform of personal income tax system. A more detail description will be given in part III afterwards.

(3) Reform the distribution of profit of enterprises

A unified system of financial management and accounting practice in accordance with the international practice is implemented. The "General guideline of Finance of Enterprises" and "Guideline of Enterprise Accounting" are implemented since July 1, 1993, under the premise of tax reform and the implementation of these two guidelines, a unified income tax rate is applied to all domestic enterprises, profit and tax contract responsibility system is abolished, adjustment tax and energy and transport charge are also dismantled[3]. There is gradual establishment of a distribution system of enterprises based on dividend on shares of the state assests, profit share based on capital investment and submission of profit after tax.

---

3. Enterprise earnings after payment of income and adjustment tax, are used to pay a transportation and energy tax or fee of 15% on the sum of after tax earnings plus depreciation.

2.04 Coming Tasks of Reform Agenda of Fiscal System

There are several tasks of further reform of the fiscal system.

1. Normalize the management of collection of fees to reduce the burden of enterprises

There is pressing need to change fees into tax. It is estimated that by the end of 1997 that the items of collection of national sectoral and administrative fees reached 344, the collection of fees under the provincial level is even more enormous. This has not only increased the social burden and caused the erosion of the tax base, it influences a healthy and sound economic and social development.

2. Reform further the fiscal management system, improve the structure of fiscal expenditure.

There will be adjustment of the structure of fiscal expenditure. Fiscal capital will be retreated gradually from the operational area of resource allocation belonged to the market, and shifted to meet the social public needs. There is the need to increase gradually public expenditure to construction of physical infrastructure, consolidation of governmental organization, development of education, cultural and scientific endeavor as well as environmental protection. There is need to improve further the budgetary system, strengthening the budgetary constraints, establish gradually the governmental public budget, state assets budget and social security budget.

Normalize further the transfer payment system, specific subsidies to local finance should be shifted gradually to transfer payment system.

3. Deepening the reform of tax collection and administration.

Part III Evolution and Reform of Tax System of China

A broad picture of evolution and reform of fiscal system of China had been described in the previous part. A relatively detailed description of the tax structure in the evolution and reform of taxation system of China will be given in this part. It is expected that it will give some reference on technical aspects of this theme. A description of the evolution of taxation system of

Chinese practice will be briefed below.

3.01 Evolution and Reform of Tax System in the Pre-reform Period

1. Chinese Tax System in the Restoration Period (1949-1952)

Since the founding of the PRC in 1949, the central role is to establish a unified political economic system: The Central People's Government promulgated "Provisions on Implementation of Major Guidelines on Taxation" in Jan. 1950. In this document, the major principles on tax policy, administrative system and organizational aspects are set up. In addition to agricultural tax, there are fourteen categories of tax: management tax, industrial and commercial tax, salt tax, customs duty, income tax on interests of deposit, income tax of salary payment, stamp tax, inheritance tax, trading tax, slaughter tax, real estate tax, land tax, specific consumption tax, and license tax for vehicles and ships.

In the period after 1950, the tax items and tax rates were adjusted and simplified.

2. Chinese Tax System in the First-Five Year Plan Period (1953-1957)

There is larger expansion of commercial networks and reduction of links in turnover tax. There is a decline of business tax in wholesale which caused a relative decline in taxable income. On the other hand, there is also a decline of the number of major taxpayers, the private enterprises. The tax system is evolved in this period based on the new circumstances.

In this period, commodity turnover tax is experimented which combines with the management tax, business tax and stamp tax in the production chain as well as the business tax in the chain of wholesale and retail into one category. It is collected once at the sales of production chains. The major tax category in this period covers fourteen: the commodity turnover tax, the management tax (merging with trading tax of grain), industrial and commercial tax, salt tax, customs duty, agricultural (husbandry) tax, stamp tax, slaughter tax, animal trading tax, urban real estate tax, cultural and entertainment tax, license tax for vehicles and ships, income tax of interest and contract tax.

3. Chinese Tax System from 1958-1978

A reform of the tax system was carried out in 1958 to adapt to the public ownership of all production means in that period. The major reforms in this period are:

(1) Merge of tax categories

The commodity turnover tax, management tax, business tax and stamp tax are merged into consolidated industrial ad commercial tax;

(2) Simplify the links of tax payment

Industrial products are taxed twice in the chain of production and retail sales;

(3) Simplify the tax collection of intermediary products

There is no levy of tax on intermediary products, with exception for cotton yarn, liquor and leather goods.

There is an adjustment of the industrial and commercial tax system in 1973. The tax categories are further simplified. The consolidated industrial and commercial tax and its surcharge paid by enterprises, urban real estate tax, license tax for vehicles and ships are merged into industrial and commercial tax. Some tax administration power is delegated to the local governments. By the end of this period, there are nine categories of tax: industrial and commercial tax, consolidated industrial and commercial tax, income tax of industry and commerce, salt tax, customs duty, agricultural (husbandry) tax, animal trading tax and contract tax.

3.02 Tax Reform- First Period (1979-1993)

The major reform in this period is the change of profit remittance into tax of enterprises in 1983 and 1984. The purpose of this reform is to realize the regulating function of tax in economy, strengthening the economic responsibilities of the enterprises, mobilizing the initiative of central and local authorities and enterprises and to create conditions of hierarchical fiscal management of central and local governmental revenue income based upon the tax categories. Due to certain negative aspects of the contract responsibility system, the purpose of the reform is not fully realized. The major contents of reform in this period are:

1. Reform of industrial and commercial tax. The industrial and commercial tax is divided into product tax, VAT, business tax and salt tax;

2. Establishment and improvement of income tax system

(1) Establish income tax system for enterprises, the submission of profit by SOEs is changed into income tax and adjustment tax;

(2) Improve the income tax system of collective enterprises;

(3) Establish income tax system for individuals and private enterprises;

3. Establish several specific categories of regulatory taxes, include tax on burning oil, resource tax, wage and bonus tax, investment tax on fixed assets, banquet tax, etc. There are thirty-nine tax categories, but many of them are abolished or merged later. For example, product tax, business tax on wholesale and retail, market transaction tax and animal husbandry tax are merged with VAT in 1994; wage and bonus tax, salary adjustment tax, adjustment tax on SOEs, banquet tax, tax on burning oil and special management tax are abolished in 1994 and later. Therefore, no detailed description of tax categories is given in this section.

3.03 Tax Reform (1994-)

The major tax reform in 1994 is:

1. Expand the scope of collection of VAT, which was introduced in 1984. VAT was formally instituted in 1986 and applied to selected commodities. The effectiveness of VAT has been limited by its gradual introduction, which has made it impossible to rebate tax payments on inputs correctly, because of cascading in the products covered by product taxes implemented before 1994. There is also unusual multiple rate structure for VAT which reflects the need to maintain revenues while not overburdening enterprises in the shift from the multiple product tax to VAT. The scope of collection of VAT in 1994 is expanded to manufacture, wholesale and retail sales. There is also a change of multiple rates (12 tax rates) to relatively simple tax rate (2 tax rates) with basic rate being 17%.

2. Implementation of consumption tax

Consumption tax is collected on part of high profitable commodities after the abolish of product tax and the introduction of unified collection of VAT on all commodities in production, wholesale and retail sales.

3. Unification of turnover tax

A unified collection of VAT, business tax and consumption tax are applied to replace the former collection of product tax, VAT and business tax of domestic enterprises and individuals and the collection of consolidated industrial and commercial tax on foreign-invested enterprises.

4. A unified income tax rate of 33% is introduced on all types of domestic enterprises.

Part IV Major Lessons of Tax Reform and Future Prospects

China was a central planned economy before the late 70's and is now in transition to a socialist market economy. The weakness of the tax system in central planned economy has been well studied in many Western literature, which points that the system lacks transparency and discriminatory, and taxes paid by enterprises are frequently subject to negotiations and there is a lack of certainty and stability in the system. China is no exception with these weaknesses in its tax system. It is impossible to discuss in detail any good reform proposal on tax reform. But two selected major lessons will be discussed.

4.01 The Central-Local Fiscal Relationship

It has been described in introduction (1.01) of this paper that the role of fiscal systems is to raise revenue to finance public expenditure. In addition, the taxes could be used to achieve three additional roles. In the former central planned economy, all these roles are generally achieved directly by the central planners and administrative means. The budgetary system, the fiscal policy and tax system are mutually supplementary and are the major means to achieve the social economic objective. It can be seen from the experience of the tax reform of China described previously that the budgetary practices, and fiscal and tax systems lag behind the economic decentralization. The central-local relationship, that is, intergovernmental finance, is one of the aspects for which lessons are to be learned. The contract responsibility system is established between the government and enterprises, between the central and local governments. The devolution of power to already deconcentrated governments has given local governments command over functions that determine macroeconomic stability. On the administrative side, China has not had a national tax service before

1994, although the central government determines the tax rates and tax base, almost all taxes have been collected by local tax authorities, and the revenues have been shared with the central government through a complex system of revenue sharing. This has allowed local governments to enjoy control over tax policy. Regardless of statutory tax rates, local administrations have been able to negotiate contracts with local enterprises to provide these enterprises tax relief and grant them tax incentives not authorized by the central government. Local governments have also been able to urge the local tax bureaus to be less vigorous in their collection of taxes to be shared with, or remitted to, the central government. As decentralization has progressd, growth-oriented local governments have used the flexibility accorded to them by China's system of tax administration to reduce their tax efforts at the margin and thereby avoid having to share local resources with the central government.

The major lessons learned from above are: There must be a clear clarification of responsibility and right of each level of government. Each level of government should also have its own substantial tax base, with which it finances functions for which it has full responsibilities. Intergovernmental fiscal relations should also be normalized by means of governmental finance law. The lack of reform of intergovernmental finance has brought up another unusual issue, high share of extra budgetary sphere.

4.02 The Extra-Budgetary System

1. Definition of Extra-Budget

The extra-budgetary fund was officially defined by the government. It is redefined by the Ministry of Finance in 1996 that the extra-budgetary fund refers to various fiscal funds collected and used by the government organizations, institutions and social communities to perform or acting to perform the government functions based upon laws and regulations. Its mainly covered administrative fees, funds and surcharges collected according to relevant laws and regulations; administrative fees collected with approval of the State Council or provincial people's governments and their bureaus of finance, planning (price) commissions; funds established with the approval of the State Council and the Ministry of Finance; funds turned in by subordinate units to related organizations; self-financing and unified financing funds of towns used for the spendings of government of towns and townships; and other fiscal funds not included in the budget.

Social security fund is managed according to the management system of extra-budget before the establishment of social security budgetary system.

2. Evolution of Extra-budgetary Fund

Evolution of extra-budgetary fund can be broadly divided into three stages.

(1) At the initial stage after the founding of the PRC, under the highly centralized fiscal and administrative system, the central government allowed the local governments, various departments and units keep a limited amount of financial resources for flexible use. In 1950, the extra-budget fund was around 8.5% of the budgeted fund. The terminology "extra-budget fund" was not used officially by that time.

(2) In the first Five-Year Plan period, the term of "extra-budgetary fund" was officially used for the first time in 1953. But it was not clearly defined. It was implicitly understood that this was the fiscal fund not to be included in the central government budget. But it was established through approval of the governmental fiscal system. In the 50's, its scope was relatively clear. Yet, its scope became blurred after several rounds of centralization and decentralization of the planning system and fiscal power, through development of the economy and the economic activities becoming more complicated. The growth of extra-budgetary fund is shown in Table 4.1.

Table 4.1 Growth of Budget and Ex-budgetary Funds
before the Launch of Economic Reform

Period	Budgetary Fund (100 million yuan)	Extra-budgetary Fund (100 million yuan)	Share of Extra-budgetary Fund in the Budget %
First Five-Year Plan Period	1,354.88	87.91	6.5
Second Five-Year Plan Period	2,116.62	391.35	18.5
1963-1965	1,215.11	193.27	15.9
Third Five-Year Plan Period	2,528.98	430.55	17
Fourth Five-Year Plan Period	3,919.71	915.29	23.4
Fifth Five-Year Plan Period	4,960.66	1,943.99	39.2

Source: *General Description of Fiscal Theory,* Li Kemu, Red Flag Press,1986.

(3) Decentralization of power to local administrative units and more autonomous power given to the enterprises are the key features of economic reform. Because China has so many administrative and institutional units, decentralization without basic regulations promotes the initiative of various levels of economic actors. A rapid growth of the extra-budgetary fund has been witnessed since 1982, which is shown in Table 4.2.

Table 4.2 Growth of Budget and Extra-Budgetary Funds Since 1981

Year	Extra-Budgetary fund (100 million yuan)	Budgetary Fund (100 million yuan)	Share of Extra-budgetary fund of within Budget %	Growth Rate of Extra-budgetary fund %	Growth Rate of Budgetary Fund %
1981	601.70	1175.79	59.1	7.8	1.4
1982	802.74	1212.33	74.1	33.6	3.1
1983	967.68	1366.95	79.9	20.5	12.8
1984	1188.48	1642.86	81.0	22.8	20.2
1985	1530.03	2004.82	83.3	28.7	22.0
1986	1737.31	2122.01	79.5	13.5	5.8
1987	2028.60	2199.35	89.7	16.8	3.6
1988	2360.77	2357.24	94.8	16.4	7.2
1989	2658.33	2664.90	94.8	12.6	13.1
1990	2708.64	2937.10	86.4	1.9	10.2
1991	3243.31	3149.48	94.5	19.7	7.2
1992	3854.92	3483.37	97.7	18.9	10.6
1993	1432.54	4348.95	30.3	-62.8	24.8
1994	1879.21	5218.10	36.0	31.2	30.0
1995	2406.50	6242.20	38.5	28.1	19.6

Source: *Fiscal Almanac 1995.*

Formerly, the retained fund of state-owned enterprises after taxation was included in the extra budgetary fund. The government changed the practice since 1993 after the promulgation of "General Guiding Principles on Financial Management of Enterprises" and "Guidelines for Enterprise Accounting",effective since July 1,1993. Since then, a negative growth was witnessed in the rate of extra-budgetary fund in 1993. This shows one of the facts that the Chinese fiscal statistics differ from the IMF standard classification in the treatment of extra-budgetary revenues. Based upon IMF's "Manual of Government Finance Statistics", the enterprise depreciation funds and retained earnings should not be included in the governmental fiscal accounts.

4.03 *Chinese Fiscal and Tax System from International Perspective*

There are various perspectives to study the tax system. Tax in general is a levy imposed by the government on the income, wealth and capital gains of persons and businesses (direct tax), on spending of goods and services (indirect tax) and on properties. In the former central planned and socialist countries, due to the denying of the capital productivity and focusing on material production, indirect tax becomes a dominant share of the taxation system. And also due to semi-isolation from global economy before the launch of the economic reform, China is a late-comer to institute the VAT which had spread very fast in public finance development of the last half century since the French instituted such a tax in the early 1950's.

This shows that much more effort is required for China, an economy in transition, to study the experience as a wave of tax reforms swept the globe in the 80's, and several common features exhibited in the reform of other countries, a focus on making taxation economically "neutral" (that is, ensuring that the tax system does not distort people's economic decisions), a trend toward lower marginal tax rates, and a consideration particularly in many developing countries of the value added tax as a broad base of tax revenue.

Part V Conclusions

In this paper, the facts of tax reform of China have been summarized in relatively greater detail, there is not enough explicit discussion to analyze in detail how a tax system can be designed well to perform its basic functions described in the very beginning of this paper. This can be got from other generous references and required a lengthy discussion. China is an economy in transition. The transitional economy has a common feature that central planning and administrative control are the major means of control and development of the economy and society. This economy is also characterized by the state ownership of nearly all enterprises, the guaranteed social security system. Due to the failure of the incentive system and organization of economic activity in contradiction with basic economic discipline and human behavior, transition is pursued nearly by all of the former central planned economies. <u>Transition is a difficult social and economic process</u>. The mankind can be well adapted through their efforts in learning, doing and adaptation to achieve a better future. This is the basic principle of evolution. It is expected that the experience provided can be served for a useful purpose for learning.

Appendix 1

State Revenues, 1958-1965 (million yuan)

	1958[a]	1959[a]	1960[b]	1961[b]	1962[b]	1963[b]	1964[b]	1965[b]	1965[c]
Agricultural taxes	3,260	3,300	2,400	2,500	2,600	2,700	2,700	2,700	
Salt tax	620	650							
Customs duty receipts	580	650							
Industry and commerce taxes	14,179	15,698	7,400	10,300	11,200	13,300	17200		
Other tax revenues	91	172							
Total tax revenues	18,730	20,470							
Profits from state farms	18,719	28,590	25,100	19,600	17,400	19,100	16,300	24,000	
Accrued depreciations and other income from state farms	3,301	4,770							
Income from domestic bonds	790								
Income from insurance trading	10								
Other income	310	330							
Total non−tax income	23,130	33,690							
Total revenues	41,860	54,160	43,300	32,900	29,500	31,400	35,000	37,600	47,330
			(34,900)	(34,400)	(31,200)	(35,100)	(14,100)	(43,900)	

Sources: Reference 4

  a. Ecklund, 1966, pp. 20, 122f.

  b. Fu Tung Chen, 1969, p. 94 f. The total revenues are derived from agricultural and industrial production (ef. Fu Tung chen, 1969, p. 174).
    Individual items of tax revenues and other income apart from tax revenues are also estimetes based on specific indicators, but their totals deviate
    (cf. the figures in parentheses) from the figures for "Total Revenues".
    Btu, 1981, No. 31 (Aug. 11), p. 12.

Appendix 2

State Expenditures, 1958-1965 (million yuan)

	1958[a]	1959[a]	1960[b]	1961[b]	1962[b]	1963[b]	1964[b]	1965[b]	1965[c]	1965[d]
Industry		19,600								
Agriculture		5,060								
Transportation		5,175								
Total economic construction	26,270	32,170	30,800	21,400	17,700	19,000	21,600	23,800	19,000	
Education		3,340								
Science		823								
Health		565								
Total social services, culture and education	4,350	5,860	5,500	5,000	4,000	4,500	5,000	5,000	6,600	
Defense	5,000	5,800	5,500	5,000	5,000	5,000	5,000	5,500	8,500	
Administration	2,270	2,900	3,000	2,500	2,300	2,300	2,500	2,500		
Other expenditures										
Foreign aid	275	350								
Interest on domestic debt	211	225								
Amortization of domestic debt	115	164								
Amortization of foreign debt	579	581								
Credit funds for state banks	1,650	4,430								
Miscellaneous	240	290								
Total expenditures	3,070	6,040	1,500	500	2,500	1,500	1,500	1,500	5,400	
Total other expenditures	40,960	52,770	46,300	34,400	31,500	32,300	35,400	38,300	42,000	46,630

Sources: Reference 4.

a. Ecklund, 1974, Col. 361 f.

b. FuTung Chen, 1969, p 99.

e. Richard Diao, 1966, p. 8.

d. Bru, 1981, No. 32 (Aug. 11), p. 12.

Appendix 3

State Revenues, 1971-1975 (million yuan)

	1971	1972	1973	1974	1975
Total tax revenues	28,680[a]				
Profits from state enterprises	42,300[a]				
Other revenues	720a				
Total revenues	71,700[a],b	(81,580[d])	(91,270[e])	(94,840[f])	98,539[f]
	(64,275[c])	72,500[g]	(76,800[g])	77,600[g]	80,500[g]
	(72,900[d])				81,560[h]

Sources: Reference 4.
   a. Tak-ming Hsu, 1974, p. 918.
   b. Calculation according to a NCNA report (September 25, 1972) which state revenues
      had inceased by "more than 10-fold" in "over twenty years".
      Miyashita, 1973, p. 314.
   c. Calculation, assuming equal annual growth rates for 1970-1973, according to the
      figure (fn.e) for 1973 and the figure for 1970 calculated from the same source
   e. Calculation, based on figures in Cheng-chich ching-chi-hsiteh chi-ch 's chih-shih, 2nd
      ed., 1975, p. 406.
   f. Estimations by the US Consulate General, Hong Kong.
   g. Kitajskaja Narodnaja Respublika, v 1976'goda, p. 181.
   h. Bru, 1981, No. 32 (Aug. 11), p 12.

Appendix 4

State Expenditures, 1971-1975 (million yuan)

	1971	1972	1973	1974	1975
Economic construction	(43,620[a])		57,204[c]		
Welfare, culture, and education	(9,150[a])				
Defense	(11,260[a])				
Administration	(4,920[a])				
Other expenditures	(1,400[a])				
Total expenditures	(70,350[a])	(74,240[b])	(81,720[d])	(84,253[e])	(86,865[e])
	(67,450[b])	71,700[f]	76,000[f]	76,800[f]	79,700[f]
	(90,000[f])				82,090[g]

Source: Reference 4.
   a. Tak-ming Hsu, 1974, p. 922.
   b. Calculation as in Table 5.1, fin.d.
   c. Miyashita 1975, p. 337.
   d. Calculation based on figures in Cheng-chih ching-chi ching-chi-hsueh chi-ch'u chih-
      shih, 2nd ed. (1975), p. 405f.
   e. Estimations by the US Consulate General, Hong Kong.
   f. Kitajykaja Narodnaja Respublika, v 1976 godu, p. 182.
   g. Bru, 1981, No. 32 (Aug. 11), p. 12.

REFERENCES

1. *Fiscal Policy Issues During the Transition in Russia,* by Augus to Lopez-claros and Sergei V. Alexashenko, IMF, Washington D.C., March 1998.

2. *The Transition to a Market Economy,* Vol. II, Special Issues, Aspects Particular OECD, Paris, 1991.

3. "China: Revenue Mobilization and Tax Policy", a World Bank country study, 1990.

4. *Economic Development and Social Change in the People's Republic of China,* by Willy Kraus, Spriner-Verlag, 1979.

5. "China: Country Economic Memorandum-Macroeconomic Stability in a Decentralized Economy 1994", the World Bank.

6. "China: Budgetary Policy and Intergovernmental Fiscal Relations 1993", the World Bank.

7. *Report of China's Macroeconomic Policy 1997* (in Chinese), chief editors: Ma Hong, Liu Zhongyi and Lu Baipu, China Financial and Economic Press, 1997.

8. "Exploration of Normalization of Governmental Income and 'Changing Fees into Tax'" (in Chinsese), by Jia Kang in *Economis Selection,* 1999 Vol. 1, China Financial and Economic Press, 1999.

9. "Fiscal Policy and Reform of Fiscal System of China" (in Chinese), by Lou Jiwei, in China's Economic and Investment Perspective International Conference, jointly sponsored by Association of China's Economic System Reform Study and Merrill Lynch, Sept. 17-18, 1998, Beijing.

10. *China's Taxation System (1994)* (in Chinese), edited by Yang Weihua and Zhou Kai, Zhongshan University Press, 1994.

11. *World Tax Reform: Case Studies of Developed and Developing Countries,* edited by Michael J. Boskin and Charles E. Mclure, Jr., ICEG, 1990.

11. Corporate Governance
— Challenge to East Asian Countries
in the Process of Globalization

Part I Introduction

Globalization, in broad sense, can be discussed in four aspects: globalization of the biosphere, i.e., the mankind shares the common biosphere for living as well as the issues in a globalized world; globalization of the technosphere, the recent rapid process of globalization is effected by the growth of technology of transportation started in the Eighteenth centuries and the rapid growth of information and communication technology in the later part of twentieth century which has shrunk the world and promoted the appearance of a truly globalized market; globalization of the econosphere, i.e., there is increasing growth rate of flow of trade and capital in the global market, and there is also change of the activity of economic actors, the allocation of the resources of factor markets and the share of global commodity markets are increasingly effected by the MNCs. There is also globalization of the sociosphere, i.e., there is emergence of certain convergence of part of pattern of consumption, life styles, cultures, etc. in the global society.

From the discussion above, it can be seen that globalization can cover a very broad area to be discussed. And the impact of globalization is different for different regions and countries in different stages of development and the four aspects of features of globalization are also related to each other.

This paper will discuss one aspect of globalization of econo-sphere, corporate governance. Corporate governance, in narrow sense, is the issue of who governs or controls joint stock companies, while a corporation is a state chartered entity that pays taxes and is legally distinct from its owners. Although corporation had a long history in Western countries and different types of enterprises played different roles in different stages of development. For example, after 1830 the great textile enterprises north of Boston were companies, but the railroads really dominated that corporate stage and poured forth the flood of securities, bonds and stocks of all varieties which gave the tone to the exchanges and banking operations of that era. The rapid development of the global economy, the growth of corporations and TNCs and the financial market, it is therefore of current great international interest and concern on the governance of the corporation, the internal means by which it accomplishes its performance. The East Asian countries, although have enjoyed a high economic growth in the past several decades, are also late-comers on corporate governance. The East Asian financial crisis erupted on July 2, 1997 has exposed further the weakness of corporate governance of them.

This paper will not focus on the discussion of concrete details of corporate governance. There are already several good international research studies focused on this subject, for example, "Corporate Governance: Improving Competitiveness and Access to Capital in Global Markets" by OECD in April 1998. This paper will focus more on factors of broad aspects influencing the performance of "corporate governance". This paper will be divided further into 5 parts in the follows.

Part II   Corporate Governance and Its Types

2.01 Definition of Corporate Governance

In most medium and large-scale enterprises, owners are usually not the managers of the enterprise. The interests of these two groups often diverge. Owners want to maximize the value of the enterprise and managers want to maximize their own returns. Managers are at an advantage over owners in having much more information about the enterprise. To ensure that managers behave in the best interests of owners, control rights and a structure of incentives has developed. This structure is known as corporate governance.

The owners of an enterprise take the ultimate risk of loss and also capture the ultimate gains. In other words, owners take the residual risk. For effective corporate governance, the residual risk bearers must have control over management decisions or be able to sell their ownership rights, or both. Because owners bear the consequences of their own decision, they have an incentive to perform efficiently. In private ownership of enterprises, the residual risk bearers are clearly identified. Thus, those who own and control the enterprise have clear and powerful incentives to be efficient. Owners appoint managers to cooperate the enterprise and provide them with incentives to maximize the enterprise value and carefully monitor management performance. If these owners do not appreciate management performance, they can replace management or sell their ownership rights.

With direct state ownership, the residual risk is born by the population as a whole, which neither has control over the enterprise nor a mechanism for selling its ownership rights. At the same time, the government institution exercising ownership rights on behalf of the population as a whole does not bear any residual risk. If the enterprises suffer losses, the monitoring government institution does not bear the loss; the population as a whole does. Thus, if residual gains or losses accrue to individuals and/or consequences of poor management performance, incentives for efficient enterprise performance are weakened.

Converting state-owned enterprises into a separate legal entities, a state-owned company, may clarify property rights but leave the residual risk situation unchanged. The population as a whole continues to bear the residual risk and have no control over the enterprise and the government ownership institution has control over the enterprise but bears no residual risk. Thus, to be effective, enterprise governance reform within the state-owned sector has to alter the risk-control to minimize the disadvantages of continued state ownership.

2.02 Types of Corporate Governance

The enterprise ownership pattern and private corporate governance framework varies among market economies. As a simplification, there are two main ownership and governance systems: where ownership and control is concentrated in the hands of stakeholders in the enterprise-financiers, suppliers, distributors, managers and employees; and where ownership is widely held by individual investors and institutions with relatively small shareholdings. The first is known as the 'insider' system of ownership and corporate governance and the second, the 'outsider' system.

The corporate governance systems of Germany and Japan are considered the best examples of the insider approach but similar systems exist in other countries such as France and Spain. The insider approach relies on stakeholder ownership and/or representation on the board of directors to reduce the cost of monitoring managers. Stakeholders/owners have a long-term interest in the prosperity of the enterprise and have the expert knowledge and information to guide and monitor management. Sale of shares is not used as a means of affecting changes in control by stakeholders. In Germany and Japan, banks hold equity affecting changes in control by stakeholders. In Germany and Japan, banks hold equity positions in enterprises although they are limited to 5 percent ownership in Japan. In a typical large German firm, three banks, own or control as custodians for individual shareholders, about 30 percent of the votes and often a majority. Banks usually occupy one or more positions on the firm's supervisory board and often the chairman's position. In Japan, banks in aggregate hold about 20 percent of enterprise equity and are represented on the board of directors. Typically, the main bank owns 5 percent and other financial institutions (including insurance companies, pension funds, etc.) in the enterprise group own another 20 percent. In aggregate, financial institutions own about 50 percent of the outstanding shares of stock exchange listed companies. Because of their vast lending and business experience, banks are well positioned to take a lead in enterprise governance. Research evidence in the past suggests that close relationships with banks improve enterprise efficiency.

In addition to bank involvement in corporate governance in Germany and Japan, other non-financial companies that have contractual links with an enterprise as suppliers or distributors also have an ownership stake. In Japan, members of an enterprise group have significant ownership cross-holdings. In total, non-financial firms own about 25 percent of all the outstanding equity of stock exchange listed companies. Corporate cross-holdings and supplier/distributor ownership reinforces good monitoring of management and also informal contract enforcement. Commercial partners can gain information on the health of each other's operations by observing directly their behaviour in commercial dealings. Thus, contractual linkages lead to greater information and an enhanced ability to monitor management and make changes in a co-operative manner. Finally, managers and other employees are also insiders with a long-term interest in the prosperity of the enterprise. There is not much evidence of management and employee ownership in enterprises in Germany and Japan, although in Germany employees are entitled to appoint one-third of the supervisory board's members under the principle of co-determination.

The foremost concern raised by stakeholder and concentrated ownership and control of enterprises is that such a system perpetuates oligarchies, encourages collusion and imposes risks in the banking system. Thus, an essential feature of insider systems is active competition in product markets which would impede collusive behaviour. Where such competition is not possible, monopoly behavior can be monitored by regulations and anti-trust agencies. Likewise, bank regulation has to take account of bank investments. Where there are high risk equity investments, higher capital requirements and more active supervision may be necessary. The German banking system, which has significant equity investments in enterprises, has not been more vulnerable to bank failures than other banking systems that have been prevented from equity ownership.

The US and UK are the usual example of the outsider approach to corporate governance. In these countries banks play virtually no role in corporate governance. Because of restrictive legislation, banks hold little or no corporate equity and generally do not sit on the boards of firms. In the US, there are increasing share of household equity in recent years, which is shown in Table 1.

Table 1 Household Equity Holdings as a Percent of Net Wealth

	1980-84	1985-89	1990-94	1995	1996	1997
United States	10.6	11.0	15.1	19.5	20.9	24.4
Japan	4.5	7.6	5.8	5.4	4.9	3.7
France	1.3	3.1	2.9	2.6	2.9	3.2
Italy	0.8	2.1	3.6	3.8	3.6	4.7
United Kingdom	5.5	6.3	9.4	11.3	11.3	12.4
Canada	13.7	13.9	14.2	15.6	16.5	18.3

Part III A General Discussion of Weakness of Corporate Governance in East Asian Countries

3.01 Toward a Framework of Analysis of Corporate Governance

Figure 1 provides a framework of discussion of corporate governance from the author's perspective by learning lessons from failure of corporate governance both domestic and abroad.

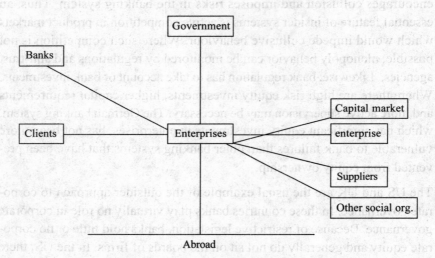

Fig 1. Stakeholders in Corporate Governance

3.02 Failure of Effective "Corporate Governance, a Description of Korean Case

In Korea, the authorities relied on the chaebol as the primary drivers of industrial development and economic growth and they soon became widely prevalent throughout the economy. For example, by 1996, 83 of the 100 largest firms in the Korean manufacturing sector belonged to the 30 largest chaebol which in turn accounted for nearly 15% of Korean GDP.

In order to maintain overall control the chaebol relied heavily on debt finance to fund their investment programs with the result that throughout much of the corporate sector debt-equity ratios in Korea have been exceptionally high. This tendency towards high leverage has been somewhat intensified by the government's role as insurer or underwriter to large investment projects encouraging banks to take out loans and then bailing them out should they turn bad. With the liberalization of controls on out loans and then bailing them out should they turn bad. With the liberalization of controls on overseas borrowing, there was a sharp rise in Korea's foreign debt to US$162 billion, much of it short-term. Following the terms-of-trade shock in 1996, there was a string of insolvencies among the major chaebols in 1997.

By aligning the interests and objectives of managers with those of investors corporate governance helps shape industrial organization as well as the mechanisms for allocating funds for investment. In most countries this is supported by the adoption of an institutional and legal framework which determines the allocation of the residual rights of corporate control.

There are broadly three types of mechanisms which may minimize the agency costs arising from the separation of ownership and control (OECD, 1996b):

— To directly induce managers to carry out efficient management, for example, by means of executive compensation plans.

— To use indirect means of corporate control such as that provided by capital market discipline, for example, through an active take-over market.

— To give more power to shareholder, creditors, institutional investors or other stakeholders by enhancing their institutional rights so that they are better able to monitor the management of those firms in which they have a vested interest.

In the Korean context, however, these mechanisms were deficient or sometimes even non-existent. In this way, governance of the chaebol, Korea's widely diversified business groups, became subject to major weaknesses.

3.03 The Financial System, an Important Source of Funding to Corporation, International Comparison

Figure 2
Relative Importance of Commercial Bank Assets, Equities and Bonds

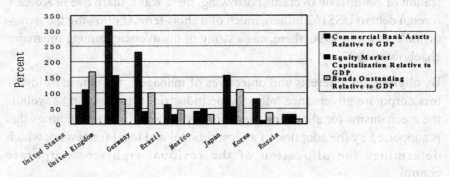

Source: Reference 3.

Figure 3
Commercial Bank Assets Relative to Equity Market Capitalization

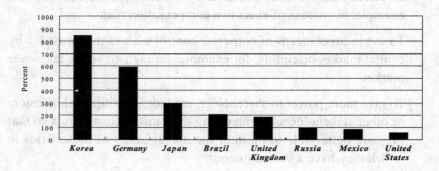

Source: Reference 3.

Corporate governance depends very much upon the financial system formed through history. Fig. 2 and 3 provides international comparison of financial system of several countries. Corporate governance should be considered within the context of the existed financial system as well as the code of good governance studied by many countries since the 90's.

3.04 Prudent and Diversified Financial System Growth Should Be Encouraged

(1) It is the general trend of change of economic structure that there is gradual shift of share of primary, secondary and tertiary (service) sector in the composition of GDP.

(2) Financial sector is a very important sub-component of the modern service sector. Modern financial services are comprised of commercial banks (SIC 602), saving institutions (SIC 6035, 6036), equipment leasing (SIC 735, 6159) which includes financial leasing (SIC 6159) and miscellaneous equipment rental and leasing (SIC 735) and property insurance (SIC 633), life insurance and annuities (SIC 631) and health coverage (SIC 6321). It should be pointed out that most of the Asian developing countries have a weak financial service. It was described by one expert of Thailand in 1996 ADB meeting that Thailand had a trade deficit in its service sector, they don't know how to develop a new service sector to take part of its traditional service sector of tourism. This is also true for a major part of other Asian developing countries. Within the financial service, the composition of the financial sector is different (refer to Fig. 2 and 3), which influences the structure of corporate governance. Besides, the performance of components of financial sector is different in different countries. For example, the financial assets of commercial banks of the USA by the year end of 1995 reached US$4,494 billion. It was told that "American banks are presently twice as profitable as European Banks..., the U.S. insurance market is second only to Japan's in size." Due to the Asian developing countries to be a latecomers in modern financial service and banking sector, they are not well equipped in management of this sector. In that sense, they are not competitive in global market in the process of globalization.

Even the banking sector of the developed countries, "the financial performance of banks deteriorated to the government where governments had to support some of the largest banks to preserve financial stability" in this new period marked by economic deregulation, the removal of cross-boarder restrictions on capital flows, financial innovation, and increased competition in financial services. Dr. Stiglitz had a very objective speech on East Asia's financial crisis in March 12, 1998 in an ADB forum. He said that the USA "established the world's first financial sector regulatory body, the office of the comptroller of the currency. It has taken more than a century before the country began to feel comfortable with a system of national banking — and even today, there are misgivings in many parts of the country". It is necessary for the Asian developing countries to learn seriously from the lessons of this crisis, and strive their full effort to overcome the weakness of their banking sector and develop their financial sector with full efforts.

On the other side, there are also weakness in the banking sector which has both roots in economic management and other non-economic factors, which has been pointed out in a popular commercial magazine in Feb. 24, 1997 that "many of Asia's banks are neck deep in the sort of bad-loan problems that have weighed down Japan for years. Too much capital has been squandered on misguided property, industrial, and financial lending. Crunching numbers and assessing risk has never been the hallmark of banking cultures heavily influenced by bureaucrats and corrupt politicians. Yet if Asia's clubby bankers don't catch on quickly, the future could be treacherous." Unfortunately, this early warning signal had not raised the awareness of the public, so that actions in response are not taken in time. The eruption of Asian financial crisis in July 1997 had its rooted weakness earlier in the economic structure.

3.05 The Industrial Policy

Although most of the Asian developing countries had pursued an industrial policies in different forms and with different measures and instruments, but there are two major issues.

(1) There is no coordination of industrial policies among different countries of the Asian developing countries, and they rely heavily upon the market of the developed countries. On the one side, there is excessive competition among Asian countries themselves in the developed market due to identity of the products group. And their economic prosperity is heavily dependent upon the demand of the developed countries. This trouble had been shown in the decline of export of computer components of most Asian countries in 1996. An unfavorable structural aspect which weakened the capacity to resist the external shocks. Appendix 1 can illustrate this phenomenon.

(2) The role played by traditional industry and industrial policies, the key structural weakness in industry existed in a number of Asian economies were the

underlying cause of the crisis had been recognized by a part of international organizations in 1999. Government, industry and trade union officials had discussed these issues at a special session of the OECD's Industry Committee, on Feb. 23, 1999. And there was also "The Asia Pacific Regional Forum on Industry" organized by UNIDO in cooperation with the Ministry of Industry, Government of Thailand from 23rd to 24th September, 1999 in Bangkok, Thailand. The general conclusions derived from these two international organizations are more or less the same, although the detail policy recommendations of them are slightly different from each other. But they are mutual complementary to each other. The general conclusion in common is: The economies struck by the crisis need to complement actions on the financial front with a series of industry-related policy reform, this is also true for some Asian countries not effected seriously in this crisis such as China and India. There is a need of strategic vision and industrial policies for the new millennium to overcome the weakness of the industrial sector.

The weakness of the industrial sector of the Asian developing countries including China can be summed up as follows:

(i) Over-capacity created by over-investment in certain sectors, but the size of the market is limited to specific regions or countries.

(ii) There is insufficient diversity of industrial structure, including excessive reliance of some industries on export market, this can be seen from Appendix 1 that many Asian countries have same category of product and exported to the US market, i.e., integrated circuits and computer + components. Therefore, the growth rate of export of NIEs is declined from 20.9% to 4.5% from 1995 to 1996. This growth rate is reduced from 24.3% in 1995 to 6.0% in 1996 for Southeast Asian countries

(iii) There is overemphasis on large enterprises to the detriment of small firms, there are unfavorable conditions for development of SMEs especially in Korea, Malaysia, and Thailand.

(iv)Lack of linkages between export-oriented industrial sector.

(v) Outdated technologies and machinery in many domestic industries.

(vi) Insufficient technological and managerial competencies.

Part IV   What Should Be a "Good" Corporate Governance

4.01 Major Public and Private Initiative to Be Focused

Defining the mission of the corporation in the modern economy: Designing long-term economic gain to enhance shareholder (or investor) value is necessary to attract equity investment capital and is, therefore, the corporations' central mission. At the same time, however, corporations must function in the larger society. To varying degrees, different national systems and individual corporations may temper the economic objective of the corporation to address non-economic objectives — both as to the national system and the individual corporation — will be necessary in the global competition for capital.

Ensuring adaptability of corporate governance arrangements: The primary role for regulation is to shape a corporate governance environment, compatible with societal values, that allows competition and market forces to work so that corporations can succeed in generating long-term economic gain. Specific governance structures or practices will not necessarily fit all companies at all times. Nor should it be taken for granted that a given design may suit the same company during different stages of its development. For dynamic enterprises operating in a rapidly changing world, corporate governance adaptability and flexibility — supported by an enabling regulatory framework — is a prerequisite for better corporate performance.

Protecting shareholder rights: For companies to attract equity investment, regulatory safeguards must emphasize fairness, transparency and accountability. These safeguards should take into account the new and growing category of non-controlling shareholders who have emerged in the form of institutional investors. The focus of current efforts to improve shareholder protection should center on investor access to performance-related information, shareholder exercise of voting rights, and promotion of active and independent (non-executive) members of boards of directors to strengthen the quality of corporate governance. But the qualification of independent members should be fully assessed.

Enabling active investing: Active owners can play a distinct role in strengthening a corporation's ability to exploit new business opportunities. Such active investment should be encouraged, but with adequate protections for more passive holders.

Aligning the interests of shareholders and other stakeholders: Corporate success is linked to the ability to align the interests of directors, managers and employees with the interests of shareholders. Performance-based compensation is a useful tool for this purpose. Independent (non-executive) members of the board of directors — or in certain nations, board of auditors — have a special responsibility in designing and approving appropriate remuneration schemes.

Recognising societal interests: companies do not act independently from the societies in which they operate. Accordingly, corporate actions must be compatible with societal objectives concerning social cohesion, individual welfare and equal opportunities for all. Reform of state-owned enterprises should also focused on this seriously. Attending to legitimate social concerns should, in the long run, benefit all parties, including investors. At times, however, there maybe a trade off between short-term social costs and the long-term benefits to society of having a healthy, competitive private sector. Societal needs that transcend the responsive ability of the private sector should be met by specific public policy measures, rather than by impeding improvements in corporate governance and capital allocation.

4.02 Perspectives for Public Policy Improvement

Protecting shareholders and promoting investor confidence are key elements in providing the access to capital needed to create and maintain a dynamic, competitive corporate sector. By focusing primarily on shareholder protection, disclosure of information and voluntary corporate governance improvements, policy makers and regulators can avoid developing overly rigid and intrusive regulatory systems.

Policy makers and regulators should be sensitive to corporations' need for flexibility in responding to the changing competitive environment and the related need for flexible, adaptive governance structures. Regulation should support a range of ownership and governance forms so that a market for governance arrangements develops.

Policy makers and regulators should consider the impact of any proposed regulatory initiative on the ability of the corporate sector to respond to competitive market environments. They should avoid those regulations that threaten to unduly interfere with market mechanisms.

Regulatory intervention in the area of corporate governance is likely to be most effective if limited to:

Ensuring the protection of shareholder rights and the enforceability of contracts with resource providers (fairness);

Requiring timely disclosure of adequate information concerning corporate financial performance (transparency);

Clarifying governance roles and responsibilities, and supporting voluntary efforts to ensure the alignment of managerial and shareholder interests, as monitored by boards of directors — or in certain nations, boards of auditors — having some independent members (accountability); and

Ensuring corporate compliance with the other laws and regulations that reflect the respective society's values (responsibility).

Policy makers and regulators should provide clear, consistent and enforceable securities and capital market regulations designed to protect shareholder rights and create legal systems capable of enforcing such regulations. Such regulations should seek to treat all equity investors — including minority shareholders — fairly, and should include protections against fraud, dilution, self-dealing and insider trading.

Regulations aimed at protecting shareholder rights should be designed to protect against litigation abuse. This can be accomplished through the use of tests for the sufficiency of shareholder complaints and the provision of safe harbors for management and director actions.

Policy makers and regulators should ensure that an adequate system of contract, commercial and basic consumer protection law is in place, so that contractual relationships are enforceable. (This is particularly relevant to those developing and emerging market nations with less established legal systems.)

Policy makers and regulators should articulate clearly the legal standards that govern shareholder, director and management authority and accountability, including their fiduciary roles and legal liabilities. However, because corporate governance and expectations concerning roles and liabilities continue to evolve, legal standards should be flexible and permissive of evolution.

Policy makers and regulators should ensure that corporations abide by laws that uphold the respective society's values, such as criminal, tax, antitrust, labor, environmental protection, equal opportunity, and health and safety laws.

Policy makers and regulators should support and encourage education and training efforts, the provision of unemployment benefits, and other similar efforts aimed at promoting the welfare of individuals.

Policy makers and regulators may wish to consider the implications of significant divergence in income and opportunity paths. In particular, government action may be necessary to promote skill acquisition in creation sections of society that do not benefit from present market trends.

Part V Concluding Remarks

Table 3 Perspective Corporations in the 21st Century*
Contrasting views of the Corporation

Characteristic	20th Century	21st Century
Organization	The Pyramid	The Web on Network
Style	Structured	Flexible
Source of Strength	Stability	Change
Structure	Self-sufficiency	Interdependence
Products	Mass Production	Mass customization
Inventory	Month	Hours
Strategy	Top-down	Bottom-up
Leadership	Dogmatic	Inspirational
Job expectations	Security	Personal Growth
Reach	Domestic	Global

Source: Reference 4.

Corporate governance practices constantly evolve to meet changing conditions. As a work-in-progress, there is no single universal model of corporate governance. Nor is there a static, final structure in corporate governance that every country or corporation should emulate. Experimentation and variety should be expected and encouraged.

Appendix 1

Top 3 Export Items to the US

Country or Region	First	Second	Third
Japan	Passenger motors	Computer components	Integrated circuits
South Korea	Integrated circuits	Office machine parts	Passenger motors
HongKong SAR	Sweater, pullover, vest	Integrated circuits	Women/girl suits
Taiwan Province of China	Office machine parts	Computers+components	Integrated circuits
Singapore	Computer+components	Office machine parts	Integrated circuits
Indonesia	Natural rubber	Shoes	Crude oil
Malasia	Integrated circuits	Computer+components	Radio broadcast
The Philippines	Integrated circuits	women/girl suits	Coconuts
Thailand	Computer+components	Integrated circuits	Crustaceans
China	Toys	shoes	Plastics

Source: U.S. Department of Commerce.

REFERENCES

1. "Corporate governance", a report to the OECD by the Business Sector Advisory Group on Corporate Governance by Ira M. Millstein (chairman) and others, April 1998, (major reference).

2. Asian Development Bank, Technical Assistance Project 1924, PRC.

3. "Choosing the Right Financial System for Growth", Feb. 28, 2000, by James R. Barth, etc., Policy Brief Milken Institute.

4. Business Week, Aug. 21-28, 2000, the 21st Century Corporation.

12. Comments on: "Rethinking the East Asian Miracle"

I. Introduction

Before I give my formal comments to the excellent presentation by Dr. Yusuf on "The East Asian Miracle at the Millennium", which is an overview of the publication *Rethinking the East Asian Miracle*, I shall quote several sentences from Helen Hughes (Achievements and objectives of industrialization) to be introductory remarks of my comments. "At the end of World War II, the developing countries had almost no industrial capacity. The severed deficiencies in their social and physical infrastructure made building such capacity difficult, and their lack of experience in economic management exerbated their problems." The above is quoted which provides the basic context of my perspective of the meaning of the former study "The East Asian Miracle" implemented by the World Bank in the early 90's. It is necessary to point out that seven of the eight HPAES of the former studies were developing economies emerged at the end of World War II. The economic performance of them differs greatly from other developing economies, that average growth rate of GNP per capita of HPAEs recorded around 5.5 percent from 1965-90 while all other developing economies in South Asia, middle East and Mediterranean, Latin America and Caribbean, with a growth rate of no more then 1.9 percent in the same period. (W.B. the East Arian Miracle, p.2). To study the difference of this economic performance is by no means meaningless either for learning lessons from the real world to have better public policy for development or for the academic interest in the exploration of "Development Economics".

It is also necessary to point out the fact that the growth of the contemporary global economy is by no means a balanced one. In the year 2000, 29 advance economies with a 15.4 percent share of global population have 57.1%

327

share of world GDP and 125 developing countries with a 75.7-percent share of global population have only a 37-percent share of world GDP and 20 percent of world export (IMF World Economic Outlook, Oct 2001). This unbalanced global development is inconsistent with the principle of sustainable development advocated by the UN which must simultaneously serve economic, social and environmental objective. This unbalanced global economic development will cause social dislocation in many parts of the world. The essence of the miracle, rapid growth with equity (the East Asian Miracle, p.8) the experience summarized in the East Asian Miracle and also the new experiences post the financial crisis is worthwhile to be reviewed and rethought, so that correct lessons can be learned by more than 75 percent of the global population to face the challenges in the pursuit of a better public policy and better development in a new globalizing world.

II. General Comment

1. As one of the editors of the publication of *Rethinking the East Asian Miracle*, Dr. Yusef has given a very nicely organized introductory overview of this book. He explained clearly in the beginning that the purpose of this publication is to cast a searching eye over a landscape rendered less familiar by an unforeseen severe event. The chapters organized in this publication reexamine the major determinants of East Asian performance from country or regional perspective. And Dr. Stiglitz had summarized also essential lessons in the concluding chapter. In this publication *Rethinking the East Asian Miracle* (Note: This expression will be abbreviated into "Rethinking" in latter part of my comments), three chapters of development experience and issues of China are also added (a part is experience of Vietnam), the gap of the former publication "The East Asian Miracle" is filled up, but also the contents of these three chapters added are not only valuable for international community, but also are ver important to the Chinese policy makers and the professionals as well.

2. Dr. Yusuf has summarized six aspects of debate in questioning the earlier consensus; the question of small TFP; doubts on the advantages of industrial policy; close symbiotic relations between banks and corporations; the efficacy of exports as an engine of productivity; a fresh look of the approach to governance in East Asia and the progressive integration of the region as well as the world which needs to be further explored. Dr. Yusuf has examined these six aspects with a balanced approach that he has extracted essential flavors expressed in other 12 chapters of this publication with good synthesis, and he has also expressed his view on issues and policy options in those aspects with in-depth analysis and concise descriptions under the headings of macroeconomic policy and stable growth, perspectives on growth in East Asia, industrial policy in the 1990's, the changing autonomy and role of bureaucracy, nature of governance and development of the legal system, trade rather than export-led growth and regional integration and policy.

3. Under the publication of rethinking, some debates have been answered through analysis in the introductory chapter, the concluding chapter, and the related chapter by respective author. For example, the debate on TFP, industrial policy and role of the government. On the debate of TFP, both Dr. Stiglitz and Yusuf have pointed out the limitation of growth accounting. And I am in agreement with the expression that "the TFP debate is much ado about nothing". There has been narrowing of the technology gap, which can be found by observing the reality happened in East Asia. It takes more than a half century for the developed countries to develop and disseminate the computer technology since the emergence of ENIAC in 1946, while the successful East Asian countries has caught up and close this knowledge gap on computer technology in general within one or two decades. The reality is the decrease in the technology gap no mather whether the gains were "purchased" or not. With respect to the debate on industrial policies, it requires a careful examination of the views expressed explicitly in five papers of this publication, "The East Asian Miracle at the Millennium" by Dr. Yusuf, "Growth Crisis, and the Future of Economic Recovery in East Asia" by Professor Ito, "Industrial and Financial Policy in China and Vietnam — A New Model or a Replay of the East Asian Experience?" by Professor Perkins, "Rethinking the Role of Government Policy in Southeast Asia" by Professor Jomo, and "From Miracle to Recovery: Lessons from Four Decades of East Asian Experience" by Professor Stigilitz. It is no wonder that there are still several aspects not in consensus among all authors on this aspect, the use of industrial policy in East Asia has given rise to much controversy that the former publication did nothing to quell. But I think all views expressed in this publication can serve better to deal this debate in spite of the controversy still existed. The debate may be derived from the perception and contents of industrial policy. If industrial policy is explained in a broader context in popular economic dictionary, for example in (Collins: *Dictionary of Economics,* 2nd edition, 1993), it is described that "Industrial policy is a policy concerned with promoting industrial efficiency and competitiveness, industrial regeneration and expansion and the creation of employment opportunities. Industrial policy can be broadly based, encompassing for example, measures to increase competition (see "competition policy") and promote regional development (see "regional policy") as well as specific across-the-board measures to stimulate efficiency and the adoption of new technology; or it can be more narrowly focused involving selective intervention in particular industries or support for particular projects and firms". If this broad definition of industrial policy is acceptable, I think debate on industrial policy can be quelled. I think the debate on industrial policy may be more on the role of the government intervention and the role of the market rather than on the content of industrial policy. If the focus is narrowed down further to Japanese style of intervention, Korean style of intervention, Chinese style of intervention, or even American style of intervention, then the debate cannot be stopped anyhow. In fact, all five papers have contributed different perspectives on industrial policy which will enrich this field for better implementation and better development.

4. Learning Lessons from Four Decades of East Asian Experience

Professor Stiglitz has prepared a very good concluding chapter "From Miracle to Crisis to Recovery: Lessons from Four Decades of East Asian Experience." His unique contribution is to express his own thinking through his evolution in contribution to the former study and current study, his perceptions and analysis are at times complementing and at other times providing a counterpoint to the views of the other authors. I expect the readers of this publication will have such awareness. He debated "Was there a miracle?" through the argument that East Asia had experienced so few crises over the preceeding three decades. He points out "The unreliability of the Solow methodology has long been recognized" and the TFP debate is much ado about nothing by looking through the reality of narrowing the technology gap of East Asian countries. I am also in agreement with his analysis on the topics of "saving," "financial market," "industrial policy and role of the government" and analysis in his concluding remarks. Hereunder, I shall quote two points essential for professionals and policy makers, especially these two points are very much relevant to current issues and options for China.

(a) Dr. Stiglitz has pointed out: Some of the governments recognized the importance of the legal reforms that would facilitate the creation of a deeper equity market; at the same time they realized that even in the most advanced of the industrial countries, well-established firms financed only a small percentage of their investment by new equity issues. I stress this message due to its relevance to consider how to deal appropriately the financing of investment in the financial system, what's the priority that should be focused in the reform and perfection of financial system of China. Of course, I don't mean that equity financing is not important.

(b) I am in high agreement with his analysis that in the light of market and government failures, there are two alternative strategies; to focus on one and ignore the other or to try to address the weakness in each, view the public and private sectors as complementary. I think the failure of policy analyst to solve the issue in reality may be due to the rooted ideology, a part of them to the market, and a part of them to the government. This may be also the major source of debate on "the East Asian Miracle". From my perspective, I am in agreement with the point that there are market failure and governmental failure, each should perform its proper role, and they should complement each other in the area of failure.

III. Specific Comments

In spite of the contribution to settle several debates for the former publication, there are several new rich information and research results generated in this "Rethinking".

(1) Trade Rather than Exported-led Growth

The earlier publication on East Asian's success have frequently stressed export orientation as a major source of growth competitiveness. In fact it is explained in the introductory chapter and chapter 10 "Trade and Growth: Import-Led or Export-Led? Evidence from Japan and Korea" by Professor Lawrence and Weinstein that imports has a stronger effect on productivity than do exports. The authors have derived their conclusions through both theoretical explanation and quantitative analysis through case studies on Korea and Japan, and challenge three central conclusions of the former publication. First there is no support for the view that exporting was a particularly beneficial conduit for faster productivity growth on Japan. Second, there is generally no support for the view (except selective corporate tax rates) that direct subsidies or other industrial policies stimulated productivity. And the third, the research results by the authors show that the former World Bank study neglected an important channel of growth — imports. It is found that imports and tariffs did stimulate productivity. Although there may be need further to do more analytic research to prove these on a sounder basis, anyhow, this preliminary result of quantitative analysis do check with economic reality. For example, when I give analysis to the components of growth rate of GDP on the demand side, I shall analyze the data of input, output, export and import, it is the net export which is shown in its contribution to the growth of GDP in simple mathematical calculation. But I generally had to add more explanations for that, I always explained that "although it is the net export which contributes to the growth of GDP from the formula, but in fact, the import does matter to contribute to the growth of GDP in reality". The contribution of import to GDP can be explained in various qualitative aspects. But I am glad that this view is now supported from this analytical approach of "Rethinking".

(2) A New Unique Contribution — "Miracle as Prologue: the State and the Reform of the Corporate Sector"

I highly appreciate some views expressed in the paper by Professor Woo-Cumings "Miracle as Prologue: the State and the Reform of the Corporate Sector". His paper has pointed out the critical weakness of the former publication. I am highly in agreement with his view that the East Asian Miracle, for all its discussion about the basics and fundamentals, failed to explore the true basics: the social and political underpinnings that have propelled economic growth in East Asia. There was precious little in the book that anticipated the charges of "Crony Capitalism" that were immediately raised in the wake of the Asian Crisis. Professor Woo Cumings has not only pointed out the weakness of the former study, but it may be also the source of debate as well as the failure of economic principle to be applied effectively under different social and political context. It is also one of the reasons of the East Asia Miracle to be a "Miracle" compared to other developing countries in other regions from my perspective.

It is impossible to achieve the same economic performance by simply replication of the same economic policy without taking the social political context into consideration (an integrated approach). On this perception, I am in agreement also with the analysis given by Professor Perkins on the implementation of industrial policy. Although the Chinese planners advocated also the industrial policy, Professor Perkins pointed out, i.e., there are three difficulties for Vietnam and China to make a Korean — or Japanese — style industrial policy work efficiently. Here I shall only discuss the first difficulty described by Professor Perkins. I shall leave the other two for the audience to study by themselves. The economic bureaucracy in both countries was built and trained to carry out a Soviet-style system of central planning, not the kind of strategic planning that existed in Korea and Japan. The later system relied heavily on "guidance", market forces, and the private sector when it came to planning implementation. And the Soviet-style central planners rely on orders backed up by direct control of most inputs to enforce the plan. This can also explain the current difficulty in the reform of planning and economic operating system of China, use my own interpretation — "a deeply rooted planning culture", i.e. It is necessary to remember that the economic planning system is operated within the established social and political context, "planning culture" means that "planning" is embedded in established social and political system.

(3) *Cultural Factor in Development* — *ultural Policy in "Rethinking the Role of Government Policy in Southeast Asia"*

There are differences in the details of perception of miracle in East Asia, i.e., the Northeast Asia differs from Southeast Asia. In this "Rethinking", professor Jamos has presented a detail analysis of differences between Northeast Asia and Southeast Asia. Analysis is given with respect to FDI, industrial policy, cultural policy. Industrial policy and investment policy in Southeast Asia are analyzed in detail in his paper. But his analysis on cultural policies interested me the most. And it is a new message generated in this "Rethinking" which I think is important to study "Miracle" in countries or regions. FDI is an essential vehicle for growth. FDI in China is admirable by many developing countries. China attracted FDI through a gradualist approach, the four SEZs of China set up in the early 80's and the opening of 14 coastal cities, Yangtze River delta area, Pudong of Shanghai have attracted a large amount of FDI. It is totaled around 446.6 billion USD from 1979-2000. But the investors from Hong Kong SAR, Macao SAR, Tapei China and overseas Chinese have a dominant share of this tremendous FDI compared to others. Therefore to study the successful experience of attraction of FDI of China without taking this cultural factor into consideration will miss an important element in policy analysis. Culture in sociology and anthropology is the way of a particular society or groups of people, including patterns of thought, beliefs, behavior, customs, traditions, rituals, dress, and language, as well as art, music and literature. The author has pointed out "In East Asia, cultural practices have consolidated and promoted trust as well as other social relations conducive to business coordination, cooperation, collaboration, or even collusion. These seem to have been crucial for the development of culturally distinctive business networks and industrial organization that do not rely on the state".

(4) The Experience of Chinese Rural Industrialization

Dr. Yusef has pointed out a piece with the East Asian miracle during its later phase, beginning in the 1980"s, the share of nonstate enterprises rose remarkably, with its share in industrial output rose from 22.4 percent in 1978 to 73.5 percent in 2000 in the face of benign neglect of the government. In fact, the successful experience of rural industrialization of China has long been focused by many international communities, not only the World Bank had several specific studies on that subject, but there are also studies from IMF and other organizations. Professor Lin and Professor Yao have made their excellent contribution in the paper "Chinese Rural Industrialization in the Context of the East Asian Miracle" included in this "Rethinking". Not only that paper has included a detail analysis of development of Chinese rural enterprises from historical perspective, its contribution to China's national economy, determinants in the reform era in capital accumulation, industrial structure and ownership as well as a search of regional diversity, but also an econometric analysis of rural enterprise development is also given. Hereunder, I like to add two more points.

(a) <u>Cultural and social factors do matter in influencing the rural industrialization of China and economic development</u>

Dr. Yusuf had a paper "The Rise of China's Nonstate Sector Presented at the KDI in 1992." I am in agreement with his analysis in that paper especially the social and cultural factors which are generally missing in general economic analysis. I shall quote several points from his paper. The Chinese have succeeded where those others failed to fashion a thriving, competitive industrial system from the stuff of traditional institution. First, it would appear that Confucian ethics imposes stronger reciprocal obligations on members of kinship group; the second, the large involvement of the state in industrial development as well as the growth of the markets, and the intertwining of communal with individual goals in business activities, enlarges the facilitative role of kinship networks. They can make both state and market work together. This social arrangements do not just substitute for market institutions, they also harness state directions most effectively for developmental purpose.

(b) The rural industrialization and the growth of non-state and private enterprises in China are also one of the source of success in managing a smooth transition from a former central planned economy to a socialist market economy. Officially, China does not adopt a policy of "privatization", instead development of various forms of ownership system was advocated since reform and opening to the outside world. It is necessary to point out the facts that in the year 1958, the share of gross value of industrial output of state-owned enterprise was 90.1 percent and the share of collective owned enterprise was 9.9 percent. The household savings (urban and rural) in the banks was only 21 billion yuan by the end of 1978, while state-owned asset was much more than 1,000 billion yuan by that time, i.e., there was no source in financing the privatization in the launch of reform and opening. And legal system, the core infrastructure of a "market" was non-existent by that time and also the nurture of entrepreneurship spirit and the managerial capability also takes time. These explain the background of the advocation of development of various ownership systems in China rather than "privatization" from political, social and economic feasibility. The lessons of "shock therapy approach" based upon pure economic doctrine can be contrasted with this gradualist approach applied in a large country under the consideration of "socio-political" context.

(5) Governance, Development of the Legal System

Dr. Yusuf has raised a very good topic and analysis titled "Nature of Governance and Development of the Legal System." This is also a new contribution in this "Rethinking" supplementary to the former study. The importance of good governance should be underscored in the contemporary technological environment driven by ICT, the social environment of consciousness-raising activities of many international NGO's and the widening acceptance of appropriate rules for democracy, the changing economic environment of further integration of economic activity in the process of globalization. Governance with the consideration of ecological environment due to growth of awareness of the limit to growth that the mankind has to live in harmony with the nature.

Dr. Yusuf has discussed the governance at two levels. Good governance at the macro level means certain procedural and constitutional rules are in place; rules for the division of responsibility between central and subnational entities, rules for relations between the different branches of the state, etc. Possibly one more level may be added, i.e., governance at the supra-national level in spite of its complexity. I think those issues of governance are essential for further reform of China. With the fiscal policy for example, I think my Chinese colleagues will be in agreement with no hesitation that if fiscal relationship between the central and lower-level governments are rule-based with clear clarification of authority and responsibility and the implementation of those rules are transparent and accountable, the budget revenue income and expenditure will be improved and better allocated, corruption can be reduced, even if not eliminated. If the role and function of every branch of the state are clearly identified, the relations between them are fully clarified and made accountable to the public, the efficiency of operation and administration of the government shall be improved.

Dr. Yusuf has also discussed governance at the micro level, i.e., corporate governance. There is also a good paper by Professor Qian dealing with lessons from China on corporate governance. There exist probably as many definitions of "corporate governance" as there have been authors on the subject (*The Director's Handbook on Corporate Governance BP*). This subject cannot be discussed in detail here. Dr. Yusuf has pointed out correctly the weakness of corporate governance in East Asia that has avoided external monitoring as well as internal oversight. "It has been characterized by ineffective boards of directors, weak internal control, unreliable financial reporting, lacking of adequate disclosure, lax enforcement to ensure compliance, and poor audits. I expect my Chinese colleagues shall not fetch their breath due to recent event of Enron Corporation. The above weakness of corporate governance in East Asia is very fundamental and basic in economic nature, and to solve those fundamentals a tremendous effort is required.

Good governance at macro and micro levels is not achievable without reform of the legal system. This weakness in legal system of East Asia is pointed out in Dr. Yusef's introductory chapter, I am in agreement with his presentation that "whereas by the 1960s and 1970s, other East Asian countries had the rudiments of a legal system geared to the market, <u>China had to commence building one from scratch</u>." In spite of the effort to establish a legal system in recent years and the guideline set up by the top leader "to rule the country by law", the unfinished agenda of reform remains vast. It is necessary to utilize the opportunity of being a membership of WTO to promote the legal system reform of China. It should also be pointed out that amendment and revision of the laws related to the accession of WTO are only a part of the picture, the legal system as a whole will cover a more broad scope than that required by WTO.

IV Concluding Remarks

1. It is described in the very beginning that there were many developing countries emerging at the end of World War II, but the economic performance and social achievement of them differ greatly. The extraordinary economic performance of East Asia with equity in growth in past four decades is a reality compared to other parts of the World. Whether we call it a miracle or not doesn't matter.

The financial crisis erupted in 1997 with several rooted weakness is a natural rather than unusual event in the history of development of the mankind. Learning by doing, improvement through rethinking will contribute a robust development in the coming future. That's the reason which I valued highly the two publications of the World Bank, the former publication *The East Asia Miracle* in 1993 and the current publication *Rethinking the East Asian Miracle* published in 2001. The above two publications contain a rich and useful sectoral and country case studies which can provide a useful reference for development. As pointed out also in the beginning, 125 developing countries with a share of 75.7 percent of global population has only a share of 37 percent of world GDP and 20 percent of world export. Development for them is an urgent task. The above two publications provide live lessons to be learned.

2. Although the above two publications have provided many related aspects in development, the global society has changed rapidly. Therefore, development strategy should not only focused domestically, countries will need to act on three fronts: domestic, regional and international as pointed out by Dr. Yusef. Globalization may require more effort at coordinating policies and institutions at the regional and international levels, so that gains from an integrated world can be fully realized.

3. There is need also in rethinking on development and to face the challenge of globalization on social and environmental aspects. The two last aspects emphasized by Professor Stiglitz in his paper, one is the city environment and the other is on social harmonization from my understanding. Therefore, development should not be narrowly focused, <u>an integrated approach of development with a balance of economy, social cohesion or social equity and improved environment is necessary</u>. This new approach will challenge all of us, and all of us can contribute our effort to that part to make a better world in this new millenium.

13. E–Governance and Human Resource Development

Introduction

Globalization is the trend of development throughout the human history. The trend of social change is increased interaction among organized groups or even individuals. The world has experienced successive waves of what we now call globalization, going back as far as Marco Polo in the thirteenth century. These periods have all shared certain features of globalization: the expansion of trade, the diffusion of technology, extensive migration, and the cross-utilization of diverse culture, which is a broader definition than perceived economically, i.e., the growth rate of cross boarder investment is higher than the growth of trade, while the growth of trade is higher than that of GDP which is shown in recent several decades.

By the end of the nineteenth century, the world was already highly globalized due to the innovation of new transport system and the falling shipping costs had led in a rapid rise in trade. The growth of trade was accompanied by unprecedented flows of capital and migration. There were some setbacks between 1913 and the end of World War II. Following the World War II, there is a new wave of globalization due to further decline of transport cost and the new actors of the global economy and the expansion of modern MNCs.

More recently, globalization has been reinvigorated by the unprecedented ease with which data and information can be processed and exchanged due to breakthroughs in computer and telecommunication technologies and its fall in the relative price has been exceptionally sharp. This revolution in technologies has promoted the emergence of an information society. Many areas can be discussed related to the theme of this conference "Globalization and ICT — The Role of Government, Private Sector and Civil Society in an "Information Society for all". This paper will be limited to discuss E-governance and human resource development related to the theme of this conference. It will be divided into four parts: part I will give a brief retrospect of the industrialization process and the emergence of information society: major lessons will be summarized for the recognition of "An Information Society for All"; part II will discuss e-governance and organizational development and performance; part III will focus on education and human resource development; part IV will be some suggestions on concrete initiatives that could be taken in connection with ASEM and finally brief concluding remarks.

I. Brief Retrospect of Industrialization Process and Emergence of Information Society

1.01 Industrialization Process in Past Two Centuries

(1) First Stage of Industrial Revolution

Began in Britain in the second half of the 18th Century, it was driven by a series of innovation of technologies, the spinning jenny (textile industry), coal energy used in smelting iron ore (material industry), James Watt's improvement of Newcomen's steam engine, etc. It took several decades for those innovations to be incorporated in the factory — new organization in the industrial age.

Trade and industrialization have reinforced each other. Britain had eliminated customs barrier and state monopoly restrictions on production by the early 1700, bill of exchange, deposit banking and insurance were well developed, simple procedure for creating a corporation was established in the Company Act of 1844. All these organizations and institutions had contributed Britain to be the cradle of Industrial Revolution.

Invention of railway had integrated national market, primitive networking of transportation through steamships in waterway and railway in land areas had enabled the agricultural producers of American Midwest to distant market of Europe.

(2) Second Stage of Industrial Revolution, 1870-1914

There were many innovations in this period, new metallurgical process for making steel, electricity, refrigeration, organic chemicals, the internal combustion engine, the transatlantic telegraph and the radio.

Some of them reinforced the trend toward greater physical integration of world market: refrigeration, for example, made it possible to ship frozen meat from Australia to London by the 1880's. Telegraph and the radio are embryoes of modern ICT.

The second differed from the earlier one in three important aspects. Technological advances became more dependent on scientific research that was systematically organized by firms and universities for commercial operation. Germany led the way in scientific area; mass production technique was developed in the USA; industrial growth in the industrialized countries become partly dependent on supplies from outside the group of industrialized countries. There came also colonization for many of the new suppliers in Africa and Asia.

There is collapse of the global market from 1913 to 1950.

Global Industrialization after World War II

By the mid-1950s postwar reconstruction was virtually complete and the world economy entered a new period of industrialization and trade expansion. Postwar growth in manufacturing was fueled by an explosion of new products, new technologies, liberalization of international trade and new participants of industrialization, i.e., the developing countries.

And the reemergence of Asia on the world economic stage has been a remarkable story in post-war global industrialization. The post-war process of industrialization is also driven by many entirely new technological advances, such as synthetic materials, nuclear energy, jet aircraft, computers and electronic products (notably televisions computers, etc.). Great strides were made in telecommunications technologies, microelectronics and robots. Some of the new technologies assisted the physical integration of word markets. The jet aircraft cut travel time. Telecommunications have facilitated the MNCs to coordinate subsidiaries in different countries. The associated electronic media helped shape a world market with increasingly similar consumer tastes.

There are three features in this global industrialization process after World War II, non-market alternative to industrialization had once been prevailed in many developing countries and transitional economies; decolonization in Asia, Africa and the Caribbean; and third which may be a dominant factor in the process of globalization, the rise of the multinational corporation to prominence in world production and trade in manufacture and service.

1.02 Lessons of Industrialization

1. Industrialization is a process of change, not only it is driven by technological change, it is driven within the context of certain institutional condition. It is also the result of interaction among technology, economy and society that had changed the mankind from pre-industrial society (agricultural society in precedence) to an industrial society.

2. There is also evolutionary change of various organizations, business firms, corporations, banks, hospitals and schools. There is also change of the governance of the government as well as the life style of the people.

3. From global perspective, the process of industrialization has not been completed. It can be seen that 125 developing countries with 78 percent of world population has a share of 37.6 percent of world GDP and a share of 20.3 percent of world export in 2001. They are still in the process of industrialization.

4. Other negative lessons for example, colonization, environmental pollution and excessive exploitation of natural resources.

1.03 Emergence of Information Society

Since the beginning of the 1990s, the term "information society" and its varieties such as new economy, knowledge-based economy, knowledge society, etc., have been used to describe the many and varied challenges and opportunities which have been created by the rapid development of modern information and communications technologies in the economy, politics and society as a whole. The European Commission is the first official organization who has presented the action plan entitled "Europe's Way to the Information Society", proposing, first and foremost, measures to create the technical, legal and regulatory standards and framework for the information. The USA has advocated "New Economy" for more than one decade, the Republic of Korea had launched an Action Plan toward a knowledge-based economy since 2000. It is interesting to note Figure 1 which shows the structure of GDP of the US. in 2002 that "Old Economy still accounts for the biggest slice of GDP", i.e., there is a long way to go to form a new economy or "Information Society". But it is a global trend of social change.

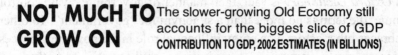

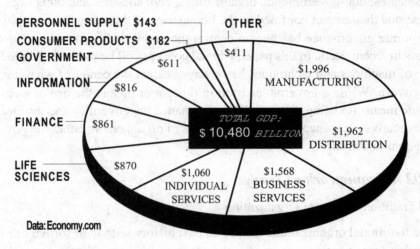

Fig.1 Structure of GDP of U.S.A. 2002

Source: *Business Week*, Jan, 14, 2002.

Therefore, developed countries will take the lead to march and shape the information society, while developing countries should take care both the opportunity and risks and pursue a pattern of development of its own to catch up this trend. China has full awareness of its own and the global trend, it is described in the report of President Jiang Zemin presented to 16th Party's National Congress that: to achieve industrialization is a difficult historical task in the modernization of China. While informatization is the necessary choice to quicken the process of industrialization and modernization, China will seize the opportunity to use ICT to serve the 21st Century. It will also be true for many developing countries if proper target is set up by them.

II. E-governance and Organizational Development and Performance

2.01 Clarification of E-Governance

The terminology "Governance" has many definitions. The basic explanation from *Oxford Dictionary* is "act, fact, manner of governing; sway, control". To some, the term is no more than a synonym for "government". To others, it embraces other actors who enjoy influential role in the governing process, businesses, non-governmental organizations, civil societies and other organizations that are not confined to the boundaries of the state, for example, corporate governance has been a central theme of study of many economists in recent years. In this paper, a broad concept will be used. The skilled use of machines and techniques has always been at the center of what it is to govern. While e-governance used in this paper means the use of electronic means (existing and new ICT) to enhance the governing capabilities of executives or managers at different levels of organization, either the government or a firm.

2.02 A Framework of Study

(1) Traditional Form of Organization

The traditional organizations formed in past history with their formal relationship (organizations emerged in the process of industrialization are only around two centuries) is shown in Figure 2. The organizational structure of them is hierarchical in nature. The larger the organization, the larger the number of layers in this hierarchy. While the governing process of an organization is mainly through collection, evaluation, transmission, analysis and diffusion of information. It had been analyzed in a Swedish study (Reference 3) that "The information technology of an economy is largely embodied in its organizational structure". It had also been analyzed in the same study that the basic industries and direct internal goods processing together has a share of 12.8 percent of GNP, while the internal information and external services of manufacturing accounted 40 percent of GNP. Therefore, application of modern ICT will improve the efficiency of operation of an organization.

(2) A System Approach of Organizational Change and Development

An organization should not be static, it is undergoing changes with changes of its internal components and external environment. To understand the impact of e-governance on improvement of organizational structure and performance, it is better to adopt a system approach.

From the perspective of system approach, organizations are: (a) goal oriented, people with a purpose; (b) psychosocial system, people interacting in groups; (c) technological system, people using knowledge and techniques; (d) structural subsystem with an integration of structured activities people working together in patterned relationships; and (e) the managerial subsystem. These five subsystems also interacted with each other. The goal and value of government, private sector and civil society differ from each other. They may also have different psychosocial systems. And different goal and psychosocial system may also influence the technological system.

Therefore, although modern ICT is existed right over there, although there must be further evolution and innovation of itself and its branches of linkages, the success and failure of its application is also constrained by goal, value and psychosocial system of an organization. Modern ICT had provided the opportunity of improvement of performance of government with e-governance and e-commerce in business firms greatly, but they may be constrained by other component systems of an organization.

2.03 Improvement of Organizational Structure through E-governance

1. Delayering in Hierarchical Level

It had been popular in Western corporations since the 80's to improve its organizational structure through delayering of its hierarchical level, i.e., to reduce its middle-level management and widen the span of control. ICT has made this restructuring of organizations to be realized with reduction of cost and improvement of efficiency.

2. Network Enterprise

(1) The beginning of the internet with on-line computer network connecting governments, companies, universities and many other network users has brought into emergence of the new organizational form of enterprise, the "network enterprise". This terminology is raised by Manual Castells that "it is increasingly impossible for organizations — be they large corporations or small businesses — to survive if they are not part of a network." With the

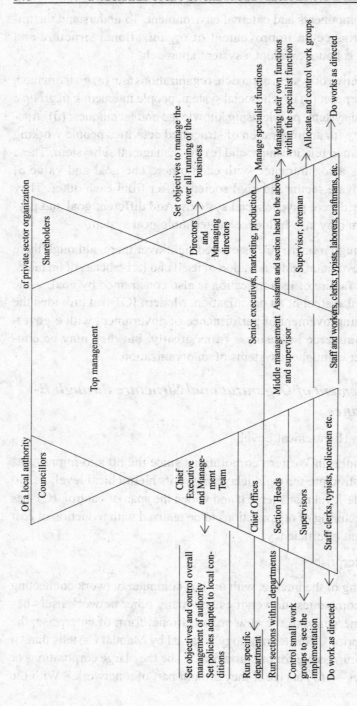

Fig 2 Formal Relations within Organizations

Derived from: S. Gregson and F. Livesey, organizations and management Behavior, Made Simple Books, 1993.

innovation of Internet and the growth of ICT, organizations around the world are able to locate each other, enter readily into contact, and coordinate joint activities through an electronic medium whether wire or wireless.

(2) Clusters of SME's

The emergence of networking has provided opportunities for new form of organization in favor of small and medium enterprises, i.e., geographic clustering of enterprises. The benefits of agglomeration arise from external economies such as the availability of information or proximity to pools of suppliers, customers and skilled workers. Clusters are of a more advanced nature in organization than passive agglomeration, where enterprises realize external economies just by being there. Combining networking, specialization and joint action, clusters could overcome many of the disadvantages associated with small size.

2.04 *Improvement of Efficiency and Transparency of Organizational Performance through E-governance at Micro Level*

(1) Efficiency and effectiveness of an organization from system perspective

Efficiency of an organization may be defined as the extent of fit between the internal psycho-social system with four other sub-systems. The effectiveness of an organization may be defined as the extent of fit between the organization's environment and all the internal subsystems of an organization. A good e-governance, i.e., an effective collection of data, processing and diffusing in an organization will improve the efficiency, transparency and effectiveness of an organization. This is especially important for the MNCs.

(2) Improvement of efficiency of operation of MNCs

The move from national to multinational corporation changes the environmental framework and in the organizational structure and behavioral responses that flow from these frameworks. There are also evolution of strategies and structures of MNCs. There are three types of MNCs evolved with different international environments. When there is significant trade barrier and costly communication and transportation, then the MNCs will adopted an stand alone, e.g., multi-domestic strategy; simple integration with outsourcing is another form of structure; while complex global production, e.g., regional core networks is relatively popular with the means of e-governance. For example, Ford motors have established cross-national networks within Europe, building on previously stand alone affiliates which tended to be geared to a single country. The final assembly is taken in the UK and Germany, while with the components produced around fourteen countries, such as Japan, Spain, the US, Canada, France, Netherlands, and with its hose clamps, cylinder bolt, exhausted down pipes, press, etc. come from Sweden. Without e-governance, the operation of such global production process will be nearly impossible, modern ICT has promoted also JIT manufacturing process and reduce greatly the cost of inventory.

(3) Opportunities and challenges of e-governance of enterprise

Not everything is positive through e-governance of enterprise in a globalizing world. It depends very much on adaptability and learning. The following box shows some aspects.

Box.1
New Ways of Organizing and Managing Enterprises

Opportunities

Clustering, networking and specialization increase efficiency and productiorty (This is especially important for SME's)

New managerial method and production techniques also enhance efficiency and productivity

Information and communication technologies provide access to new knowledge on management methods, production technologies, marketing and export opportunities (e-commerce)

Challenges

Increased competition at all levels in both export and domestic markets due to trade liberalization

New skills and capabilities required to master information technology — especially for new designs, production and marketing system.

Source: Industrial Development Report 2002/2003, Competing through innovation and learning, UNIDO.

2.05 E-governance (government)

Current situation of e-governance

E-governance of government refers for the most part to the delivery of government service.

It is a very complicate issue in spite of the fact that e-governance can improve the transparency and better delivery of the service of government to its people.

Currently, nearly most of the countries in the world are putting e-government on the agenda. The potential benefits of new information and communication capabilities for the services delivered by public agencies are well known on principles, i.e., it will lower administration costs; it provides faster and more accurate responses to requests and queries; it provides access to all departments and levels of government from any location; it improves governance capability; it gives assistance to local and national economies by facilitating the government to business interface and it provides additional means of public feedback. But in the process of implementation, it is far from satisfactory. Generally speaking, the developed countries are in a better position in pushing forward e-governance, because they have both the hardware (computer infrastructure, internet infrastructure and information infrastructure) and software (social infrastructure, legal system, etc.) relatively well developed than those of developing countries in general. And it is also true that e-government in the public sector, for example, on-line sales, electronic purchasing, web-based order entry, supply chain integration, enterprise resource planning and electronic data interchange, etc., had became popular in the past decade. There is also organizational changes and the emergence of the global value chain in the manufacturing sector of the world. But in the public sector, the organizational changes may be more difficult than in the private sector, it is difficult to change a lot of routine call for apaper trail for approval. With China for example, although there are 5846 gov.cn websites, including central and local governmental organizations by the end of 2001, reduction of the amount of approval by the governmental agencies is one of the major item on China's reform agenda. Therefore, e-government, the use of information and communication technology to promote more convenient government services cannot substitute for good public management and control.

Prospects

Anyhow, e-governance of government is a mega trend towards an information society. In order to make e-governance to be effective, the following points are essential.

— Establish necessary physical and social infrastructure, development of ICT should go hand in hand with improved rules and processes.

— It is necessary to aim at an integrated strategy and avoid a piecemeal approach.

— E-governance should be fitted to user requirements.

III. Human Resource Development

3.01 Meaning of Human Resource Development

1. Human resources are personnel pool available to an organization. It should be emphasized that they are the most important resources in any organization, either the government or a private firm. Appropriate human resources assure an organization that the right number and kind of people are available at the right time and place so that organizational needs can be met. It had been point out by Daniel Bell that the strategic resources in a post-industrial society is human capital, rather than the financial capital in an industrial society.

2. Human Resources Management (HRM) is a term emerged in recent years to replace personnel management and implying that the responsibility of personnel managers should not merely handle recruitment, pay and discharging, but should maximize the use of an organization's human resources. This is a style of management introduced in many Western organizations in order to boost productivity and competitiveness. HRM regards a company's work force as vital to economic competitiveness; if the employees are not completely dedicated to the firm and its product, the firm will not become the leader of the product. In order to generate employees' enthusiasm and commitment, the entire organizational culture must be retooled to make the workers feel they have an investment in the workplace and in the work process. Based upon HRM, human resources issues should not be the exclusive domain of designated personnel offices but should be a top priority for all members of company management.

3. Necessity of Human Resource Development

It can be seen from above the importance of human resource which is vital to a business organization. It is also true for organizations in general, either for the government or for the civil society. Narrowly speaking, in an information society, there is rapid growth of new information and knowledge, and there is rapid change of the market, products and processes. Therefore, there is a continuous development of the human resources within an organization, continuous upgradation of their knowledge and skills to meet the challenges of high rate of "depreciation" of the human capital in order not to be outdated. Broadly speaking, continuous improvement of cohesion towards a common goal and value is also a realm of HRM.

3.02 Traditional Means of Human Resource Development and Skill Acquirement

1. Skill and competence means "ability to do something expertly and well", skills are of various types: management skill (including administrative skill of a government official), technical skill, marketing skill or a specific skill in certain activity. Various skills in the industrial society require in general various formal educational background of the personnel.

2. Evolution of formal education in the process of industrialization

The process of industrialization and the growth of urbanization had influenced greatly the development of the education system. Until the first few decades of the nineteenth century, most of the population had no schooling whatsoever. As the industrial economy expanded rapidly, there was a great demand for specialized schooling that could produce an educated, capable workforce. By the mid-1800s, the Netherlands, Switzerland and the German states had achieved more or less universal enrollment in elementary schools. There were evolution and expansion of education system in all countries, but there are wide differences between countries both in the number of years children are expected to be in school, and in ways of organizing education systems. But there are great achievements of education system and knowledge development of human beings in the past hundred years (see Table 1) which provides one of the foundation of the information society.

It can be seen from the above Table that developed countries had build up a work force with higher level of educational background. And it can also be seen that the enrollment ratio of tertiary education of high-income economies is 51 percent in average, while it is only 19 percent for upper-middle- income economies and 5 percent for low-income economies respectively in the year 1992. This may be a fact of concern in marching towards an information society. But application of ICT will provide a great opportunity to narrow the gap.

Table 1 Years of Education Per Person Aged 15-64, Six Countries 1820-1992
(average for both sex)

Country / Year	USA	France	Netherlands	UK	Germany	Japan
1820	1.75	n.a.	n.a.	2.00	n.a.	1.50
1913	7.86	6.99	6.42	8.82	8.37	5.36
1992	18.04	15.96	13.34	14.09	12.17	14.87

Note: Abstracted from "Monitoring the World Economy 1820-1992," (Reference 8).

3. Skill creation   The skill created by the workers, staff, engineers and management with different levels of educational background is generally through on-job training. A part of Western corporations had once adopted an apprenticeship system around the 30's in the 20th Century, i.e., a person under apprenticeship will rotate through all departments of a company to get a general knowledge, and then specialize in certain position. This system had been abandoned in the West around the 40's due to high training cost. It is interesting to note that some Westerners had attributed the distinctive characteristics of Japanese large corporations to the successful economic performance during the 1980's, one of the characteristics is "Less specialization". In Japanese organizations employees specialize much less than their counterparts in the West. Young workers entering a firm in a management training position will spend the first year learning generally how the various departments of the firm operate. They will then rotate through a variety of positions in both local branches and national headquarters in order to gain experience in the many dimensions of the company's activities. This illustrates that upgradation of skill is a must in order to be competitive. But there are various approaches and lessons to be summarized and learned.

3.03 New Means of Human Resource Development and Skill Acquirement through ICT

1. Changing mode of education

The current education system is established and evolved in the process of industrialization in the past two centuries. Teachers and students have to group together in school at definite location. There is transfer of knowledge face to face between the teacher and the students. With the ICT revolution, audio tape and disc, video tape and disc, TV college and vocational school, distance learning, the multi-media have provided the opportunity to upgrade any individual's knowledge and skill through lifelong learn process.

2. E-universities

Distance learning through the Internet is now available. Students study in small groups of ten to fifteen individuals, with whom they exchange ideas on an ongoing basis. Course instructors are able to offer individual assistance and answer questions by e-mail. Internet-based courses attempt to replicate all the elements in traditional learning in an on-line environment.

Conventional universities are now taking steps to become e-universities; a consortia of institutions are sharing their academic resources, research facilities, teaching staff and students on line. Universities around the world are acknowledging the benefits of these partnerships with other institutions whose offerings complement their own.

It was reported that the UK is going to create distinctly new Internet-based learning programs for a global network of students. In Feb. 2000, David Blunkett, the UK Education and Employment Secretary, announced plans to create a web-based UK university that would bring together elements of the best of British education and made it available to students around the world.

In spite of the benefits of emerging e-universities described above, in reality, there is emergence of a "computer underclass" within Western societies, but Internet access has become the new line of demarcation between the rich and the poor. Underdeveloped regions of the world struggling with mass illiteracy and lacking telephone lines and electricity need an improved educational infrastructure before they can truly benefit from distance learning programs. Also, the Internet cannot be substituted for direct contact between teacher and pupils under these conditions.

3. Innovation of Knowledge Management in Corporation

There is evolution of knowledge management in corporation. It was reported that knowledge management at Monsanto focused on five objectives:

(1) Connecting people with other knowledge people

(2) Connecting people with information

(3) Enable the conversion of information into knowledge

(4) Encapsulating knowledge to make it easier to transfer

(5) Disseminating knowledge around the firm

It can be conceived from these trends that without further cooperation among universities, research institutions and firms, it is possible to upgrade continuously the skills of the human resources and contribute better to the growth of an information society.

3.04 Current Distance Learning System in China

China has established 45 radio and TV universities with new student enrollment around 165,000 and 109,000 graduates respectively in 2001. At the end of 1999, there were 8.9 million Internet users in China, 21 percent of them students. And over the past 20 years, more than 2 million Chinese have graduated from radio and television universities. China learned from its experience that greater use of these technologies would expand access for all people of China. This will also be true for other developing countries too.

There are issues of current Chinese distance learning system. It is advised by the World Bank that "A wholesale change in focus and mindset is needed to meet the requirement of an efficient distance learning system. Integrating the curriculum and offerings of the various distance education providers requires a coordinated and networked national education and training system or a learning network to connect all providers". This advice has correctly pointed out the current institutional weakness of the administration of the education system of China. Although China had implemented its educational system reform in the 80's. But the concept and mindset have not been changed greatly due to the implanted former Soviet model of education and deep-rooted planning culture. For example, private sector involvement in the education system is prohibited in the past, the textbooks are unified, the students are narrowly trained, different ministries established their own universities and colleges, and the focus is on basic literacy and test scores rather than on applying knowledge to solve problems. The government had not created a sound environment for lifelong learning process. There is the need for institutional improvement to utilize the opportunity offered by modern ICT appropriately, i.e., the government and the enterprise must create an environment to encourage lifelong learning of its people and employees, soft skills (skills required for management and capability in adaptation) should also be emphasized.

Generally speaking, most of the developing countries are in shortage of qualified personnel with high grade of education and skill. ICT can provide a great opportunity to bridge the gap of knowledge and skill, if proper institutions can be established. This is related to the necessity of upgradation of skill and competence of other organization, and the government should also participate this learning process.

IV. Some Suggestions of Concrete Initiatives in Connection with ASEM

4.01 General Reconmmendation

It should be emphasized that both Asia and Europe are very much heterogeneous in nature. For example, Japan is already a developed country within G-7, or G-3. The four newly industrialized economies have already been included in the advanced economies in the statistics of some international organizations. Within them, Singapore has taken the lead in its rank either in the world competitiveness scoreboard of the IMD or in the industrial competitiveness index of UNIDO. The Republic of Korea has already implemented its 3-year action plan towards a knowledge-based economy since 2000. While Indonesia, the Philippines and Vietnam within ASEAN have a somewhat lower standards of living than the NIEs and the rest of Southeast Asia. The specific requirements of them may be different from other Asian countries. This is also true for Europe, Northern Europe, Southern, Western and Eastern Europe have also unique features of their own. But one theme is true for all, i.e., to utilize the maximum opportunity of ICT and globalization and to minimize the risks of ICT and the volatility of a globalizing world. Some Asian countries had already experienced the negative side of globalization — the Asian financial crisis erupted since July 1997. Internally, this is the financial and corporate sector weakness combined with macroeconomic vulnerabilities to spark the crisis. Although a large part of Asian countries had caught up with the developed countries in the global industrialization process, they are still weak in modern service sector, especially the financial sector, including banking sector, the capital market as well as the insurance sector. The Asian countries in general, should strengthen these services by learning more from the international experience in order to be better adapted in an information society.

There are many areas of collaborations possible from the above general descriptions, two general recommendations are presented. The first, it is the human resource who will play a crucial role in shaping the emerging information society. And there is also the need to have continuous upgradation of skill of the human resource. The second, due to the diversity of ASEM, the nature of its heterogeneity, and the complexity of the issue, its seems feasible to begin with a few of small pilot programs, and then extended to whole Asia and Europe, in Chinese saying, "A thousand miles of journey is started with the first step." Some small experimental programs can help in the achievement of larger programs.

4.02 Agreement to Collaborate on the Upgrading of Competence

1. I agree to establish a joint program for skills upgrading among decision makers of various organizations through an open learning system. The decision makers should include both the public sector officials at different levels of a country as well as the private sector. It had been described in previous part of this paper that management contributes an important role to the success and failure of a firm. This is also true for the government, in spite of the ideological debate on government intervention, the role of the government on economic growth has been confirmed by the two studies of the World Bank *The East Asia Miracle* and *Rethinking the East Asian Miracle* respectively in 1993 and 2001. It is commented in later that "In the light of market and government failures, there are two alternative strategies: to focus on one and ignore the other or try to address the weakness in each, viewing the public and private sectors as complementary." The role of government have to be redefined in a changing global environment. Therefore, to establish a distance-training program for the Asian decision makers are of crucial importance.

2. I also agree to develop an educational program for enhanced human resource development on a broad basis. Linking up the European School Net with the ASEAN School Net Pilot Project and the Asia e-Learning

Initiative could be an option. The crucial issue is: how effective educational material can be designed and prepared given the diversity of the Asian region and even in the ASEAN.

3. A special program should be designed to assist SMEs. On the one hand, there is need to promote growth of SMEs to meet the great challenge of employment pressure either in Europe or Asia, on the other side, there is the need to improve the innovative and competitive capability to move up in a global value chain of SMEs.

4. Experimenting a pilot innovation system of ASEM

National innovation system had been prevailed in recent years. There is no single accepted definition of a national innovation system, what is important is the web of interaction of the system as a whole. Innovation is a complex interaction among actors on producing, disseminating, acquiring and applying various kinds of knowledge. The major actors generally involve the private enterprises, universities, and research institutes. The linkage can take the form of joint research, personnel exchange, equipment purchase, etc. It can also came from national initiative, the former Eureka program of Europe from my personal understanding was a cross-boarder innovation system inside Europe. It is also feasible to experiment innovation system of ASEM, start with a small scale with the initiative coming from governments or from private enterprises to be the core. This experimental program can focus on manufacturing of new ICT products or others. It is a complex issue from organizational aspects, but it can be implemented by start small.

4.03 Other Recommendations

1. The issue of technology parks

China has established around 53 technology parks, which account for about 10 percent of industrial production. Foreign enterprises of non-Chinese origin were responsible for more than 62 percent of the parks' exports while Hong Kong SAR, Macao and Taiwan China enterprises add another 14 percent. In spite of the high growth rate in number and employment in these parks, the technology diffusion beyond the parks are limited. It is expected that improvement of the performance of those technology parks can be derived by learning experience from Europe. Of course, a large part of the issue may be institutional, which can only be overcome by ourselves.

Institutions are rules, enforcement mechanism, and organization, institutional structure effects behavior. China had inherited from the former Soviet Union the whole institution. Although China has implemented a market-oriented reform for around two decades, but a top-down approach and bureautic administrative means are deeply rooted, with technology parks as an example (this is also true for financial system described below). All 53 national technology parks were established through provincial or national initiative, rather than from universities, research institutions or private sector. There are too many technology parks with redundant construction, technology import and production. The terminology "high technology" used in China is inconsistent with international practice. R&D of high technology parks has a share of only 2.71 percent of total sales in 1996. And the performance of those technology parks differ greatly: the labor productivity of Shenzhen in 1997 is 592,674 yuan per capita while the lowest one in Anshan is only 45, 819 yuan per capita. All these institutional issues should be overcome through further reform in the coming decade.

2. In the Sino-EU Agreement on China's Accession to the WTO, China and the EU have agreed to establish a regulatory dialogue on the development of the securities market in China. In fact, the Chinese financial system is dominated by the banking sector, stock market the second, and bond market is underdeveloped. There is a great potential on improvement of the securities market and improvement of the performance of the banking sector in further reform. We welcome the European experience for that.

Concluding Remarks

There are opportunities in the process of globalization and for the ICT to play a role. But technology-driven efforts will not create an information society for all. It is the role of various organizations and the continuos development of the human resource (not only intellectually, but morally) that may shape an information society for all with lessons of industrialization process of the past two centuries to be kept deeply in mind.

REFERENCES

1. *World Economic Outlook,* Oct. 2001, "The Information Technology Revolution", IMF.

2. "World Development Report 1987", the World Bank.

3. "The Knowledge Based Information Economy", Gunnar Eliasson, Stefan Fulster, Thomas Lindberg, Thomas Pousetts and Erol Taymaz , Telecon, The Industrial Institute for Economic and Social Research, 1990.

4. *The New Palgrave Dictionary of Economcis,* edited by John Eatwell Murray Milgate and Peter Newman, the Macmillan Press Limited, 1987.

5. *World Investment Report 1999,* UNCTAD.

6. *The World Since 1500 — A Global History* by L.S. Stavriano, 2nd edition, Prentice Hall Inc.

7. *Sociology,* by Anthony Giddens, 4th edition, 2001, Polity Press.

8. *Monitoring the World Economy 1820-1992,* by Angus Maddision, OECD, 1995.

9. *The Coming of Post Industirla Society — A venture in social forecasting,* by Daniel Bell, Basic Books, 1999.

10. *World Investment Report 1993,* UNCTAD.

11. Industrial Development Report 2002/2003 — Competing through innovation and learning.

12. OECD Science, Technology and Industry Scoreboard 1999 Benchmarking Knowledge — Basec Economies, OECD, 1999.

13. "E-Governance", by Graham Leicester, Feb. 2001 — a paper presented to Strategic Policy Forum on Using Knowledge for Development Wilton Park, U.K., March 2001.

14. "ICT Policy and E-government of China", by Xinxin Fang, a paper presented to "Joint Seminar on Strategies for Knowledge-Based Economies in Korea and China" held in Seoul Korea, Oct.16-17, 2002.

15. *China and the WTO,* Supachai Panitchpakdi and Mark L. Clifford, John Wiley & Sons Ltd., 2002.

16. *Barrons Disctionary of Business Terms,* third edition, Jack P. Friedman, Barrons Educational Series Inc., 2000.

17. *EC/EU Fact Book,* by Alex Roney, sixth edition, Kogan Page, 2000.

18. "China and the Knowledge Economy — Seizing the 21st Century", by Carl Dahlman and Jean Eric Aubert, the World Bank, 2001.

19. *The East Asian Mirade,* the World Bank, 1993.

20. *Rethinking the East Asian Miracle,* editors: Joseph E. Stiglitz and Shahid Yusuf, the World Bank, 2001.

21. "Pension Fund Investment From Ageing to Emerging Markets", by Bernhard Fischer and Helmut Reisen, OECD Development Center Policy Brief, No. 9, 1994.

22. "Governance in the 21st Century", OECD, 2001.

Part IV

Some Social Aspects of China

Social aspects include many areas to be studied — education, public health (the recent event of SARS is one example), poverty, gender issue, social harmonization, culture, religion, etc. Especially culture in broad sense, it includes the pattern of thought, belief, behavior, customs, traditions, rituals, dress and language as well as art, music and literature. China has five thousands of years of culture. Cultural factor does have its great influence on development. The author should apologize that due to the limitation of his study, activities, time constraints and knowledge, only two papers are collected here.

14. Social Security System
and Alleviation of Poverty in China

Introduction

A. The social security system

The social security system in a country can be studied from two aspects:
(a) an active social security system which will enhance the capacity of
the poor to satisfy basic needs through economic and social development strategies, policies and programs; and (b) a passive social security
system which includes targeted programs for specially disadvantaged
segments and programs that provide relief and insurance against
contingencies.

In the present paper, "social security" is defined in the comprehensive sense
to refer to the condition that would enable the poor to satisfy their basic
needs in a sustainable manner. The unique characteristics of this system in
China are described in Fig. I and the coming chapter.

B. The social security system — A dynamic concept

As discussed in section A above, although a broad and general definition
can be given to social security, the coverage, scope and level of protection
are different in countries at different stages of development. The social
security system is undergoing changes owing to changes in the social and
economic structure and the emergent problems in the historical process.
For example, many developed countries have been trying to reform their
social security systems since the 1970's. They are facing the problems of
heavy financial burden and shortage of financial resources for the existing
social security systems owing to an accelerated ageing process of the
population and an increase in the rate of unemployment owing to the low

rate of economic growth and high rate of inflation. In the initial period of industrialization in 1952 there were only 1.5 million employees in the secondary sector and 1.9 million in the tertiary sector of the public-owned enterprises. That social security system could be afforded by the public enterprises and the state. But there are now more than 135 million and 127 million employees in the secondary and tertiary sectors respectively. In the urban areas, which has become a heavy financial burden, the economic reform launched in the late 1970s has also given rise to the need to reform the enterprise-based social security system initiated in the early 1950s in the context of an economy managed almost entirely by the state, because it is also a major obstacle to economic efficiency owing to the surplus labour force in nearly every public enterprise. The old social security provisions have also, so far, not allowed for the needs of individuals and non-state-run enterprises that have sprung up in recent years. Therefore, China's social security system becomes an important element in the current reform process.

C. The Chinese social security system

China had established a unique social security system with a wide scope derived from the model of the former Union of Soviet Socialist Republics. China's social security system (in the broad sense) is shown in Fig. I in the next chapter, but detailed discussion will be given for these aspects listed from (a)-(e) given in the outlines of the country study by the Marga Institute.

Statistical figures will be provided for the discussion. However, China has not established a unified system for the measurement of poverty. It is clear from Fig. I that there are many different line ministries involved in the provision and administration of the social security system. (The public enterprises providing the social security system are administered by more than 50 ministries and more than 30 provinces, autonomous regions and municipalities.) The definition of poverty also changes. There are variations in the data even from the same institutions. Therefore, there may be some discrepancies among the data obtained. However, much effort has been expended on the selection and preparation of the data and tables. The major discrepancies are pointed out in the discussion.

**Figure I. Framework of China's existing social security system and
its administrative structure**

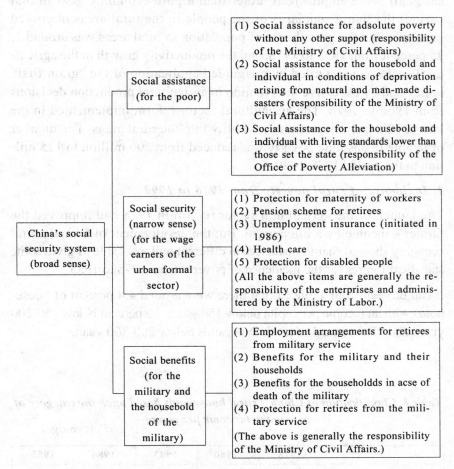

I. **Poverty and Social Insecurity — the Present
Situation and Trends**

A. Analysis of the prevailing situation relating to poverty

Introduction

The incidence of poverty in China is generally concentrated in the rural
areas. Because a full employment policy was implemented in the urban
sector, the incidence of poverty is very minor in that sector. Although an

egalitarian strategy was pursued from 1952 to 1978, the social and political goals were emphasized rather than a pure economic goal in that period; the living standards of the people in the rural areas improved generally, but the growth rate of population in rural areas was around 1. 75 percent from 1952 to 1978, and the productivity growth in the agricultural sector was retarded by misguided application of the "grain first" policy and by excessive intervention in agricultural production decisions from 1966 to 1976. The agricultural sector reform implemented in the late 1970's had injected a new vitality into the rural areas. The number of people in absolute poverty was reduced from 200 million to 125 million in the period 1978-1989.

1. Incidence of rural poverty from 1978 to 1992

The launch of the agricultural sector reform in 1978 had improved the farmer's income by a big margin. But the development of China's rural economy showed sharp imbalances in different regions. Table I.I gives some statistical figures for the incidence of poverty from 1978 to 1985.

It can be seen from Table I.I that there were around 4.4 percent of households with an income per capita below 150 yuan, 7.9 percent below 150-200 yuan, and 25.6 percent of rural households below 200-300 yuan.

Table I. Classification of China's rural households based upon the category of average net income per capita   *(Percentage)*

	1978	1980	1983	1984	1985
Above 500 yuan	2.4	1.6	11.9	18.2	22.3
300-500 yuan	2.4	11.5	34.5	38.6	39.8
200-300 yuan	15.0	25.3	32.9	29.2	25.6
150-200 yuan	17.6	27.1	13.1	9.4	7.9
Below150 yuan	65.0	34.5	7.6	4.6	4.4

Source: Outline of Economic Development in China's Poor Areas (1989).

A recent report by the Director of the Poor Area Development Office (PADO) defines the incidence of poverty as follows:

The level of absolute poverty in rural areas is defined on the basis of net income per capita in 1995. In general, for counties with net income per capita below 150 yuan, for counties in minority areas with a net income per capita from 150 to 200 yuan, and counties of the old revolutionary area base from 200 to 300 yuan, there are 331 poor counties identified to be assisted by the State. The average net income per capita was 208.6 yuan, which is around US$70.95 based upon the exchange rate of 1 dollar to 2.94 yuan in 1985. Based upon this definition of the poverty line, the daily calorie intake is around 2,200 kcal, and protein around 50 grams. All the provinces and regions had identified an additional 368 poor counties to be assisted by themselves. Altogether, 699 poor counties with a population of around 125 million (which is 14.8 percent of the population in rural areas) are to be assisted by the central and provincial governments in the Seventh Five-Year Plan (1986-1990).

Based upon the data from the State Statistics Bureau, the population of rural poverty was reduced to 80.83 million in 1992; this represents 8.8 percent of the total population in rural areas.

2. *Features of the poor counties and socio-economic profile of the rural poor*

The features of the poor counties are characterized by the following:

(a) Low level of economic development

Generally the poor counties are characterized by primitive methods of production, outdated production skills, small-scale markets, non-diversified production structure, poor infrastructure and insufficient supply of food for local residents. Based on the statistics of 1986, the population and arable land of the 664 poor counties accounted for 25 percent of the total in China[1], but the overall gross output of all sectors accounted for only 14 percent of the national total. Some economic and technical indicators of the 664 poor counties in comparison with the national average are shown in Fig. II.

---

1. The poor counties identified numbered 664, based upon the official announcement of the Office of the Leading Group of Economic Development in Poor Areas under the State Council in 1989. But this number was later changed to 699 in the Seventh Five-Year Plan (1986-1990).

(b) Low levels of social and physical development of infrastructures

The basic features of social development of the poor counties are inconvenient transport, blockage of information, shortage of scientific and technological personnel, unskilled farmers, poor health-care equipment, and rampant endemic diseases. Statistics in 1986 show that 16.1 percent of townships in the 664 poor counties could not be reached by highways, and 22.2 percent of townships had no electricity. A comparison of 11 provinces (or autonomous regions) with concentration of the poor to that of relatively developed provinces (or municipalities administrated by the central government) shows there are 68.4 scientific and technological personnel/10,000 people in the former which is 3.2 percent lower than the latter with 89 scientific and technological personnel/10,000 people. Table 1.2 gives a comparison of some indicators of 11 provinces (or municipalities administrated by the central government) to the national average[2].

Figure II. Comparison of the economic and technical indicators of 664 poor counties with the national average

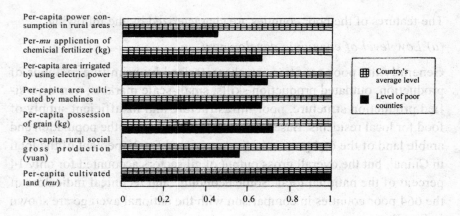

---

2. It will be difficult to understand the descriptions in this paper without some explanations on the terminology used in China.

(c) Poor natural and geographical conditions and serious ecological imbalances

Many of the poor regions suffer from poor agricultural conditions. There is serious soil erosion in the deep mountainous areas; the arid areas in northwest China (see Table 1.3) are frequently affected by drought; the karst region, both soil and water, the red soil region in areas south of the Yangtze River and the poor region in North China have experienced natural disasters such as drought, flood and salinization of land almost every year. These adverse factors have led directly to a vicious cycle in these regions.

Table I. 2. Comparison of some social indicators among 11 poor provinces and the national average

Year:1985	Number per 10,000 presons, national average	Number per 10,000 presons, 11 poor provinces	B/A (percentage)
Primary school education	6,127	5,000	81.6
Illiterate persons	2,361.9	2,943	124.6
Hospital beds	23.8	21.7	91.0
Medical workers	32.5	30.3	93.2

Source: Outline of Economic Development in China's Poor Areas (1989).

Urban and rural — There is no exact definition of "urban" and "rural" in China. The administration level is county, prefecture, municipality (municipality is also classified as municipality administered by the central government or provincial government) and county. There are urban and rural areas in a country. "Urban" in a county or municipality includes cities and townships. An area with more than 3,000 people with 50 percent of the people of permanent residence engaged in non-agricultural activities is classified as city and township. (Before 1993, the threshold was 2,000.)

Agricultural population and non-agricultural population — This is classified based upon profession and the way of supply of grain and food. Agricultural population refers to the workers and their dependants engaged in agricultural activities, and their food and grain supply is based upon the regulation of commodity grain supply of non-city and township residents. The non-agricultural population refers to the workers and their dependants engaged in non-agricultural activities, and their food and grain are supplied through the standard amount of commodity grain supply from the government.

Township — In China the status of township has not been clearly identified because it is derived from the former commune, while the commune in rural areas is in the realm of rural areas; therefore, town and village enterprises are under the administration of the Ministry of Agriculture. The population in townships classified as urban population in the Chinese statistical system.

Table I.3. Distributon of poor counties in provinces and autonomous regions

Name of province or autonomous region	Number of poor counties	Percentage share of poor counties in related provinces
1. Hebei Province	49	35
2. Shanxi Province	35	35
3. Inner Mongolia Autonomous Region	37	44
4. Liaoning Province	11	24
5. Zhejiang Province	3	4
6. Anhui Province	17	23
7. Fujian Province	16	25
8. Jiangxi Province	54	64
9. Shandong Province	14	13
10. Henan Province	24	21
11. Hubei Province	37	52
12. Hunan Province	38	29
13. Guangdong Province	30	30
14. Guangxi Zhuang Autonomous Region	48	59
15. Sichuan Province	46	25
16. Guizhou Province	31	38
17. Yunnan Province	41	33
18. Shaanxi Province	46	49
19. Gansu Province	43	57
20. Ningia Hui Autonomous Region	8	47
21. Qinghai Province	19	50
22. Xinjiang Uygur Autonomous Region	27	32
Total	664	30 percent of total counties

(d) Excessive growth rate of population

Studies indicate that "the poorer the people are, the more babies they will have", and the population growth rate in the poor regions often exceeds 2-3 percent[3]. This is also a widespread vicious cycle in many poor regions.

3. Regional and geographical distribution of rural growth

The regional and geographical distribution of rural poverty is relatively concentrated with explicit features of regional characteristics. The 664 coun-

---

3. China had a national average natural growth rate of population 1.145 percent in 1993.

ties targeted for poverty alleviation from 1986 to 1990 had a share of 64.4 percent (430 counties) distributed in 18 extensive regions (see Table 1.4) in relatively underdeveloped central and western China. Tables 1.3 and 1.4 give the distribution of the poor counties in provinces and autonomous regions and the extensive poor regions (characterized by geographical features) related to the poor counties and provinces.

Table I.4. Distribution of 18 extensive poor regions

Number of poor regions	poor regions (geographical features)	Provinces and regions involved	Number of poor counties
2	Yimeng mountain	Shandong	9
	Southwestern and northeasterm Fujian	Fujian, Zhejiang and Guangdong	23
7	Nuluerhu mountain region	Liaoning, Inner Mongolia, Hebei	18
	Tahang mountain region	Shanxi, Hebei	25
	Luliang mountain region	Shanxi	21
	Luhang mountain region	Sichuan, Shaanxi, Hubei, Henan	68
	Qinling-Daba mountain	Sichuan, Hunan, Hubei, Guizhou	40
	Dabie mountain	Hubei, Henan, Anhui	27
	Jinggang mountain and southern Jiangxi	Jiangxi, Hunan	34
9	Dingxi dryland	Gansu	27
	Xihaigu region	Ningxia	8
	Northern Shaanxi	Shaanxi, Gansu	27
	Tibet		77
	Southeastern part of Yunnan	Yunnan	19
	Hengduan mountain	Yunnan	13
	Jiuwan mountain	Guangxi, Guizhou	17
	Wumeng mountain	Sichuan, Yunnan, Guizhou	32
	Northwestern part of Guizhou	Guizhou	29

4. Brief summary of rural poverty

It was stated in the introduction that the incidence of poverty was concentrated in rural areas. Generally, those provinces have a high share of the primary sector (that is at a low stage of industrialization) and those with a poor natural agricultural endowment have a high share of poor counties because they are generally located in mountainous regions or areas. This can be illustrated from the facts presented in Table 1.4. Owing to the large territorial size of China, there are poor counties in almost every province and autonomous region, because there are disadvantaged locations in every province, for example, although Liaoning and Shanxi provinces have a high degree of industrialization (Liaoning is the heavy industrial base of China) with a low percentage share of the primary sector, they have 24 and 35 percent of their counties as poor ones owing to the presence of Nuluerhu, Taihang and Luliang mountainous regions. The disadvantageous geographical location and low level of industrialization have resulted in poor access and poor human resources development. The high population growth rate is another social factor that accentuates the vicious cycle. The previous section presents the features and socio-economic profile of the rural poor.

Jiangsu Province is a rich province with no poor counties, and Gansu a poor Province with per-capita GDP ranking twenty-eighth among the 30 provinces, autonomous regions, and central administered municipalities of China (Taiwan Province excluded). Table 1.5 presents the comparison between these two provinces.

It can be shown from Table 1.5 that the absolute difference and the relative difference between Gansu and Jiansu provinces show a general increasing trend of the gap. This is the background of the poverty alleviation program which was launched in 1986 and lasted until 1992. Although there are improvements in the poor regions, owing to the differences faced in geographical locations, the regional distribution has not changed very much. Therefore, the statistical data presented in Tables I.I, 1.3 and 1.4 remain valid up to 1993. The "'8-7' Poverty Eradication Program"[4], launched in 1994, was based

Table 1.5. Comparison of annual average per-capita net income in rural areas of Jiangsu and Gansu provinces

	1978	1980	1981	1983	1984	1985
Per-capita net income, Gansu(A)	98.4	153.33	153.63	213.06	221.05	269.4
Per-capita net income, Jiangsu(B)	152.1	217.94	257.99	357.47	447.87	492.6
Absolute difference (C=B-A)	53.7	64.61	99.36	144.41	226.82	237.38
Relative difference (C/B)	35.3	29.6	38.5	40.4	50.6	48.2

---

4. A seven-year program to help 80 million poor eradicate poverty; started in 1994 by the government.

upon those data, which is discussed in detail in Section B of this chapter.

5. Urban poverty

(a) The unique characteristics of China's urban poverty

It was mentioned in the introduction to the present chapter that, because a full employment policy was implemented, the incidence of poverty was very minor in the urban sector. It has also been pointed out in a World Bank report[5] that in 1990, average per-capita income among the poorest 5 percent of urban residents was 689 yuan[6], or more than double the urban absolute poverty line of 321 yuan and greater than the per-capita income of 65 percent of rural residents. Less than 1 percent of the urban population, or

Table I.6. Government price subsidies *(100 million yuan)*

Year	Total	Grain, cotton and edible oil price subsidies	Subsidies for increases in meat prices	Other price subsidies
1978	11.24	11.14	-	-
1979	79.20	54.85	-	24.35
1980	117.71	102.80	-	14.91
1981	159.41	142.22	-	17.19
1982	172.22	156.19	-	16.03
1983	197.37	182.13	-	15.24
1984	218.34	201.67	-	16.67
1985	261.79	198.66	33.52	29.61
1986	257.48	169.37	42.24	45.87
1987	294.60	195.43	42.74	56.43
1988	216.82	204.03	40.40	72.39
1989	370.34	259.47	40.53	70.34
1990	380.80	267.61	41.78	71.41
1991	373.77	267.03	42.46	64.28
1992	321.64	224.35	38.54	58.75
1993	299.30	224.75	29.86	44.69

Source: *Statistical Yearbook of China 1994,* China Statistical Publishing House.

---

5. China: *Strategies for Reducing Poverty in the 1990s,* Washington, DC, 1990.

6. This is equivalent to 185.2 US dollars based on an exchange rate of 1 US dollar = 3.72 yuan up to December 15, 1989.

about 1 million people, had income levels falling below the estimated absolute poverty line each year from 1983 to 1990. The government also has a policy of giving consumer food subsidies (as shown in Table 1.6) to the urban residents, and therefore the registered urban population are much better nourished than their rural counterparts. Therefore, more discussion will be included on the poverty problem in the rural areas in this chapter and a broad background of the urban social welfare system and the social security system will be presented in chapter II, together with the development strategy and experience. Annex tables A. 2 and A. 3 supplement the above quotation from the World Bank report.

(b) Regional distribution of urban income and urban poverty

China has not carried out any studies on identification of the urban poverty line. Various provinces and municipalities are setting their own poverty lines and programs of assistance based upon their own fiscal capability. It was said that the poverty line set by the Poor Area Development Office (see section A.I) also applied to urban poverty. However, after checking with other related ministries, this was found not to be the case. Therefore, a part of the results of the study on the "poverty line" carried out by the World Bank is also provided in annex Tables A.I and A.2. These tables seem to be generally applicable to the Chinese situation; the discrepancies between the official statement and the World Bank study are very small; on real terms in calories, the Chinese set a standard of 2,200 kcal, while that of the World Bank is 2,150 kcal.

The available statistics cannot support the regional distribution of urban poverty. The aim of the following analysis, based upon available statistics, is to explore the regional distribution of urban poverty for reference purposes.

In 1993, the average GDP/capita was 2,915 yuan. There were four provinces and municipalities which were higher above the average: Shanghai (11,700 yuan), Guangdong Province (4,938 yuan), Zhejiang Province (4, 431 yuan) and Beijing (8,240 yuan). There were seven provinces and autonomous regions with GDP/capita lower than the national average: Gansu, Henan, Jilin, Helongjiang, Jiangxi, Shanxi and Inner Mongolia. Those provinces have an GDP/capita ranging from 2,382 yuan (Inner Mongolia) to 1, 867 yuan (Henan Province). If the average annual income of these provinces is checked against Table 1.7, which is a household survey of cities and townships in 1993 (there is no data on household survey of province and municipalities described above). It can be seen that the average annual income of Inner Mongolia, the lowest average income in the above seven, was near the level of low income, the second decile of the whole nation. Therefore, it is reasonable to assume that the regional distribution of urban poverty will have a close relationship to the regional distribution of poor provinces, with a low average annual income. Further exploration of the national and provincial development strategy will derive useful experiences and lessons, in view of the fact that strategy development and policies are of importance in effecting active poverty alleviation rather than passive poverty assistance in urban areas. This point will be elaborated further in chapter II.

Table I.7. Basic indicators of urban household income and esenditure

	Average	Lowest income	First 5 per cent	Low income	Medium-low income	Medium income	Medium-high income	High income	Highest income
Total living expenditure	2 110.81	1 261.36	1 183.15	1 528.68	1 770.17	2 055.72	2 404.13	2 810.3	3 533.5
Food	1 058.20	744.58	700.33	869.27	957.57	1064.65	1 169.4	1 284.6	1 464.7
Grain	129.96	119.14	115.70	124.77	126.40	128.97	132.57	141.60	145.1
Meat poultry and related products	250.36	178.10	166.87	207.39	229.62	252.69	278.41	303.92	329.23
Eggs	47.07	35.46	32.92	39.97	43.34	47.60	51.22	56.54	60.39
Aquatic products	71.35	47.61	43.49	57.16	63.09	71.77	80.17	88.13	101.84
Milk and dairy products	19.76	10.18	9.00	14.07	16.56	20.27	23.68	26.72	30.42
Clothing	300.61	142.50	127.01	195.79	246.43	303.32	367.20	418.16	492.62
Household facilities articles and services	184.96	66.51	60.00	94.42	120.06	163.10	220.27	314.16	446.75
Medicine and medical services	56.89	36.05	36.02	41.92	50.09	53.59	61.52	74.58	100.34
Sport and communications	80.63	28.34	24.18	35.69	51.04	68.72	99.60	127.27	212.16
Recreation, education and cultural services	194.01	113.29	101.43	136.40	158.43	182.91	221.37	256.21	356.23
Residence	140.01	93.28	92.88	103.74	119.33	132.98	150.50	83.37	240.87
Miscellaneous commodities	95.50	36.81	34.69	51.45	67.21	86.45	114.26	147.76	219.88

Source: *Statistical Yearbook of China 1994,* China Statistical Publishing House.

Table 1.8 gives a comparison of data of the richest municipality, Shanghai, and the poorest autonomous region, Inner Mongolia, from the available sample survey of 1989. Although the 1993 data are not available, the above compilation will provide a useful reference for discussing the development strategy in the next chapter.

Table 1.8. Comparison of sample survey of household living

| | Rural household | | | | | | City and township Household | | | | | |
| | Shanghai | | | Inner Mongolia | | | Shanghai | | | Inner Mongolia | | |
	A	B	C	A	B	C	A	B	C	A	B	C
1978	1.60	280.69	192.52	2.8	130	-	-	-	-	-	273.65	268.77
1979	1.52	359.99	247.44	2.7	156	-	-	-	-	-	357.12	350.64
1980	1.51	401.94	322.92	2.6	181	158	1.69	559.80	552.84	-	370.12	353.04
1981	1.48	444.02	389.84	2.5	228	177	1.65	589.32	548.52	-	380.28	377.85
1982	1.47	536.36	444.29	2.4	273	203	1.62	606.36	575.64	-	411.58	397.12
1983	1.44	562.97	511.60	2.1	294	227	1.58	641.16	615.24	-	431.13	411.38
1984	1.46	785.06	619.04	2.0	336	246	1.56	787.08	726.00	1.96	498.98	448.98
1985	1.50	805.92	778.45	1.8	360	291	1.64	1011.84	991.80	1.99	615.33	594.82
1986	1.48	936.73	895.76	1.8	340	307	1.60	1214.76	1170.24	2.00	703.26	680.04
1987	1.47	1059.12	977.40	1.8	389	349	1.61	1347.48	1282.08	2.01	745.14	711.85
1988	1.43	1300.94	1229.02	1.8	500	404	1.62	1615.56	1645.44	1.95	832.57	843.86
1989	1.42	1520.00	1319.00	1.7	478	448	1.63	1860.00	1812.00	1.92	957.09	913.47

Source: *A Compilation of Historcal Srotistics of Provinces, Autonomous Regions and Munici-palities Administered by the State, 1949-1989,* China Statistical Publishing House, 1990.

A = Number of people supported / laborer

B = Net income/per capita

C = Net living expendimre/per capita

B. Past and current trends in the alleviation of poverty

1. Background information — before 1978

In order to have a better understanding of past and current trends in the alleviation of poverty, several important aspects should be considered. China's development strategy can be classified broadly into two periods: a closed and semi-closed condition on the external side and an egalitarian growth strategy applied domestically before 1978, social equity being emphasized rather than the pursuit of economic efficiency. If the criteria of pure social equity are used, it can probably be said that China had a very small Gini coefficient before 1978, although the living standard of the whole is low by international standards, because China started from the historical background of a very much underdeveloped state in 1949. The result of the development effort implemented before 1978 was that notwithstanding their low income share, the poorest people in China were far better off than their counterparts in most other developing countries[7].

The egalitarian development strategy implemented before 1978 was characterized by a balanced regional development strategy with less emphasis on the locational advantage; a full employment policy for the urban workers with a very low wage growth rate and also a low rate of inflation; and a social security system which covered a wide range of benefits for the urban workers. All able-bodied rural residents were assigned jobs on commune lands or in sideline industries in the commune system implemented before 1978 in rural areas, and for those who could not work, many work teams in the commune used a distribution system based on a minimum per-capita grain ration. The above facts are illustrated in Tables 1.9, 1.10 and 1.11. Table 1.9 shows the growth of output from 1952 to 1978 of six provinces selected from six regions, from which it can be seen that the difference in the growth of these regions is small. Table 1.10 shows that the average wage growth rate of state-owned enterprises from 1952 to 1978 is only 65 percent. Table 1.11 presents the social security cost for state-owned enterprises.

Table I.9. Comparison of total output of society, 1952-1978
(millioms of yuan)

Unit: 100

Year	Total output of society (output indes 1952=100)					
	Liaoning	Inner Mongolia	Shandong	Guangdong	Guizhou	Gansu
1952	76.2 (100)	15.61 (100)	69.82 (100)	49.92 (100)	12.69 (100)	16.78 (100)
1978	483.7 (775.6)	109.76 (525.21)	445.01 (614.18)	350.31 (541.1)	87.95 (487.9)	125.21 (612.66)

Source: *A Compilation of Historical Statistics of Provinces, Autonomous Regions and Municipalities Administered by the State, 1949-1989*, China Statistical Publishing House, 1990.

7. World Bank, *China: Socialist Economic Development*, Washington, DC, 1982.

Table I.10   Average wage rate of state-owned enterprises
(yuan)

Year	Departments									
	Average	Industry	Construc-tion	Agri-culture, irrigation	Trans-port, postal	Com-merce	Urban public utility	Science, education and health	Finance, insu-rance	Insti-tution
1952	446	515	564	375	583	360	634	368	458	376
1957	637	690	744	501	752	529	651	580	613	631
1962	592	652	705	392	702	494	631	542	559	626
1965	652	729	730	433	774	579	687	598	624	684
1970	609	661	650	419	709	553	660	555	588	678
1975	613	644	704	460	699	562	639	574	609	645
1978	644	683	748	492	733	587	652	582	643	662

Source: *China Statistics Yearbook 1984.*

Table I.11. Expenditure on social security of state-owned enterprises

Year	Expenditure on social security	Percentage equivalent to wage total
1952	9.52	14.0
1957	27.94	17.9
1962	28.25	13.2
1978	66.91	14.3

Source: *China Statistical Yearbook 1981,* China Statistical Publishing House, 1990.

2. Past and current strategy in the alleviation of poverty

The launch of the economic reform in late 1978 had created the vitality of the rural sector. Therefore, absolute poverty in rural areas declined rapidly from 260 million in 1978 to around 96 million in 1985, and declined further to 80 million in 1992. A new poverty alleviation program in rural areas was established by the central government in 1994. While poverty alleviation in the urban sectors is different, there was a very minor proportion of urban poverty before 1978, and urban workers enjoyed lifetime employment and a high social security system that was much better than that of the rural poor. Reform of the social security system was implemented gradually from 1985, and there are many areas of reform in the social security system of the urban sector; these reforms are still under experimentation and are ongoing.

A relatively detailed discussion of this is given in chapter II; the focus will be mainly on poverty alleviation in rural areas in this chapter.

(a) The past strategy in the alleviation of poverty in the rural area is passive in nature (before 1985)

It is explained in section A that the farmers who could not work in the commune system were provided a minimum per-capita grain ration, and social relief facilities and programs were also provided for the elderly and the weak. This system has continued up to the present time but the available financial resources and level of security and welfare depend very much upon the local capability and capacity of the village, the township or the local government. A national security system for rural areas is in preparation. Tables 1.12 and 1.13 give the data for two types of social security for the rural people. Table 1.12 gives numbers for those with no working capability and with no financial resources; generally these are the elderly, the weak, orphans and the disabled. Their daily living is supplied by the collectives to guarantee their food, clothing, housing, medical care and funeral expenses and education for orphans. Table 1.13 gives data on social welfare homes run by rural collectives, which is protection for the elderly. These two systems are continued from the past (before 1978), but can only cover some of the rural poor, and therefore, a scientific reform program should be pursued. The poverty alleviation program in the Seventh Five-Year Plan was described in section A.I and the "'8-7'Poverty Eradication Program" (1994-2000) will be discussed in the next paragraph.

(b) Current strategy for the alleviation of rural poverty

The Chinese have learnt from their own development experience of past strategies that an active poverty alleviation program is more important for the rural poor than a passive assistance programme. The State Council has clearly defined the basic targets for development in the country's poor areas in the Seventh Five-Year Plan for National Economic and Social Development (1986-1990). The targets are: to supply people in most of the poor areas with enough food and clothing; to help such areas generate a self-development capability in developing the local market economy; and gradually wipe out poverty and bring prosperity.

This new development strategy emphasized the following:

(i) Provision of development assistance for developing income-generating

Table I.12. Statistics of rural households of "five guarantees"

Year	Number of peopte in household of five guaran- tees (hundred of thousands)	People in the program (hundred of thousands)	Rate of support (percentage)	Financial resources supplied by collective (hundred of thousands)	Yuan/capita
1985	300.8	223.8 (274.7)	74.2	52 854	214.5
1986	293.2	220.4	75.2	50 526	227.5
1987	287.6	219.0	76.3	60 000	273.1
1988	282.6	207.2	73.3	64 574	303.0
1989	321.4	222.4	69.1	74 922	348.6
1990	283.7	206.4 (250.6)	72.8	73 410	342.4
1993	-	(244.7)	-	-	-

Source: *China: Reference Material for Social Development (1992)*. Data for 1993 are obtained
from *China Statistical Yearbook 1994*. There are some discrepancies between these two
data sources, but both are quoted for reference. The numbers in parentheses show data
from the *China Statistical Yearbook 1994*.

Table I.13. Data on homes for the elderly (rural and urban)

Year	Number of homes for elderly	Number of elderly accommo- dated (hundreds of thousands)	Expenditure (hundred thousand of yuan)			Cost/capita
			Total	Assistance from the State	Support from the collective	
1985	27 103	30.9	13 459.6	3 356.9	10 102.7	485
1986	32 792	36.8	18 304.5	3 638.3	14 666.2	541
1987	35 015	40.7	22 641.4	4 117.7	18 523.7	589
1988	36 665	43.4	23 013.7	3 902.3	19 111.4	547
1989	37 377	45.3	28 813.6	3 992.8	24 820.8	649
1990	38 161	47.8	33 555.9	4 396.5	29 159.4	721
1993	26 281	35.2	-	-	-	-

Source: *China: Reference Material for Social Deveiopmint (1992)*. The data inlude both rural and
urdan;separate data for rural are not available. Data for 1993 were obtained from *China
Statistical Yearbook 1994*, the data are for rural areas.

activities based on local resources and local organization;

(ii) Continued provision of direct relief aid and social services, as shown in Tables 1.12 and 1.13, but shifting the financing burden from the central to local levels;

(iii) Preferential tax, pricing and other measures devised to stimulate the development of poor areas;

(iv) Targeting assistance funds to poor areas based on a standard set of income criteria for determining need.

Since the launch of this new strategy, the incidence of poverty is defined as explained in section A.I, and 699 poor counties were identified in the Seventh Five-Year Plan; the population of rural poverty was reduced to 80.8 million in 1992.

3. "8-7" Poverty Eradication Program

The "8-7" Poverty Eradication Program is an active poverty eradication policy announced by the central government in 1994, the target being to solve the basic needs of food and clothing for 80 million poor people within seven years.

(a) Basic characteristics of the poor counties in the "8-7" Poverty Eradication Program

The new poor counties identified by the government include 592 counties with a population of around 210 million and a rural population of around 195 million. The poor people in rural areas who cannot have their basic needs in food and clothing met accounted for around 60 million. They have a share of arable land of around 22.3 million hectares, a total grain production of around 64.3 million tons, and grain per capita of 307 kilograms.

The geographical distribution is nearly the same as shown in Tables 1.3 and 1.4, but even more concentrated in Shanxi, Inner Mongolia, Henan, Hubei, Sichuan, Guizhou, Yunan, Shaanxi, Gansu and Xingjiang. These features have been fully described in section A.3. Those poor rural areas are dominated by mono-agricultural structure; the share of plantation and husbandry production is over 80 percent.

(b) Target of the "8-7" Poverty Eradication Program

Criteria set for poverty alleviation

(i) The net income per capita of most of the households in absolute poverty will reach above 500 yuan based on the constant price of 1990;

(ii) To assist poor households in creating the basic conditions for meeting their needs for better food and clothing;

(iii) To create 0.5-1 mu[8] of basic farm land with stable high productivity in areas with appropriate conditions;

(iv) To create 1 mu of land with fruit or trees, or 1 mu of farm land with cash crops;

(v) Every household will transfer one person on average to the labor force in town and village enterprises or the developed regions;

(vi) Every household will have a sideline activity.

For households in the animal husbandry area, hedged grassland or a "grass warehouse" will be created, to foster the result of poverty alleviation to reduce the reentry of the poor.

To strengthen the establishment of infrastructure

(i) To solve the difficulty of obtaining drinking water for people and animals;

(ii) To establish highways to reach most poor villages and townships to enable them to have access to community markets and the production base of commodities;

(iii) To ensure that there are no counties without electricity supply, as most poor counties should have access to this.

To change the backward state of education, culture and health care

(i) To universalize primary education, and to abolish illiteracy of adults and young people;

(ii) To establish vocational and technical training for adults, so that most of the labor force in adolescence master one or two practical skills;

(iii) To improve sanitary and health-care conditions, to prevent and reduce endemic disease, and to prevent disabilities;

---

8. 1 mu = 0.066 ha.

(iv) To strengthen family planning and control the natural growth rate of the population in accordance with national targets.

Guidelines and method

The major guideline is to alleviate poverty through development. The basic method is to develop plantations, fisheries and related processing and sales activities, to develop labor-intensive town and village enterprises for resources development, and to organize labor force output in a planned and orderly manner.

To guide poor villages in creating enterprises in other places with a good in vestment environment; and to expand the exchange of cadres and economic and technical cooperation between developed regions and poor regions;

The individual economy, private economy and stock partnership economy should be developed at the same time in the development of the public economy.

Management and institutions for poverty alleviation

The strength of the economic development and poverty alleviation of China depends very much on its organizational effort and the participation of different line ministries, although if too many ministries are involved the problem of difficulty in coordination will arise. Even then, sectoral interests may sometimes affect successful achievement of the overall target. This is a very complex issue requiring study of a specific topic: this paper can only present the background information.

The office of the Leading Group of Economic Development of the Poor Areas (LGEDPA) is a task force executive agency established by the State Council in 1986, responsible for poverty alleviation in the Seventh Five-Year Plan and the "8-7" Program (1994-2000). Its organizational structure is shown in Figure III. The provinces, prefectures and counties have established their institutions based on the central model.

Nearly all related ministries and regions are requested to include concrete measures in the "8-7" Program, for example:

State Planning Commission

The commission will be responsible for improving the regional planning of the poor areas and the allocation of funds for the Program[9]. The commission had allocated 10 billion yuan for the "Food-for-Work" Program for poverty alleviation for the period 1984-1993; 1 billion yuan is allocated every year from 1991 to 1995, the sixth allocation from the plan will be 2 billion yuan per annum from 1993 to 1997, and the seventh allocation (1994-2000) from the plan will be 1 billion yuan \ per annum: the commission will inte-

Figure III. Organization Chart of the Leading Group of the Economic Development in Poor Areas under the State Council

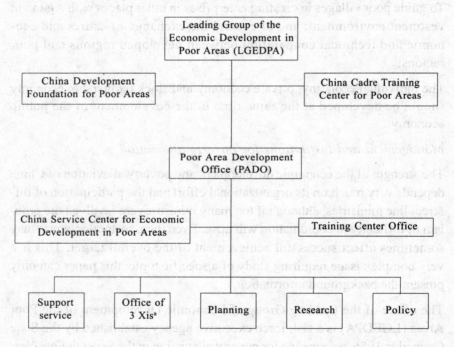

Note: a 3-Xis or Sanxi Area, are three poor areas in China, Dingxi and Hexi Corridor in Gansu Province and Xihaigu Region of Ningxia Hui Autonomous Region.The government had a special program for the alleviation of poverty in these regions.

9. The "Food-for-Work" Program is also a special program for the alleviation of poverty. It was designed to use surplus commodity stocks or necessities as in-kind payment for construction work on water supply systems and building in rural areas or underdeveloped regions.

grate the "8-7" Poverty Alleviation Program into the national Ninth Five-Year Plan (1996-2000) and the preparation of long-term planning to 2010.

Ministry of Finance

The ministry had implemented the poverty program to give subsidies to 331 poor counties amounting to around 2 billion yuan in 1993, which is equivalent to 30 percent of the budget revenue income of these poor counties. From 1980 to 1993, the central government had a budget expenditure of around 27 billion yuan for poverty alleviation. In 1993, this figure was around 8 billion. The government is aware of the fact that a poor ecological environment is common in poor regions, and it is also one of the causes of poverty. The central government had a budget expenditure of around 16.5 billion yuan from 1984 to 1993 in the form of the "Food-for-Work" Program to assist the poor regions in constructing roads, irrigation systems and hydropower. A special program was also provided for tree-planting and soil and water conservation in the upper Yangtze River. Tax-sharing system reform[10] was implemented in 1994. The central government may have more financial reserves for transfer payments to poor areas. And it is necessary to be considered in the reform of the public finance. In addition, there will be adjustments in the distribution structure of funds for poverty alleviation; a part of the poverty alleviation fund for the coastal development region should be allocated to the central and western poor regions.

State Science and Technology Commission

The commission had organized to send around of 27,000 scientific and technological personnel to the poverty regions to push forward the application of advanced appropriate technology to improve production technology. A demonstration project to improve agricultural productivity with new plantation techniques had been implemented in the mountainous region of Anhui and Shaanxi provinces, and the productivity was improved. The commission will continue to arrange for scientific personnel in different disciplines to study the development strategy of poor regions, to push forward the "Sparks

---

10. Before the fiscal system reform implemented in 1994, the government had implemented fiscal contract system reform between the central and local governments. The revenue of the central government declined to 14 percent of GDP in 1993. This implementation of fiscal system reform in 1994 will strengthen the fiscal position of the central government.

Program"[11], organizing experts to assist town and village enterprises in improving production and management techniques and profit; implement policies to encourage scientific and technological personnel to stay in poor regions and to establish industrial development groups using their technology with the town and village enterprises; and to prompt the exchange of cooperative arrangements between poor regions and developed regions.

Ministry of Education

There are one or two agricultural professional middle schools in most of the poverty regions among 2,000 national counties, and there are evening schools for farmers in 30 percent of the villages, providing technical training. A special program was experimented on by the Ministry of Education in different provinces, and the demonstration villages reached 7,056 people within 1,553 counties. The ministry has emphasized that reform and adjustment of the educational structure are necessary. The basic education of the poor areas should be combined with vocational education at an early stage; proper professional and technical content should be introduced based upon local features. Because in many poor areas there are no primary schools, very few graduates from primary schools will have a chance to study in junior middle schools and most of the primary school graduates will go back to their native villages to work; they should therefore be provided with the means to learn the necessary production techniques adapted to local needs in various forms.

The Ministry of Education is beginning to adopt a targeting policy for the development of education of the poor areas. In the Eighth Five-Year Plan, 250 million yuan was spent to rebuild the dangerous housing of primary schools of the poor regions; 1,000 million yuan in education subsidies is spent in the minority region. The World Bank loan of US$110 million is used to develop basic education for 114 poor counties of six provinces and autonomous regions. A second poverty alleviation project from a World Bank loan of US$100 million will be used to make education compulsory for 103 poor counties of five provinces.

---

11. The Sparks Program, launched by the State Science and Technology Commission (SSTC), includes a number of demonstrated projects implemented in rural areas to improve the application of appropriate technology, technical skills of the workers, and management of the enterprises.

There are around 143 poor counties in the minority-inhabited regions within the poor counties at the state level. The Ministry of Education and the Ministry of Civil Affairs, together with universities and colleges, are making arrangements to organize educational assistance in partnership. The ministry also arranges training programs for cadres, teachers and technical personnel for the poor region. Staff from institutions of higher learning and scientific and technological institutes are also encouraged to participate in development projects in the poor regions. Some professors and researchers are assigned to posts of deputy county chiefs (temporarily, they still hold their posts in universities, etc.) to provide technical consultation transfers of technical projects, training of teachers and so om. The ministry organized a National Conference for Comprehensive Rural Education Reform to accelerate compulsory education at the level of junior middle school in the poor regions and areas inhabited by minorities in compact communities.

Commission of Family Planning

It has been stated by the commission that the slow growth of the economy of poor provinces is due to the high growth rate of the population. Statistics from Guizhou Province from 1949 to 1987 show that the average annual growth rate of the population was 16.7 percent higher than the national average. It is estimated that during that period an additional 2.77 million people were born, which had lowered the 70.52 yuan per-capita gross value of industrial and agricultural output of that province, and increased consumption expenditure by around 950 milhon yuan and grain consumption by around 691.6 thousand tons. A sample survey by the commission in 1989 showed that a birth rate in excess of 20 percent of the national average was generally seen in the economicly underdeveloped provinces. Of the 16 provinces with a population growth rate in excess of the national average, 15 are also provinces with a high concentration of poor counties. Therefore, the State Council had approved and distributed the report submitted jointly by the State Commission of Family Planning and LGEDPA in the form of Document No. 59, asking every region to integrate the work of poverty alleviation with family planning in the poor regions. It is stated in this document that poor households that implement family planning seriously should be given priority assistance while those poor households that did not follow the family planning policy would be assisted only under certain conditions.

Ministry of Agriculture

The ministry will strengthen the agricultural infrastructure and establishment of the commodity bases of the poor region. A targeting policy will be implemented for crucial poverty alleviation counties. The major measures include: establishment and perfection of the system of diffusion of agricultural technology — it is planned that agricultural diffusion centres will all be established in crucial poverty alleviation counties; establishment of a breeding system for a better strain of seed; establishment of a group of agricultural commodity bases; and pushing forward the progress of integration of trade, industry and agriculture.

The Ministry of Agriculture will also accelerate the development of town and village enterprises in the relatively underdeveloped regions of China (100 East-West[12] Cooperative Development Demonstration Region). It will collaborate with the State Science and Technology Commission to popularize 1,000 items of new technologies, new products and new processes.

Professors and staff of universities, colleges and research institutes belonging to this ministry should be organized to develop the work of human resources development for the alleviation of poverty. Since 1983, these universities and colleges have initiated the absorption of students from the poor regions; the quota had been set at 15 percent, and more than 40,000 students had been enrolled. It is planned to absorb around 6,000 to 7,000 students from the poor regions.

Ministry of Health

The health-care system set up by the Ministry of Health to the year 2000 has two major aspects: prevention of diseases and improvement of the rural health-care system. Its concrete targets are as follows:

(i) To establish a sound basis for a primary health-care system. Health-care offices should be established and perfected in more than 90 percent of the villages to provide comprehensive health-care services for the community;

(ii) To develop and establish a rural health-care security system actively and gradually, to develop cooperative medical-care systems and various forms of social medical insurance systems to make the people in the poor area less

---

12. Generally, the eastern region is located in coastal areas, while the western part of China is a landlocked region; the former is generally a developed region while the latter is underdeveloped.

vulnerable to diseases;

(iii) To provide the people with basic education in hygiene and safe drinking water.

The Ministry of Health is also responsible for medical human resources development for the poor regions. Since 1987, around 400 senior medical professionals have been trained every year for the poor regions. Foreign assistance and loans from the World Bank are also allocated to those provinces with a high share of poverty counties on a priority basis.

Because China is a vast country, and only limited financial resources were created in the short period of industrialization. It is almost impossible to solve the health-care problems of the rural areas satisfactorily. It has been observed by foreign experts that an important policy question for the government is whether to postpone sustained concern for health-care improvement in good areas until after further gains have been made in cities and well-off rural areas. This point can be understood better in the discussion in chapter II.

Ministry of Civil Affairs

This ministry is responsible for social assistance for the urban and rural poor, households of "five guarantees" and also the old-age insurance system. The State Council had assigned the responsibility to this ministry for reform of the old-age security system (including township and village enterprises) in rural areas. Rural old-age security administrative organizations had been organized in more than 1,000 counties based on the "Guidelines for Old-age Social Security at the County Level" set up by this ministry. It was reported that the accumulated funds of insurance reached 140 million yuan, covering around 45 million rural people. It can be seen that this is a small amount on a per-capita basis. However, the process is an ongoing one which will improve with time.

Other Ministries

There are seven other ministries involved in the "8-7" Poverty Eradication Program: the Ministry of Forestry, which is responsible for assisting the poverty areas in the development of forest with economic returns; the Ministry of Water Resources which is responsible for solving the water supply and clean drinking water problems for the poor people and large domestic animals; the Ministry of Transportation, for roads; the Ministry of Electricity, for the electricity supply; the Ministry of Labor, for the training of the labor force and organized migration of the labor force from the poor regions to the developed regions; the Ministry of Broadcasting and Television, for the coverage of a wide area in poor regions in broadcasting and television; the Agricultural Bank of China, which will be responsible for increasing the special credit for poverty alleviation with interest subsidy (to increase 1 billion yuan of credit every year from 1994 to 2000); and the Ministry of Communications and Post, which has set the target that more than 50 percent of the villages and all townships of poverty counties will have access to the telephone service before the year 2000.

The above brief introduction to the poverty alleviation program and the responsibility of different ministries will illustrate the special features of government intervention in poverty alleviation in China with its unique size and large population.

II. Policy Framework for Social Security and the Existing System

A. China's Development Strategy — Active Policy of Poverty Alleviation

1. China's development strategies and policies (before 1978)

China had adopted a Soviet model of industrialization and rural collectivization before 1978 but added some ingredients of its own after 1958. With regard to industrialization, the First Five-Tear Plan for National Economic Development was carried out in the period 1953-1957, and an initial basis of industrialization was established through the construction of 694 above-norm projects (including 156 key projects). In the agricultural sector, the Agrarian Reform Law was promulgated in June 1950. After the land reform, the agricultural production system was changed through three steps: the mutual aid teams, the elementary agricultural producers cooperatives and advanced agricultural producers cooperatives.

The new ingredient of China's development strategy is that it had not rapidly followed the rigorous central planning system in development. The

"Great Leap Forward" development policy was launched at the end of 1957, but several cycles of decentralization and recentralization had occurred after 1957. The basis was simultaneous development in all types of industry and agriculture. People's communes were established in 1958 and, although these helped to involve rural labor in industrial activities, they removed much of the incentive to work by taking away private landowning, and an adjustment policy was implemented for three years. Some objective comments were made by foreign experts. "The success of this venture has been very difficult to assess because of other events which were occurring simultaneously.... However, one clear lesson was learnt, in that extensive use of labour-intensive techniques requires trained experts to guide it..."[13]. This experience gained in the period of the "Great Leap Forward" induced the rapid development of town and village enterprises in the reform period.

Industry has been the leading sector of economic development. Its net output grew in real terms at around 10 percent annually in the period 1957-1978. The World Bank estimated that on a per-capita basis (at Chinese prices and official exchange rates) it was close to three times the average for other low-income countries. Special efforts had been made to spread manufacturing into remote regions and rural areas, with much reliance on small plants and older techniques, and in the energy sector, whose technology is generally outmoded, China had developed a technological lead in biogas and small-scale hydropower[14].

In the agricultural sector, gross agricultural output grew in real terms at 2.1 percent annually. This improvement in agricultural production was achieved through the refinement of traditional labor-intensive cultivation techniques; an increase in the rate of multiple cropping up to an average of 1.5 in 1978; extensive irrigation (45 percent of the land was irrigated by that time) — flood control and land improvement were carried out with commune labor; improvement of seed varieties, and increased use of machinery and chemical fertilizers.

Moreover, an egalitarian development strategy is pursued at the regional

13. *MIT Dictionary of Modern Economics*, third edition, David W. Pearce, ed. Macmillan Press Ltd., 1989.
14. World Bank, *China: Socialist Economic Development,* Washington, D.C., 1982.

level, and equity is pursued as the major goal.

The development strategy before 1978 depended mainly on massive mobilization of resources and full employment in the urban sector rather than on improving the efficiency of resource use. The remarkable progress made in industrialization to meet basic needs has not been matched by a demand for a rapid rise in the general level of living standards. The low level of efficiency in Chinese industry is also partly the result of technological isolation from the international environment. In the agricultural sector, especially from 1966 to 1976, growth in productivity was retarded by misguided application of the "grain first" policy, by excessive intervention in agricultural production in decisions from a high level to the communes and the production brigades. There were also political constraints on the cultivation of private plots. The commune system before the economic reform was an experiment to combine the function of public administration and production in the rural areas; the commune is still responsible for social security at the grass-roots level, as shown in Table 11.2. But because of the large size of China, it was not possible to eliminate rural inequality in spite of the egalitarian growth strategy implemented. This rural inequality is primarily due to differences between communities in the quantity per capita, quality and location of land. Poverty thus persists in some areas. This is also the background of the "8-7" Program described in chapter I.

Table II.1. Development of the commune system

Year	Number of communes in rural areas	Number of prodution brigades (ten thousands)	Number of proluction teams (ten thousands)	Number of households in communes (ten thousands)	Number of people in the communes (ten thousands)	Average number of production brigades/communes	Average number of production teams/brigades	Average number of people/production teams
1958	23 630	-	-	12 861	56 017	-	-	-
1965	74 755	61.8	541.2	13 527	59 122	8.7	8.3	109
1975	52 615	67.7	482.6	16 448	77 712	12.9	7.1	161
1979	53 348	69.9	515.4	17 491	80 739	13.1	7.1	157
1981	54 368	71.8	600.4	18 016	81 881	13.2	8.4	136

Source: *Modern Chinese Economic Diclionary,* China's Social Science Press.
Note: The commune system was elininated gradually at the beginning of the 1980s.

Table II.2. Responsibility of rural institutions before the 1980's

Institution	Responsibility
Family	Private plots, distribution of consumption among individuals, government policy explicitly requires children to be responsible for aged parents.
Production team	A small village or traditional neighborhood of a large village. It is responsible for the management of agricultural production, ownership of land, makes most production decisions and is responsible for income distribution among families.
Production brigade	The production brigade is responsible for the delivery of social services to the brigade rural population and production activities requiring large skillled operations. Primary schools are organized at the brigade level; there are usually one or two auxiliary health workers in each production team and a brigade medical station, responsible for sanitation, immunization, vaccination, maternal, child health and elementary curative care.
People's commune	Owns and rents out large machinery; it is responsible for production skills or management not available to the production team. It is also responsible for organizing larger or technically intensive industrial enterprises. Commune and brigade enterprises have become an inportant source of income for the rural setor since 1970. In the period of economic reform,they came to be called "town and village enterprises". The commune is responsible for secondary schools, health clinics, small industries, marketing services and civil adninistration.

2. China's development strategies and policies — The ongoing economic reform and opening to the outside world (after 1978)

Much has been written about China's progress and experience since the launch of economic reform late in 1978.China recorded an average annual GDP growth rate of around 9.5 percent in the 1980's. The successful achievements in economic reform were laid down by the initial conditions set in the past development strategy. In the agricultural sector, where reforms were launched in changing the commune economy of egalitarian income distribution to a household responsibility system, the households can farm the land as they wish and retain whatever they produce after their obligations to the state and to the collective have been met. This greatly increases the incentives for the farmers in production. But the former commune system of socialized agriculture had developed a rural infrastructure and a rural management system to foster social aims such as preventive medicine and attainment of universal education, as well as the diversification of the rural sector. Much has also been written about the growth of rural industry. There are different statistics for the rural industry. Based upon the statistics of the Bureau of Town and Village Enterprises of the Ministry of Agriculture, it was reported that the rural industry had approximately 19 million enterprises employing around 96 million employees in 1991. Based upon the *China Statistical Yearbook 1994*, it was reported that the township-run and village-run industry had around 97 thousand enterprises and employed around 93 million employees in 1993. The successful development in rural industry is due to the agricultural reforms which had created a surplus available for investment and released a pool of labour eager and available for new sources of employment. This has improved the welfare of the rural people in general.

In the industrial sector, China had changed from being an essentially rural peasant economy in 1949 to one in which industry was very significant. The share of industry in national income had grown from 20 percent in 1952 to 49 percent in 1978. The gross value of industrial output was raised from 423.7 billion yuan in 1978 to 5,269.2 billion yuan (at current prices) in 1993; the average annual growth rate is 14.2 percent.

3. Successful experience of economic reform in the transition from a central planned economy to a socialist market economy

China's successful experience of economic reform has been summed up by the World Bank, which indicated that China's reform style has the following features: gradualism and experimentation, partial reform, decentralization, and self-reinforcing reforms. Although China has been successful in its economic reform, such reform is also related to the social security system which was patterned after the Soviet model. Urban workers received a higher social security than the rural people. The number of workers employed in the secondary sector increased from 15.28 million in 1952 to 135.17 million in 1993. In the tertiary sector, the number increased from 18.85 million in 1952 to 127.37 million in 1993. This large increase in the number of workers in the urban sector imposed serious difficulties on the reform of the social security system — a difficult problem in the transition process. This point is made clear in the following paragraphs.

B. Evolution of China's Social Security System

1. Review of the establishment of a social security system (1949-1957)

(a) Social insurance

The social insurance system in China was divided into two categories for employees in different organizations — the enterprises and government organizations or other state institutions (these are called *shi ye dan wei* in Chinese).

The social insurance system for employees in enterprises was called labor insurance. It was announced by the government in February 1951, with concrete protection for sickness, disability, death, maternity and old age in the Labor Insurance Regulation of the People's Republic of China. Based upon this regulation, this social security system would be implemented in mining, railway, transport, communication and postal service enterprises having more than 100 employees. This, was also applicable to state, joint venture and private enterprises and enterprises cooperatives. The regulation was revised in 1953, with two major revisions and amendments. In the first, the scope was extended to enterprises in general, the mining field, capital construction units of transport and state construction companies; and in the second, the retirement pension was increased from 35-60 percent of the wage to 60-80 percent.

In 1957, the Ministry of Health issued the Regulation on Occupational Diseases, which defined the scope of occupational diseases and the content of social welfare.

Social insurance for government organizations or other state institutions was initiated in 1950. It was based upon the supply system[15] established in the old revolutionary base and military base areas, and the specific regulations related to sickness, pension, maternity and death care were formulated gradually. Formal regulations related to health care were issued in June 1952, regulations related to vacation and maternity of workers were issued in April 1955 and 1956, and those related to the pension system of employees working in governmental organizations were issued in December 1955.

---

15. The supply system was established in the Red Army and the old revolutionary base areas. The government is responsible for providing cadres, officers and soldiers with food, and dairy necessities based upon their ranks, but with small differences. The distribution of income is not through the wage system.

China had established the social insurance system by the end of 1957.

(b) Features and components of the Chinese social insurance system before economic reform

Although there were several revisions and amendments after 1957 to various regulations of the social insurance system, the basic features and contents of the system before the reform can be summed up as follows:

(i) The social insurance fund is the sole responsibility of the government and the enterprises, the employees not being responsible for any payment;

(ii) The benefit received from social insurance is calculated on the basis of the standard wages of the wage earners, with proper consideration given to the number of years worked. For example, the age of retirement is 60 for male workers, 50 for female workers, and 55 for women office staff. The pension received is 60-90 percent of the wage, depending on the number of years worked. The retiree still enjoys the benefit of health care from public expenditure;

(iii) The Chinese social insurance system before economic reform covered a wide range of benefits from birth to death; it included benefits for work-related disablement, assistance in case of sickness, subsidies for maternity (the normal maternity leave is 56 days), assistance for disabled people in general, assistance in the case of death and for funerals, benefits for the dependants of employees whose death was work-related, subsidies for funerals of direct relatives supported by the employees, and so on. The enterprises were responsible for all these expenses;

(iv) All medical expenses, including medicine, operations and living costs in the hospital, were the responsibility of the enterprises. Direct relatives supported by the employee could receive half the cost of the health care. For sickness under six months, the employee could receive 60-100 percent of the wage, depending on the number of years worked of the employee. From 40 to 80 percent of the wages would be paid for sickness over six months.

(c) Social assistance

The social assistance in rural areas includes assistance in the case of natural disasters, households of "five guarantees" and also assistance for the rural poor. This is the responsibility of the Ministry of Civil Affairs. The guidelines and organization of social assistance in rural areas were laid down

Table II.3. Composition of labor insurance and welfare benefits for state units
(Billion yuan)

	1978	1979	1980	1981	1982	1983	1984	1985	1986	1987
Retired and disabled staff and workers										
Pension	-	-	-	-	-	-	-	-	11.18	13.60
Medical care	-	-	-	-	-	-	-	-	1.59	2.34
Welfare benefit	-	-	-	-	-	-	-	-	3.00	3.70
Total	1.41	2.61	4.01	5.00	5.89	7.08	3.16	11.55	15.77	19.64
Active staff and workers										
Funeral expenses and assistance to survivors	0.26	0.37	0.38	0.39	0.40	0.44	0.48	0.53	0.65	0.35
Medical care	2.73	3.17	3.64	3.90	4.44	5.00	5.54	0.46	8.49	8.42
Hardship allowances	0.60	0.68	0.63	0.60	0.60	0.63	0.66	0.66	0.61	0.64
Agriculture sideline production subsidies	0.12	0.12	0.10	0.08	0.08	0.08	0.09	0.10	-	-
Culture activities and recreation expenses	0.26	0.30	0.32	0.29	0.32	0.33	0.45	0.49	0.35	0.59
Public welfare subsidies	0.44	0.57	0.66	0.74	0.83	1.02	1.45	1.64	1.63	1.97
Welfare facilities subsidies	0.43	0.61	0.78	0.90	1.05	1.13	1.48	1.65	1.98	2.29
Other welfare benefits										
Commute subsidies	-	-	0.49	0.53	0.59	0.63	0.70	0.84	0.97	1.09
Family planning subsidies	-	-	0.21	0.27	0.40	0.55	0.55	0.61	-	0.80
Subtotal	0.44	0.78	1.08	1.34	1.77	2.24	2.73	3.91	6.22	7.27
Total	5.28	6.60	7.59	8.24	9.49	10.87	12.88	15.44	20.13	21.53
Grand total of all labor insurance and welfare benefits	6.69	9.21	11.60	13.24	15.38	17.95	21.04	26.99	35.90	41.18
(As share of total)										
Retired and disabled staff and workers										
Pension	-	-	-	-	-	-	-	-	31.1	33.0
Medical care	-	-	-	-	-	-	-	-	4.4	5.7
Welfare benefit	-	-	-	-	-	-	-	-	8.4	9.0
Total	21.1	28.3	34.6	37.8	38.3	39.4	38.8	42.8	43.9	47.7
Active staff and workers										
Funeral expenses and assistance to survivors	3.9	4.0	3.3	2.9	2.6	2.5	2.3	2.0	1.8	0.8
Medical care	40.8	34.4	31.4	29.5	28.9	27.9	29.3	23.9	23.6	20.4
Hardship allowances	9.0	7.4	5.4	4.5	3.9	3.5	3.1	2.4	1.7	1.6
Agriculture sideline production subsidies	1.8	1.3	0.9	0.6	0.5	0.4	0.4	0.4	-	-
Culture activities and recreation expenses	3.9	3.3	2.8	2.2	2.1	1.8	2.1	1.8	1.5	1.4
Public welfare subsidies	6.6	6.2	5.7	5.6	5.4	5.7	6.9	6.1	4.5	4.8
Welfare facilities subsidies	6.4	6.6	6.7	6.8	6.8	6.3	7.0	6.1	5.5	5.6
Other welfare benefits										
Commute subsidies	-	-	4.2	4..0	3.8	3.5	3.3	3.1	2.7	2.6
Family planning subsidies	-	-	1.8	2.0	2.6	3.1	2.6	2.3	-	1.9
Subtotal	6.6	8.5	9.3	10.1	11.5	12.5	13.0	14.5	17.3	17.7
Total	78.9	71.7	65.4	52.2	61.7	60.6	61.2	57.2	56.1	52.3
Grand total of all labor insurance and welfare benefits	100.0	100.0	100.0	100.0	100.0	100.0	100.0	100.0	100.0	100.0

Source: *Statistical Material on Labor and Wages, China,* p. 191; and *Statistical Yearbook of China, 1987 and 1988,*China Satistical Pubishing House.

Note: State units refer to enterprises, governments, parties, and non-profit making organizations.

in 1952 and 1951 respectively in the official documents of the State Council.

Social assistance was also implemented for the urban poor with living standards lower than the minimum. The government issued a document to define the scope, standard and financial resources of social assistance for urban poverty.

Generally, this system of social assistance has been changed several times in scope and standards. It is broadly classified into two categories: permanent assistance and temporary assistance. These are counted on a perhead basis. For the assistance of "households of 'five guarantees'," it is also classified into concentrated type and distributed type. Table 11.4 presents some ideas for these.

Table II.4. Amount of social assistance

Year	Amount in 100 million yuan	Within which; city, township	Within which; rural	Within which; assistance for natural disasters
1985	22.46	8.62	12.75	9.58
1986	23.23	7.97	14.06	-
1987	22.66	8.35	13.05	9.87
1988	26.82	10.65	14.81	-
1989	28.57	11.16	15.95	-
1990	29.74	11.56	16.66	13.07

Source: *Data on China Social Development,* China Statistical Publishing House, 1992.

(d) Social welfare

The government had issued the Act of Trade Union of the People's Republic of China in 1950 to clarify the responsibility of the trade union for improving the physical and cultural life of the workers and establishing welfare facilities. In 1954, the All-China Federation of Trade Unions organized a working conference on kindergartens of important cities. A document for the development of kindergartens was issued jointly by the Ministry of Education, the Ministry of Health and the Ministry of Internal Affairs. In 1957, the State Council issued "Some Guidelines Related to the Life of Employees" which had set up concrete regulations related to housing, transport to the workplace, supply of necessities and assistance for employees in difficulties.This practice has continued into later periods.

(e) Assistance for family members of martyrs and the military

This kind of assistance was initiated early in the period of revolution. Five regulations were issued by the government in December 1950, as follows: Tentative Regulation for Benefits for the Family Members of Martyrs and the Military, Tentative Regulations for Benefits for the Disabled Military People, Tentative Regulations for the Revolutionary, Military, Sacrificed or Dead, the Regulations for Benefits for Disabled Workers, and the Tentative

Table II.5. Basic statistics on major social welfare relief funds

Item	1985	1990	1992	1993
National total	218 349.0	426 771.9	468634.8	572 589
Government funds	71 097.0	202 445.8	226 718.1	267 468
Collective funds	147 252.0	224 316.1	255 916.7	305 121
Funds for family members of				
martyrs and disabled veterans	106 982.6	242 732.1	270 434.8	301 728
Government funds	35 327.6	141 163.1	153 861.9	170 173
Collective funds	71 655.0	101 569.0	116 572.9	131 555
Funds for poor households	28 688.3	38 743.7	38 312.9	53 222
Government funds	11 852.6	18 649.5	18 973.9	21 616
Collective funds	16 862.7	20 094.2	19 339.0	31 606
Funds for orphans, disabled,				
elderly and young persons				
in society	55 195.5	85 051.5	98 382.1	110 587
Government funds	6 692.9	11 850.7	14 315.2	16 334
Collective funds	48 502.6	73 200.8	84 066.9	94 253
Funds for urban and rural				
welfare Homes of all types	27 482.6	60 244.6	75 505.0	107 052
Homes for disabled veterans	3 039.7	6 212.7	8 499.8	9 858
Government funds	2 910.7	5 920.0	8 050.2	9 345
Collective funds	129.0	292.7	449.6	513
Social welfare homes	24 442.9	54 031.9	67 005.2	97 194
Government funds	14 340.2	24 872.5	31 516.9	50 000
Collective funds	10 102.7	29 159.4	35 488.3	47 194

Source: *China Statistical Yearbook 1994,* China Statistical Publishing House.

Table II.6. Persons receiving subsidies or relief funds

Item	1985	1990	1992	1993
Persons in rural poor households receiving relief funds	3 800.4	2 631.7	2 432.7	2 886.9
Persons in rural households receiving "five guarantees"	274.7	250.6	231.8	244.7
Persons receiving periodical and fixed government relief funds	22.6	21.8	18.6	14.2
Persons receiving collective subsidies	197.6	173.3	154.3	202.5
Persons in urban poor households receiving relief funds and subsidies	376.9	632.7	908.0	200.4
Laid-off, retired, elderly and disabled staff and workers receiving relief funds	53.4	56.4	54.6	54.6
Persons receiving 40 percent of their original wages	24.5	25.1	24.8	24.5
Persons receiving periodical and fixed government relief funds	28.9	31.3	29.8	30.1
Number of households in the Poor Household Support Program	857.0	755.8	720.9	701.9
Households leaving the Poor Household Support Program	214.2	261.4	212.9	186.1

Source: *China Statistical Yearbook 1994,* China Statistical Publishing House.

Regulations for Benefits for Disabled Civil Workers and Civil Soldiers. These five regulations set up the basic pattern of system of assistance, although the level changed from time to time.

2. Background of social security reform

Social security reform is a part of China's economic reform, and is also related to labor market reform. Before the launch of economic reform, China had a lifetime employment system and full employment system in urban areas. These resulted in low economic efficiency in the enterprises. In 1982, as part of urban economic reform, the government encouraged the employment of workers under contract. In 1986, the central government regulations required that all new workers be hired under the labor contract system. There is also need for reform of the labor insurance system, as the old system (or social security system in the narrow sense) has the following major problems:

(a) The old social insurance system gives the responsibility mainly to the state and the enterprises. Their financial burden has increased rapidly owing to the ageing of the population and the increase in the number of retirees. For example, the amount for pensions was 6.91 billion yuan for the state enterprises in 1978. It reached 138.6 billion yuan in 1993. This can hardly be borne by the enterprises;

(b) The traditional social security system had narrow coverage. The pension and health-care insurance systems were implemented only in the state-owned enterprises and large collective enterprises in cities and townships. The "waiting for employment" system was only applicable to employees of state-owned enterprises. Pension, health care, and the "waiting for employment" system were not implemented in joint ventures, joint cooperatives, private and individually operated enterprises or for people in rural areas;

Table II.7. Labor insurance and welfare funds of staff and workers

Year	Total Funds	State-owned units	Paid by employer units	Paid by the Civil Adminis-tration Depart-ments	Urban collective-owned units	Other ownership units	Total funds as percentage of total wages
1978	78.1	69.1	66.9	2.2	9.0	-	13.7
1980	136.1	119.3	116.0	3.3	17.1	-	17.7
1983	212.5	182.7	179.5	3.2	29.8	-	22.7
1984	257.7	213.4	210.4	3.0	43.4	0.9	22.7
1985	331.6	273.6	269.9	3.7	56.8	1.2	24.0
1986	420.1	343.9	340.0	3.9	74.1	2.1	25.3
1987	508.7	415.9	411.8	4.1	89.8	3.0	27.0
1988	653.1	537.6	533.4	4.2	110.8	4.7	28.2
1989	768.0	635.5	628.0	7.5	126.5	6.0	29.3
1990	937.9	777.3	770.1	7.2	152.9	7.7	31.8
1991	1 094.7	912.5	904.9	7.6	171.8	10.4	32.9
1992	1 309.5	1 095.8	1 086.6	9.2	198.8	14.9	33.2
1993	1 670.2	1 386.5	1 374.5	12.0	238.6	45.1	34.0

Source: *China Statistical Yearbook 1994,* China Statistical Pulishing House.

(c) There was fragmentation in the administrative organization: a unified management system had not been established in the social security system. It can be seen from the previous discussion that many ministries are involved in the management of the system. The current social security management system is separated according to the type of security and objective and can generally be divided into four parts:

(i)   The social insurance and social welfare of employees in enterprises of townships and cities are managed comprehensively by the department of labor at various levels of government;

(ii) The labor department of government at different levels is responsible for the medical insurance of workers. "Public medical care offices" set up at different levels of government are responsible for the health care of employees in governmental organizations and other state institutions;

(iii) Types of social insurance other than health care of the employees working in government and other state institutions are administered by the personnel departments at different levels of government; the organizational-department of the Party is also responsible for part of this administrative work;

(iv) Urban and rural social security assistance, social benefits and specific social welfare are managed comprehensively by the department of civil affairs at different levels of government.

3. Current state of reform of the social security system

The government started the reform of the pension system in 1984. The Ministry of Labor has been promoting resource pooling for permanent workers' retirement to ease the uneven burden of retirement expenditure on enterprises. In 1991, the State Council issued the document "Decision on the Reform of Pension and Insurance System for Enterprise Employees". In 1995, it issued a further document, "Notice for Deepening the Pension Insurance System Reform of City and Township Enterprises". The major points in these are the following.

The target of the reform is to establish by the year 2000 a pension and insurance system that will cover all laborers in cities and townships, which is multi-channel in financial resources and multi-level in protection, with the combination of social pooling and individual contribution. The management and service should be taken care of by the society as a whole. There are four principles in the reform of the social security system. First, the level of protection should be consistent with the level of economic and social development, and should also be adapted to the support capability of the various parties concerned. Second, social mutual assistance should also be combined with self-protection and equity with efficiency. Third, there must be a unified policy and legalized management. And fourth, administrative management should be separated from the operation of insurance funds.

The old-age insurance system will be extended to employees in townships, and foreign-funded and private enterprises (originally, the system covered state enterprise staff only).

The basic old-age insurance funds will be shared by both the enterprises and the employees. Reform will be implemented to promote the personal income explicitly in the form of wages[16]. The personal share will be increased gradually based upon the decision of the governments of provinces, autonomous regions and municipalities directly under the leadership of the central government. This decision is based upon the wage increase at the local level.

The basic old-age insurance fund is implemented based upon a combination of social pooling and personal account. This basic old-age insurance system is implemented compulsorily through legislation. In the meantime, supplementary old-age insurance established by enterprises and personal saving old-age insurance are also encouraged.

Explanation of the reform of the pension system

Some explanation is necessary to supplement the above summary of government documents. So far, nearly 2,000 cities and counties have extended this reformed old-age pension system to employees in collective-owned enterprises, and around 1,000 to those of non-publicly-owned enterprises. Currently, more than 60 million employees are handing in

---

16. Formerly, China had a low wage system. But there were many subsidies from the government, such as low house rent, low cost on public utilities, and nearly all large and medium enterprises had established kindergartens or even schools, hospitals, etc.

2-3 percent of their wages as insurance funds, and the proportion contributed by individual employees will be increased by one percentage point every two years. The aim is to have employees contribute half of the insurance funds.

This old-age insurance will connect the mutual assistance funds with individual accounts. All fees paid by employees and part of the fees paid by enterprises will go into the employees' individual accounts. Those earning more will hand in more money and receive correspondingly more after retirement. Another part of the money will be handed in on the basis of the average salary level of the region. All employees in the region will receive the same treatment.

Unemployment insurance

The unemployment insurance provisions were introduced in 1986. The main features are shown in the box. In 1993, the State Council issued "Regulations on Employees of the State-owned Enterprises Waiting for Employment"[17]; an initial "waiting for employment" system has been established.

Other reforms of the social security system

It has been mentioned previously that Chinese employees in the urban sector enjoy a full range of security from birth to death. This is not sustainable for a developing country like China. Therefore, reform of the health-care system is under way and tried out. Jiujiang Municipality in Jiangxi Province, Zhenjiang Municipality in Jiangsu Province have been assigned by the central government to carry out the health-care system reform developed by the Ministry of Labor in 1992.

With regard to social security for work-related disability, the system has lasted for more than 40 years without revision. A new system was tried in Guangdong, Fujian, Hainan and Jilin provinces. The Ministry of Labor had issued the draft of "Regulations on Insurance for Disabled Workers of Enterprises". This draft is under review and revision. A social pooling fund for maternity benefits is also tried out.

---

17. Generally, the Chinese do not use the term "unemployment" in statistics or official documents. Academically, "waiting for employment" has the same implications as "unemployment".

Main features of unemployment insurance, 1986

Eligibility

    (a) Workers of bankrupt enterprises

    (b) Workers made redundant by near-bankrupt enterprises during a process of reorgani-
        zation

    (c) Contract workers on expiration or cancellation of contract

    (d) Workers dismissed for disciplinary reasons

Relief allowance

    Five or more years of service: up to 24 months, of which for the first 12 months 60-75
    percent of the standard wage is received; for the rest 12 months, 50 percent is received
    Less than 5 years of service: up 12 months, 60-75 percent of the standard wage is
    received (standard wage = worker's average monthly standard wage over two years
    before leaving the enterprise)

Other benefits for those in categories (a) and (b)

    Medical expenses, funeral and burial subsidies for workers and immediate families,
    retirement pensions (where no centralized retirement pension plan exists), and early
    retirement pensions for those less than five years from retirement age

Other benefits for those in categories (c) and (d)

    Medical subsidies

Ineligibility

    Where twice refused for no legitimate reasons to accept jobs recommended by relevant
    agencies

Funding

    Enterprises contribute 1 percent of the standard wage bill; in addition, financed by
    interest paid by banks on unemployment insurance funds and local government subsi-
    dies

Administration

    Administered by local labor service companies

The employees have been paying very low rent for housing (formerly, only 1-2 percent of the average wage). This is also undergoing reform.

4. Role of non-governmental organizations

It can be seen from the above discussion that domestic NGOs are not well developed in a centrally planned economy. Therefore, this part of the contribution to social security is nearly non-existent. Many international NGOs have been active in China, but their assistance represents less than 1 percent of total assistance.

5. Independent evaluations of the social security scheme by international organizations

There are many recent studies on the schemes of China. The study of two major agencies are described briefly below.

Evaluations by the World Bank

(a) Quotation from the World Bank country study, "China: Strategies for Reducing Poverty in the 1990s"

Poverty alleviation and social security are closely related to the development policy, as can be seen from the following evaluations:

Incidence of Absolute Poverty.   Broad participation in strong rural economic growth brought about a tremendous reduction in absolute poverty in China during the period 1978-1985. World Bank estimates show the number of absolute poor to have declined from roughly 270 million in 1978 to 97 million in 1985, or from about one third to less than one tenth of the total population. However, no further reductions in poverty were achieved during the second half of the 1980s.... The stagnation of poverty during 1985-1990, which contrasts the strong overall economic growth of those years, is consistent with the modest observed increase of rural income disparity.

... Since virtually all of China's rural population received land-use rights as part of the production responsibility system during the early 1980s, there are few if any landless labourers. Instead, the majority of the rural poor are now concentrated in resource-deficient areas.

... Steady adoption of a range of economic reforms is expected to sustain overall growth of the Chinese economy at about 7 percent per annum during of 1990s.... growth alone would not be sufficient to achieve desired levels of poverty reduction. Reducing poverty requires that economic growth be coupled with expanded and new social service and rural development programmes directed to the poor.

Reform of state-owned enterprise, another priority for the 1990s with important implications for the poor, could be associated with some increase in unemployment in cities where there is a large concentration of state enterprises. However, it should be possible to maintain the welfare of the urban population ... by (i) shirting welfare functions from urban enterprises to specialized government agencies and (ii) making adequate provision, in advance, for unemployment insurance...[18]

(b) Summary of comments derived from the World Bank study, "China: Reforming Social Security in a Socialist Economy"[19]

China's social security systems cover a wide range of benefits. For workers in the urban formal sector, these benefits are provided almost entirely by enterprises, which are thus responsible for nearly all their employees' living, needs throughout their lifetime. Three developments during the 1980's have given rise to the need to reform China's enterprise-based social security system instituted in the early 1950s. First, with greater enterprise autonomy, the state-owned enterprises shared a heavy financial and social burden while existing social security provisions have not allowed for the needs of the individual or non-state-run enterprises that have sprung up in recent years. Second, a key element of enterprise reform is to separate enterprise and government budgets. The payment of social security benefits through grants from the government to enterprises compromises their financial autonomy seriously. Third, because the benefits are provided almost entirely by enterprises, and beneficiaries do not contribute to them, this system cannot be sustainable.

The following is extracted from a paper entitled "Economic Transition on the Other Side of the Wall: China".[20]

Evaluation by overseas experts

The Chinese social security system has two central features. First, it consists of two separate subsystems, urban and rural, with different organization and benefits. Second, the urban system is segmented according to the ownership status of the employment unit. Compared to cities, social security provision in rural areas is sparse and highly variable. In rural areas it is primarily meant to relieve extreme poverty and is narrowly targeted. In sum, rural social security provisions rest on the increasingly questionable assumption that the rural population is self-employed and is able to insure itself against deprivation, barring rare cases.

The Chinese social security system has the problem of segmentation, that is,

---

18. World Bank, *China: Strategies for Reducing Poverty in the 1990's,* Washington DC, 1990. pp.ix.x and xiii
19. ibid.
20. By Professor A. Hussain and N. Stern of the London School of Economics.

the administrative distinction between the urban and the rural population which is increasingly discrepant with the division between the wage-employed and the self-employed labor force. Aside from segmentation, the Chinese social security system is characterized by three inter linked features: first, the absence of a specialized administration, and fragmented management; second, a wide variation in benefits within the same scheme in some cases; and third, highly decentralized financing.

6. Conclusion

The above independent evaluation of the schemes, by the World Bank and experts abroad, can illustrate and explain further the discussions presented in the present paper. It can also serve as a brief evaluation of the prevailing system in China — its strengths, shortcomings and gaps in the coverage of disadvantaged groups and security needs.

III. Financing of Social Security

A. Public expenditure on social security

It has been discussed in previous chapters that the expenditure on social security is very much decentralized. The urban sector has a high share of the benefits of social security, but the financial resources come mainly from the enterprises. While, in the rural areas, there are official statistics on disaster assistance and expenditure on "households of five guarantees", there are generally no exact data on expenditure in the commune or brigade. Therefore, the source of financing of the social security of China before the economic reform is generally the role of central government and local governments. Financing from state enterprises may be said to be from the government, because the state-owned enterprises have to submit nearly all its profits to the central government by deduction of expenditure on social security. This is also the cause of the loss of a fair part of state-owned enterprises. There was no contribution by beneficiaries before the economic reform. It was also explained in section B.6 above that the contribution from the beneficiaries (the employees) represented only 2-3 percent of their wages. The contribution by NGOs was also non-existent before the economic reform, and is accounted less than 1 percent of the total assistance. Public expenditure from the state budget is shown in Table III. 1.

Table III.1. Expenditure on social benefits and social welfare from the state fiscal budget

100 mil. Yuan

Year	Total	Expen- diture on benefits	Expen- diture on retirees	Assistance for social welfare	Assistance for natural disasters	Others
1952	2.95	1.23	-	0.66	1.06	-
1962	8.14	1.73	-	2.39	4.02	-
1978	18.91	2.93	2.34	4.62	9.02	-
1980	20.31	4.51	3.41	5.36	7.03	-
1982	21.43	4.86	3.48	5.45	7.64	-
1983	24.04	5.39	3.62	6.58	8.45	-
1984	25.16	6.20	3.64	7.92	7.40	-
1985	31.15	7.13	4.88	7.71	10.25	1.18
1986	35.58	8.77	5.77	8.69	10.64	1.71
1987	37.40	9.87	6.68	9.04	9.91	1.90
1988	41.77	11.32	7.59	9.73	10.64	2.49
1989	49.60	14.43	8.56	10.80	12.88	2.93
1990	55.04	16.61	9.60	12.07	13.33	3.43
1991	67.32	17.21	10.32	13.18	22.51	4.10
1992	66.45	-	-	-	-	-
1993	75.27	-	-	-	-	-

Source: *China's Fiscal Statistics Yearbook, 1994*, China Fiscal Publishing House.

B. Data on social security

Table III.2-5 shows the composition of social security and amounts of social welfare. The major source is the government and the enterprises. The tables further illustrate the necessity for reform of the social security system in China.

Table III.2. Total amount of labor insurance (100 nillion yuan)

Year	Total amount of national labor insurance			
	Total	Living expenses for retirees of those who have left their jobs	Health care	Benefits related to funerals
1985	229.0	145.6	78.1	5.3
1986	278.2	169.1	102.7	6.4
1987	342.6	204.3	131.0	7.3
1988	461.5	270.2	182.1	9.2
1989	549.2	313.3	224.4	11.5
1990	672.1	388.6	268.6	14.9

Source: *China Statistical Yearbook 1994*, China Statistical Publishing House.

Table III.3. Total amount of labor insurance of employees of state-owned enterprises

Year	Total (100 million yuan)	Within which; health care	Benefits related to funerals	Average medical cost (yuan/capita)
1985	67.6	64.6	3.0	71.9
1986	72.4	69.0	3.4	75.7
1987	87.7	84.2	3.5	89.2
1988	117.1	112.9	4.2	114.1
1989	140.5	135.2	5.3	135.4
1990	170.2	163.7	6.5	160.8

Source: *China: Reference Material for Social Development, 1992,* China Statistical Publishing House.

Table III.4. Average living expenses of retirees and people who have left their jobs

Year	Total mumber of retirees and people who left their jobs, year-end (ten thousands)				Total amount of living expense of retirees and people who left their jobs (100 million yuan)				Average living expense per capita (yuan)			
	Total	State-owned enterprises	Other Collective enterprises		Total	State-owned enterprises	Collective	Other owner-ship	Total	State-owned enterprises	Collective	Other owner-ship
1985	1 637	1 165	465	5	145.6	116.1	29.1	0.4	935	1 043	662	839
1986	1 805	1 303	496	6	169.1	137.5	31.0	0.6	983	1 114	643	1 000
1987	1 968	1 424	538	6	204.3	168.2	35.3	0.8	1 083	1 233	683	1 333
1988	2 120	1 544	538	8	270.2	215.6	53.1	1.5	1 322	1 453	960	1 875
1989	2 201	1 629	562	10	313.3	252.8	59.1	1.4	1 450	1 593	1 046	1 556
1990	2 301	1 724	566	11	388.6	313.3	73.6	1.7	1 726	1 868	1 305	1 619

Source: *China: Reference Material for Social Dvelopment, 1992,* China Statistical Publishing House.

Table III.5. Cost of social welfare

Year	Cost of social welfare (100 million yuan)	Within which: welfare expenses for government organizations, enterprises
1985	125.3	77.9
1986	169.9	133.3
1987	200.4	152.3
1988	250.2	195.2
1989	284.9	223.6
1990	374.6	294.1

Source: *China: Reference Material for Social Development, 1992,* China Statistical Publishing House.

C. Foreign assistance for poverty alleviation

Foreign assistance for poverty alleviation from outside donors can be classified into two types. The first type has provided grant and loan assistance to support China's long-term development process. Total concessional aid amounted to US$2 billion in 1988 and US$2.2 billion in 1989. Total World Bank lending to China over the period 1981-1991 amounted to US$10 billion. Other agencies within the United Nations system provided another US$10 billion over the same period. Bilateral assistance totalled US$5.8 billion during the period 1985-1990.

There are also International Fund for Agricultural Development (IFAD) and World Food Program (WFP) programs which are directed to poverty concerns. Since its lending program to China began in 1984, IFAD has provided US$136 million in support of six projects targeted at poor households. WFP also targets its assistance at low-income households in resource-poor counties; between 1985 and 1990, it approved 50 development projects and two emergency operations totalling US$5,851 million. UNDP, in its third country program, provided resources of US$189 million over the period 1991-1995.

D. Analysis of the macroeconomic implications of financing social security

A unique system of financing the social security system existed prior to the launch of social security system reform in the mid-1980's. Because the government and the enterprises are responsible for nearly the whole expenditure on social security, and the state-owned enterprises are also directly related to the government, a loss in the enterprise due in part to the heavy financial burden of expenditure on social security means no profit to the government — and no subsidy will be provided by the government. Therefore, this type of financing of social security is not only a cause of the low efficiency of state-owned enterprises but has imposed serious constraints on the fiscal capability of the government in exercising macroeconomic control or to allocate the budget expenditure properly. This aspect shows the serious difficulty of a former centrally planned economy following the Soviet model, especially in view of the rapid process of industrialization and large expansion of the labor sector in urban areas. Although this will contribute to growth in the medium term, <u>difficulties will emerge in the long term owing to the large number of elderly workers</u>.

One major lesson from Chinese or international experience has been summed up in section B of the introduction: a flexible approach should be maintained for the social security system. For example, the old-age pension system in the United States of America dates from the 1935 Social Security Act, and the United Kingdom system from the post-Second World War period. In recent years the social security system has come into trouble in both western Europe and the United States because of the mounting costs and the heavy burden on the fiscal aspect of the government owing to state-provided social security.

E. Sources of financing social security and the options available

The options for sources of financing social security depend upon the stage of development and cultural background. For example, in an underdeveloped economy of a family-based agro-society, there may be no need to finance social security for old age. But a contribution from the family base to take care of emergencies and mutual assistance may be helpful. Still, there is the role of the community organized at the local level to take care of health, education, and mutual assistance. If the government has the fiscal capability, it is its role to finance the assistance of disasters which cannot be handled by the community in general.

For a country under industrialization, a provident fund scheme with contributions from both the employers and employees may be a good solution. If this scheme is managed properly, the fund can also be used for growth. In the reform of the social security system, China sent several delegations abroad to learn about international experience in social security. The social provident scheme of Singapore is advocated generally by officials and people in the academic field.

It is also learned from international experience that the sources of financing social security can be divided into three categories:

(1) If the whole population is to be focused as the object of social security and social assistance, then the source of financing is generally from fiscal expenditure of the state or local governments;

(2) If the wage earner is the major object of social insurance, then the

source of financing is insurance fees;

(3) The source of financing of provident funds adopted by some developing countries is the contribution of employees and enterprises.

The current old-age insurance system of China is to follow the model of the providen fund scheme. The income from operation of the old-age fund will receive exemption from tax. But an in-depth study is necessary for the social security system in China, because its unique feature of huge population and huge number of employees.

IV. Summary of Conclusions and Future Strategies

A. Summary of main conclusions

The social security system must be considered an integral part of the development strategy.

1. The social security system is a part of social goals: government intervention is necessary to correct "market failure"

Industrialization and economic development have been the major tasks focused upon by most of the developing countries since the 1950's. But the social security system has not been well studied or designed as an integral process of economic development in general. Social systems, economic systems, and science and technology systems are systems at the hierarchical level but are mutually interactive. The purpose of the development of science and technology is for economic developments and that of economic development is achieving a proper social goal. Economic development and reform, with market orientation, must recognize the problem of "market failure". Social security and poverty are areas of "market failure." Active intervention should be undertaken by the government to establish a social security system and achieve poverty alleviation.

2. Growth and equity should be properly balanced

A balanced and coordinated strategy on social economic and technological development is necessary. China paid considerable attention to the social goal, exceeding its economic capability during the process of industrialization before the economic reform, which resulted in low economic efficiency and a heavy burden on enterprises. Therefore, the social security system should be designed and implemented adapted appropriately to the stage of development.

3. Order of priority for implementation should be established

It can be seen from Figure I that there are many stages in a social security system. The design and implementation of a social security scheme should proceed in stages. Social assistance and social preference should come first, followed by social insurance (social security in the narrow sense) and finally social welfare in general.

4. Population policy — a key factor

The population problem is an essential element in effecting a social security system, and must be basic in the national development strategy. Failure to recognize this aspect will result in serious difficulties in long-term development. China had a baby boom in the 1960's, and the family planning system implemented in the late 1970's cannot modify the effect of that boom in the past — it can only attempt to improve the situation for the future. A carefully designed family planning system is needed which takes into account the long-term effects of the age structure of the active labor force and the number of the elderly. Although China has been successful in general in family planning, in the long term to the next century, the share of the active labor force will be reduced; the active labor force has to support both the old and the young generations if a proper social security system cannot be implemented.

B. Key elements of a strategy for enhancing social security

In the success and failure experience of China in the social security system, there are two major elements:

(a) An active social security policy, rather than a passive social security policy is important

An active social security policy has the following implications:

(i) A sound economic development policy to promote the economic growth which will enhance the social security is one important lesson from the Chinese experience. The successful agricultural sector reform implemented in the late 1970's reduced the absolute poor from 270 million in 1978 to 97 million in 1985. This active social security policy is also implemented in the

Eighth Five-Year Plan and the "8-7" Poverty Alleviation Program which is characterized by promotion of the production activity of the poor rather than passive assistance, to use the Chinese term, that is, try to change the poverty alleviation process from injection of blood to creation of blood;

(ii) The social security system should not provide over-protection, which may induce a disincentive to hard work. In the meantime, the beneficiary of the social security system must contribute a fair part of the social security system fund himself or herself. The failure of the lifetime employment system in China had a bad effect on economic efficiency as a whole. The high degree of waste in the health-care system in China is another evidence of the failure of over-protection on the part of the government with almost no contribution on the part of the beneficiary.

(b) The social security system in rural areas has not been properly designed and implemented since the launch of economic reform: it is still in the period of exploration and experimentation. Traditional family-based security should not be disturbed abruptly in the process of industrialization, and community-based mutual assistance should be encouraged.

C. Future trends

Future trends will be discussed in two aspects: those in China and those in the world:

(1) For the future, the social security system in China will be promoted. The government target is to extend the section of the population covered by the old-age pension system. The employees in townships and in foreign-funded and private enterprises will also be covered gradually. The level of contributions by the employees will also be raised, that is, a pattern of provident fund schemes will be followed. Other categories of social security will also be implemented. A commercial insurance system will be developed. But it must be developed based upon law with proper supervision, given the current weakness in shortage of qualified financial and managerial personnel. The social security system in the rural areas will also be implemented gradually through further rural industrialization and further encouragement of the development of town and village enterprises;

(2) With regard to future trends of the social security system in the world, it is evident that there is reform of the social security system in the developed

economies with a trend towards reducing the financial burden of the government resulting from a welfare state. In the developing economies social security systems will be established since most of them have been successful in the industrialization process and have rid themselves of the stage of Maslor's theory of motivation. But a framework of analysis to design and implement the social security system should be established based upon the study of papers and other sources of information:

(a) A dynamic social security system should be considered with the benefits it provides, the conditions attached to the receipt of benefits, and the part of the population covered. The part covered should start from the most disadvantaged section.

(b) A proper system of organization should be set up to collect the data and information needed for the proper operation of the schemes.

(c) With regard to proper sources of financing, generally speaking, in the initial stage there must be government involvement in financing, and the contribution of the beneficiaries should be increased gradually based upon increase in income.

(d) A proper economic and social development policy will be a precondition for a successful social security system.

(e) Economic incentives

These are the major conclusions derived from the experience of China on a social security system. It is to be expected that a better social security system can evolve in a more prosperous global society.

REFERENCES

Compilation of Historical Statistics of Provinces, Autonomous Regions and Municipalities Directly under the Central Government, 1949-1989, China Statistical Publishing House, 1990.

China: Reference Material for Social Development, China Statistical Publishing House, 1992.

Office of the Leading Group of Economic Development in Poor Areas under the State Council: *Outline of Economic Development in China's Poor*

Areas, Agricultural Publishing House, 1989.

Task Force of Ministry of Labor, *Establishment and Perfection of China Social Security System*, Economic Publishing House, 1994.

China Statistical Yearbook 1981, China Statistical Publishing House.

China Statistical Yearbook 1986, China Statistical Publishing House.

China Statistical Yearbook 1994, China Statistical Publishing House.

Hussain, A. "Reform of the Chinese Social Security System", London School of Economics, 1993.

World Bank, *China: Strategies for Reducing Poverty in the 1990s*, Washington, D.C., 1992.

China: Socialist Economic Development, Washington, DC, 1982.

ANNEX TABLES

A.1. China's achievement in poverty alleviation

	1978	1985	1990
Total population (million)	963	1 059	1 143
Urban	172 (17.9%)	251 (23.7%)	302 (26.4%)
Rural	790 (82.1%)	808 (76.3%)	841 (73.6%)
Average per-capita income (1978 yuan)			
Urban	-	557	685
Rural	134	324	319
Poverty line (yuan/year)			
Urban	-	215	319
Rural	98	190	275
Incidence of poverty (million)			
Total	270 (28.0%)	97 (9.2%)	98 (8.6%)
Urban	10 (4.4%)	1 (0.4%)	1 (0.4%)
Rural	260 (33.0%)	96 (11.9%)	97 (11.5%)
Gini coefficient			
Rural	-	0.28	0.29
Poverty gap (index)			
Rural	-	2.1	2.5

A.2. National poverty line and incidence

	1978	1980	1981	1982	1983	1984	1985	1 986	1987	1988	1989	1990
Poverty line (yuan)												
Urban	-	-	171	169	178	190	215	226	247	289	304	321
Rural (planned)	98	134	158	167	175	179	190	199	210	231	262	275
Rural (procurement)	99	135	160	170	175	178	193	206	222	249	292	301
Poverty line index												
Urban (1985=100)	-	-	80	79	83	88	100	105	115	134	141	149
Rural (planned)	52	71	83	88	92	94	100	105	111	122	138	145
Rural (procurement)	51	72	83	88	91	92	100	107	115	129	151	156
Retail price index												
Urban (1985 = 100)	74	81	84	85	87	89	100	107	117	142	164	165
Rural (1985 = 100)	81	86	88	90	91	93	100	105	112	131	155	160
Procurement price index												
Grain (1985 = 100)	63	87	92	94	94	95	100	112	122	135	180	172
Absolute poverty (percentage of households)												
Urban	-	-	1.5	0.6	0.5	0.2	0.2	0.1	0.2	0.2	0.2	0.3
Rural (planned)	32.8	26.8	23.4	16.3	14.0	10.0	10.7	11.2	10.0	9.5	11.4	10.7
Rural (procurement)	33.0	27.2	24.3	17.4	14.1	9.9	11.1	12.5	12.1	11.7	14.7	13.3
Absolute poverty (millions of people)												
Urban	-	-	4	2	1	1	1	1	1	1	1	1
Poverty line + 20%	-	-	5	2	1	1	2	2	2	3	3	3
Poverty (planned)	260	218	194	140	123	89	96	97	91	86	103	97
Poverty line + 10%	306	272	255	186	163	119	131	133	124	113	128	121
Poverty (procurement)	262	221	202	148	123	88	100	108	109	106	132	121
Poverty line + 10%	310	276	264	195	164	118	138	146	144	136	168	160

A.3. Distribution of annual per-capita income, poverty line, and incidence of absolute poverty

	Unit	1978	1981	1984	1985	1989	1990
ANNUAL PER CAPITA							
Income Urban							
<240	%	–	2.1	–	–	–	–
240–300	%	–	5.5	1.7	11.1	–	–
300–420	%	–	31.8	10.5	–	4.8	7.4
420–600	%	–	42.3	38.9	24.8	–	–
600–720	%	–	11.9	22.7	19.5	5.0	–
720–840	%	–	–	12.8	16.0	6.9	5.7
840–960	%	–	–	–	11.0	9.3	7.0
960–1080	%	–	–	–	7.0	10.8	8.8
1080–1200	%	–	–	–	4.1	11.2	8.8
1200–1320	%	–	6.5	13.4	2.6	10.2	9.8
1320–1440	%	–	–	–	–	8.6	9.2
1440–1560	%	–	–	–	–	7.5	8.0
1560–1680	%	–	–	–	3.9	6.0	7.4
1680–1800	%	–	–	–	–	4.4	5.8
>1800	%	–	–	–	–	15.8	22.3
Average	Y	–	500	660	749	1388	1523
Rural							
<100	%	33.3	4.7	0.8	1.0	0.6	0.5
100–150	%	31.7	14.9	3.8	3.4	1.3	0.9
150–200	%	17.6	16.0	9.4	7.9	2.8	2.2
200–300	%	15.0	34.8	29.2	25.6	10.9	9.5
300–400	%	–	14.4	24.5	24.0	15.6	14.4
400–500	%	2.4	5.0	14.1	15.8	15.6	15.1
>500	%	–	3.2	18.2	22.3	53.2	57.4
Average	Y	134	223	355	398	603	630
Rural Gini coefficient		0.21	0.24	0.26	0.26	0.31	0.31
POVERTY LINE							
Urban							
Expenditure on food	Y	–	108	117	132	190	197
Food budget share	%	–	0.63	0.62	0.61	0.62	0.61
Poverty line	Y	–	171	190	215	304	321
Rural							
Expenditure on food	Y	74	105	112	120	165	173
Food budget share	%	0.75	0.66	0.63	0.63	0.63	0.63
Poverty line	Y	98	158	179	190	304	275
INCIDENCE OF							
ABSOLUTE POVERTY							
Urban	Millions of people	–	3.9	0.8	0.9	0.9	0.3
	Percentage of urban population	–	1.9	0.3	0.4	0.3	0.4
Rural	Millions of people	260.5	194.3	88.7	96.4	102.5	96.8
	Percentage of urban population	–	24.3	11.0	11.9	12.3	11.5
Total	Millions of people	–	198.2	89.5	97.3	103.4	98.2
	Percentage of urban population	–	19.8	8.6	9.2	9.2	8.6

Source: World Bank China: *Strategies for Reducing Poverty in the 1990s*, Washington. DC, 1992.

15. Urban Poverty Alleviation and Development — The Chinese Experience

Introduction

The Second UN Conference on Human Settlement had brought to the attention of the world that urban poverty and its attended human cost is the greatest challenges of our time. The issue of urban poverty in China is different from other developing countries due to its unique features of industrialization and urbanization of its development process before the 90's. Dynamically, the warning is also given correctly in a very recent UNDP report *China: Human Development Report* that among the new kinds of poverty alluded to above is urban poverty, a relatively "new phenomenon." Therefore, this issue should deserve new focus in the national development policy. Presentation of this paper will be divided into four parts: Part one will give a retrospect of China's urban poverty, development process and human settlement before the 90's; part two describes the emerging urban poverty and its alleviation in the 90's; part three and part four are briefings of essential messages from the Chinese side on the International Forum on the Role of Private Sector in Poverty Alleviation through Social Efforts and Balanced Regional Development, held in Beijing, July 1-2, 1998, jointly sponsored by UNCRD, DRC and the "Brilliant Cause"; part three will summarize one of the new approach of poverty alleviation in China (the Brilliant Cause Program, launched by the organization of non-public sectors, a relatively recent initiative in China's economic reform; part four is some concluding remarks of that forum with some modifications to adapt to this conference. Some lessons of development and related development thinking will also be presented in the part IV. I expect this approach of presentation can meet the two basic objectives of this symposium to provide a better understanding of poverty issues of China in the struggle against urban

420

poverty for our organizers and all participants here; to illustrate one of the operational means of poverty alleviation — public private partnership; to explore the potential for organizing a forum on urban poverty for the region for the exchange of knowledge and experience.

Part I Urban Poverty, Development Process and Human Settlement of China — A Retrospect before 90's

1.01 The Urban Poverty before 90's

Unlike in most of the developing world, poverty in China has been largely a rural phenomenon before the 90's. There was no urban poverty line declared officially before the mid-1990's. This is due to the unique feature of development policy that the Chinese government has limited urban poverty to extremely low levels through full employment policy linked with narrow ranges of earned income which is illustrated in Table 1.1. There are price controls on basic needs of foodstuffs, cloth and nearly universal access to education and health care.

Table 1.1 Average Wage Rate of State-owned Enterprises (yuan)

	1952	1965	1975	1978
Averages Wage Per Year	446	652	613	644
Industry	515	729	644	683
Construction	564	730	704	748
Agriculture, Irrigation	375	433	460	492
Transport, Postal Service, Communication	583	774	699	733
Commerce	360	579	562	587
Urban Public Utility	634	687	639	652
Science, Education and Health	368	598	574	582
Finance, Insurance	458	624	609	643
Institution	376	684	645	662

Source: *China Statistical Yearbook 1981,* China Statistical Publishing House.

China had also implemented an urban food and cloth ration system which had ensured the China's urban population in enjoying preferential access to staple foods and cloth below market prices. Urban enrollment ratios at the primary and secondary schools levels have risen faster and now are higher than those of most other developing countries. It can be seen from Table 1. 2 the comparison of Chinese education and the world in the year 1970 and 1990. The widespread availability of primary health services provided at little or no cost brought the most serious contagious and parasitic diseases under control in urban areas by the early 1960's. There is great improvement of social indicators which can be shown from Table 1.3.

Table 1.2 Comparison of Education Indicators of China and the World

Enrollment Ratio / Country/ Region	Percentage of Age Groups Enrolled in Age Groups							
	Primary				Secondary			
	Total		Female		Total		Female	
	1970	1990	1970	1990	1970	1990	1970	1990
China	89	135	-	129	24	48	-	41
Average Low-income Economies	74	105	-	98	21	41	-	34
Middle-income Economies	94	103	88	99	33	126 (55)	28	59 (57)

Source: *World Development Report 1993.*
      The figure 1990 is doubtful. The number in the bracket is 1989 figure in WRD 1992.

Based upon the above information, the urban poverty alleviation in China before the 90's can be judged a major success. It is also observed by the World Bank that "Supreme income levels, complemented by annual consumer food subsidies of at least Y200 per urban resident (World Bank 1990d), leave the registered urban population much better nourished than their rural counterparts, SSB household income and expenditure surveys show, for example, that urban residents among the bottom 5% of the 1988 urban income distribution consumed 15% more vegetable oil, 27% more meat, and 117% more eggs than did the average rural inhabitant." It is also noted by

UNICEF that "The maternal mortality rate dropped to an estimated 95 per 100,000 births in 1989 from 1500 before 1949. Though the proportion of children with at least moderate malnutrition is still significant, severe malnutrition among children under five has been virtually eliminated except in several remote areas."[1]

Table 1.3 Selected Indicators of Social Development of China in the World

	Expectancy of Life at Birth	Crude Death Rate	Infant Mortality Rate	Adult Illiteracy %		Per-capita Availability of Food Energy	GNP per capita
	Years	Per 1000	Per 1000	Female	Male	Calories/ day	1990 US$
China: 1950-1955	34	31	236	80		1,894	
1990	70	7	29	38	27	2,639	370
1990 Average							
Low-income Countries	62	10	69	52	40	2,406*	350
Middle-income Countries	66	8	48	27	22	2,860*	2,220

Source: 1. *China: Strategies for Reducing Poverty in the 1990s.*
 2. World Bank Report 1992.
 3. * 1989 data.

1.02 Features of Development Process and Its Impact on Urban Poverty

It had been described in the beginning of 1.01 that "poverty in China has been largely a rural phenomenon before the 90's, this phenomenon was closely related to the development process before the 80's. This development process was characterized by the following characteristics:

1. Background of the Development Process before the 80's

Prior to 1949, the Chinese economy relied mainly on the production of

---

1. UNICEF in *China 1996.*

its agricultural sector, in 1950, the share of the primary, secondary and the tertiary sector in GDP is 50.5%, 20.8%, and 28.7% respectively. Since the founding of the PRC, whole effort of the government is devoted on two major aspects: industrialization and alleviation of poverty. Before the launch of economic reform, a Soviet model of development strategy was adopted, since the launch of economic reform and opening to the outside world in late 1978, a gradual transition from a central planned economy to market economy is implemented. In the development process of both periods, the unique characteristics of China are taken into consideration. There are both large achievements and issues in these two periods. These are not subjects of discussions in this paper, only the relevant aspects to urban poverty and human settlement will be decrisbed in the following.

2. Major Features of the Development Process before 80's[2] and 90's

(1) Industrialization — a major focus

China has been successful in its process of industrialization in spite of political upheavals and issues in this period.

The Soviet model of industrialization process was followed with massive investment in heavy industry. Before 1978, it was thought that in the drive to raise the rate of industrialization, while keeping price stable by ensuing the supply of an adequate quantity of agricultural goods at fixed prices to the non-agricultural sector, the development process had tended to discriminate against the rural producers. China had also pushed forward a commune system of socialized agriculture and small scale of rural industries in that period, that had developed a rural infrastructure and management system which facilitate the rapid growth of town and village enterprises since the launch of economy reform. Therefore, the structure of the Chinese economy has been changed greatly. The share of primary, secondary and tertiary sector in GDP is 30%,48.5:21.5% and 27%:41.5%:31.5% respectively in 1980 and 1990. A full industrial production capability is established which is shown in Tables 1.4 and 1.5.

---

2. "80's" and 90's are used here, because from 1980-1989 is a period in transition, some characteristics before the 80's are kept.

Table 1.4 Structure of Manufacturing Sector in China
(value added in millions US$)

Sectors	Value added	1980	1990
311/2	Food products	3764/e	4489
313	Beverages	1587/e	2414
314	Tobacco products	3545	6210
321	Textile	13409	10299
322	Wearing apparel	1866	2109a
323	Leather and fur products	911	949
324	Footwear	a	a
331	Wood and wood products	751/e	502
332	Furnitures and fixtures	653/e	455
341	Paper and paper products	1929/e	1949
342	Printing and publishing	1042	1036
351	Industrial chemicals	7125	8459
352	Other chemical products	2924	3372
353	Petroleum refineries	4223	2714
354	Miscellaneous petroleum and coal products	154	208
355	Rubber products	2175	1603
356	Plastic products	1256	1736
361	Pottery, China and earthward	439	504
362	Glass and glass products	838	705
369	Other non-metal mineral products	4425	4524
371	Iron and steel	6538	6571
372	Non-ferrous metals	1868	2050
381	Metal products	4861	3946
382	Non electric machinery	13418	10116
383	Electric machinery	3216	7445
384	Transport equipment	3013	3918
385	Professional and scientific equipment	810	843
390	Other manufacturing industries	1838/e	2125
Value added total		88577	90259

Note: The Chinese statistics did not provide a classification of manufacture based upon ISIC,
therefore, Table 1.4 is quoted from *Industry and Development Global Report 1993/94*,
UNIDO, e: UNIDO estimates.

Table 1.5 Change of Order of China's Industrial Products

Item	1949	1957	1965	1978	1980	1985	1990	1993	1994	1995	1996
CrudeSteel	26	9	8	5	5	4	4	3	2	2	1
Coal	9	5	5	3	3	2	1	1	1	1	1
Crude Petroleum	27 [1]	23	12	8	6	6	5	5	5	5	5
Electricity	25	13	9	7	6	5	4	4	2	2	2
Cement		8	8	4	4	1	1	1	1	1	1
Fertilizer		33	8	3	3	3	3	3	2	2	2
Chemical Fiber		26 [2]		7	5	4	2	2	2	2	2
Woven Cotton Fabric			3	1	1	1	1	1	1	1	1
Sugar			8	8	10	6	6	3	4	4	4
Television				8	5	3	1	1	1	1	1

Source: *China Statistical Yearbook 1997.* The 1950 data and 1960 data are estimates.

(2) Pursuit of an egalitarian growth strategy before the 80's

Before 1978, social equity is emphasized rather than pursuit of economic efficacy. The result of this development effort implemented before 1978 was that notwithstanding their low income share, the poorest people in China were far better off than their counterparts in most other developing countries. A balanced regional development strategy was also pursued before 1978 with less emphasis on locational advantage. Table 1.6 shows the growth of output from 1952 to 1978 of six provinces selected from six regions, which can illustrate the difference of growth of output of those regions is small. Provinces in the hinterland such as Gansu Province (located in northwesten region of China) even has a higher growth rate of total output than Guangdong Province (along the coastal region) which is well known for its extra-ordinary high economic growth since the reform and opening. The output of the Liaoning Province is highest because it received the highest share of state investment designated to be the basis of China's heavy industry before 1978. Since the launch of economic reform and opening to the outside, this egalitarian growth strategy is changed.

Table 1.6 Comparison of Total Output of Society (1952-1978)
Unit: 100 million yuan
(number in the bracket is times of output refered to base year 100)

Year	Total Output of Society					
	Liaoning	Inner Mongolia	Shandong	Guangdong	Guizhou	Gansu
1952	76.2(100)	15.61(100)	69.82(100)	49.92(100)	12.69(100)	16.78(100)
1978	483.7	109.76	445.01	350.31	87.95	125.21
	(775.6)	(525.21)	(614.18)	(541.1)	(487.9)	(612.66)

Source: *A Compilation of Historical Statistics of Provinces, Autonomous Regions and Munici-palities Administered by the State,* China Statistical Publishing House.

(3) Public ownership was the main goal before 1978

Due to the socialist ideology, state ownership and collective ownership were the main goal. All types of enterprises were transformed into state owned or collectively owned before the 60's, and from 1966-1975, there is further increase of the state ownership, and the private ownership system is abolished. It can be seen from the labor statistics that the number of individual workers were reduced from 8.83 million persons in 1952 down to 0.15 million persons in 1978. Table 1.7 presents the labor statistics of various ownership systems of selected years.

Table 1.7 Number of Social Labor Force Employed in Urban Areas
(year end) unit:10^4

	1952	1957	1965	1978	1990
Sub-Total	2486	3205	5136	9514	6616
State-owned Units	1580	2451	3738	7451	10346
Urban collective-owned Units	23	650	1227	2048	3549
Jointly Owned Economic Units					96
Foreign-funded Economic Units					62
Funded by Hongkong Macao, Taiwan					4
Private Enterprises					2
Other Types					57
Individual					614

Source: *China Statistical Yearbook 1997,* China Statistical Publishing House.

Since the launch of economic reform, the growth of various types of owner-ship system is encouraged gradually. It is clearly expressed in President Jiang Zemin's Report to the 15th National Party's Congress in 1997, that "The non-public sector is an important component of China's socialist mar-ket economy. We should continue to encourage and guide the non-public sector comprising self-employment and private businesses to facilitate its sound development."

(4) Relationship of state urban enterprises and employees before 80's

Full employment and lifetime employment policy were implemented by the state. Early in Feb. 26, 1951, the government of PRC had officially promul-gated the First Labor Insurance Regulation, the employers and workers had the right to receive pension after retirement and other social welfare.

1.03 Industrialization, Urbanization and Human Settlement

The process of industrialization had great impact on the pattern of urban-ization process of China. Based upon the practice of industrialization of China before the 80's, the new enterprise established will also be respon-sible to provide housing, medical service and even education system for their employees, especially the large enterprises. A lot of new municipali-ties were established due to establishment of new large enterprises. It was defined by the central government of the PRC that for towns with population in excess of fifty thousand can become an administrative municipality. Table 1.8 shows the number of new municipalities estab-lished in different periods.

Table 1.8 Number of New Municipalities Established in Different Periods

Period	Number of New Municipalities Established (Net)
1949	137
1950-1957	40 (63 established, 20 canceled)
1958-1965	-7 (22 established, 29 canceled)
1966-1976	19 (21 established, 2 canceled)
1977-1985	136
1986-1994	299

Before 1949 these were only 66 municipalities in China, which can show clearly the low level of urbanization that China was nearly a peasant society before 1949. By the end of 1985 and 1994, there are altogether 325 and 622 municipalities respectively, wit total number of urban population around 1.18 hundred millions and 1.91 hundred million respectively. The newly established municipalities are closely linked to the industrialization process, there were urban planning and housing planning during the set up of the new industrial plants. Schools and hospitals were also established in the planning process. The social safety net was provided by the SOEs and the government. Security department was set up in every large or medium state-owned enterprises, and rural urban migration was not free before the 80's. Therefore, there was little crime in that period. Public transport such as bus or trolley bus were constructed in large and municipalities, besides, bicycles were popular in the urban area before the 80's, nearly every household owned one or two bicycles. There is nearly no informal city, little crime, relatively convenient urban transport and available social service (education, medical care) to the urban dwellers in general.

Part II The Emerging Urban Poverty and Its Alleviation

2.01 Introduction

Before the mid-1990's, the urban poverty of China was not a serious issue which had been explained in part I. Traditionally, the Ministry of Civil Affairs was responsible to handle target groups for relief both for the urban and rural. But there is few urban poor before 80's. In the transitional process from a former controlled planned economy to the socialist market economy, three new issues have emerged. There is increasing unemployment revealed from labor shedding in state and collective enterprises due to restructuring of the national economy and redeployment of the labor force; there was increasing number of the retired, elderly and disable staffs and workers, who cannot get their normal pensions or wages due to the inefficient operation of these enterprises; the third, there is a large amount of migrants form rural to urban areas, although their living standard is far better off than their rural members, a part of them even remit the surplus of their income back to their families, generally, however, they cannot enjoy the social welfare of the local workers, such as low cost housing, medical care, etc. Some of them are living in a poor condition, poor housing in surroundings of metropolitans. Therefore, <u>there is emerging urban poverty in this transitional process</u>. As there is no unified national rule on the one side, and the urban poverty alleviation is a new issue on the other, only selected aspects and case study will be described for this new issue.

2.02 National Urban Poverty Line (Case Study of Guarantee Line of Minimum Living Standard)

1. It was reported in 1997 that China had set up the poverty line for urban residents at per-capita annual income of 1,700 yuan based on the statistics of SSB (the annual per-capita income of average urban household in 1997 is 5,160.3 yuan, the number of the urban poor totaled 11.76 million in 1996). The Ministry of Civil Affairs had spent more than five years of effort to set up the guarantee line of minimum living standard. Box 2-1, a case study from the Bureau of Civil Affairs of Xiamen Municipality will provide a relatively in detail of this system in establishment.

2. Guarantee line of minimum living standard — set up and implementation

It is reported by the *Family News* on August 18, 1998 that the Ministry of Civil Affairs had pushed forward this system "Guarantee Line of Minimum Living Standard" with full effort. There are around 486 municipalities which had implemented this system, a share of 73% of the total number of municipalities. It can bee seen from Box 2-1 that a large part of the relief fund will be imbursed by the Bureau of Civil Affairs of the municipalities. The fiscal capacity of these municipalities does matter. It can also be seen form Box 2-1 that the relief fund of the non-targeted group by the Ministry Civil Affairs will be imbursed by the Employees' Welfare Fund of concerned enterprises. If the enterprise is in difficulty, it is not sure whether the payment to the poor can be guaranteed or not. This point has not been checked yet.

Implementation of "Provisional Regulations on Guarantee Line of Minimum Living Standard", Bureau of Civil Affairs of Xiamen Municipality

1. General

In Oct. 1993, the "Provisional Regulations on Guarantee Line of Minimum Living Standard" is promulgated. It is officially implemented in Nov. 1993. In 1995, the relief fund was imbursed at two levels of public finance, the municipality and the district. It was amounted to 1,705.8 thousand yuan, the number of urban people in poverty received this benefit reached 15,892 person/times.

2. Set up of "Guarantee Line of Minimum Living Standard"

A special team is organized by the Bureau of Civil Affairs and the Bureau of Public Finance. A survey visit on items of basic living commodities (rice, oil, salt, soybean oil, fuel, electricity, water, vegetables, meat, house rent, cloth and cover, etc.) and cost of medical care, transportation is made to "Households with Livelihood Guaranteed in Five Aspects" and urban poor households. In combination with the data base supplied by the Bureau of Statistics and Bureau of Price, a "Provincial Regulation" was drafted and sent to various departments to get opinions. This "Provincial Regulations" is sent to the municipal government, and it is discussed and approved on Oct. 22.

3. Major Contents

There are four major aspects of this "Provincial Regulations".

(1) The basis of Guarantee Line of Minimum Living Standard of the urban people is clarified.

The Bureau of Statistics and the Bureau of Price of this municipality will provide the price index of the basic necessities of living of the household last year, the Bureau of Civil Affairs will announce them once every year.

(2) Scope and Target of Guarantee

All municipal urban residents (restricted to local residents only) with monthly real income lower than that announced by the Bureau of Civil Affairs described in 3-(1) will be covered in the guarantee.

The target group of guarantee is divided into two categories:

Category 1: The targeted group of Bureau of Civil Affairs who have no fixed jobs, no fixed income with difficulties in living, who are qualified with the conditions of social relief;

Category 2: The non-targeted group of Bureau of Civil Affairs with difficulties in living whose family have members with jobs (include retired).

(3) Procedures of Application and Approval

Category 1: Procedure of application (omit), approved by District Bureau of Civil Affairs.

Category 2: Application should be sent to the trade union of an enterprise and unit in which a family member has a job. It will be approved by the trade union of the concerned enterprise and the relief fund will be allocated to and issued from the employee's welfare fund of the concerned enterprises.

(4) Source of Relief Fund, Imbursemment, Management and Supervision

The relief fund approved by the district civil affairs will be imbursed monthly by the offices of neighborhoods;

The relief fund approved by the trade union of the enterprise will be imbursed by the enterprise or its supervisory department.

2.03 Off-Job³, Diversification of Employment and Implementation of Reemployment Program

1. General

The Chinese government has not implement the "Anti poverty programs" with urban poverty taken into consideration. The well-known "'Eight-Seven' Poverty Alleviation Program" refers mainly to the rural sector, i.e., to rid eighty millions of people (rural) of poverty within seven years. There was social assistance for the urban poor which is responsible traditionally by the Ministry of Civil Affairs. There is no specific leading group established at national level to deal with urban poverty issues. Formerly, the Ministry of Labor was responsible to assist the unemployed and retired workers, the Ministry of Civil Affairs takes care of those target groups of traditional relief, the Ministry of Personnel is in charge to help those low-income groups associated with the public institutions. A new Ministry of Labor and Social Security is established this year, traditional work division is followed more or less, whether there is new division of work has not been fully clarified when this paper was written.

2. The newly added urban poor is generally consisted of off-job workers from staff of state-owned and collectively owned enterprises. But this is not the case that all off-job workers live under the urban poverty line. There are institutionalized reemployment programs started around 1993-1994. Table 2.1 presents some statistics.

Table 2.1 Statistics on Unemployment Relief and
Reemployment Programs 1986-1995

Item	1986-1995	1994	1995
Number of unemployed workers receiving relief (million people/times)	6	1.96	2.61
Number of reemployed workers (million people)	3	0.99	1.38

Source: Ministry of Labor (1997): *Outline of Social Security Reform,* April 1997, Beijing.

---

3. These are official terms used currently.

3. The Reemployment Programs

The objectives of the reemployment program includes follows:

(1) To facilitate the unemployed to find new jobs by providing intermediary service. There are around 8,700 intermediary service institutions established up to May 1997, within which 2,000 are private, 2,700 are established by social community and around 4,000 are established by labor departments at different levels of governmental administration. The clients of these services include the off-job workers and staffs, the newly added labor force and the retired workers who are seeking new jobs. There were around 70 million urban people seeking jobs in the period from 1983-1996, and most of them have got assistance from these labor intermediary services.

(2) To assist the unemployed with training courses to get access to new skills. The training programs are organized either by the labor departments, trade unions and women's federations or by "corporations" or "companies" derived from the former bureau of industries. The courses are financed generally by the contributions of enterprises and local governmental budgetary expenditure. There are also a number of private-funded vocational schools offering the training courses. A few of the unemployed also pay the cost of training with their own savings and from the subsidies provided by their former enterprises.

In 1997, experiments to establish reemployment service centers in several cities, the cost of these centers are born by the contributions from the local governmental budgetary expenditure, the enterprises and the labor departments.

(3) The unemployed workers and staffs are also encouraged to do self-employed business, preferential policies will be implemented for loans and rent, facilitation of application of business licenses will also be provided.

(4) To Encourage Enterprises to Recruit the Unemployed

4. Current Situation and Issues

(1) Recent Situation

It is reported in the beginning of 1998 that by the end of 1997 the off-job workers and staffs make up around 17% of the total labor force employed in the SOEs, more than 50% of them was reemployed. Within the remaining 50% off-job workers and staffs, 10% had entered into the program of Reemployment Service Centers, 90% of them was left out. But around half of them had received the basic living cost, a half of them had not received this type of payment. It is estimated by the labor departments that the number of off-job workers or staffs in difficulty will be around 3 million.

(2) Issues

There are five major issues in implementation of reemployment program. Insufficient job opportunities; insufficient financial resources; narrow coverage of social security system; outdated concept on employment for the off-job workers, or low skill of off-job workers without adaptability to new jobs; the arrangement for different enterprises has not followed closely the rule set up for off-job workers by the central government.

(3) Regional Disparity

The solution of problem of urban poverty depends very much on the fiscal capability of the local municipal government. It can be seen from Box-2, the case study of social assistance in Shanghai, i.e., the poor residents have the opportunity to receive better benefits than the urban poor of other municipalities.

5. Theory and Practice — Academic Debates

(1) Urban poverty is a new phenomenon of China. It is also a new issue for the transitional economies in general. It is described in Reference 8 to be one of the unfinished agenda for the transitional economies that "major changes in social policies must complement the move to the market to focus on relieving poverty, to cope with increased mobility, and to counteract the adverse intergeneration effects of reform." The economic reform of China has come to a stage that major changes in social policies are necessary.

Box 2-2
Evolution of Social Assistance of a Socialist Market Economy, Shanghai

Since 1980's Shanghai had implemented a large-scale economic reform, the traditional social assistance program established in the planned economy cannot adapt to the needs of a market economy and social development. The structure and contents of the social assistance program are also adjusted. These adjustments include:

1. 1993 The municipal government has set up a system of three-security lines — the

minimum income line; waiting for employment (unemployment) employee's security line and urban residents "Guarantee Line of Minimum Living Standard."

2. May. 1994   "Notice on Provision of Material Subsidies within Definite Period to Specially Difficult Local Urban Residents." Material subsidies are provided monthly to retired people with difficulties in daily life and jobless elders aged more than 60 years. Prepared by six departments led by the Bureau of Civil Affair, and approved by the municipal government.

3. June 1994   Standard of Poverty Alleviation in rural area was set up.

4. July 1995   "Notice on Issue of Supply Certificate of Grain and Oil for Low-income Urban Families" was issued by the municipal government. This assistance is given to poor family with per-capita income lower than "minimum income line" of Shanghai. By the end of 1996, 500,000 people had benefited from this assistance.

5. Nov. 1996   "Social Assistance Means of Shanghai Municipality" is promulgated by the Shanghai Municipal People's Government, and went into effect on July 1, 1997. The document has clarified the main agency responsible for social assistance, target of social assistance, standard and conditions of social assistance and management of social assistance. This is the first time that social assistance is normalized in the form of legislation.

6. Shanghai has also established a dynamic adjustment mechanism of standard of social assistance. The budget expenditure of social assistance, material assistance, assistance through grain and oil reached 280 million yuan in 1995 and 1996.

Source: Derived from Reference 7.

(2) At the current stage of implementation of reform, there may be insufficient focus on the research of social aspects. It is argued by the academic field that "the reemployment programs implemented in the urban formed a part of employment policies, this urban biased employment policies can be thought a heritage of the planned economy."[4] And also in the current transitional stage, some people may still not master fully the speech given by President Jiang to the 15th Party's National Congress. It is pointed out in his speech that "It remains a major task in economic restructuring to continue readjusting and improving the ownership structure so as to further release and develop the productive forces". In fact, the non-public sector is not only important in the contribution to economic growth and prosperity, it is also an essential component in the alleviation of urban and rural poverty. With the complex issue of implementation of reemployment program, the regional disparity, and the

---

4. Refer to reference 3.

emerging issue of urban poverty, the role of the non-public sector should be fully realized to contribute to the solution of these complex issues. In the next part, the role of non-public sector in the alleviation of poverty will be described.

Part III New Initiative of Poverty Alleviation in China — the Activity of Brilliant Cause

3.01 Introduction

Poverty and poverty alleviation are dynamic in nature. There is nearly no urban poverty in China before the 80's, but it emerged in the 90's. This issue of urban poverty will become even more serious if static concept of poverty and poverty alleviation is kept. UNCRD is actively involved in regional development issues and policies. An international forum on the role of the private sector in poverty alleviation through social efforts and balanced regional development was jointly sponsored by UNCRD, Development Research Center of the State Council and the Brilliant Cause in Beijing, July 1-2, 1998. We have the honor that Dr. Disa Weerapaua, the deputy director of UNCHS Fukuoka office had joined us in that conference.

It is my honor on behalf of the Chinese sponsor of that conference to give you here a briefing of the activity of Brilliant Cause (a new initiative from the private sector in the alleviation of poverty in China. The meaning of the role of private sector in poverty alleviation had been pointed out clearly by the opening address given by Dr. Hideki Kaji, Director of UNCRD. "Our belief is that we can never overcome our problems of poverty unless we also see the economic sides of the coin. We have to link poverty with employment generation and promotion of the productive sectors, and within the broader framework of spatial and regional development." Hereunder, the major activities of the Brilliant Cause will be briefed in general, special activities related of alleviation of urban poverty ("The concept and practice of alleviation of poverty and market development" will be described in relatively detail and also a unique case of poverty alleviation through reallocation of the poor will be introduced.

3.02 A brief Introduction of the Development and Activities of the "Brilliant Cause"

1. The Launch of the "Brilliant Cause" Program

The Chinese government had launched the national "'Eight-Seven' Poverty Alleviation Program" in 1994, the target being to solve the basic needs of food and clothing for 80 million of poor people within seven years. A Leading Group of Economic Development in Poor Areas (LGEDPA) was established by the State Council in 1986, Poor Area Development Office (DADO) was established under LGEDPA to look after the day-to-day affairs. Nearly all ministries were involved in this program.

In the Second Session of the Seventh Standing Committee of the All-China Federation of Industry and Commerce, ten non-public sector entrepreneurs put forward a proposal entitled "Let's all join in the Brilliant Cause of Poverty Alleviation." This proposal was accepted and got wide support. In the past four years since the launch of the "Brilliant Cause" program up to June 30, 1997, there are around 2,296 non-public sector entrepreneurs who had joined and implemented the project of the "Brilliant Cause" program, the number of projects implemented reached 2,731, with more than 5 billion yuan of investment and training around 255,600 people. Moreover, 547,100 poor people had got rid off poverty through the implementation of this program.

2. Types of Project Investment

There are many forms of project investment. The investment activity can be broadly classified into the following nine types. Descriptions will be given to some types closely related to urban poverty alleviation. The nine types of investment are:

(1) Agricultural development;

(2) Resource development;

(3) Chain-plant was located in poverty-ridden regions to manufacture the product of the same brands of the parent plant;

(4) Integration of production activity of agriculture, industry and trade, agricultural and industrial production bases are set in poverty-ridden regions, trade of the products is developed in the domestic market and abroad;

(5) Development through relocation of population in difficult regions;

(6) Market driven development (refer to 3.03);

(7) Export of Labor Force Labor mobility and emigration from poverty-ridden regions are effective means for the alleviation of poverty. The Brilliant Cause-Shenzhen municipal branch had collaborated with the Municipal Bureau of Labor and Municipal Economic Commission, supported by local labor department of poverty-ridden regions, had imported a large amount of rural labor force from Guizhou and Jiangxi, having them employed in non-public enterprises in Shenzhen.

(8) Development through training This is also important for urban poverty alleviation;

(9) Grant for public benefit

3. Features and Basic Concept

It had been described in 1.01-1-(3) that China had discriminated against other types of ownership other than public ownership before 1978. Change of ideology and development policy has been observed since the launch of economic reform. There is emergence of non-public economies in the beginning of the 80's. It had opened a new path of development for the younger generation who wish to realize the human value through honest work and creations. The concept of the Brilliant Cause program does recognize this as a type of poverty alleviation through developmental investment. The inherent requirement of investment is return, is the profit, is the value added of the capital input. But it is also a development process and investment shared between the investors and local community in sharing the profit, in sharing the profit with common effort, in sharing the view that poverty alleviation is a global task advocated by UN.

It is realized by the advocators and participants of the "Brilliant Cause" program that the basic concept is to abolish poverty, not elimination of disparity. On this basis of concept, it is possible to compromise the contradiction between righteousness and profit making.

4. Proposal to contribute to "Reemployment" program of workers and staffs of state-owned enterprises by the "Brilliant Cause" Program

It is proposed by the Chief of Board of Directors of Brilliant Cause Investment Company that it is ready to invest 10 million yuan in collaboration with

"ReEmployment Center" and the "All-China Federation of Industry and Commerce" in different regions on the following: If the off-job worker prefers to create business by oneself, it is necessary to contribute two-thirds of the investment by oneself and the company can complement one-third of the investment for projects under 100,000 yuan. The risk of investment will be shared by both sides. If the investment is successful, profit will be received by both sides according to their share of the investment; if the investment fails, there is no need for the collaborator to reimburse the capital investment to the company.

3.03 Poverty Alleviation and Market Development — Practice and Exploration

1. Market-Driven Type of Poverty Alleviation

In the implementation of various types of investment development, it is found that the market-driven investment has achieved very good results. There are seventeen markets organized, coordinated and constructed by the "Brilliant Cause" program. Seven markets have been established (3 in Inner Mongolia, 1 in Shanghai, 2 in Shenzhen, 1 in Jiangxi); three markets are in establishment (1 in Shenzhen, 2 in Jiangxi); seven markets are under planning (1 in Shenyang, 1 in Jingdezhen, 1 in Jujiang, 1 in Nanchang, 2 in Guangdong Province, 1 in Guizhou Province). The locations of those markets varied, some are located directly in the poverty-ridden regions of central and western China, such as the Brilliant Grand Market in Southern Jiangxi, the specific market of Mihao Peach of Guizhou. Some are established in developed coastal regions to develop trade with the central and western regions with preferential policies to provide conditions to facilitate the entry of their product to markets of developed regions. This is precisely the role of Shanghai Brilliant Small and Miscellaneous Wholesale Market. All "Brilliant" markets are established with the objective of poverty alleviation, aiming at promoting the circulation of products. Commerce, wholesale and retail service can accommodate a relatively large amount of employment with low capital to labor ratio. This will also provide a favorable condition for the "re-employment" program.

2. Unique meaning and role of "Market-Driven Type" of Poverty Alleviation

People in poverty are mainly distributed in remote mountainous regions in central and western parts of China. Most of the people in poverty live in rural areas with harsh natural environment, backward means of production, simple economic structure and small scale of market. "Market-Driven Poverty Alleviation" has the following unique role and meaning.

(1) It is favorable to break the closed status of the natural economy, to upgrade local people's awareness of commodity transaction and trade.

The closed natural economy is the basic cause of socio-economic underdevelopment of the poverty regions. The establishment of a market with definite scale can perform the function to link together the widely-scattered individual small agricultural economy to get access to the market operation and concepts. For example, the formation of the economy of scale of Baigou market in Xincheng County, Hebei Province is mainly due to the emergence of a new generation of farmers working in the market. They have acquired the capability of production and operation, have a broad perspective and got wide accessible information. The Shanghai Brilliant Small and Miscellaneous Commodity Wholesale Market has offered one third of general price level to invite business operations, to provide conditions to facilitate the entry of products of poverty-ridden regions into the Shanghai market and coastal regions. The market-driven poverty alleviation facilitates the establishment of urban-rural linkages which are not only beneficial to the alleviation of rural poverty, but it will also promote further the development of both urban and rural areas in linkage.

(2) It is favorable to the reasonal spatial location and regional economy, push forward the development of tertiary sector, promote the reasonable transfer of surplus rural labor force and re-employment of urban off-job workers and staffs. The growth of the market will perform the function of attraction and radiation to promote the prosperity of regional economy. Ganzhou Prefecture, an old revolutionary base, is located in southern part of Jiangxi Province. There are around 800,000 people in poverty there. Following the concept of market-driven proverty alleviation, the Gannan Brilliant Grand Market is being built. This market will occupy a ground area around seventy hectares and will be divided into ten operation districts, including agricultural products, daily-use goods, foods, textiles, household electric appliance, house decoration material, etc. This market can rely upon the Ganzhou Station on the Beijing-Kowlong Railway for transport of commodities. Around ten thousand of people will enter into operation after

the completion of the construction of Gannan Brilliant Grand Market. It will provide a channel of entry for local agricultural and subsidiary products into national market. It will also be favorable for the processing and export of local agricultural and subsidiary products, promote the formation of economy of scale of industrial production. It will also promote the development of communication, electricity and water supply, postal service, financial service and transportation service. It will help tap fully the potential of the market-driven poverty alleviation program.

Part IV Poverty Alleviation and Better Human Settlement — A Challenge in Human Development

4.01 Introduction

Poverty alleviation and human development are essential subjects and challenges faced by the global society as a whole. In 1995, the World Summit for Social Development was held in Copenhagen, Denmark. It is recognized that "Beyond economic growth, which is an engine and not an end in itself, development is first and foremost social." It is also recognized that "People's participation in social development is essential in combating poverty." The Chinese experience of development and poverty alleviation have been described in previous parts. We shall summarize and explore further some pragmatic and theoretical aspects of this subject in this part.

4.02 Socialist Market Economy — A Target of China's Economic Reform

China has defined its target of economic system reform, that is, to establish a socialist market economy. This target of economic system reform is derived from both positive and negative experiences from the development and reform in the past four and half decades since the founding of the PRC. (Please refer to paper 2, paper 8 of this book) The human race is the aim of the development. It is also the driving force of development. Only through the development of the human race as a whole, then the development of the society can be expected. Many foreign friends came to China generally raised the question "What do you mean the so-called socialist market economy?" There are many means for development. We use market economy as a means of development rather than depending upon allocation through planning, and the social goal is kept in mind. The social goal includes the human development and equity in development. Recently, the East Asian countries are faced with the "East AsianCurrency Crises". It is the poor who suffered the most. Therefore, poverty alleviation is a very important subject to be studied in the process of economic and social development.

4.03 Exploration of Some Aspects of Poverty Alleviation

1. Industrialization is an important means for alleviation of poverty

China had put heavy emphasis on industrialization and poverty alleviation. This development experience can be proven by the following quotations from the *Human Development Report 1997*. "In the past 50 years, poverty has fallen more than in the previous 500. The accredited progress in reducing poverty in the 20th Century began in Europe and North America in the 19th century in what can now be seen as the first Great Ascent from poverty and human deprivation. The ascent started in the foothills of the industrial revolution, with rising incomes, improvements in public health and education and eventually programmes of social security."

2. Sum up experiences of early stages of industrialization and corrections

The early stages of industrialization gave rise to social traumas (a widening gap between the rich and poor. Therefore, there are three new development.

(1) The state became interventionist and was compelled to enter the field as the protector of the weak. But the state is also aware of its weakness in taking all responsibilites. Public-private partner is a must.

(2) Development was the self-protection movement where effected segments of socially organized to promote their own cause. This aspect is also important in poverty alleviation. Poverty alleviation is not limited to let the people to have the basic needs, the food, the cloth and the shelter. It is important to change the mind of the people, they must receive the education and skill to adapt to a changing environment; they must receive the education and skill to adapt to a changing society; they should also be endowed with intellectual inspiration to be a true human beings to contribute their part to a better society, i.e., an active poverty alleviation policy should be broader

in sense.

(3) There is gradual recognition by industry of its social responsibilities for long-term sustained growth. This can be illustrated by the initiatives of "Brilliant Cause" Program of China.

3. *Growth of Economy is a prerequisite of poverty alleviation (The Chinese experience of poverty alleviation and the experience of the "Brilliant Cause" Program).*

It had been described in previous parts that China had pursued an egalitarian pattern of economic growth before the launch of economic reform (please refer to Tables 1.1 and 1.6). By that time, the social indicators of the hinterland in the western part improved at a higher rate than that of the coastal regions. Since the launch of economic reform the economy of the eastern part grows very rapidly. I don't think this is a failure of policy of economic reform. Before 1978, nearly all Chinese people lived in the same standard (a lower living standard). But the whole living standard of the Chinese people improved very rapidly even in the hinterland since the launch of economic reform. We should also realize the fact that the income disparities became wider between the rich and the poor, the coastal regions and the western regionws. But unless the people became rich by themselves, it is difficult for them to show concern for others. There was a saying by Guanzhui, an ancient Chinese politician around the year 600 B.C., "People can be educated with ceremony and politeness if the warehouse of grain is full. People will have a sense of glory and shame if they are supplied with enough food and cloth". This 2,000-year-old saying can be interpreted into western thought by using Maslow's modern theory of management in which he classifies the needs of mankind into a hierarchy of five stages. In this hierarchy, mankind cannot strive for the intangible, higher levels of safety security, love belongings, esteem, and self actualization without first attaining basic physiological needs such as food, shelter, clothing, etc.

The "Brilliant Cause" Program is initiated and operated by those people who had got rid off poverty and became rich in the period of economic reform. They can show concerns for people in poverty. And it is important in current China that market mechanism should be fully utilized, public-private partnership is important for alleviation of poverty. In a country such as China with 1.2 billion people currently and which may have its population reach 1.5-1.6 billion around 2030, it is nearly impossible to have correct government intervention without the participation of large non-public sector. Therefore, the experience of the "Brilliant Cause" Program is meaningful and it is worth while to be diffused. It may be not only important for China, but it may be a useful reference for other countries in general.

4. Information is essential for poverty alleviation and human settlement

In the poverty alleviation and the utilization of market mechanism for development, it is the role of the government, international organizations and others to disseminate the information. The developed countries had long advocated that the 20th century will be the information society, and a knowledge-based economy is in emergence. From the history of the human race, in the analysis of trend of change of human society, a long-term perspective should be taken rather than a short-term policy of development. With a long-term perspective, the information society or knowledge-based economy will come sooner or later. The important element of a knowledge-based economy is information. It is hardly imaginable that a knowledge-based economy will emerge that the people have not the basic education, that there is no dissemination of knowledge and information. The international symposium held in Fukuoka by UNCHS this time and held in Beijing by UNCRD in July had provided a rich information exchange on poverty alleviation and human settlement. There are more chances for the participants and organizers to learn from each other and to disseminate information and knowledge learned. A proper action can then be undertaken by appropriately combining the knowledge learned with the concrete conditions of every country for the betterment of poverty alleviation and human settlement. Therefore, there is reason to be optimistic that "The world has the material and natural resources, the know-how and the people to make a poverty-free world a reality in less than a generation," as pointed out in the foreword of *Human Development Report 1997*.

4.04 The Challenges

This is a dynamic and changing world. There is absolute poverty and relative poverty. Even in developed countries, such as the USA, there are no less people living under the poverty line; there are inequality between rural and urban; even in the urban area, there is micro-region with population in poverty. There is also changing conditions of human settlement. In the developed countries, "Ecological settlements including ecological planning and building, experiences in new housing and in the renewal of existing housing quarters in European countries is emerging. Therefore, alleviation of poverty and seeking for a better human settlement are a dynamic challenging subject for all of us. Let's join our efforts to face these challenges and to create a society with better development.

REFERENCES

1. China: Human Development Report: "Human Development & Poverty Alleviation," UNDP, China.

2. *China Strategies for Reducing Poverty in the 1990s — A World Bank Country Study 1992,* the World Bank.

3. "Poverty Alleviation during the Transition in China", Zhu Ling, Institute of Economics, CASS, paper presented to UNU/WIDER project meeting, "Well Being in Asia During the Transition," August 21-22, 1997, Beijing.

4. *World Development Report 1992,* the World Bank.

5. *Industry and Development,* Global Report, 1993/1994, UNIDO.

6. "Social Security System and Alleviation of Poverty in China", Wang Huijiong, in *Toward Social Security for the Poor in the Asia Pacific Region,* ESCAP, Published by the UN, New York, 1996.

7. "Theory and Practice of Development of Social Assistance in Shanghai", Zhao Min, Shanghai Academy of Social Sciences (paper in Chinese).

8. *World Development Report 1996,* the World Bank.

9. *Human Development Report 1997,* UNDP, New York, Oxford University Press, 1997.

10. "Towards the Preparation of the World Summit for Social Development", position paper presented by the Director-General of UNESCO, July 1994.

11. *Social Progress through Industrial Development,* position paper pre-

sented by UNIDO to the World Summit of Social Development, March 1995.

12. "Global Environment and Local Action", the Club of Rome Conference in Fukuoka, Kyushu, May 1992.

13. *Designing Ecological Settlements,* chief editors: Margirt Kennedy & Declaan Kennedy, Dietrich Reimer Verlag, Berlin, 1996.

14. Papers from international forum "The Role of Private Sector in Poverty Alleviation through Social Efforts and Balanced Regional Development", July 1-2, Beijing, China UNCRD, DRC, China Promotional Commission of Brilliant Cause.

Part V

Some Environmental
Aspects of China

16. Toward a Sustainable Development Society: a System Approach

In dealing with the theme of this session, sustainable development in Asian, I have to focus on two aspects of this subject, one is sustainable development, the other is Asia. The former is entity-oriented, including dimension of time, because development means growing larger, fuller or more matured. Therefore, time or stage should be taken into consideration. While the later is space-oriented. we are focusing at the sustainable development in Asia, not in Europe or North America. Therefore, the regional features of Asia should be fully assessed. My understanding of sustainable development society includes four interrelated overlapped systems, the ecosystem, the social system, the economic system, S&T subsystem. An understanding and recognition of the laws of the ecosystem which governs the mechanism of the organisms of a natural community together with their environment is a recent development of science and technology system, the knowledge of mankind to nature in his historical development process, while development of S&T and economic system can be tentatively put in the lowest rank order of this interlinked hierarchical system, in spite of it is the cornerstone of development of the social system or ecosystem. Because in the stage of development, a sound economic system is to be established at first. But this is not absolute in sense, the order of ranking is mutually interactive, a disruptive ecosystem or social system will impair the sound growth of an economic system, and economic system will also have its effect on the development of S&T system.

With the above aspects and a framework of systems in mind, I shall present my views in sustainable development in Asia into four parts.

I. Asia Economic Development — A part of global industrialization process (interaction between S&T system and economic system is explored)

The Asian countries, specially countries in the East and Southeast Asia region, have enjoyed a rapid economic development after World War II; they are the successors of the forerunners. Emergence of modern industry, the first stage of industrial revolution from 1770 to 1870 had brought about the industrial dominance of UK, USA, Germany and France, innovation that allowed coal to be used in smelting iron and James Watt's improvement of the New-Commen steam engine between 1776 and 1781 had played a proper role in this stage. The second stage of industrialization from 1870-1913 had invited further the participation of Japan and Russia as members of the industrial club. Electricity, refrigeration, organic chemicals, the internal combustion engine, the telegraph and the radio made the economy enter a period of unprecedented output and growth, manufacturing led the way in this global industrialization process. There is an integration of world markets, and some of the new technologies, such as the jet aircraft, telecommunications, electronics, had helped the growth of this process. There was the exponential growth of the national economy, of energy use and also of waste loads. The population shifted from farms to urban and from urban to sub-urban were also accelerated. Many Asian countries and China have enjoyed a rapid economic development in the past several decades. Based upon the statistics of ADB and the World Bank, the average annual growth rate of GDP of Japan, China, NIEs and Southeast Asia from 1971 to 1980 is 5.0%, 6.5%, 9.2% and 7.9% respectively. (Japan has a high growth rate of 10.9% from 1960 to 1970). The growth rate of VA in China, South Korea, Malaysia, Indonesia and Thailand ranges from 8.9% to 14.2% in 1971-80, and it is 5.8%-12.7% from 1980-1989. The process of urbanization also proceeds rapidly, the urban population as percentage of total for China, South Korea and Malaysia in 1960 was 19%, 28% and 25%, and it is 33%, 72% and 43% respectively in 1990. While the trend for developed countries in population shift from urban to sub-urban, this rapid economic development and urbanization through industrialization and increase of use of energy brings along also serious environmental issues, which are common consequence of industrial and economic development. Atmospheric pollution, problems on freshwater resources and water quality, toxical chemicals and hazardous waste, land degradation and desertification, these are not known by people in general for ozone depletion and climate change. It is known in a narrow circle because of their invisibility. But we must look upon the Asian economic development as a part of history of global industrialization, a diffusion of industrial development in time spectrum to spatial spectrum. Countries in Asia are now undergoing what developed countries had experienced in the past two centuries. The latecomers can learn much from the positive and negative development experience from the developed countries, and they are at a better position to quicken the tempo of development, from economic development to social and sustainable development.

II. Sustainable Development — A stage of development of high hierarchy (interaction between economic system and social system is explored)

In consideration of sustainable development society in Asia, it is necessary to clarify the conception of sustainable development. I have mentioned in the very beginning that a sustainable development society includes four interrelated systems, the ecosystem, the social system, the economic system and science and technology system. It is impossible to realize a sustainable development society without an integrated approach of these four. I think sustainable development society is a society in the higher hierarchy generally. There is no acceptable standard definition of sustainable development. China has also used this phrase as one of the guidelines in the development of its national economy in Ten-Year Development Perspective. Two definitions can be clearly explained how contradictory issues in development could be solved. In its simplest form, sustainable development is a process which meets the needs of the present without compromising the ability of future generations to meet their own needs. And sustainable development can also be defined as a process of change in which the exploitation of resources, the direction of investment, the orientation of technological development and institutional change are all in harmony. The former definition has outlined a conceptual framework of balanced development in the time span while the later definition gives concrete actions in related fields. Both definitions are useful references for our discussions here. I shall emphasize the former definition in the discussion of this part.

In the former definition of sustainable development, two needs are pointed out, the present needs must be met and the needs of the future generations should not be sacrificed. It sounds good. But there are difficulties in implementation. Because the needs of the people of different regions are so diversified and the word "needs" need further clarification. There are many types of needs. I arbitrarily classify them into social needs and economic needs, the former includes mental and cultural aspects mostly and the economic needs are mainly physical. Although different people may have different needs, and the Eastern and Western culture are quite distinguished in their philosophies, i.e., their attitude and activities toward problems may be different, their needs may be different, but the basic nature of the human beings is common to all. The mankind in different stage has different needs, generally economic needs come first and then the social needs. An ancient great Chinese politician, Guanzhui, in the *Spring and Autumn Annals* around 600 B.C. had a saying, "The people can be educated with ceremony if the warehouse of cereal is full; the people will have the sense of glory and shame if the supply of food and cloth is enough". This statement two thousand years ago can also be interpreted with modern Maslow's theory of management. Mankind has a hierarchy of needs that must be satisfied in a certain order. The bottom of this hierarchy is physiological needs, then goes up to safety security needs, then the love-belongingness, esteem and finallyself-actualization. Both ancient Chinese saying and modern Western management theory explore a universal nature of the mankind, a pragmatic approach of development. Man starts at the bottom of this needs hierarchy and first strives to meet his physiological needs, such as food, shelter and clothing, or tangible needs and material substance. He does not proceed higher, to a higher needs of something intangible, the social needs (the sound social relationship between the human beings) and ecological needs (the sound relationship between the mankind and the nature). Sustainable development pointed out the action of mankind to the nature for their present economic needs should not endanger the economic needs of the future generation. This is a contradiction between the present and the future. But our world is full of contradictions. In the real world faced by us, countries of different regions are generally in different stages of development. A majority of countries in Asia are developing countries with different needs from that of developed countries. Economic development is a major concern of these countries. A key element in economic development is that the people of the countries must be major participants in development process that brought about the changes in per-capita income and also the fundamental changes in the structure of the economy, sustainable development requires the people of the globe to be major participants in the process that the global actions should be in harmony on the exploitation of resources, the direction of investments, the orientation of technology and also institutional changes.

III. Environmental Issues of China and China's Strategy towards Sustainable Development (China's responsibility to the global ecosystem)

China is the largest country in terms of population and size, and we have very rapid economic development in the past four decades, in recent decade specially. But the environmental issue is also serious and this may be a subject of concern by bur neighboring countries in Asia. A brief introduction of environ mental issues in China and her strategy toward sustainable development must be of interest here.

There are two major trends of problems faced by China in the economic development process: one is the trend of ecological-environmental problems, the other is the trend of environmental pollution problems. Some problems of them are local in nature, i.e., they will have not great effect on our neighboring countries, for example, habitat of some endangered species are gradually shrinking. I shall mention essential trends of problems that may have regional or global impact.

For the trends of ecological-environmental problems, China has relative fragility of the ecological function of forests and acute contradiction between supply and demand for forest resources. Forest is important in economic development because it not only provides timber and firewood, but also medical and other plants of use to mankind. Forest also has an important role environmentally, because it serves as carbon sinks to reduce the effects of carbon dioxide in the atmosphere, thereby help to contain global warming. This two points should be kept in mind in talking about the preservation of tropical forests in this panel discussion. China has now an forestry area of 124 million hectares, representing 12.98% of the land area of the nation, the per-capita forest area is 0.11 hectare, accounting for only 11.3% of the world average. Great efforts are spent by the government in this respect. Based upon our projection "China Toward the Year 2000" study, the coverage of the forest will reach 17% of the land area of the nation by the year 2000. It is mentioned in an UNDP report that "China is one of the few countries that has had success in reforesting major areas of its land. Between 1979 and 1983, 4 million ha. were planted each year: in 1985, the area rose to 8 million ha." In 1990, the growth rate of forests in half of the provinces and automous regions was higher than that of consumption.

For the trend of environmental pollution problems, we have the issues of relying coal as a major resource of energy, as coal will continue to be the major source of energy, air pollution from coal combustion is and will be a serious problem in the near future. Because China depends on coal as a major source of energy which provides 73% of total commercial energy consumption. Coal accounts for 75% of industrial fuel and power, 65% of raw materials for chemical industries. And coal will remain its importance in these sectors through the 1990's. China has already made great effort in preservation of atmospheric environment. With my initial background as chief electrical engineer, I know that many small power plants (in Western standard) have adopted electro-precipitators which are quite costly for this size of plant. China has an emission of SO_2 around 14.95 million tons in 1989. Removal of SO_2 is very costly although technically possible. But Chinese government will continue to make efforts to implement energy policies, encouraging energy saving and using better means to reduce air pollution, such as accelerating development of hydro-power, reducing the share of coal in energy structure, and utilizing coal of low sulfur content, etc.

For the environmental problems accompanied with urbanization, China has strains caused by rapid urbanization and lagging infrastructure; partial improvement can be expected of the urban environment quality and China has set up guidelines for urban development, i.e., "strictly control the scale of large cities, properly develop medium and small cities". This guideline is what China has learned from international experience in urbanization.

As a member of the international community and a country with population that accounts for about one fifth of the total of the world, China is keenly aware in protecting the global and regional environment and the major role she can play in this regard. The Chinese government has set up the following objectives in her national environmental protection plan by the year 2000.

1. Environmental pollution should be basically brought under control;

2. Environmental quality in major cities should be improved;

3. The trend of ecological degradation should be alleviated;

4. The integration of environmental protection with the national economic and social development should be achieved step by step.

IV. A System Approach toward Sustainable Development Society

(Sustainable Development Society is evolved through four interactive systems, the social system will play an important role in System Approach toward Sustainable Development)

Sustainable development is a new phase or new stage of development when the mankind knows more about the laws of nature so that a harmonious relations can be established between the man and the environment. The welfare of the present generation and the right of living for the future generations, the life of ourselves and our neighbors can be properly balanced. Sustainable development society is a high goal of society that we should achieve.

1) To achieve this goal and to meet the needs of this stage of development is a quite complex issue. No single means or single mind approach can solve this problem. A system approach is required. Because environmental problem itself is a system problem, there are many interrelated elements. There are five-level model of environmental issues: local (the developed environment), regional (the landscape), fluvial (the basins of rivers and coastal area), continental (air and ocean currents), and global (the higher air layers). Each level has its "own" problems, yet they all affect each other. Local problems can contribute to problems at "higher" levels. Ozone layer depletion and climate change is a global issue, coordinated action must be taken at global level for its solution. Therefore, in the space span, achievement of sustainable development requires coordinated action between local, national, regional and global. It is the local action which forms the basis for global

protection. Policy and planning may be a proper area for coordination.

2) In the time span, most of Asian countries are developing countries, economic development and elimination of poverty are the main aims of present stage of development, because poverty is one of the course of worsening of environment. Economic development of Asian developing countries should be recognized. But economic development should be properly balanced with long-term issues. I remember an old Chinese saying says, "One will face immediate trouble if one has not a longer perspective". We shall keep this in mind.

3) Sustainable development society includes interaction of four systems, the ecosystem, the social system, the economic system and the science and technology system.

(1) Action to be taken in science and technology system is to study better substance cycle so as to contain few "leaks" as possible in the chain of production process; to conserve energy and improve the efficiency and utilization of renewable energy sources; to promote the quality of production process and products. Proper regulations of technology transfer should be established internationally so that developing countries can obtain environmental non pollutant technology under favorite terms.

(2) Action to be taken in economic system is to establish proper financing system at different levels to assist the developing countries to combat against environmental problems. The developed countries have established their capacity in capital and technology through centuries of industrialization. They can contribute more. Even in a developed country, there are still developed and developing regions. Developed region should assist the developing region in all countries.

(3) What is important is the social aspects, the social system. A sense of environment awareness, a sense of concern for the neighbor and the future generation, a sense of local action and global responsibility is necessary. These senses of society may be a prerequisite to solve the contradictions of many issues, the contradictions between long term and short term, between national, regional and global. Sustainable development is a high standard of morality. Confucius had a saying, "Respect my old man as well as the old man of others, take care of my young ones as well as the young ones of others". This is a type of social relationship in dealing with others, one kind

of morality. Sustainable development society may mean more than that. It requires the change of life style, to create a sense of preservation of environment, to devise an innovative approach to development, to live harmoniously with nature and living organisms in general. To create this social awareness requires education. To educate ourselves as well as the people in general. All of us here can do and should do, every effort should be spent to advocate, to popularize the conception of sustainable development, so that sustainable development will become a mass action with involvement of grassroot participation. After all, development is done for the people and by the people. Mr. Toffler had once created "The Third Wave", information age had once been widely popularized to every corner of the world. Sustainable development, a new age of development should become a "Fourth Wave" rush around the world, deeply rooted in the hearts of the people, all preservative actions for the environment are widely undertaken in the household, in the factory, in the urban and in the rural area. Then, a sustainable development society is achievable, to be sure.

17. Economic Development and the Environment in China[*]

China has achieved rapid economic growth since initiating economic reform and opening to the outside world in the late 1970's, and it has emerged as an indispensable component of the "East Asian Miracle." It is worth emphasizing, however, that China has been committed to industrial growth and technology development since the 1950's. Industrialization has been a primary objective of development strategy since the establishment of the People's Republic of China (PRC), despite occasional debate about the best means to achieve this objective. Four decades of effort to industrialize the country have resulted in pervasive changes in economic structure. The shares of total value-added attributable to the primary, secondary, and tertiary sectors has shifted from 52, 22, and 26 percent in 1952 to 21, 48, and 31 percent in 1995.

This rapid industrialization has inevitably affected the environment. In the latest decades of a much longer period of industrialization, the international community has gained deeper understanding of linkages between economic development and the environment. Although China is a latecomer in this process, it can benefit from many precedents and experiences originating elsewhere.

There are many environmental issues in China, but the most prominent one today is the use of coal, the country's major energy resource. Burning this fuel with current technologies emits CO_2 — the greenhouse gas most important in quantity, thereby contributing to climate change — and SO_2, the primary constituent in acid rain. Because of the importance of global warming and acid rain to China and the world, this chapter focuses on links be-

---

[*] The author and co-author of this paper are Huijiong Wang and Shantong Li.

tween the economy and these two environmental issues, with emphasis on energy-related CO_2 and SO1 emissions. Other environmental problems will be surveyed more generally.

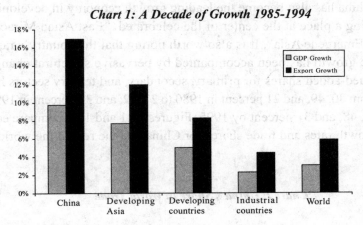

Chart 1: A Decade of Growth 1985-1994

Source: IMF, "World Economic Outlook", October 1994.

In section 2 of this chapter, we provide and overview economic growth patterns and the structure of energy demand and supply in China. This provides a basis for discussion in section 3 of industrialization and its impact on the environment. Since these issues have arisen relatively recently in China, evidence is still limited, section 3 still provides some general inferences about development-environment linkages. Section 4 surveys long-term and short-term policy options for the Chinese government in dealing with environmental problems and economic growth. Section 5 examines Chinese environmental issues from an international perspective, and section 6 closes with concluding remarks.

2. Economic Growth and Energy Consumption

2.1. China's Economic Growth from an International Perspective

China has experienced remarkable economic growth in recent years, with the external sector acting as the primary engine of growth and opening this vast country to the outside world. The growth rate of GDP averaged 9.3 percent during 1980-90 and 12.0 percent during 1990-95. These high economic growth rates are even more remarkable when compared to the relatively slow growth experienced by industrial economies during the same period. China has also become the leading growth economy in developing Asia, taking a place at the center of the celebrated "East Asian Miracle" and the "Emergene Asia". It is also worth noting that the country's rapid economic growth has been accompanied by pervasive structural change. Total valued-added shares for primary, secondary, and tertiary sectors had shifted from 30, 49, and 21 percent in 1980 to 27, 42, and 31 percent in 1990, and to 21, 48, and 31 percent by 1995. Figures 12.1 and 12.2 compare economic growth rates and trade shares for China and the rest of the world.

Chart 2: China's Share in World Trade

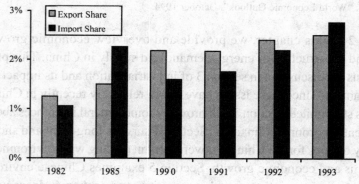

Source: IMF, "Direction of Trade".

2.2. Pattern of Economic Growth and Energy Consumption

2.2.1. Measurement of Economic Growth

To better understand links between economic growth and energy supply and demand patterns, a brief description on the features of the Chinese System of National Accounts (SNA) is warranted. Prior to its economic reforms, China used a framework of national accounts modeled on the Soviet system of the 1950's, but this system differs in significant ways from SNA. As one growth indicator in the Chinese statistical system since the 1950's, national income, measured from the production side, represents value added to a country's material wealth by the five "material production sectors".[1] Deductions from gross output of each sector are made for depreciation and other intermediate inputs to arrive at value-added; the figures for each sector are then aggregated to obtain national income produced (or "Net Material Product", NMP). China's Bureau of Statistics has used two basic adjustments — depreciation and nonmaterial services not covered by the original framework — to arrive at the value of GDP. Official values of GDP are available since 1978, with the value of GDP generally 19-23 percent higher than national income.

2.2.2. GDP and Energy Consumption Growth

Energy is the lifeblood of an industrial economy, and in a rapidly industrializing country like China, national economic growth is closely related to the growth of energy consumption and production Figure 12.3 plots the growth rates of energy consumption and GDP from 1978 to 1995, over which period their correlation coefficient is 0.6683.

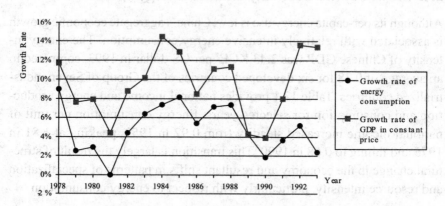

Fig. 3. Growth Rate of Energy Use and GDP

Source: *Statistical Yearbook of China.*

---

1. The sectors are agriculture, industry, construction, transport communications, and commerce.

Table 12.1. Income and Energy Use in Different Planning Periods

Year	National Income (billion yuan)	Energy Production (MTCE)	Energy Consumption (MTCE)	Energy Consumption/ National Income (MTCE/ billion yuan)
1952	58.9	51.92	54.11[*]	0.9187
1957	90.8	98.61	96.44	1.0621
1962	92.4	171.85	165.40	1.7900
1965	138.7	188.24	189.01	1.3627
1970	192.6	309.90	292.91	1.5208
1975	250.3	487.54	454.25	1.8148
1980	368.8	637.35	602.75	1.6344
1985	702.0	855.46	766.82	1.0923
1990	1442.9	1039.22	987.03	0.6841

*1953 figure. Since an energy consumption figure for 1952 is not available in national statistics, the statistics of 1953 are used.
Source: *China Energy Statistical Almanac1991*.

2.3. Growth of the Economy and the Energy Sector

Although its per-capita energy use is low, China's aggregate economic growth is associated with relatively intensive energy consumption. The energy intensity of Chinese GDP was 2.43 KCE[2] per US dollar in 1993, compared to an average of 0.38 for six developed countries of the Group of Seven industrialized countries. Table 12.1 provides national income and energy production and consumption for selected years. Energy consumption per unit of national income increased steadily from 0.92 in 1953, peaking at 1.81 in 1975 and falling to 0.68 in 1990. This transition is largely the result of structural change in the economy and resultant shifts in patterns of specialization and resource intensity, particularly with respect to energy consumption.

For several decades, China's strategy for industrialization was modeled on that of the former Soviet Union. This was characterized mainly by an accelerated buildup of heavy industries and large-scale production with capital-intensive and modern technical processes. In both countries, this pattern of

---

2. KCE, Kilogram of Standard Coal Equivalent, which is coal with 7,000 kilocalorics per kilogram of coal.

industrialization proved to be less successful in raising living standards than one that targeted light industries first and then moved to heavy industries as the newly industrialized economies (NIEs) have done. Nevertheless, this pattern of development established an extensive foundation of industry and technology in China. From the Second Five-Year Plan to the Fifth Five-Year Plan (1976-1980), development of heavy industries was the dominant priority, despite the fact that Chairman Mao once assigned the opposite priorities for sectoral development in industrialization (agriculture, light industry, and heavy industry). This is a major reason for high energy intensity of consumption in the pre-reform era. This trend has moderated since the launch of economic reform in late 1978, as the ratio of light to heavy industries increased from 0.89 in 1980 to 0.97 in 1990.

Table 12.2. Change of Value and Structure of National Income

Year	Growth Rate of Energy Production (%)	Growth Rate of Energy Consumption (%)	Growth Rate of National Income (%)	Elasticity of Energy Production	Elasticity of Energy Consumption
1953	6.59		14.00	0.47	
1957	19.64	9.59	4.50	4.37	2.13
1962	-19.03	-18.88	-6.50	2.93	2.90
1965	9.24	13.61	17.00	0.54	0.80
1970	34.13	28.86	23.30	1.46	1.24
1975	17.12	13.24	8.30	2.06	1.60
1980	-1.28	2.88	6.40		0.45
1985	9.88	8.15	13.50	0.73	0.60
1990	2.25	1.15	4.80	0.47	0.23

Source: China Energy Statical Almanac 1991.

It can also be seen from Tables 12.1 and 12.2 that before 1980 the growth rate of energy demand increased rapidly in comparison with the growth rate of the national economy. This is mainly due to the process of industrialization and the priority given to heavy industry before the 1980's. In 1953, the growth rate of national income (N1) is much higher than the growth rate of energy supply because China was predominantly an agrarian society before 1952.

It can be seen that the elasticity of energy consumption was as low as 0.23 in 1990, due to structural change in the economy as well as improvements in efficiency of energy utilization.

Table 12.3. Average Annual Growth Rate of Energy Production and Consumption across Different Planning Periods

	Average Annual Growth Rate during Different Planning Periods*						
	First 5-Second 5	Second 5-Adjustment	Adjustmt-Third 5	Third 5-Fourth 5	Fourth 5-Fifth 5	Fifth 5-Sixth 5	Sixth 5-Seventh 5
Production (%)	25.5	-9.1	7.8	12.8	7.9	4.1	5.7
Consumption (%)	24.0	-8.4	8.5	12.5	7.1	3.9	6.4

*First 5 means the First Five-Year Plan period, and Second 5 the Second Five-Year Plan period, etc.

Source: *China Statistical Yearbook*.

3. Patterns of Growth in Energy Supply and Demand

3.1. Historical Energy Supply and Demand

Energy demand in China has in the past been met through domestic resources and production. Table 12.3 shows the average annual growth rate of energy production and consumption between different planning periods (i.e., comparing five-year intervals begmning about 1950). These trends will facilitate understanding of more detailed patterns of economic growth and energy consumption, discussed in the following subsection.

3.2. Structure of Energy Production and Consumption of Energy

The data in Figure 12.4 summarize the structure of consumption for different energy resources. These figures clearly reveal the dominant role that coal plays in consumption, although a declining trend in the share of coal since the 1960s is discernible. The latter effect is largely due to the discovery of petroleum in the northeastern provinces and northern, central part of China (Hebei, Henan, Hubei) and a large gasfield in Sichuan Province. Hence, there were increasing shares of petroleum and natural gas in domestic energy production and consumption from the 1960's to the 1970's. The production of petroleum became sluggish in the 1980's, however, with a growth rate of only 3.5 percent from 1981 to 1990, and the share of coal in total energy production and consumption in China increased slightly during that period. Figure 12.4 also illustrates the low share of hydro-electricity energy of consumption in China, only 5.1 percent of consumption in 1990. Apparently, the country is seriously under-utilizing the rich potential of its water resources. The development of electric power in China is interesting in comparison with other countries, such as Japan, Norway, Switzerland, France, the USA, and Canada. Those countries generally give hydro-energy resources higher exploration priority then thermal plants. In China, however, most of the hydroelectric potential is located in relatively under-developed regions (especially the mountainous Southwest), far from large cities and commercial centers. In addition, institutional and technical challenges to hydroelectric capacity development are formidable.

It can be seen from Figure 12.4 that a conspicuous feature of Chinese energy consumption is the high share of coal in total energy use — over 90 percent during the first two five-year periods; it remains around 73 percent by 1986-90. This is extremely high compared to other countries. Even in India, where coal is also a major energy source, it accounted for only 60

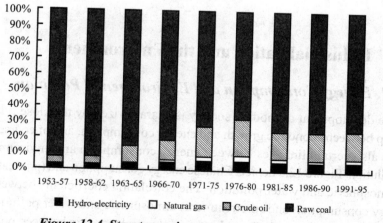

Figure 12.4. Structure primary energy consumption.

(Sources: *China's Energy Statistics Almanac 1991; Statistical Yearbook of China 1995.*)

percent of total primary energy use in 1980. The unique features of energy source shares are apparent in Table 12.4, which gives international comparisons of energy source shares around the 1990s. Although this table cannot provide completely up-to-date information because China has commissioned nuclear power plants in the decade of the 1990s, it does capture the general picture.

Table12.4.Energy Source Shares of Country Energy Production,1989
(percent)

Country	Comparison of Energy Sources					
	Coal	Oil	Natural Gas	Hydro-electricity	Nuclear Electricity	Total
China	74	19	2	5	0	100
India	60	23	6	11	1	100
Japan	8	1	2	26	63	100
USA	33	27	27	5	10	100
USSR	19	36	39	4	3	100
Rest of World	...	...	...	...	...	...
World Total	27	38	21	7	6	100

Source: Lawrence Berkeley Laboratory (1992), *China Energy Databook*, Berkeley: University of California, Berkeley.

4. Industrialization and the Environment

4.1. Energy Consumption and Environmental Pollution

The development of modern society is characterized by the close relationship between economic growth and energy consumption, and of course there are also certain linkages between energy consumption and environmental pollution. Figure 12.5 depicts Chinese energy consumption and (pretreatment) atmospheric and water pollution. The correlation coefficients between energy consumption and (pretreatment) atmospheric and water pollution are 0.97 and 0.41, respectively, indicating a close relationship between pollution and energy consumption.

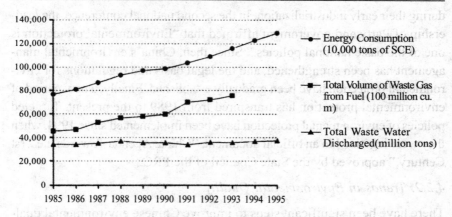

Figure 12.5. Energy Consumption and Pollution of Atmosphere and Water

Source: *China Statistical Yearbook.*

4.2. China's Environment Protection and Trends in Environment Quality

4.2.1. Environment Protection in China: A Retrospective

China focused its attention on industrialization in the early 1950's but because of its relative isolation, the history of environmental protection is only about two decades old. China's environmental protection was initiated only in the early 1970's (whereas the Clean Air Act was established in 1956 in some developed countries), *Limits to Growth* was published in 1972, and the Stockholm Declaration was negotiated in 1972. China participated in the Stockholm Conference and soon afterward (1973) launched its first national conference on environmental protection. The period 1973-83 was the real inception of environmental protection in China. In the first national conference on this subject, China for the first time began to recognize its environmental problems, which were already relatively serious. After this conference, a temporary environmental protection policy group and office were set up. A limited amount of work on environmental protection was done, and an environmental administration team was trained at this time.

The period 1983-89 marked an important transition in Chinese environmental management. The country began to realize that it could not simply relive the "pollute first, clean up afterward" cycle adopted by the developed countries during their early industrialization. In the second national conference, the leadership of Party and government affirmed that "Environmental protection is one of the basic national policies." Since then, China's environmental management has been strengthened, and the legal basis and regulations for environmental protection have been gradually established. Finally, a new period of environmental protection has transpired from 1989 to the present. Targeted policies of environ mental protection have been implemented since 1994, when they were legalized in an official document, "China: Agenda Towards the 21st Century," approved by the State Council of the PRC.

4.2.2. Trends in Environmental Quality

There have been significant steps to improve Chinese environmental quality in recent years, and these come from several sources. The scope of the present exposition allows for only an overview of this subject. A more in-depth examination of these issues is currently being undertaken in China by several departments, including the Development Research Center of the State Council.

Examination of data in Table 12.5 reveals that China's energy consumption per unit of GDP decreased during the 1978-93 period. The resulting gain in energy efficiency over the fifteen-year period is 48.3 percent. This improvement is likely to have resulted from changing economic structure and more efficient energy utilization, but it is difficult to separate these two factors.

There have been noticeable improvements in environmental protection measures in the past decade.[3] For example, in 1986, 57 percent of all fuel gas was treated, and 50.7 percent of treated industrial wastewater met water quality standards. By 1993, these two figures had increased to 68.8 percent and 75.4 percent, respectively. They reflect both more extensive monitoring and greater levels of average conformity with environmental quality standards. Two atmospheric pollutants, SO_2 and particulates, are of special concern to Chinese environmental experts and are coming under intensified official

---

3. At the national level, the State Administration of Environmental Protection of China publishes an official report every year giving assessments of environmental quality. The government also published "Technical Guidelines on Environmental Impact Assessment" (HJ/T2-93) in 1993, which consists of three parts: general, atmospheric environment, and under-ground water environment.

scrutiny. Although more favorable aggregate trends in environmental quality have now been established, several special categories remain relatively
hazardous. We discuss them in more detail in the following sections.

Table 12.5 Energy Consumption per 10,000 Yuan of GDP

Year	Energy Consumption (10,000 ton of SCE)	GDP of 1978 billion yuan	Energy Consump. per 10,000 yuan of GDP
1978	57,144	362.4	15.8
1979	58,588	390.0	15.0
1980	60,275	420.4	14.3
1981	59,447	442.5	13.4
1982	62,067	482.4	12.9
1983	66,040	534.9	12.3
1984	70,904	616.1	11.5
1985	76,685	699.1	11.0
1986	80,850	761.1	10.6
1987	86,632	849.1	10.2
1988	92,997	944.8	9.8
1989	96,934	983.2	9.9
1990	98,703	1,020.9	9.7
1991	103,783	1,114.8	9.3
1992	109,170	1,273.5	8.6
1993	115,993	1,445.3	8.0
1994	122,737	1,628.3	7.5
1995	129,000	1,800.1	7.2

Source: *China Statistical Yearbook 1996.*

4.3. Statistics on Atmospheric Pollution

Complete statistics and data on atmospheric pollution are not available before 1986. The following paragraphs summarize the available statistics on
essential components of atmospheric pollution. It should be emphasized that
the pollution statistics may be biased on the lower side, because official
monitoring and statistics are confined to state-owned enterprises. Township
and village enterprises contribute about 30 percent to total value-added in
industry, yet their pollution from them is not included in the national accounts

for pollution. It is estimated that a factor of 1.3-1.4 should be applied to correct the following data for atmospheric and water pollution.

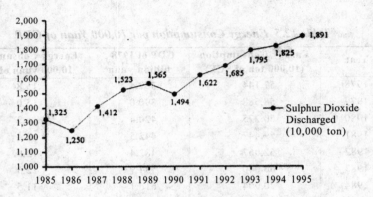

Figure 12.6. Discharge of SO₂, 1985-95.

Source: *China Statistical Yearbook, 1986-96.*

4.3.1. Statistics for SO₂

Discharge of SO_2 is mainly due to combustion of fossil fuels, especially soft coal. Therefore, those sectors that have a higher share in coal consumption are also the sectors with higher share of SO_2, discharged. Figure 12.9 shows that the electricity sector, nonmetallic mineral processing, chemical engineering, and metallurgy each represent more than 10 percent of all SO_2, discharges, while the electricity sector has a share as high as 46.1 percent.

4.3.2. Statistics for Particulates

The data on industrial soot refer to the soot discharged into the atmosphere after the process of gas treatment. This includes the suspended particulate matter (SPM) produced in combustion processes and in various industrial processes. Several sectors contribute the majority share; for example, in 1991, the electricity sector, the chemical sector, and the nonmetallic mineral processing sector contributed 29.6 percent, 6.1 percent, and 32 percent shares of the total discharge, respectively The electricity sector had a high share of soot produced in combustion, and the nonmetallic mineral processing sector (mainly cement) had a high share of soot produced in the manufacturing process.

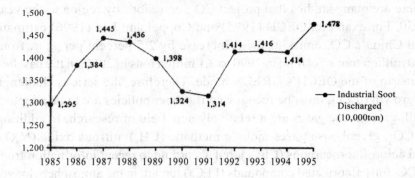

Figure 12.7. Discharge of Industrial Soot,1985-95.

Source: *China Statistical Yearbook.*

It is also interesting to note the shape of the graph (the clip from 1988-90 is a result of the economic austerity program in this period) and also improvements due to environmental protection measures. Industrial soot in 1995 is 102.3 percent of that in 1987, the previous peak.

4.3.3. Statistics for CO_2

CO_2 is the most important greenhouse gas (GHG), representing about 55 percent of all GHG emissions and 75 percent of energy-related GHG emissions. It is widely believed that the rising atmospheric concentration of GHG could result in a change in the global as well as regional climate, entailing severely detrimental economic and ecological effects. China has not estimated its CO_2 emissions in the past, although early estimates of climate change due to CO_2; concentration had been done in developed countries. Several international organizations and groups of scholars such as the OECD, the International Panel on Climate Change (IPCC), the International Institute for Applied Systems Analysis (IIASA), and the World Bank have estimated CO_2 emissions in China and other countries/regions. At the moment, a Chinese research institution is carrying out research to estimate a proper coefficient to be applied to the combustion of coal, petroleum, and natural gas to derive induced CO_2; emissions. One value of CO_2 emissions, calculated by the Energy Research Institute of China, is 564 million tons of carbon equivalents based upon statistics for consumption of fossil fuels; another figure, from IPCC, is 630 million tons.

There are many studies that project CO_2; emissions by region to the year 2050. For example, OECD (1995) and Coppel and Lee (1996) estimate that China's CO_2 emissions will increase by 2.5 percent per year, from 600 million tons of carbon in 1990 to 3.1 billion tons in 2050, in the baseline scenario of the OECD's GREEN mode. Therefore, the serious challenge of growth of CO_2 must be recognized if proper policies are to be adopted. Still, greenhouse gases are a relatively new field of research. In addition to CO_2, greenhouse gases include methane (CH_4), nitrous oxide (N_2O), and chlorofluorocarbons (CFCs), but according to recent information from IPCC, fully fluorinated compounds (FFCs) remain in the atmosphere longer and trap more heat per molecule emitted than almost any other gas. It has been suggested by the World Resources Institute (WRI) that "the international community should not allow FFC emissions or new uses to grow unchecked." The effects of those greenhouse gases will be examined in a separate study.

4.3.4. Acid Rain-pH Concentration

Although a large number of monitoring stations for acid rain have been established, detailed official information and academic research for China are still unavailable in this important area. The formation of acid rain is a very complicated process, requiring a lot of coordinated studies on climate, soil characteristics, and pollutants. Much work of this kind is already extant for Western countries, but it will require years of determined effort for China to catch up. For example, a research team organized by the World Resources Institute and the Energy and Resource Group at the University of California at Berkeley worked for more than eighteen months on research for "The American West's Acid Rain Test." In the Netherlands, the study of emission reduction objectives for acidifying substances included NH_3, NO_2, SO_2, and volatile organic compounds (VOC). By contrast, at present one can find only an index of SO_2 in China's official statistics. This succinctly but persuasively clarifies the difficulty in explaining the causes of acid rain in China. In any event, SO_2 is the main contributor to acid rain. Cities with more than 1.5 percent share of national total SO_2 discharged are listed in Appendix Table A12.2. Appendix figure A 12.1 provides a map of China with cities with high frequency of acid rain.

It is claimed in the National Report on Environment in 1993 that acid rain is restricted in certain local areas where, based upon statistics for seventy-three cities, the range of annual average pH value of precipitation is 3.94-7. 63. In this group, 49.3 percent of the cities had an annual average pH below 5.6. The frequency of acid rain in Ganzhou, Changsha, Nanchong, Yibin, Huaihua, Chongqing, Wuzhou, Nanchang, Luzhou, Hangzhou, Hengyang, and Guilin was higher than 70 percent." An "Outline on Comprehensive Prevention and Abatement of Acid Rain" was drafted by China's State Administration of Environmental Protection in 1993, and research and policy development in this area is very active.

4.4. Statistics for Water Pollution

Organic compounds dominate China's water pollution. Heavy metal pollutants had once been under better control in the Seventh Five-Year Plan period, but the situation has worsened in recent years. Pollution of the water system is described separately later.

4.4.1. Rivers

China has seven major river systems, and nearly one-half of them are polluted. The quality of 86 percent of the urban river section is below official standards. For example, an evaluation of a 200-km section of the Huai River revealed that 78.8 percent of this stretch of river is below standard for drinking water, 79.7 percent of the river section is not adapted to the standard of water for fisheries, and 32 percent of the river section is not adapted to irrigation use. Many regions of the Huai River have rates of cancer incidence more than twenty to thirty times the normal rate of incidence. According to incomplete statistics of twenty-nine rivers in fifteen provinces and municipalities, there are around 2,800 km of river courses where fish populations are negligible.

4.4.2. Lakes

The lakes of China are generally polluted, especially with heavy metal contaminants that are among the most serious waterborne pollutants. Dianchi Lake, for example, is the largest source of drinking water for Kunming municipality (over 2 million people) in Yunnan Province. It provides 54 percent of the total water supply to this city. But due to the discharge of industrial waste water and sewage by households surrounding the lake, it is seriously polluted by heavy metals and remains well below the minimum official standard for drinking water.

The state of pollution in urban rivers monitored by the state is summarized in

Table 12.6. State of Pollution of City Rivers Monitored by the State

Pollutant	Statistics of number monitored		No. of rivers with sampling exceeding the standard	No. of river sectors with rate of exceeeding standard>50%	No. of river sections with annual average value exceeding the standard
	City	River			
pH	98	131	47	4	4
Suspension solids	95	126	89	35	49
Total hardness	93	126	39	23	25
Dissolved oxygen	96	129	79	37	31
Index of manganic acid salt	97	129	90	59	64
BOD	97	130	83	51	59
Ammonia nitrogen	98	131	78	44	42
Nitrite	98	131	70	15	24
Nitrate	96	128	0	0	0
Volatile pheno	96	128	77	32	46
Total cyanidel	96	128	9	1	1
Total arsenic	96	128	21	101	3
Total mercury	89	119	49	24	29
Chrome 6 valence	97	130	13	0	0
Total lead	92	124	28	7	8
Total cadmium	91	123	29	8	9
Petroleum	83	108	94	73	84

Source: *China Environmental Yearbook 1995.*

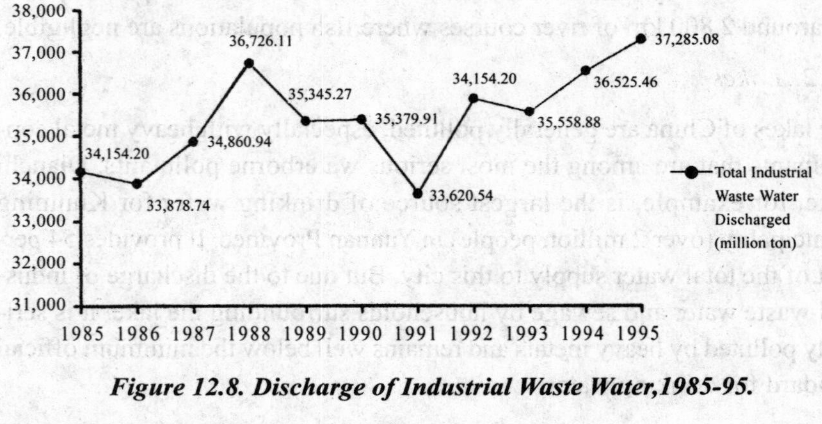

Figure 12.8. Discharge of Industrial Waste Water, 1985-95.

Source: *China Statistical Yearbook, 1986-96.*

Table 12.6, which shows that the number of rivers with toxic metals exceeding standards is quite high. Generally, rivers in the northern part of China have more excessive annual values exceeding the standard than do rivers in southern China.This may be due to the fact that rivers in the southern part of China, coming mainly off the Himalayan Plateau, have larger annual flows than those of northern China.

4.4.3. Water Quality

One leading environmental issue for China is the quality of its water resources. Total annual average surface water in China is around 2,638 billion m^3, ranking sixth in the world. But per-capita water resources measure 2,500 m^3, less than one fourth of the average per-capita water resources for the world. Moreover, water resources per-hectare land measure only 87.9 m^3, which is about one-half the world average. Therefore, China is classified as one of thirteen countries experiencing water shortage. The spatial distribution of the water resources is also quite uneven, rich in the southwest and poorer in the northwest. This shortage of water must inevitably affect production in industry and agriculture, as well as public health generally.

Figure 12.8 shows the trend in discharge of industrial waste water from 1985-1995. It can be seen from Table 12.7 that the sectors with the highest share of

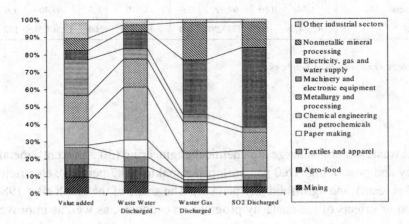

Fig.12. 9. Structure Comparison of Sectoral Output of Value and Pollution

Table 12.7. Comparison of Sectoral Output of Value and Pollution

Industrial Sector	Value-added (share of industrial output)		Waste Water Discharged (share of total W.W.)		Waster Gas Discharged (share of total W.G.)		SO₂ Discharged (share of total SO₂)	
	100 million yuan	%	10,000 ton	%	100 million cum.	%	ton	%
Mining	1,202.85	9.4	148,675	6.7	3,518	3.4	463,653	3.4
Agro-food	960.7	7.5	192,716	8.7	2,832	2.8	561,452	4.1
Textile and apparel	1,276.09	9.9	129,410	5.8	1,800	1.8	401,307	3.0
Paper making	151.06	1.2	215,810	9.7	1,731	1.7	280,770	2.1
Chemical engineering and petrochemicals	1,738.19	13.5	676,528	30.5	13,912	13.6	1,610,667	11.9
Metallurgy and processing	1,994.33	15.1	355,736	16.0	18,574	18.1	1,410,585	10.4
Machinery and electronic equip.	2,632.46	20.5	136,747	6.2	4,220	4.1	410,779	3.0
Electricity,gas,and water supply	691.11	5.4	265,675	9.7	32,264	31.5	6,283,378	46.1
Non-metallic mineral processing	897.82	7.0	82,807	3.7	22,107	21.5	1,941,594	14.4
Other industrial sectors	1,348	10.5	69,099	3.0	1,570	1.5	197,400	1.6
Total	12,842.6	100	2,237,203	100	102,528	100	13,561,585	100

Source: *China Statistical Yearbook 1994.*

total waste water discharge are chemical engineering (30.5 percent), metallurgy and processing (16.0 percent), paper making (9.7 percent), electricity (9.7 percent), and agro-food (8.7 percent). The shape of the graph after 1988 captures effects of the austerity program on economy, as well as improvements in waste-water discharge due to more rigorous enforcement of environmental standards. This explains the lower value of discharge of waste water in 1993 than in 1988, although GDP in 1993 is 1.51 times that of 1988.

4.5. Effect of Industrial Structure on the Environment

An Initial Exploration

Different sectors of economic activity have different impacts on the environment. For example, the electricity, gas, and water sector has a lower share in value-added of total industrial output but very high shares of total discharge for waste gas and SO_2. Likewise, industrial activities are generally more pollution-intensive (even with modern technologies) than services, a fact that highlights one of the central environmental dilemmas facing developing countries. As they make the transition from agrarian to industrial society, they pass through a structural bottleneck that concentrates their output, employment, and value-added into activities that are more pollution-intensive at any level of technological advancement. This can foster an impression of environmental irresponsibility, even though the pollution intensity of their GDP is inevitably higher than more advanced countries because of differing economic structure. Indeed, the world's most modern societies are no longer really industrial economies. Obtaining up to 75 percent of their GDP from tertiary activities, they have relegated industry to the marginal status that agriculture attained there after World War II.

For the Chinese case, a detailed sectoral analysis is given in the appendix. Figure 12.9 and Table 12.7 also provide a comprehensive picture.

5. Government Policies for Environmental Protection

Government environment policies at the national level are best discussed from two perspectives: (1) long-term policies, and (2) short and medium-term policies.

5.1. Long-term Environmental Policy at the National Level — "China: Agenda Towards 21st Century"

Following the Earth Summit in Rio de Janeiro in 1992, the Environmental Protection Committee of the State Council prepared a white paper titled "China: Agenda Towards 21st Century." This policy document dealt with population, the environment, and development. The project was led by the State Planning

Box 12.1.
Abstracts from Chapter 13 of "China: Agenda Towards 21st Century"

Sustainable Energy Production and Consumption

Introduction

13.1-13.4 ...

13.5 Four programs are set up in this chapter:

A. Comprehensive energy planning and management;

B. Improvement of energy efficiency and energy saving;

C. To push forward pollutantless coal-mining technology and clean coal technology;

D. Development and utilization of new energy and renewable energy resources.

Program

A. Comprehensive Energy Planning and Management

Basis for Action

13.6-13.8 ...

13.9. Before the end of this century, the strategy and public policy for the development of China's energy and environment are to place emphasis both on development and saving, as well as to improve the composition of energy and its location. The development of the energy sector should be based upon coal, be centered around electricity, and strive to develop hydroelectric power fully, petroleum and natural gas actively, nuclear energy properly, and new and renewable energy sources appropriately, based upon local conditions. To reduce environmental pollution, energy needs to be utilized more efficiently through scientific and technological progress.

Target

13.10-13.12 ...

Action

13.13-13.20 Essential action in these articles is to increase the share of electricity in the energy sector, develop nuclear energy both through domestic effort and joint ventures, extend rural electrification, and promote energy-saving cookers, biogas, and new and renewable energy resources.

13.23 (International cooperation) Proceed with extensive international cooperation and exchange; learn the experience of international advanced comprehensive planning, management measures, and policy instruments adapted to Chinese concrete conditions; import and transfer advanced technology and process from abroad through various channels to upgrade the domestic technological level of energy production and utilization; obtain access to international grant and financial resources through bilateral and multilateral means to strengthen the construction of Chinese energy industry; promote academic exchange and training of personnel.

B. Improvement of Energy Efficiency and Energy Saving

Basis of Action 13.24-13.27

Target 13.28-13.29

Action 13.30-13.37

C. To Push Forward Pollutantless Coal Mining Technology and Clean Coal Technology

Basis of Action

13.41 ... To develop pollutantless coal mining technology and clean coal technology; to control the discharge of greenhouse gases such as CH4 and CO_2...

Target 13.42

Action

13.43-13.51 The efficiency of utilization of conversion of energy, to lower the production cost, increase the share of new energy resource in energy supply structure.

13.56 The hydropower capacity should reach more than 80,000 M.W. before the year 2000; utilization of solar energy should reach 2-3 million TCE, energy from wind power should reach 200 M.W., capacity of utilization of geothermal power should reach more than 800,000 TCE to raise the efficiency of utilization of biomass; the method of utilization will be transformed gradually mainly to biogas production and clean liquid.

Commission (SPC) and the State Science and Technology Commission (SSTC), with the participation of fifty-two ministries and 300 experts. The final draft was completed and approved by the State Council on May 25, 1994. It is claimed to represent a national policy for sustainable development over a long term.

Sustainable development is an integrated approach of basic policy measures and instruments of social, economic, and ecological systems. The concept and approach of this document are illustrated in Box 12.1, quoted with targets and action on "Sustainable Energy Production and Consumption." A more detailed discussion of policy response to environmental issues related to this document is provided in subsequent sections.

5.2. Short- and Medium-term Policy Responses

Four areas of medium- and short-term energy policy response to environmental issues are worthy of special emphasis.

5.2.1. Price Distortions in the Energy Sector

There are significant and extensive price distortions in various types of energy. But reform of the price system is beginning to reduce these disparities. The government as tried to correct price distortions with a gradual approach, and we can only summarize its main features here.

China's reliance on coal as a major source of energy and its effects on the environment were clearly recognized in the national report:

As coal will continue to be China's primary source of energy for a considerable period of time, in the absence of major breakthroughs in combustion technology and in coal conversion, atmospheric pollution and acid rains are likely to worsen. The government's policy on price reform generally is to liberalize prices gradually. Table 12.8 summarizes the historical record of energy sector price reform.

This gradual approach seeks to achieve convergence between the market price and planned price. Now that the government has liberalized the coal price and adjusted crude oil prices in the direction of international market prices, more than 10 percent of crude oil is traded below the planned

Table 12.8. Plan and Market Prices for Selected Energy Sectors,1985-91
(yuan per ton)

	1985		1988		1991	
	Coal	Crude oil	Coal	Crude oil	Coal	Crude oil
Planned price(a)	26.4	100	61		83	204
Non-planned price(b)	77.4	545	148		141	580
(b)-(a)	51.0	445	87		58	376
(b)/(a)	2.93	5.45	2.43		1.70	2.84

Sources: Tian Yuan and Qiao Gang (1991),*China's Price Research,China Price 1992* (February).

price. In the case of electricity, too many planned prices are currently being implemented without a coherent, unifying rule. A new power plant, built through joint venture or with imported equipment, might be allowed to sell its electricity at a higher price to cover actual production cost, while the existing power plants have to sell their electricity at a lower, planned price. Much remains to be done to achieve significant price reform in the energy sector.

5.2.2. Development of New Coal Technologies and Nonfossil Fuel Energy

These issues have been emphasized in the long-term strategy section of the "Agenda Towards 21st Century" document (see 13.9 of Box 12.1). These are high priorities, targeted by the SSTC for research on clean coal technology in particular. Emphasis in this area is hardly surprising, given the country's vast endowments of coal and the adverse environmental consequences of exploiting it with existing technologies. Among the many technical areas addressed in this study are technologies of ash and sulfur removal, preparation of coal slurry, fluidized bed combustion technology, coal gasification, and combined cycle generation technology. Coal-based, fuel-cell, and MHD-generation technology will also be studied and developed over the long term.

The Ministry of Electricity is also committed to increase significantly the shares of hydropower among China's energy sources. There are some practical engineering problems, but exceptionally rich hydropower energy resources are located in the southwest (e.g., Yunnan Province and Tibet). They are far from the land center, however, and the key issue will be balancing high transmission costs against the environmental costs of local generation with imported fossil fuels.

5.2.3. Improvement in Energy Efficiency

China is a country with very high energy intensity — 1.69 tons of coal equivalent per US$1,000 GDP in 1990 against a world average of only 0.43. A recent study shows that if PPP is used to measure GDP, China's energy intensity may be around two times the world average.[4] In any case, there is

---

4. These PPP calculations are from independent sources and are not officially recognized in China.

great potential for improvement in China's energy efficiency, and this will translate into improved environmental quality. It is recognized in 13.9 of Box 12.1 that "to reduce environmental pollution, energy needs to be utilized more efficiently through scientific and technological progress." It is also a guiding priority of energy development strategy to the year 2000 that emphasis should be placed on both energy resource development and energy conservation. The SSTC has identified several areas of energy-saving technology in the guidelines for S&T development from 1990-2020. These include the following:

- utilization of waste heat and heat pumps;
- energy-saving techniques for industrial boilers;
- energy-saving technology for auxiliary equipment in power plants, such as fans and pumps;
- energy-saving techniques in petroleum and petrochemical enterprises;
- energy saving for household electrical appliances;
- co-generation of heat and electricity;
- improvement of various types of manufacturing processes and establishment of an energy-management information system;

All these approaches are relevant to the future of China's energy policy and practices.

5.2.4. International Cooperation

In a modern society and in the context of economic globalization mankind increasingly shares its common biosphere. Developed countries are leading in the effort at pollution abatement because of their accumulated knowledge, wealth, economic structure, and institutional coherence. The United Nation's Framework Convention on Climate Change (FCCC) recognizes the potential gains from international cooperation and endorses principles that share the benefits and encourages universal implementation of GHG abatement policies. OECD (1995) and Coppel and Lee (1996) suggest that "joint implementation" (i.e., the implementation of policies and measures jointly by developed and developing countries to curtail GHG emissions) could improve welfare in both regions while meeting the CO_2 abatement targets. Therefore, active policies to promote international cooperation are very important for the protection of the environment. China is fully aware of this, as can be seen in item 13.23 of Box 12.1, where international cooperation is emphasized.

5.3. Environmental Institutions, Monitoring, Management Policies, and Major Issues

5.3.1. Environmental Administration

Since 1973, the State Council had established an environmental administration directly under its control; later on, a separate ministry was established as the Ministry of Urban and Rural Construction and Environmental Protection; and finally the State Administration of Environmental Protection was established. Corresponding organizations exist at the provincial and municipality levels.

There are fifteen official responsibilities of the organizations of environmental protection:

1. Organize and prepare programs and plans for environmental protection;
2. Organize and prepare guidelines and policies of environmental protection;
3. Draft laws and regulations on environmental protection;
4. Set up environmental standards;
5. Supervise environmental protection work of various departments and regions;
6. Approve, supervise, and monitor the implementation of "Three Simultaneities";[5]
7. Promote more advanced management and treatment technology;
8. Environmental supervision, survey, and evaluation;
9. Plan nature preservation zones;
10. Organize for management of the marine environment;
11. Supervise and manage poisonous chemical materials;
12. Organize and develop research in environmental science;
13. Organize and develop environmental education;
14. Organize publicity activities related to environmental protection;
15. Guide and coordinate environmental protection activities between the various ministries, various regions and various units.

5.3.2. Monitoring and Supervision System

Monitoring and supervision systems have been established at the national,

---

5. The Chinese term "Three Simultaneities" means that whenever there is any kind of new project, environmental protection should be simultaneously implemented with (1) the design, (2) construction, and (3) operation of the project.

provincial, municipal, and country levels, even at the village and township levels in favorable circumstances. Also have been built were environmental monitoring stations. Currently, there are around 2,200 environmental monitoring stations with a total staff of around thirty-five thousand. Various resource-related ministries, such as agriculture and forestry, and various industrial health and military departments have also established sectoral environmental monitoring and supervision institutions. Based upon the "Law on Environmental Protection of the PRC," the State Administration of Environmental Protection has established the National Environmental Monitoring Network in concert with various other ministries of the State Council. The National Environmental Monitoring Network is shown schematically in Figure 12.10.

5.3.3. Guidelines and Policies of Environmental Management

The six principal official guidelines for environmental management are:

1. The major guideline for environmental protection is set up in Article 4 of the "Law on Environmental Protection of the PRC."
It is stated in eight sentences, each with four words (a Chinese characteristic):
  • overall planning;
  • reasonable location;
  • comprehensive utilization;
  • transform detrimental into useful;
  • rely upon the masses;
  • everybody takes action;
  • protect the environment;
  • benefit the people.

2. Environmental policy for industrial location (includes relevant urban environmental policies).

3. Energy-related environmental policy (including relevant urban and rural environmental policy, industrial and transportation energy policy).

4. Water-related environmental policy, particularly in the context of regional water distribution.

5. Natural environment protection policy.

6. Promote techno-economic policy congenial to environmental protection

(which includes encouragement of comprehensive utilization, control of industrial pollution through technological rehabilitation of enterprises, pollutant discharge fees for discharge in excess of standards, promote the polluter pays principle).

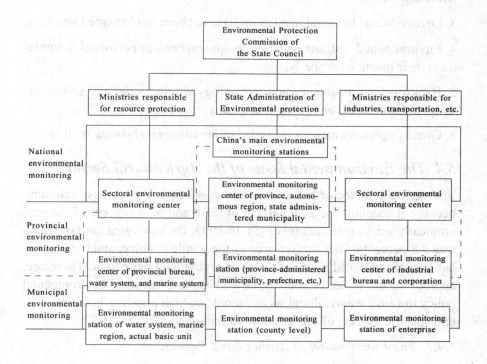

Figure 12.10. National Environmental Monitoring Network.

5.3.4. Major Issues

Although the state has made considerable efforts to catch up by establishment of institutions, environmental problems in China remain serious, as is evident from the data on air and water pollution. The major issues in this area are:

1. Environmental protection has not become an integrated part of the national economic and social development plan. For example, in the investment planning for fixed assets, there is no separate item for the investment of environmental protection.

2. Insufficient financial inputs for environmental protection; generally, the financial input for environmental protection represents less than 1 percent of GDP; there is no treatment of SO_2 discharges; a fair part of urban sewage from households, and industrial waste and rubbish, are often discharged without treatment.

3. Environmental laws and regulations have not been implemented seriously.

4. Environmental institutions lack enough authority or personnel to implement their functions properly.

5. Backwardness in science and technology would hinder any serious attempt to improve the environmental quality.

6. Greater public awareness is needed of environmental issues at all levels.

5.4. The Environmental Issue of the Agricultural Sector

The agricultural sector has an essential position in the Chinese economy because it accounts for 20.9 percent of GDP and 52.9 percent of the economically active population (1995). In 1993, the cultivated land of China was 9.8 percent of the surface area of the whole country, and the country has one of the world's lowest ratios of arable land per capita. Therefore, appropriate use of land resources, as well as more informed environmental policy toward the agricultural sector, should be high priorities in China. Several specific aspects of this are now summarized .

5.4.1. The Preservation of Arable Land Resources

Rapid rural industrialization in China (i.e., development of town and village enterprises, or TVEs) has made important contributions to economic growth and rural prosperity of the Chinese population generally. But it has also had a negative effect by competing for limited land resources. This fact has come to the attention of the state, and the central government has put priority emphasis on development of the agricultural sector. Hence, strict records are now kept, and supervision is maintained on sublets of state-owned land and transfers between regions.

5.4.2. Detrimental Effects of Pesticide and Chemical Fertilizer Use

It is estimated that the area of annual pesticide utilization in China is 15 billion "hectare times" (i.e., the same hectare may be sprayed more than once and is counted each time), and the annual fertilizer use is around 29.3

million tons. The effective rate of utilization is only 30 percent, however, which is around one-half of the advanced agricultural area abroad. The other 70 percent is either volatized into the atmosphere or flows through the soil, lakes, or rivers, leading to the major cause of the excessive nitrate content in drinking water.

5.4.3. Environmental Impact of Town and Village Enterprise Development

The development of TVEs in China has its positive contribution to the national economy and the living standard of the rural household, but its negative impact on the environment is also serious. This situation is exacerbated by the low technological level of production processes in TVEs and insufficient local monitoring capacity by environmental protection institutions. For example, TVEs will consume three tons of coal for one ton of coke, and SO_2 discharged by TVEs is around 15.1 percent of total discharge in 1990, under incomplete monitoring conditions. It is projected that the industrial waste water discharged by TVEs may reach 6.15 billion tons by the year 2000, with an average annual growth rate of 6.6 percent during 1990-2000. COP discharges may reach 1.84 million tons, with an average annual growth rate of 2.3 percent during 1990-2000. All these issues must receive enough attention to better secure sustainable economic growth. Recently, the state has taken decisive action to close down some TVEs with serious pollution problems.

6. Chinese Economic Growth and Environment from an International Perspective

6.1. International Comparison of Economic Activity and Environmental Loading

China has enjoyed very rapid and unprecedented economic growth for more than a decade. To put its environmental experience during this period in context, it is useful to compare economic activity and environmental loading across several countries. This provides a reference for projecting future environmental impact on China as it continues its growth and economic development.

Table 12.9. International Comparison of Economic Activity and
Environmental Loading (1992)

Indicator	China	Japan	USA	OECD Europe
Area(1,000km²)	9,597	378	9,809	4,490
Population (million)	1,162	124	255	439
Population density (person/km²)	121	328	26	98
GNP (1987 prices, billion US$)	491	2,988	4,924	5,767
GNP/capita (US$)	423	24,094	19,311	13,141
Energy consumption (million tons of oil equivalent)	710	451	1,984	1,439
Energy consumption (ton/capita)	0.61	3.64	7.78	3.28
Energy consumption (ton/km²)	7.4	119.3	20.2	32.0
Energy consumption (ton, oil equivalent/GNP in million US$)	1,445	151	403	250
CO_2 discharged (million tons of carbon equivalent)	733	349	1,581	1,071
Carbon (ton/capita)	0.63	2.81	6.20	2.44
Carbon (ton/km²)	7.6	92.3	16.1	23.9
Carbon (ton/GNP in millions of US$)	1,493	117	321	186

Sources:Imura, Hidefumi, and Takeshi Katsuhara (1996), *Environmental Problem of China*,
    2nd Edition, Tokyo:Toyo Keizai Sinposha.

6.2. Response and Experience of Neighboring Countries to China's Environmental Issues

Japan is one of China's most prominent neighbors and trading partners, and
its perspective on Chinese environmental issues exemplifies the regional
experience of China's more industrialized neighbors. We use Japan as an
example in the following discussion.

6.2.1. Urban Economic Development and Environmental Issues

China has a high share of secondary or industrial activity in GDP, more than
56 percent in 1993. Most Chinese cities are industrial cities, as was the case
with Japan in the 1960's. Industrial restructuring, modernization of equipment and relocation of industry, promotion of equipment renewal, and investment on key projects for improvement of production equipment and
environment are as likely to be part of modernization in China as they were
in Japan. Moreover, technological differences between the two countries

create the basis for a collaborative approach to China's technological renovation.

6.2.2. The Pressing Necessity to Deal with the Issues of Urban Environmental Infrastructure

It is correctly noted by outside observers that high economic growth of China will induce serious shortages in urban environmental infrastructure, such as sewage disposal. Our center has recently been involved in a UNDP project entitled "Sustainable Development of the Yellow River Delta," which could represent a pilot project for studying sustainable development of the nation in the future. This study found that sewage disposal and treatment are very serious problems that must receive attention in China's future urban planning. This experience may also be relevant to new industrial economies in east and southeast Asia. The high economic growth of the "East Asian Miracle" may have a dark side if infrastructural needs are not correctly anticipated.

6.2.3. Lifestyle of the Urban Population

Much of the impetus for economic modernization, particularly on the demand side, has historically been modeled on Western consumption patterns. In populous Asia, one issue where this tendency is likely to have very serious environmental ramifications is in the transportation sector. Private car ownership and use patterns need to be balanced properly with public transportation from the point of energy consumption and environmental issues.

6.3. China's Energy-Environmental Issues from the Japanese Perspective

China's energy and environmental issues have raised major concerns in neighboring countries such as Japan and South Korea. The Research Institute of the Ministry of International Trade and Industry (MITI) has implemented joint research programs on energy and the environment. We abstract from this report to conclude this part of the chapter.

Observations of air pollutant emission in the two countries show that their extent of air pollutant generation, removal, and emission depends largely on the difference in their industrial structures and final demand structures, which are indications of their economic states of development, as well as the differences between their technical coefficients for energy emission factors and outputs. The tasks for conserving the environment on the global level must of necessity be set at levels which can be achieved by a variety of countries at different development stages, without hampering the attainment of their targets for economic development. If not, this will likely pose a hurdle to the making of any international accords regarding such issue.

7. Conclusion

7.1. China's Awareness of Its Responsibility in Global Environmental Issues

Compared with other countries at similar income levels, China has made significant gains in recognition of environmental policy challenges, capacity development for environmental monitoring, and more rigorous control of environmental damage arising from economic activity. China is a latecomer to industrialization as well as in environmental science, technology, and management. But it is making serious efforts to catch up. In the process of industrialization, China has achieved high economic growth rates since the late 1970's. China participated in the United Nation's Conference on Human Environment in Stockholm in 1972, enunciated environmental protection as a basic national policy in 1983, and participated in the Earth Summit in Rio de Janeiro in 1992. A series of environmental policies are being implemented by a variety of different ministries, in coordination with regional and local governments.

7.2. The Role of Energy

Energy plays a dominant role in economic growth and Chinese environmental issues. This chapter has surveyed the links between energy supply and demand and economic growth, including a quantitative assessment of their environmental impacts. Although data of this kind are still limited in China, the analysis presented here clearly illustrates the importance of anticipating energy-related environmental damage as this arises from continued industrialization. Macro and micro policies toward energy development and utilization have been examined in some detail in this chapter.

7.3. Sustainable Development and Policy Challenge

The general recognition of global environmental issues is of recent origin. Caldwell points out in 1984, for example, that "at the beginning of the twentieth century, neither environment as an integrated ecological concept nor the biosphere as the planetary life-support system was an object of public concern." But sustainable development had been accepted worldwide by the late 1980's, especially after the Earth Summit in 1992. Achieving sustainable development requires the effort of one generation even for developed countries. This can be illustrated from the quotation from an official document of one developed country that "It is understood that this will not be possible within a generation in all cases. This is because the consequences of man-environmental problems may only become manifest after several decades and because some problems can only take longer to solve." Rec-

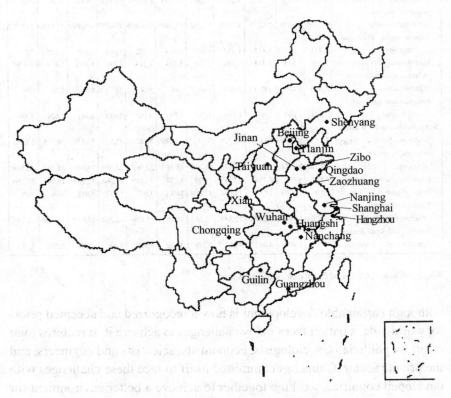

Figure A.12.1 Chinese cities with high frequency of acid rain

ognizing the nature and scope of the problem takes time, and so does the technological innovation needed to solve it economically. A recent study by WRI points out that industrialized countries are struggling to curtail their greenhouse gas emissions to 1990 levels by the year 2000, but lifetime commitment points to curbing emissions of fully fluorinated compounds (FFC) — a family of little-known but extremely potent and long-lived greenhouse gases — as a cost-effective way toward this goal.

Table A12.1. GDP, Energy Consumption, and Pollution, 1985-95

	1985	1986	1987	1988	1989	1990	1991	1992	1993	1994	1995
GDP (100 million yuan)	8,964	10,202	11,963	14,928	16,909	18,548	21,618	26,638	34,634	46,622	58,261
Total energy consumption											
(10,000 tons of SCE)	76,682	80,850	86,632	92,997	96,934	98,703	103,783	109,170	115,993	122,737	129,000
Atmospheric pollution:											
Total volume of waste gas											
from fuel (100 million m³)	45,373	46,467	52,624	56,417	57,613	59,478	69,941	72,028	75,401	N.A.	N.A.
Waste gas emission											
(100 million m³)	73,970	69,679	77,275	82,380	83,065	85,380	101,416	104,787	109,604	113,63	123,407
Sulphur dioxide discharged											
(10,000 tons)	1,325	1,250	1,412	1,523	1,565	1,494	1,622	1,685	1,795	1,825	1,891
Soot discharged (10,000 tons)	1,295	1,384	1,445	1,436	1,398	1,324	1,314	1,414	1,416	1,414	1,478
Industrial dust discharged											
(10,000 tons)	1,305	1,075	1,004	1,125	840	781	579	576	617	583	639
Industrial dust retrieved											
(10,000 tons)	1,431	1,644	1,603	1,861	1,786	1,987	2,161	2,451	2,641	2,629	2,895
Water pollution (million tons)											
Total waste water discharged	34,154	33,879	34,861	36,726	35,345	353,780	33,621	35,878	35,559	36,526	37,285
Industrial waste water											
discharged	25,740	26,024	26,375	26,839	25,209	24,869	23,567	23,385	21,949	21,551	22,189
Industrial waste water treated	5,682	6,321	6,784	7,234	7,539	8,024	15,589	17,568	17,934	19,845	21,566
Industrial waste water untreated	20,058	19,703	19,591	19,605	17,670	16,845	7,977	5,817	4,015	N.A.	N.A.
Reaching industrial											
discharge standards	9,870	11,059	12,072	12,389	12,033	12,461	11,820	12,362	12,049	11,970	12,287
Reaching industrial discharge											
standards after treatment	3,197	3,470	4,042	4,157	4,348	4,639	4,233	4,449	4,503	4,756	4,814

Source: *China Statistical Yearbook*, various issues.

Although sustainable development is now a recognized and accepted priority worldwide, a nation faces many challenges to achieve it. It requires joint effort by politicians, sociologists, economists, scientists and engineers, and the private sector. China has committed itself to face these challenges with developed countries, working together to achieve a better environment for all future generations.

Table A12.2. SO$_2$ Discharged in Waste Gas of Selected Cities (thousand tons)

City	Sum of 5-6th Plan	1981	1982	1983	1984	1985	Sum of 7-8th Plan	1986	1987	1988	1989	1990
Beijing	1,410	263	260	277	300	310	1,657	323	321	321	344	346
Tianjin	1,050	187	193	213	271	186	1,235	256	267	251	241	220
Taiyuan	726	142	138	144	132	170	841	175	171	173	166	157
Shenyang	783	133	139	156	167	188	731	147	140	131	155	158
Shanghai	1,391	233	223	267	324	344	2,000	355	434	405	391	415
Nanjing	694	146	133	138	148	129	742	141	131	150	150	170
Hangzhou	323	59	63	65	66	70	474	93	92	98	98	93
Nanchang	284	45	55	54	71	59	288	60	57	56	60	55
Jinan	725	106	130	115	178	196	1,054	196	208	229	211	210
Zibo	718	168	134	150	130	136	1,248	163	243	273	287	282
Zaozhuang	609	113	129	105	133	129	544	126	110	113	98	99
Qingdao	921	146	180	190	199	206	1,406	278	261	284	279	304
Wuhan	703	144	133	128	141	157	644	120	127	130	132	135
Huangshi	508	112	86	118	109	83	432	80	87	101	78	86
Guangzhou	478	117	98	84	89	90	537	95	92	99	119	132
Guilin	176	64	24	25	30	33	156	38	30	29	31	27
Chongqing	632	115	120	126	132	139	3,610	682	746	762	711	709
Xi'an	708	164	146	125	130	143	923	195	194	196	196	143
Total	12,839	2,457	2,384	2,480	2,750	2,768	18,522	3,523	3,711	3,801	3,747	3,741

REFERENCES

China State Statistical Bureau (1991): *China: Energy Statistics Almanac 1991*, Beijing: China Statistical Publishing House.

China State Statistical Bureau (1986-96): *Statistical Yearbook of China, 1986,. . . , 1996*, Beijing: China Statistical Publishing House.

Coppel, Jonathan, and Hiro Lee (1996): "The Framework Convention and Climate Change Policy in Asia," in R. Mendelsohn and D. Shaw, eds., *The Economics of Pollution Control in the Asia Pacific*, Brookfield,

Vermont: Edward Elgar.

Imura, Hidefumi, and Takeshi Katsuhara (1996): *Environmental Problem of China*, 2nd edition, Tokyo: Toyo Keizai Sinposha.

Lawrence Berkeley Laboratory (1992): China Energy Databook, Document LBL-32B22 UC-350, Berkeley: University of California, Berkeley.

OECD (1995): *Global Warning: Economic Dimensions and Policy Responses*, Paris: OECD.

Comment
Mark Paffenberger

First, I compliment the authors on producing such a useful summary of the energy situation in China. Looking into the future, there are few issues that will have as much environmental impact, within a nation or globally, as China's energy policies and programs. This is due to a number of factors. First, China is the world's largest user of coal; per-capita use is low and likely to grow rapidly in the future. Coal, as an energy source, creates many environmental problems due to gas emissions and water requirements. With an economic growth rate currently over 8 percent per annum, industrial demands for coal-based energy will continue to expand rapidly. As the authors point out, China's industry is heavily energy intensive, using about seven times as much coal to produce a dollar of GDP as the average G-7 economy.

Although China does possess immense hydroelectric potential, analysts still project that coal will continue to be the primary component of power generation. It will also be a major source of energy for domestic consumers. Household coal consumption doubled between 1979 and 1984, and this trend is likely to continue. To meet these demands in recent years, over 80,000 small coal mines were opened throughout the country, creating immense regulatory challenges for this industry.

The problems of water pollution associated with coal use within the energy sector are very significant in China. In the northeast particularly, where water resources are already reaching scarcity levels, water availability for power generation becomes a critical problem. At least one hundred kilos of water are required for each kilowatt hour generated by coal. In Shansi

Province, for example, where a third of the nation's high-quality coal is located, plans to establish a power plant generating 20 to 24 gigawatts would require 12 billion tons of water for cooling alone. Currently, the province's entire water requirement for industrial, agricultural, and domestic use is only 7 billion tons.

The development of the coal-driven energy sector also has significant ramifications for land resources. By the end of the 1980's coal mining activities and ash disposal areas occupied over 100,000 hectares of land, with another 60,000 being added during the 1990's. Perhaps even more serious is the impact of emissions of air quality SO_2 gases already contribute significantly to acid rain, which threatens agricultural and forested areas in southeastern China in particular. The health implications of deteriorating air quality in highly populated urban environments would seem to justify careful monitoring.

The authors, as well as other China energy specialists, predict that the nation will continue to consume increasing quantities of coal to meet its growing power needs, and the environmental and social costs will be enormous if cleaner practices are not adopted. With a vast and growing population and limited water, farm, and forest resources, China needs to be especially conservation-minded to improve its living standards sustainably. A number of strategies should be considered by policymakers to minimize the impact of coal use in the energy sector on the natural resource base and society.

The efficiency of coal use in China is low compared to other countries. Energy conservation is approximately 30 percent of total energy input into service-generating power, versus 60 percent in Japan. This in part reflects management by state enterprises that have little incentive to boost performance. Commercial rates are set for state enterprises and often have no relation to production costs or demand conditions. As a consequence, many government run coal and gas operations are running at a constant loss. If cleaner, more efficient industries are to evolve, new policies will need to be developed to provide energy enterprises with economic incentives to adopt improved technologies and strengthen operation and maintenance systems.

Experience from the United States with command and control environmental regulations has been mixed, and there are many indications that this approach may not be effective within the Chinese context. The lack of advocacy groups or judicial mechanisms to monitor and prosecute polluters effectively will undermine the efficacy of environmental controls. Even in the United States, confrontational systems to leverage change and achieve compliance with environmental regulations have not worked well. The question is, "What type of incentives can be created that will encourage the Asian energy sector to move toward better technologies?" It is argued by economists that, given the high rates of growth in the Asia region, there is a window of opportunity to replace technology from the 1950's. Economic incentives that reward energy enterprises for restructuring now could be extremely strategic in establishing clean technology and longer-term competitiveness in the Chinese economy.

The authors have noted that the Chinese government has subscribed to international environmental conventions, and is setting ambitious targets to deal with gas emission problems, but operational mechanisms need to be established that strongly encourage managers of enterprises to make the huge investments needed in new technologies. In looking at the environmental problems facing the countries of the former Soviet Union, it is clear that postponing these investments is ill advised. The cost of "end-of-pipe" clean-up approaches is far higher, in terms of both direct costs and externalities, than making a timely transition toward a cleaner energy sector.

18. Sustainable Development in a New Millenium

I. Introduction

The mankind learned lessons from economic and social development in the history as well as the development experience of themselves. It is recognized that there are "the limits to growth", the resource is declining through the physical expansion dominated by the behavior of the human society. It is also recognized that the mankind is facing many social ills today — crime, (including cyber crime), drugs, disease, urban decay, shortage and declining standards of education, those social problems which once could be confined within borders, now spread across the world. Therefore, it is necessary to pursue the establishment of a sustainable society that can persist over generations, that will not undermine either its physical or its social systems of support. These are the major themes of the Rio Declaration on Environment and Development signed by 169 nations in 1992. In fact, one essential goals of the World Summit for Social Development 1995, conquest of poverty had also been included in section 1 of "Agenda 21". The mankind have to live in harmony with nature as well as in harmony by themselves in order to achieve sustainable development. It is worthwhile to review the progress and insufficiency of the implementation of the main outcome of UNCED "Agenda 21" a decade after "Rio", so that confidence can be confirmed, experience can be learned from the positive and negative aspects of the progress, and priority areas to be identified for further action. Proper targets and efforts can be focused through such process to achieve a better results toward the solemn goal — sutainbalbe development which may require the successive effort of UN and all of us.

This paper will be divided into 5 parts: major accomplishments and major lessons; major issues and constraints; new challenges and opportunities;

institutional framework and suggestions of priority areas.

In each part, discussion of East Asia and the Pacific will be presented in general and followed a specific description of China.

II. Major Accomplishments and Major Lessons

2.01 Major Accomplishments of Implementation of "Agenda 21" of East Asia and the Pacific

East Asia and the Pacific is a part of ESCAP region composed of Northeast Asia, Southeast Asia and the Pacific sub-regions. ESCAP had prepared "The Regional Action Program on Environmental Sound and Sustainable Development 1996-2000" (RAP 1996-2000). This "RAP1996-2000" includes four objectives: Pollution Reduction, Prevention and Enhancement of Environmental Quality; Conservation and Management of Natural Resources and Ecosystems; Sustainable Development Policy Improvement and Sustainable Development Indicators and Assessment. There are 24 program areas included in these 4 objectives. These program areas have transformed the principle of "Agenda 21" into specific actions. And in the subregions of East Asia and Pacific, around 26 countries had prepared national "Agenda 21" or "Green Vision 21", such as China, Japan, Mongolia, Republic of Korea, Indonesia, Malaysia, Singapore, etc., a number of countries have also prepared and adopted national conservation plans and strategies for sustainable development, such as Australia and other island countries in the Pacific Ocean. The above facts show that in the post-Rio period many countries in the East Asia and Pacific region have responded actively in general to the emerging challenges of achieving sustainable development. And it is shown in Reference 1 and 2 that there are significant achievements nearly in all related aspects on sustainable development for many countries in this regions.

These active responses of most of the countries of this region represents the major accomplishment of outcome of UNCED "Agenda 21". Those countries are in awareness of the principle of Rio Declaration that "The right to development must be fulfilled so as to equitably meet developmental and environmental needs of present and future generations." That "all states and all people shall cooperate in the essential task of eradicating poverty as an indispensable requirement for sustainable development."

2.02 Major Lessons of "Implementation of 'Agenda 21'"

1. Although the system of concepts of sustainable development is outlined in 1992, the major concepts of sustainable development had been evolved for several decades. The International Conference on Human Environment held at Stockholm in 1972, "Concern for Tomorrow" in 1988. In fact, various environmental issues had been responded quite early in developed countries, such as Public Law 90-148, Air Quality Act of 1967 of the US Government. Therefore, the road toward sustainable development is a process. The year 1992 of World Summit represents a turning point of this process. Action plan developed for the implementation of "Agenda 21" makes words into action. Many lessons had been summarized in Reference 1, for instance, there is the need to improve the sustainable development performance review, there is the need to adopt good practice and governance. It is expected that diffusion of these informations and exchange of views of further improvement of the implementation can be done by various related UN agencies in the coming period.

2. Another major lesson learned is environmental legislation and effective enforcement of environmental legislation. This will promote to establish a new behavior toward sustainable development.

2.03 "China's Agenda 21"

1. China had prepared "China's Agenda 21". It was adopted at the 16th Executive meeting of the State Council of PRC on March 25, 1994. This document contains 20 chapters, several program areas are covered in each chapter. Major accomplishment of implementation of "China's Agenda 21" can be briefed into five aspects in "2".

2. Major accomplishments of implementation of "China's Agenda 21"

(1) Reduction of growth rate of the population, improvement of the education level of the people, and reduce the number of people in poverty

These are targets outlined in chapter 7 (Population, Consumption and Social Services) and 8 (Eradication of Poverty) of "China's Agenda 21".

China has full awareness of the relationship between population, resources, environment and development. China is known for its successful perfor- mance of family planning. Based upon the Fifth National Population Survey implemented in 2000, the total number of population of China by the end of 2000 reached 1.266 billion, the average annual growth rate in the 90's is 1.07%, which is 0.4 percentage point lower than the population growth rate in the decade of 80's. There is improvement of living standard and level of education of the people in general due to high growth of the national economy. China had implemented a "'8-7' Poverty Eradication Program" since 1994, that is to eradicate 80 million[1] of people in poverty within seven years. The number of rural people in poverty had been reduced from 80 million in 1994 to 25 million by the year 2000. The per-capita income of rural people in 592 targeted poverty county assisted by the State has been increased from 648 yuan in 1994 to 1348 yuan in the year 2000.

(2) There are progresses in prevention and control of environmental pollution, larger accomplishments were achieved in key regions and key sectors. China has changed its strategy of industrial pollution control. For basic pollution control, China changed from "end of pipe" control of pollution to control of whole production process; for control of pollutant discharge, China changed from control of intensity of pollutant to combined control of intensity and total amount of pollutants.

China generated around 644 million tons of industrial solid waste every year, around 2.4 percent of them is toxic, radioactive or explosive in nature. China paid attention to the comprehensive utilization of solid industrial waste and also control of the production process, the industrial solid waste discharged is reduced from 33.76 million ton to 11.54 million ton in 1999.

There is better control of discharge of TSP and SO_2. The area suffered from acid rain and pollution of SO_2 had been widened since the 90's. China promulgated the "Law of PRC on Prevention and Control of Atmospheric Pollution". China has defined two areas of control, "acid rain controlled area" and "SO_2 controlled area". By the end of April 1999, 175 prefectures and municipalities of these two controlled areas and two key sectors, elec- tricity and coal mining, have completed programs of prevention and control.

---

1. The national poverty line of China is lower than that set up by the World Bank, i.e., 1 US dollar per capita per day. China's national poverty line is around 0.6 USD/day.

390 projects of rectification were accomplished in 1999 which can reduce the amount of discharge of SO_2 around 239.8 thousand tons per year.

With respect to water quality, China focused on controlling the total load of pollutant discharged into "Three Rivers (Huai River, Liao River and Hai River) and Three Lakes (Tai Lake, Dianchi Lake and Chao Lake) under a major project. This project has accomplished the target of its first stage, and is proceeding to the second stage.

More than 84 thousand small enterprises with serious pollutant discharged were closed.

There are around 24 provinces and municipalities launching the demonstrative and experimental project of cleaner production. The implementation is not up to expectation due to institutional barrier and inconsistent policy.

Development of sustainable human settlement (chapter 10 of "China's Agenda 21") is also in progress with better urban planning and construction.

(3) Strengthening and Improvement of Conservation and Sustainable Use of Natural Resources

China has prepared "China's Irrigation: Agenda 21" and also "Long- and Medium-term Plan of Supply and Demand of Water", to deal the problem of water scarcity. China is actively pushing forward reform of the water pricing and quota system of industrial water use in the northern part of China, water saving spraying technique is also applied partly in agricultural production.

Significant achievements have been made in managing land resources in China, including the establishment of basic farmland reserves. "Law of Land Management" is promulgated in August 1998.

China had prepared "China's Forestry: Agenda 21". Recovery and growth of stock volume and area of forest are seen since the 90's. In 1990, the area of forest, stock volume of forest and the rate of forest coverage are 12,465 x 10⁴ hec., 10.572 billion m³ and 12.98% respectively, while in 1999, they are 1,5894 x 10⁴ hec., 12.49 billion m³ and 16.50% respectively.

China had also prepared "China's Marine Management: Agenda 21" and its action plans. The Standing Committee of the Nationaql People's Congress of China had revised "Law on Protection of Marine Environment". Monitoring network of marine environmental information, forecasting and service system are also formed gradually.

Energy plays a very important role in economic development. But it is also an important source of pollution, especially the unique structure of energy production and consumption of China is dominated by more than 67% share of coal. China had paid attention on energy conservation. "Outline of Energy Saving Technological Policy" had been promulgated in 1996. There is large reduction of energy consumption per 10,000 yuan of GDP; it is 5.3 Ton Standard Coal Equivalent (TSCE) per 10,000 yuan of GDP in 1990, and it is reduced to 1.3 TSCE/10,000 yuan in 1999. This is both due to energy saving and industrial restructuring. Development of renewable energy resource has also been achieved, biogas, solar energy, wind energy, geothermal energy and small hydro power are developed in the rural area. The generating capacity of wind power plant in Dabancheng region of Xinjiang Uygur Autonomous Region reached 100 mw, the largest unit capacity is 600 kw.

(4) Improvement of ecological environment and achievement in mitigation of disaster

China had launched a series of important projects to improve the ecological environment. Protective forest is constructed in northern part, upper and middle reaches of the Yangtze River, middle reach of the Yellow River, Pearl River, Huai River and Tai Lake basin. The planned area of protective forest reached 120 million hectare, which is around 73.5% of national total, and it covered major areas of soil erosion of China. In the development of the western region of China, major strategy implemented is improvement of ecological environment. The policy of "replanting the farming with trees and grass and greening the mountains" is implemented.

By the end of 1999, China had established 1,146 Natural Preserves with an area reaching 88.152 million hectare, or 8.8% of national land area.

China had made efforts to mitigate disaster to establish a sound management system of disaster mitigation, "China's International Commission of 10- Year Mitigation of Disaster" is established, which is consisted by 28 ministries or bureaus. "Outline of the China International Action for Mitigation of Disaster" is prepared. Various engineering construction related to mitigation of disaster is organized, such as flooding prevention, combating drought, earthquake combating engineering, prevention and rectification of agricultural and forest disaster, etc.

(5) Actively participate international exchange and cooperation on environment and development

China participated with an active attitude the negotiation of international convention on global environmental issues, participate and ratify international convention of environmental and resource protection and agreements around 30 items. China has fulfilled its commitment based upon principle of equality of right and responsibility. For example, China has played its active role in "Agenda 21", "Convention on Biological Diversity", "Vienna Convention for the Protection of the Ozone Layer 1985", "UN Convention to Combat Desertification", etc.

China has strengthened bilateral and multilateral international cooperation on environment protection and development. In the preparation, organization and implementation of "Priority Programs and Projects of China's Agenda 21", China has taken an active part in and made efforts to push forward global cooperation in environmental protection and developmental.

III. Major Issues and Major Constraints

3.01 Issues and Constraints of East and Pacific Region (general)

1. Demographic Dynamics

Countries in East Asia and the Pacific are in different stages of development. The demographic dynamics of them is also different. It is projected that there will be a further increase of the population by around 215,282 thousand in East and Northeast Asia from 2000-2025, within which, China shall account for 94.2% of the total increase. But the annual compound growth rate of this region will be reduced to 0.4% from 2020-2025. There will be an increase ofthe population by 157,014 thousand in Southeast Asia and 4,206 thousand in the Pacific Island economies. For the three developed economies in this region, all countries have a growth rate less than 1% while Japan will have -0.4 growth rate from 2020-2025. The aged people, 60 and older, will be 30% for East Asia, 23% for Southeast Asia by 2050 — a severe social challenge.

2. State of the environment and trends

Population Pressure

The further increase of the population in huge amounts, especially in the developing countries, will consume more natural resources and produce more waste. Although the Southeast Asian countries and most countries in Northeast Asia have enjoyed rapid economic growth (more than 7% in general) in the 90's except in the period of economic downturn caused by the Asia financial crisis. Energy consumption for industrial and household uses increased at an annual rate of 4.8% from 1990 to 1997, compared with the world rate of 1.3%. Heavy dependence on fossil fuels also effects the air quality, and most power plants in the Asia and Pacific region have no strict pollution control in general.

Shortage and Quality of Water

The per-capita fresh water resources in the Asia and Pacific region is the lowest in the world. Irrigation remains by far the largest consumption of water in Asia and the Pacific region, accounting for 60 to 90 percent of annual water withdrawl in most countries of this region. Growth of demand for water due to the growth of population, industrialization and urbanization have created competition between the urban and rural sectors for its allocation. Due to institutional weakness, national governments are fragmented between ministries that govern water respectively for irrigation, transportation and urban use. An integrated policy is absent. The acute water shortage is also accompanied by irresponsible activities of enterprises and households, agricultural runoff, domestic sewage and industrial waste water discharge. Water pollution is very severe in Southeast Asia and then Northeast Asia in general.

Poverty

One of the major issues of this region is poverty. According to the international poverty line of US$1 a day per-capita at 1993 prices, around 800 million poor people lived in the Asian and Pacific region in 1998[2], accounting for around 67% of the world"s poor. This was significantly lower than that in 1987 (75%). But this decline is entirely attributable to the reduction of

---

2 . This data covers the broader region Asia and the Pacific; it includes that of South Asia and Central Asia.

poverty in East Asia and Southeast Asia. This also illustrates that economic prosperity will promote the eradication of poverty. If South Asia is not counted, the number of the poor in this region will be around 278 million, with around 85 million poor persons in Southeast Asia. It should be pointed out more than 10 million people are added in the wake of the Asian financial crisis.

3. *The sub-regional priorities related to environment can be shown in Table 1.*

Table 1 Sub-regional Priorities in Asia and the Pacific

	Northeast Asia	Southeast Asia	Small Island Developing States	Australia/New Zealand
Land	*	*		*
Water		*	*	
Forest and biodiversity	*	*	*	*
Marine environment	*	*	*	*
Energy	*		*	*
Population	*			
Poverty		*		
Pollution	*	*	*	*
National disaster	*	*	*	
Climate change	*		*	
Solid and hazardous waste	*	*	*	
Water supply and sanitation	*	*	*	

Source: "State of the Environment in Asia and the Pacific 2000", executive summary, ESCAP.

4. Major Constraints

(1) Common constraint — policy and institutional challenges

The common constraint to all countries concerned is a further awareness of the implication of sustainable development. Environmental issue is created and accumulated by the mankind in time and space that the earth and the nature have almost reached the limit of their bearing capacity currently. There is no simple solution to this multi-dimensional issue.

Appropriate legal system and policy should be designed to change the socio-economic behavior of a national system to adapt to sustainable development. This can be done by the nation itself without resort to external resource in general.

The major constraint is political will, the art of implementation and coordination among various perspective and various interest-vested groups. Continuous reform is required of the unsustainable tradition in production and consumption at general level.

(2) <u>Specific constraint 1:</u> The financial resources

The developing countries of this region are deficit in financial resources to improve the environment. There is no detailed estimate of the financial resource requirement for environment-related infrastructure. The widely used data is from Reference 6. The funding needs for water supply sanitation, education, agriculture, forestry, control of acid rain, improvement of global climate, etc., may be up to US$70.2 billion in 2000 and the amount will reach US$244.6 billion in 2025, with an average annual growth around 5.1%. No matter whether this figure is correct or not, the high cost is hardly bearable by developing countries. Much will depend upon the inputs and assistance provided by the developed countries in terms of the provision of new and additional financial resources.

(3) <u>Specific constraint 2:</u> Clean Production Technology and EST

Many countries in East Asia and the Pacific are still in the process of industrialization, only a minority are marching toward a knowledge-based economy.

It is necessary to acquire CP technology or EST in the development process. Developed countries are well ahead of the developing countries in technology and in production and management process. The USA produced around 80 million tons of coke in 1950, and the output droped to no more than 20 million tons in 2000. Consequently, the USa closed many of the coke producing plants around the 1980's due to strict environmental regulation. The USA then switched to imported coke from China, India and others. Now China has become the largest producer and exporter of coke at the expense of the environment. This case may be of a general trend for industrial re-structuring of other countries. Developed countries have the advantage in the field of CPT and EST. It is expected that developed countries will transfer environmentally sound technologies to developing countries on favorable and non-commercial terms.

3.02 Issues and Constraints of China in the Implementation of "Agenda 21"

There are seven major issues confronted by China in the implementation of "Agenda 21".

1. Huge population and severe task in anti-poverty

China has a large population, 70% of them are in the rural areas. "Poverty" is mainly a rural phenomenon in the past. There are still more than 25 million of people in poverty after the implementation of "'8-7' Poverty Alleviation Program". As most of these people live in mountainous or desert areas in the western part of the country with poor ecological environment and inconvenient transportation, assistance program for them is very difficult. Moreover, there is increase of regional disparity. The share of GDP of China's western region is reduced from 14.2% in 1995 to 13.7% in 1999. For poverty-ridden people living in places with unfavorable natural conditions, 20% or 30% of the rural people who have rid off poverty will fall below the poverty line again annually. In addition, urban poverty has emerged due to laid-off labor force through the restructuring of SOEs. Therefore, anti-poverty and the reduction of income disparity between different regions will be a major challenge faced by China in the new millenium.

(2) Poor utilization of water resource

It is reported in a research that China is in deficit of 21.8 billion m³ of water annually, within which, the shortage in northern China amounts to 18 billion m³. Moreover, there is serious waste in the utilization of water resources, which is common in the agricultural sector. The recycled rate of water used for industry is only around 50%.

Water pollution is severe. Water discharged from industrial production and household sewage reachs 40.1 billion m³, 44.5% of it is untreated and discharged to the surface of ground, causing serious pollution of rivers and lakes.

(3) Atmospheric pollution is worsening

China has a rapid economic growth around 10% in the 90's, along with increasing discharge of SO_2, smoke dust and industrial dust, although the growth rate of discharge of pollutants is lower than the growth rate of GDP. Yet, the absolute total amount is large. The amount of SO_2, smoke dust and industrial dust discharged in 1999 reached 18.57 million tons, 11.59 million tons and 11.75 million tons. The share of those pollutants discharged by TVEs accounted for 20.6%, 34.2% and 61.1% respectively. The TVEs of China are generally small- and medium-sized enterprises providing a large amount of job opportunities. The total number of employees of the TVEs reached 127 million in 1999, and they also contributed 2.48 trillion yuan in value added and 774.3 billion yuan of export. This constitutes a major conflict between environment protection and social and economic development. Besides the traditional types of atmospheric pollutants, a new one has emerged, characterized by NOx and CH compound, etc. This pollutant is the result of new types of consumption, arising from the increase in the number of automobiles.

(4) Increasing amount of solid waste discharge

There is increasing amount of solid waste discharge. China has a lower rate of comprehensive use of industrial solid waste, with the rate of utilization being around 50%. The municipal solid waste (MSW) of China reached around 100 million tons. Treatment of MSW mainly relies on filling the low land and burying. This kind of treatment also adversely affect the agricultural land, soil and quality of water.

(5) Natural disasters

The Asia and Pacific region has a high share of natural disasters. Of the total number of 689 disasters in the world from 1997-1998, those happened in this region account for 42%. It is also reported by the country team of the UN in China that "China[3] is one of the most naturally hazard-prone countries in the world." China has witnessed an increasing number of natural disasters since the 90's. The serious flood in 1998 has caused a direct economic loss ammounting to around 3.2% of the GNP that year. And during the year of drought, 20 million of people and large animals were affected

---

3. "A current perspective", by the UN Country Team in China.

because of shortage of drinking water. The rate of damage to agriculture caused by meteorological disasters has increased from 33% in the 50's-60's to 53% in the 90's. As a whole, due to the low level of socio-economic development, the input to disaster prevention is low.

(6) The trend of loss of biodiversity has not improved basically

Seven out of 17 mega-diversity countries of the world are located in Asia and the Pacific region. China is one of them. Due to historical and several interrelated factors, the loss of biodiversity is severe in China, especially due to the long period of expansion of agriculture into primitive forests, wetlands and grassland. Of the 640 species of wild fauna and flora listed as protected ones under the Convention on International Trade in Endangered Species of Wild Fauna and Flora (CITES), 156 of them are found in China. It was reported that some 15% of country's fauna and flora species are endangered, which is higher than the world average of 10-15 percent.

(7) Climate change

China has been aware of the issue of climate change. It is also serious on its international commitment. Therefore, China is not involved in Kyoto pact[4]. "It is true that China and India are already big emitters of greenhouse gases, and in a few decades, may even be the biggest. Today, however, their contribution pales beside America's (see Fig.1). It was the rich world that created todays' problem by emitting greenhouse gases while industrialising over the past century; it is only fair, goes the argument, that rich countries act first to curb emissions."[5] China has done a lot to save energy to reduce carbon emissions per unit of GDP output. Fig. 2 is reproduced from a very recent study of MIT (Reference 11) shows that carbon intensity of China (Kg/GDP 1990 U.S. dollar) is reduced from 2.0 in 1980 to around 0.6 in 1998.

(8) Possible constraints from global development and changing conditions

China has a high share of trade dependency ratio and high inflow of FDI in recent decade, there may be changes in the tradition of trade protectionism through more strict environmental regulation, standard, labeling, procedure or through increasing greening barrier.

4. In the world summit on Sustainable Development in Johannesburg 2002, China announced that it had ratified the Kyoto Protocol to the United Nations Framework Convention on Climate Change. (Author, May 2003)
5. Rrom Reference 13.

Fig. 1* America Exhales

America exhales

Emissions per person, 1997
tonnes of carbon

— Qatar — 18

Broken scale ⚡

— Singapore — 6

United States — 5

— Australia

Finland — Germany — 3

Russia — Japan
Britain
— Italy — 2
France — Switzerland
Mexico — China
India — 0

Selected countries

Source: Oak Ridge National Laboratory

19

7

4

1

2

Source: See Reference 13

Fig.2 Carbon Intensity China, U.S.,
and World (1980-1998)

(CO₂ EMISSIONS/ GROSS DOMESTIC PRODUCT)

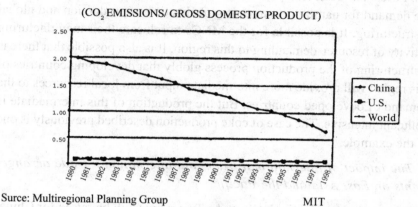

Surce: Multiregional Planning Group

MIT

IV. New Challenges and Opportunities for East Asia and the Pacific

4.01 Challenges and Opportunities in the Process of Globalization

In the process of globalization, there are both challenges and opportunities for developing countries in East Asia and the Pacific. Because the developing countries are in the process of industrialization, this process of globalization will promote further the restructuring of the global economy. The developed countries are moving toward a post-industrialization society, i.e., knowledge-based economy or service-oriented economy. While the developing countries will become industrialized in the coming future. And the emerging new technology, especially ICT, will promote further the process of industrialization with less energy consumption and pollution. Several aspects will be analyzed in next section.

4.02 Analysis of Impact of Globalization

1. The impact of globalization on the demand for natural resources

It is of great uncertainty to identify the impact of globalization on the demand of natural resources in the region. The natural resources demanded from this region are coal, oil and gas, metallic ores, gold, timber, minerals, etc. Forest has been studied widely. One of the impact of globalization on the demand for natural resources is globalization of production and global restructuring. It is possible for the MNCs to relocate their manufacturing activity of resource demanding to this region. It is also possible that there is restructuring of the production process globly that developing countries of this region will provide more intermediate input from local resources to the demand of developed countries. But the production of this intermediate is pollutant intensive. The case of coke production described previously is one of the example.

2. *The impact of international trade and international trade arrangements on East Asia and the Pacific*

This is a point requires in-depth study. Two points will be raised for China.

(1) It had been analyzed by us that China's accession to the WTO will require the transfer of surplus labor force from rural to industrial or tertiary sector, i. e., the requirement to provide more job opportunities for the rural people.

(2) Under current stage of development, the developing countries have less strict environment regulations. There is further need to have effective environmental policies, including those internalizing environmental cost. Otherwise, increased economic activity generated from trade liberalization can contribute to environmental problems. Therefore, the environmental effects of trade liberalization — both positive and negative will vary, depending on the country, sector and particular circumstances.

3. *Impact of new technology*

The new technology, especially the new generic technology, ICT and biotechnology, emerged to have a large impact on the economy and society. Many countries in this region is catching up with the train. Australia, Japan and Singapore are ranked in the foremost of ISI by IDC in this region. South Korea has achieved a growth rate of IT with 41% respectively in 1999 and 2000, with the users of internet reaching 19 million. It was reported that in China the network users has reached 25 million and the users of mobile phones has reached 100 million in the first quarter of 2001.

The impact of this new technology, from the negative perspective, may be a new digital divide. In 2000, 29 advanced economies with 15.4 percent of the global population has a share of 57.1% of GDP and 75.7% of global export; while 125 developing countries with 77.9% of global population has a share of only 37.0% of global GDP and 20.0% of global export, and 28 countries in transition with 6.7% of the global population has a share of 5.9% of global GDP and 4.3% of global export. This is the reality of the world today. The impact produced by new technology may possibly create a new digital divide if no appropriate policy is undertaken.

4. Negative aspect of globalization

The negative aspect of globalization is largely social. A research report done by OECD shows the following.

"The latest report[6] brings to light the following facts:

• In 1820, the ratio between the richest and the poorest nations was 3:1. In 1913 it had increased to 11:1, in 1950 to 31:1, in 1973 to 44:1 and in 1992 to 72:1.

• In the world today, the 200 richest people have a fortune equivalent to the annual income of the group of least developed nations. Of these 200 people, 65 are found in the US, 55 in Europe, 13 in other industralised nations, 3 in Eastern and Central Europe, 30 in Asia and the Pacific, and 16 in Africa and 17 in Latin America.

But it cannot be disputed that there is a correlation between the growing disparity and the growing internationalisation of economies."

These negative aspects have been shown fully in the Asian financial crisis, during which, it is the poor who suffered the most.

V. Perspective in the New Millenium — Some Suggestions

5.01 Brief Summary of Previous Parts

1. There are many accomplishments and many lessons well summarized in Reference 1 and 2. There is an increasing number of countries adhering to

---

6. Reference 10.

various agreements related to sustainable development. This shows the increasing acceptance of the outcomes of the 1992 UNCED. The regional action program has transformed "Agenda 21" into various actions adapted to different regions. Various international organizations, NGO's and governmental agencies are involved in the action program. This is the major accomplishments. It gives confidence to the global society to follow the path of Rio.

The major lesson is: there is need to have better coordination and better information sharing among institutions concerned to make the implementation to be more effective.

In China's case, it has the same major accomplishments and lessons. The concept of sustainable development is widely accepted. China's "Agenda 21" is prepared to guide SD. There is the same major lesson and issue of coordination and information sharing among various institutions.

2. The major constraints

(1) The common constraint faced by all countries across the region is the institutional rigidity to adapt to change.

(2) A particular constraint faced by the countries in the region is that the region contains three developed countries, most of the remaining are developing countries and they are in different stages of development. The major target for these countries is further industrialization within the context of sustainable development. Thereby, the major constraints are three:

(a) Shortage of financial resource;

(b) Environmentally sound technology is urgently needed, but there is high cost in transfer; and

(c) Lack of qualified people.

3. Challenges and opportunities in the process of globalization

(1) Accelerated process of globalization since the 80's is promoted by ICT and other technology. The production process is becoming increasingly global; there is increasing growth of trade and capital flow; the major actors are the MNCs. Developing countries in this region can be benefited from this process to promote their development through FDI and export-oriented strategy.

(2) The negative aspects of globalization are largely social and partly economic. There is an increase of income disparity between rich nations and poor nations since 1820, along with tremendous income disparity between the rich and poor people.

(3) The Asian financial crisis shows our ignorance on globalization. It has raised the issue of reform of the international financial structure. This issue has to be solved yet. It has brought to light the fact that nearly all countries in this region are latecomers in the financial sector. Perfecting the financial system is a remaining issue. It also shows that it is the poor who suffers the most in this crisis.

(4) In the transition from traditional industrial society to post-industrial society, ICT will play a dominant role. Negative lessons should be learned from the history of formation of the industrial society. How serious is the effect of digital divide must be studied seriously.

(5) The new trade regime will promote the growth of trade, many issues remained to be studied, and the global industrial restructuring and trade may have negative impacts to the environment.

5.02 Some Suggestions

1. Reconfirm "Agenda 21" to be a common paradigm for collective action in the World Summit 2002; this sustainability paradigm also serves as a new international relationship that:

- The needs of all countries (big or small) should be incorporated to international agreements and policies;

- A partnership in which the strong help the weak is necessary;

- Differential treatment is justified;

- Integration of environment and development (economic and social) concerns is the only road towards sustainability; and

- Intervention of the state and the global community on behalf of the public interest to control market forces so as to attain greater social equity and bring about more sustainable patterns of production and consumption is of paramount importance. There are market failures. Partnership involves governments, inter-governmental community,

NGOs and citizen groups, who should unite to temper the market with social and environmental priorities and programs.

2. Suggestions for improvement of RAP

Sustainable development is a new paradigm in development, including complexity of interaction of technological, economic and social systems. The solution of it is complicated. The space effect of various environmental issues is different. Five levels of space can be identified, including local, regional, fluvial, constinental and global. The environmental issue at the global level includes ozone layer depletion and climate change; the environmental issue at the local level includes indoor environment, soil sanitation, disruption, etc. (Reference 12). Solution of the issues of different levels requires different timing periods. The experience can be learned from the argument on debate of the treatment with Kyoto Agreement "the approach of the existing agreement — abrupt reduction in emissions in the short term and no commitments yet agreed for more distant years is not well suited to the challenge of global warming. Better would be a longer-term plan, based on milder reductions at the start following by more demanding targets further out." This argument can be applied to "Agenda 21" and regional RAP in medium term. "Agenda 21" should be system-oriented, while RAP can be more issue-oriented.

3. Five priority areas for this region

(1) Appropriate Social Program (poverty alleviation, education, health, and other social issues)

(2) Increase the funding resources for the implementation of "Agenda 21"

Increase the fund from multilateral funding such as GEF as well as the number of projects supported by GEF. Expand bilateral assistance from donor states for the implementation of "Agenda 21".

(3) Promote Technology Transfer

Environment-sound technology, clean production technology should be transferred on concessional terms.

(4) Several critical resource-conservation programs, such as "energy program" and "water program," should be designed and implemented.

Most of developing countries are in the stage of industrialization and consume increasingly various amounts of natural resources, especially energy and water. This region is in acute shortage of water resources, water-saving techniques in agriculture and sewage-water treatment in the urban areas should also be focused.

(5) Research on sustainable development indicators, natural resources accounting, etc. The difficulty to have a consensus on sustainable development is the issue of accounting. If appropriate sustainable development indicators can be developed and accepted. Then it will be easier to make progress in the assessment of sustainable development.

5.03 Ways of Strengthening the Institutional Framework for Sustainable Development

1. The role of commission on sustainable development should be further strengthened

It can be seen from previous discussions the complexity in the implementation of "Agenda 21". The role of CSD must be strengthened in directing and coordinating various regional action programs, coordinating action of various UN agencies, NGOs, etc.

The major issues on the implementation of "Agenda 21" should be reviewed, and appropriate solutions be recommended. It is necessary to establish a global network of SD for dissemination of information.

2. Realize appropriately the function of various UN organizations

There are many UN organizations with different roles. The role of various organizations should be brought into full play and better coordinated, these organizations include UNEP, UNDP, ESCAP, UNIDO, the World Bank, ADB, UNICEF and others.

3. Regional cooperation

Different regions are different in their natural resources endowment, and ecological environment. They are also in different stages of development, cultural aspects, etc. Strengthening the regional cooperative efforts toward SD is essential. Concerted action plan should be studied and implemented.

REFERENCES

1. Review of the Implementation of Agenda 21, International Environmental Conventions, the Regional Action Program on Environmentally Sound and Sustainable Development, 1996-2000, and the Program of Action for the Sustainable Development of Small Island Developing States. (RAP) ESCAP/SO/MCED(00) IMF. 8, August 28, 2000.

2. "State of the Environment in Asia and the Pacific 2000", ADB, ESCAP, UN.

3. "State of the Environment in Asia and the Pacific 1990", ESCAP, UN.

4. *China's Agenda 21,* China's Environmental Science Press, 1994.

5. "Economic and Social Survey of Asia and the Pacific 2001", UN.

6. *Emerging Asia,* ADB, 1997.

7. The Global Coke Industry, H. Erica Chan.

    MIT Multiregional Planning Group, July 2001.

8. "Economic Globalization and the Environment", OECD, 1997.

9. *World Economic Outlook,* IMF, May 2001.

10. "The Creative Society of the 21st Century", OECD, 2000.

11. "Comparative Analysis of Carbon-intensity Differences from Coal Consumption", Karen R. Polenske, MIT, presented in China, July 2001.

12. "Highlights of the Dutch National Environmental Policy Plan", Ministry of Housing, Physical Planning and Environment Department for Information and International Relation.

13. *The Economist,* April 7-13, 2001.

14. "The Future of the Global Economy", OECD, 1999.

15. "Supplemented: A Current Perspective", by the UN Country Team in China, "Updated Common Country Assessment," Beijing, April 2003.

Conclusions

An Integrated Approach to Development and Reform is a challenge faced both by the global society and China in the 21st century.

I

1. Five aspects related to development and reform of China have been presented in the eighteen papers. In fact, the later four parts can also be included in the first part. A proper development strategy must take all four components, i.e., S&T, economy, social and environmental aspects and the mutual interaction among them, into consideration. The global society and China had accepted the concept that "sustainable development must simultaneously serve economic, social and environmental objectives".

2. At international level, virtually every United Nations' body has adopted new policies and strategies to promote sustainable development (or integrated approach perceived by the author). But the progress is not up to expectation. It is recognized in an UN document that "the state of the world's environment is still fragile and conservation measures are far from satisfactory".[1] "There has been at best limited progress in reducing poverty", etc.

3. Integrated approach to development and reform is by no means a simple task in the real world. First, it should be rooted in the national planning; second, there is need to have mutually coherent policies in the areas of finance, trade, investment and technology, and especially, the economic, social and environmental policies should not be compartmentalized either

---

1. All quotations in this paragraph are from E/CN. 17/2002 PC. 2/7, "Implementing Agenda 21", report of the Secretary-General.

at the national level or international level.

4. A sustainable pattern of consumption and production requires change in the pattern of human behavior, which is effected very much by cultural traditions on the one side and dominant global trend on the other.

5. Implementation of an integrated approach to development and reform is also constrained by many other factors, such as institutional framework, the need for policy integration (cooperation among relevant organizations), knowledge-based decision making and participation, finance, transfer of technology and dissemination of information, etc.

Therefore, it must be recognized that integrated approach to development and reform is an object to be pursued. But it is a challenging and enduring task both for the international society and China. Full effort should be exercised for the improvement of planning and implementation to achieve it.

II

6. China had worked out its "Five-Year Plan" for ten consecutive periods; much of its experience is summarized in part I of this book. It is worthwhile to point out here that, in spite of China's rapid economic growth since its reform and opening-up, China is still a developing country. Although China had entered the ranks of lower middle-income developing countries[2] in 2000 classified by the World Bank. We must fully recognize the entire range of development problems confronting a large country with a population around 1.28 billion in 2002, with 50% of its labor force (368.7 million persons in 2002) still employed in the agricultural sector. It is also observed by an international organization that "China's rapid economic development is occurring in the midst of major systematic transformations — from central planning to markets, from an agrarian to a manufacturing/services-based economy, and from being relatively closed to fast-paced globalization." China needs to widen further its opening to learn more international experience in combination with its own concrete conditions. Hereunder, several important international documents on China's development and reform will be

---

2. *China Country Assistance Strategy 2003-2005,* the World Bank Group, Jan. 22, 2003.

quoted to be a source of information to supplement China's studies on planning and implementation.

7. The United Nations had launched a program for reform in 1997, with the aim to prepare the UN to meet the challenges of the 21st century. The establishment of the United Nations Development Assistance Framework (UNDAF) is aimed at enhancing the capacities of various UN agencies to implement their development. It is a planning framework to harmonize the development cooperation work of all UN agencies in providing assistance to a given country, identifying joint goals, objectives and strategies. Programs and projects of assistance are set up based on the goals and objectives. The first key input to UNDAF is the Common Country Assessment (CCA), which is a country-based process that the United Nations Country Team (UNCT) undertakes to reviewing and analyzing the national development situation and identify key issues as a basis for advocacy, policy dialogue and preparation of the UNDAF.

8. In UNDAF for PRC (2001-2005), there are three goals and twelve objectives. The three goals are "Promote Sustainable Development to Reduce Disparities," "Support Favorable Conditions for the National Reform and Development Process" and "Assist China's Efforts in Meeting Global Challenges and Promote International Cooperation." It can also be pointed out that nearly five objectives (Goal One) out of twelve of UNDAF, are mainly social. The five objectives of goal one are: "improve the quality of, and equal access to, basic social service," "reduce the burden of HIV/AIDS," "enhance food security and nutrition, especially at the household level," "improve access to, and opportunities for, employment" and "strengthen the social security system, including health benefits, disability benefits and pension schemes in both rural and urban areas." There five objectives covered large areas to be studied. This can illustrate the insufficient study covered in part IV of this book.

9. Integrated approach of development and reform includes a design phase and implementation phase. A sound management is required in both phases. It is impossible to discuss in detail here. The author recommends Reference 3 for the readers.

10. A part of international studies are quoted and recommended in this part is to show the complexity of this study — An Integrated Approach to

China's Development and Reform. Both development and reform are a process. It is expected that we Chinese, through learning and reviewing its own experience of development and reform, through learning widely the global experience, through our enduring and concerted efforts, can do better in this process generation after generation, and achieve our objective in revitalizing China and contribute also our part of to a prosperous global society.

REFERENCES

1. "United Nations Development Assistance Framework for the People's Republic of China (2001-2005)", Oct. 2000, prepared by the United Nations Country Team in China and the Government "Mirror Team", Beijing, Oct. 2000.
2. "China Country Assistance Strategy 2003-2005", the World Bank Group Document of the World Bank Report, No. 25141, Jan. 22, 2003/5/21, China Country Management Unit, East Asia and Pacific Region.
3. "Development Management", Asia Development Bank, 2002.

NOTES

The author had the chance to participate in many designing and construction projects in the engineering field, especially in the power system and power plant field over the past 33 years before 1980. He spent 20 years in producing a book titled *An Introduction to Systems Engineering*, which summed up his experience gained in more than thirty years. The book was published in 1980 (in Chinese). Then, he has the chance to work in the Development Research Center of the State Council, focusing on strategic planning and policy studies. He has taken part in several large domestic and international joint research projects on integrated economic development planning and policies and other aspects. He has been invited by many international organizations and academic personages to give speeches and present his papers abroad. Some of these speeches and papers have been published in books and journals overseas. The author thinks it is feasible to select eighteen papers in different disciplines to form this *An Integrated Study of China's Development and Reform — A Preliminary Exploration of Social System (Engineering)*. The author is hesitated to use the word "Engineering" in social systems in order to avoid academic debate, as there may need much to say and much to be explored further. The papers collected here were written in different styles, as they were presented and written in different years. To unify them in a certain style requires lot of editing work. Therefore, every paper in this book keeps its original form and content to show that policy study should be forward-looking with a sense of retrospect. Only a very minor part is supplemented (wherever necessary, the author has put a note). There may be duplication in some of the papers although they make up a very minor share. The papers selected in this book as a whole is integrated to form a preliminary exploration of a social system and an integrated study of China's development and reform. The author holds it is useful to international and domestic readers because the papers selected cover a span of around 50 years of the development process and twenty years of the experience of reform and the lessons there. The original source of each paper in each part is given below:

Part I Overall Perspective of Development of China

1. System Concept of Sustainable Development—Sustainable Development of the Mode of Production and Consumption and the Impact of Social Culture

(Speech given to national scientific and engineering academicians, 1998)

2. The Experience of Development Planning in China, Oct. 1998

(Speech given at the National Planning Conference of Iran)

3. Redefining Regional Development Strategy: the Chinese Experience — Toward a Framework of Study of Regional Development Strategy of China

(Speech given at Global Forum on Regional Development Policy held in December 1-4, 1998, Nagoya, Japan. Abstract published in UNCRD Proceedings, Series No. 37, July 1999)

4. Two Decades of Policy Modeling of DRC

(Paper presented to the International Conference of Economic Modeling in Beijing, China, Nov. 2001)

Part II Development of Science and Technology of China

5. Chinese Experience of Technological Independence

(Published in *Technological Independence – The Asian Experience*, edited by Saneh Chanarik and Susanlta Goonatilake)

UNU Press, 1994

6. Technology Innovation and Enterprise Management and a Case Study in China

(Published in *International Journal of Technology Management 1994*, Vol. 9, No. 5/6/7, editor in chief: Dr. M.A. Dorgham. Publisher: Inderscience Enterprise Ltd. Switzerland)

7. Some Issues of Technology Management in China: A Challenge Towards the 21st Century

(Published in *International Journal of Manufacturing Technology and*

Management, Vol. 3, No. 1/2, 2001), chief editor: Dr. M.A. Dorgham, Inderscience Enterprises Ltd. U.K.

Part III Economic Development and Reform of China

8. Industrialization and Economic Reform in China, Feb. 1993

(Speech given in Vargas Foundation)

Published in: *A EconomiA mundial EM Transformaçao,* Fundaço Getulio Vargas, 1994 (in Portuguese)

9. Foreign Direct Investment Policies and Related Institution-Building in China

(Published in *Foreign Direct Investment in Selected Asian Countries: Policies, Related Institution-Building and Regional Cooperation*), ESCAP Development Papers, No. 19, 1998

10. Experience with Tax Reform in China

(Speech given in Kyrgyz Republic on Nov. 1999, jointly sponsored by Ministry of Finance of Kyrgyz Republic and ESCAP. Published in ESCAP Development Papers)

11. Corporate Governance—Challenge to East Asian Countries in the Process of Globalization

(Speech given to an international conference for foreign visiting students at Beijing University, Beijing, China Aug. 2000)

12. Comments on: "Rethinking the East Asian Miracle"

(Speeches given at the launch of the Publication of the World Bank *Rethinking the East Asian Miracle* in Tsinghua University, March 2002)

13. E-Governance and Human Resource Development

(Paper presented at the ASEM Conference and ICT, March 10-12, 2003, Sweden)

Part IV Some Social Aspects of China

14. Social Security System and Alleviation of Poverty in China

(Published in *Toward Social Security for the Poor in the Asia-Pacific Region*), UN, ESCAP, 1996

15. Urban Poverty Alleviation and Development

(Published in *Regional Development Dialogue,* Vol. 20, No. 1, Spring 1999, UNCRD, Nagoya, Japan)

Part V Some Environmental Aspects of China

16. Toward a Sustainable Development Society: A System Approach

(Speech given in the Club of Rome Conference in Fukuoka, Kyusu, May 1992. Published both in English and Japanese, titled "Global Environment and Local Action" by Club of Rome, Japan)

17. Economic Development and the Environment in China

(Published in *Economic Development & Cooperation in the Pacific Basin,* edited by Hiro Lee and David W. Roland-Holst, Cambridge University Press, 1998)

18. Sustainable Development in a New Millenium

(Paper presented to the expert group meeting of UN in July 2001, Malaysia, for the preparation of World Summit in 2002)

图书在版编目（CIP）数据

中国发展与改革的综合研究／王慧炯著

－北京：外文出版社，2003.7

ISBN 7-119-03335-2

I. 中⋯ II. 王⋯ III. 体制改革－研究－中国－英文

IV. D61

中国版本图书馆 CIP 数据核字（2003）第 036566 号

责 任 编 辑：崔黎丽　于　瑛
英 文 审 定：李振国
封 面 设 计：张　韬
印 刷 监 制：韩少乙

中国发展与改革的综合研究

王慧炯　著

*

ⓒ 外文出版社

外文出版社出版

（中国北京百万庄大街 24 号）

邮政编码　　100037

外文出版社网址：http://www.flp.com.cn

外文出版社电子信箱：info@flp.com.cn

sales@flp.com.cn

三河市汇鑫印务有限公司印刷

2003 年 7 月（小 16 开）第 1 版

2003 年 7 月第 1 版第 1 次印刷

（英）

ISBN 7-119-03335-2/Z・641（外）

09800（精）